Jacob Haberman earned his doctorate from Columbia University where he specialized in the Philosophy of Religion and Middle East Languages and Cultures, and received his rabbinical ordination *(Semichah)* from the Rabbi Isaac Elchanan Theological Seminary of Yeshiva University. He also obtained a J.D. degree from New York Law School and is active in the real estate and construction business. Dr. Haberman has contributed essays to the *Jewish Quarterly Review* and other learned periodicals and is the author of more than 50 articles in the new sixteen-volume *Encyclopaedia Judaica.*

Maimonides
and
Aquinas

A Contemporary Appraisal

Maimonides
and
Aquinas

A Contemporary Appraisal

by
Jacob Haberman

With a Foreword by
Professor Joseph L. Blau

KTAV Publishing House, Inc.
New York
1979

Library of Congress Cataloging in Publication Data

Haberman, Jacob.
  Maimonides and Aquinas.

  Includes bibliographical references and index.
  1. Moses ben Maimon, 1135-1204—Philosophy. 2. Thomas
Aquinas, Saint, 1225?-1274—Philosophy. 3. Faith and reason (Jewish
theology) 4. Faith and reason. 5. Loewe, Herbert Martin James,
1882-1940. I. Title.
B759.M34H27   121   78-27626
ISBN 0-87068-685-2

For
HENRYKA JUDYTH

I fondly remember you for the unfailing devotion of your youth,
    the love of your bridal days:
How you followed me in the wilderness,
    in a land not sown—You and I!

Jeremiah 2:2

If love has joined two people in this life, we have good reason for believing that their existences are bound up with one another, not for one life only, but for ever. This would not involve their meeting in every life, any more than it would involve their meeting every day of each life. Love can survive occasional absences, and is often even stronger for them. And the universe is on a large scale, which might require long absences.

McTaggart, Some Dogmas of Religon, sec. 108

TABLE OF CONTENTS

"It is a remarkable fact that no canonical writer has ever made use of nature to prove God. They all strive to make us believe in Him. David, Solomon and the rest never said: 'There is no void, therefore there is a God.' They must have had more knowledge than the most learned people who came after them, and who have all made use of that argument. This is highly significant and worthy of attention."

Blaise Pascal, *Pensées*, iv. 243, in Brunschvicg's arrangement.

"I was obliged to destroy knowledge in order to make room for faith."

Immanuel Kant, *Critique of Pure Reason*, Preface to 2nd edition.

"The feeling of reverence should itself be treated with reverence, although not at the sacrifice of truth, with which alone, in the end, reverence is compatible."

George Santayana, *Reason in Religion*, New York, 1905, p. 13.

Foreword

One of the recurrent dreams of Western man is that he will be able to develop a theological statement that will satisfy at one and the same time the emotional needs of his faith and the intellectual demands of his reason. For Western man is the offshot of the conjunction of Athens and Jerusalem—Athens symbolically the birthplace of the intellectual critique we call philosophy, and Jerusalem symbolically the birthplace of the spiritual outreach we call faith. From the time when these two cultural worlds first began to interact, in or before the fourth century before the common era, there have been many systematic efforts to harmonize the conflicts of the two great human imperatives of religion and rationality.

Judaism, Christianity, and Islam, the three great religious structures of Western man, are all, in varying degrees, products of the conjunction of Athens and Jerusalem. Each, in its development, was affected by other influences, but the basis of the mixture in each case was Hebrew faith and Greek reason, in an everlasting tension. In the Middle Ages, particularly between the tenth and the fourteenth centuries, a series of major thinkers in the three religions made the most persistent and determined efforts to establish a firm philosophic foundation for the synthesis of the deliverances of the scriptural tradition and the conclusions of scientific thought. Of all the Jewish contributors to this effort, Moses Maimonides made the most significant impact on later thought. An analogous place in the development of Christian thought is held by Thomas Aquinas.

Until quite recent times, the theological synthesis of Aquinas was the dominant intellectual force in Roman Catholic life. Even today, in Neo-Thomism, a version of the tradition of Aquinas still holds the loyalties of many Catholic thinkers. The theological philosophy of Maimonides never had the like authority in Judaism, but has had a comparable prestige. For Jewish tradition, Moses the son of Maimon was *the* philosopher even as the biblical Moses was *the* lawgiver.

It is these two major thinkers and their whole tradition of synthesis of faith and reason that the brilliant young author of the following pages dares to challenge. Dr. Jacob Haberman completed his preparation for the rabbinate before his twenty-first birthday. He earned a doctorate in religion at Columbia University, producing for his degree a translation of and commentary on a medieval Hebrew philosophical work. Since then, while active as a businessman, he has completed his study for a degree in law. The studies whose fruits are before us continue the interests of his period of rabbinic and graduate work.

Dr. Haberman's challenge to Thomas Aquinas and Moses Maimonides is firmly grounded in the author's study of the modern critical tool of philosophical analysis. To the extent that this is so, this work could not have been written save in the last fifty years. From other angles, however, it might have been produced at any time since the philosopher-theologians it criticizes. For philosophy is often spoken of as "a dialogue between generations," which means that the solutions that satisfy the needs and the knowledge of the age of their genesis must always face anew, in each later generation, the questions of their relevance and their adequacy.

The glory of the philosopher lies not in supplying solutions that never lose their force, but in being thought worthy of being put to the tests of relevance and adequacy. We do not challenge those of our predecessors who seem to us unworthy of these tests; we ignore them. It is, then, a sign of respect that Dr. Haberman not only challenges these two earlier masters, but also that he pulls no punches in his critique. He does not try to soften the blows he aims at Aquinas and Maimonides precisely because he can still consider them as worthy antagonists.

Finally (for the prologue should merely invite to the play, not replace it), philosophic criticism, vigorously maintained, can destroy any attempted synthesis of faith and reason that man has yet produced. If this destruction should be followed by a rejection of faith—its most usual result—it is called *skepticism.* From time to time, the destruction of the synthesis of faith and reason is followed by the vigorous reassertion of faith as able to stand in its own right, without support or justification by reason. This is called *fideism.* It is in fideism that Dr. Haberman finds a solution to satisfy himself. I invite you (on his behalf) to discover whether his solution satisfies you.

JOSEPH L. BLAU
Head
Department of Religion
Columbia University

Preface and Acknowledgments

Not long ago I stood by the grave of Maimonides in Tiberias in the Galilee. The whitewashed tomb is a half-cylinder of plastered stone mounted lengthwise on a foundation of rough blocks. No trace remains now of the inscription, penned by an unknown hand, claiming an almost divine parentage for Maimonides. "Here lies a man, and yet not a man; / Wert thou a man, then heavenly beings produced thee." Likewise vanished or obliterated is the inscription which took its place and which read: "Here lies Maimuni, the banned heretic."

But the quarrel and the intellectual ferment which evoked these inscriptions has not subsided over the centuries and is with us still. And what is true in the case of Maimonides holds *a fortiori* in regard to Aquinas. Admittedly his popularity has suffered a serious setback since the Second Vatican Council. Perhaps Dom Aelred Graham, the learned English Benedictine, was not thinking exclusively of the Council of Lyons when he wryly remarked that Aquinas seemingly found the invitation to an Ecumenical Council in 1274 so distasteful that he died on his way there. Certainly some of the most vigorous and original theologians in the Catholic tradition today have deliberately adopted an intuitionist and existentialist Augustinianism in place of the rationalist and realist Thomistic Aristotelianism. Other seminal Catholic theologians have espoused a Whiteheadian "process" philosophy in preference to the traditional Thomistic approach. Will these trends continue, and are these shifts permanent? It is too soon to say. But even in the post-Conciliar Church, the influence of Aquinas is far greater than it was in the Middle Ages and we have it on the *auctoritas* of the *magisterium* of the Church as embodied in the Code of Canon Law (*Codex Iuris Canonici,* cc. 1366, #2; 589, #1) that Thomism should be taught as the correct system in all Catholic educational institutions that teach philosophy. Only recently Pope Paul VI told an international congress marking the seventh centenary of the Dominican philosopher's death that his teachings are "still valid and relevant." The Pontiff urged scholars to "learn above all the art of thinking well" from St. Thomas and others associated with his philosophical thinking.

The problems which Maimonides and Aquinas treated and the issues which they dealt with are still with us today. Professor John Hick has recently reminded us that two of the most pressing problems in contemporary religious philosophy are formulated right near the beginning of the *Summa Theologica.* As is his wont, Aquinas states the difficulties fairly and with great force. In the second article of the third question, two objections are raised to the belief in the existence of God. The one difficulty is that every aspect of our experience, including the religious aspect, is capable of naturalistic explanation, and the other is the ancient and grisly problem of evil. Of course, Aquinas is not content to raise objections, he marshals evidence on the other side and seeks to resolve the difficulties and vindicate Christian theism. We are not here concerned with whether his resolution is acceptable or not, but at any rate he was aware of the difficulties. It is precisely because I view the philosophies of Maimonides and Aquinas as very much "alive" and "relevant" that I have at times considered modern developments and alternatives to their positions. This is entirely in the spirit of their philosophizing. As Aquinas puts the matter so magnificently in his triumphant and often-quoted retort to the Parisian Averroist, Siger of Brabant: "The aim of philosophy is not merely to know what other men have thought, but to learn what the truth of things is" (*In De Caelo,* I:22.8). And not only have the medieval notions regarding the existence and attributes of God not changed significantly, even the medieval heresies have been resurrected. Some forty years ago a group of radical and iconoclastic intellectuals issued a *Humanist Manifesto,* comprehensively summing up their philosophic and religious viewpoint in fifteen brief propositions. Yet the majority of the propositions enunciated by these most "advanced thinkers" can be found in the writings of the Jewish and Latin Averroists! (The more recently issued *Humanist Manifesto II* concerns itself more with current social and political problems.) The sociology of knowledge has indeed a legitimate function, but that function does not pertain to the fundamental problems of religious philosophy. There is more faith to be found in the writings of Brand Blanshard, McTaggart, Broad, and Hook, who very earnestly and with an open mind examined the arguments for the existence of God and found themselves faced with intellectual difficulties which forced them reluctantly to reject theism, than in the glib assertions of many a modernist theologian. These avowed unbelievers are not beyond the hope of redemption, and there is good cheer for honest doubters in the biblical reminder that "You shall seek the Lord your God, and you shall find Him, if only you search after Him with all your heart and with all your soul" (Deut. 4:29), as well as in the memorable utterance which Pascal puts into the mouth of God: "Be comforted, you would not be seeking Me unless you had already found Me" (*Pensées,* vii, no. 553, in Léon Brunschvicg's arrangement).

What Loisy once said of history is even more true, I believe, of philosophy: "On n'écrit pas l'histoire à genoux." I make no apology, therefore, for my apparently harsh criticism of certain aspects of Maimonides' and Aquinas' work. At the same time, I have been generous with praise where I thought it was deserved, and I have not hesitated to refer to the metaphysical systems of both Maimonides and Aquinas as works of the first order of genius. I am aware, of course, that in certain circles, the works of Aquinas and Maimonides, respectively, are considered quasi-infallible. Not being in the religious tradition of Aquinas any remarks on my part concerning him on that score would be impudent. Suffice it to say that if a Christian reader should find anything objectionable in what I have written, I can only state that I have honestly set forth my views according to my own lights, however mistaken, and I would remind him of the injunction of the gospel Jesus to "know the truth, and the truth will make you free" (John 8:32). Since I am a committed Jew who finds in normative Judaism the basis of my personal faith and religion, a few words may be in order regarding the status of Maimonides' philosophy in Judaism. It is quite true that an epitome of Maimonides' theological creed, the so-called Thirteen Principles of the Jewish faith, was incorporated into the Jewish prayer-book, but its acceptance was never made *de fide* by the Synagogue, and it was never practically employed as a test of membership in the Jewish community. Far from it; in the most orthodox of all rites, that of "The Sacred Lion," Rabbi Isaac Luria ben Solomon Ashkenazi (1534–1572) of Safed, may his merit protect us, the Thirteen Principles are left out of the liturgy both in their prose (*Ani Ma'amin*) and poetic (*Yigdal* hymn) forms. This omission was no mere accident; we are told by the saintly Ḥayyim Vital, who was Luria's beloved disciple and successor, that his teacher was opposed to the singing of the *Yigdal* hymn on ideological grounds.[1] Evidently the eminent Cabbalist felt that God is too great to be shackled and confined (if we may use the expression with becoming reverence) within the articles of a paralyzing creed. "Élargissez Dieu!" he might well have exclaimed with Diderot (*Pensées philosophiques,* #26). Surely, the formulation of the highest truths needs constant revision in the face of new thinking, and each age must, in the words of prophet and psalmist, sing unto the Lord new songs.

Moreover, if in my ignorance and stupidity I have presumed in an offensive manner, to handle matters and speak of personalities hallowed alike by

Jewish tradition and sentiment, I wish it to be known that this is due solely
to want of skill and not to purpose, and with the Synagogue-poet I appeal
from the strict justice of God to His infinite mercy: "I shall flee from Thee
unto Thyself, O Lord . . . and to the skirts of Thy mercies I will lay hold until Thou hast mercy on me" (Solomon ibn Gabirol, *The Royal Crown* xxxviii).
I would also make my own the pious petitions and reflections of the soul
with which Baḥya ibn Pakuda concludes his ethical work, *The Duties of the
Hearts,* but I feel in all sad sincerity that I am not even worthy to repeat
them.

Nor do I think that I have been unfaithful to the ideal of Maimonides in
my sometimes harsh strictures. Writing in the 1954 *Yearbook of the Central
Conference of American Rabbis* on the contemporary relevance of
Maimonides' philosophy, Professor Samuel Atlas, who was not only a
profound student of medieval Jewish thought but a most accomplished
talmudist in his own right, sums up his evaluation in these words: "A proper
understanding of the deep motives and tendencies underlying Maimonides'
thought allows, yea, even demands, a process of thought leading away
from Maimonides. That is to say, *with* Maimonides we can and should go
beyond Maimonides. The most significant lesson which the understanding of
Maimonides' philosophy teaches is that with Maimonides we can supersede
Maimonides."

It behooves us to remember that their contemporaries viewed both
Maimonides and Aquinas as radical and dangerous innovators whose views
were to be opposed at all costs. The antagonism to Maimonides' ideas
already began in his lifetime and it intensified after his death. And numerous
doctrines and theses taught by Aquinas were condemned by Etienne Tem-
pier, Bishop of Paris, three years to the day (March 7, 1277) of the Saint's
death following a request by Pope John XXI (Petrus Hispanus) that he inquire into the heterodox Aristotelianism being taught by the professors at
the University of Paris. The exact number of basic Thomist philosophical
theses that were condemned in 1277 is one of the "disputed questions"
heatedly debated by the learned historians of scholastic thought. Professor
Gilson observes with wry humor: "The list of Thomistic propositions involved in the condemnation is longer or shorter according as it is compiled
by a Franciscan or by a Dominican" (*History of Christian Philosophy in the
Middle Ages,* p. 728). But here the analogy between Maimonides and
Aquinas ends. Soon after his canonization in 1323 the Parisian censures
were withdrawn insofar as they related to Aquinas, and the Church accepted
him as its authoritative spokesman. His theologico-philosophical system
became the official doctrine not only of his own Dominican Order, but also

of the Benedictines, the Carmelites, the Augustinians, the Jesuits and the other sacred orders. The Popes, too, gave their approbation to, and lavished praise upon, the teachings of St. Thomas who was declared to be the Common, or Universal Doctor of the Church. With no stretch of the imagination can Maimonides be described as occupying a similar place of distinction in Jewish thought. To be sure he is generally recognized and revered as a foremost jurist and codifier of Jewish law (halakah), but the attitude of normative Judaism to his philosophy can be described as ambivalent at best. It is still unsettled whether his philosophy is compatible with Jewish orthodoxy; the matter is still *sub judice,* we might say. The Columbia University Nobel laureate in physics, Isidor Isaac Rabi, is the son of Eastern European immigrant Jews who were deeply pious and extremely rigid in their orthodoxy. "Even Maimonides was a bit suspect" in their circle, the professor emeritus observed in a recent interview. "In fact," he added, "*more* than a bit suspect—a great man, but still . . . ."

My absence for some time from the groves of Academe will acount for what well may appear at times a flippant style for a scholarly work. Like Dr. Johnson's friend Oliver Edwards, I tried hard to think and write like a philosopher; but despite all my efforts, I note (with embarrassment) that cheerfulness kept breaking in. But I shall soon make amends for this. A second monograph of mine is in the course of preparation and, if the auspices are favoring, will appear in Switzerland in German in the not very distant future under the rather ponderous title, *Eroerterungen zu einer quellenkritischen Untersuchung der inneren Voraussetzungen der Grundlinien der Entwickelungsgeschichte der mittelalterlichen juedischen Religionsphilosophie.* But all this has reference only to the style and the form of presentation. The substance of my critique is based on a study in depth of the primary sources. I have studied all the classics of medieval Jewish philosophy (a not very formidable task) and all the secondary literature listed by Georges Vajda in his invaluable bibliographical study *Juedische Philosophie* (Berne, 1950), and I have kept abreast of the periodical literature. It would be rash for anyone to make a similar claim regarding Thomist texts and thought, and I am not about to do so. But one does not have to eat all of an apple to decide whether it is good or bad or merely edible. I have, during many years, examined extensive portions of Thomas' literary output. This sampling and careful study of hundreds of pages leads me to believe that I have an adequate basis for a judgment as to its quality. The standard accountant's certificate reads, in part: "Our examination was made in accordance with generally accepted auditing standards, and accordingly included such tests of the accounting records and such other auditing procedures as we considered necessary in the circumstances." If such a technique is proper for the accountant it seems equally proper in evaluating a stupendous mass of work which would take a lifetime to master. It is only fair to add that two auditors in possession of the same data may construct two entirely different reports, although both follow "generally accepted auditing standards." I do not claim that my interpretation of Aquinas' philosophy is *the* correct one, only that the exposition and critique offered is a reasonable one. And while I have termed it a contemporary appraisal this does not mean that I have not availed myself of the scholarship of others. It has been said that the notion that we can dismiss the views of all previous thinkers leaves no basis for the hope that our own work will prove of any value to others. Particularly in regard to Maimonides, the medieval commentaries on the *Guide* are a quarry which has scarcely been scratched and all responsible Maimonidean scholarship must first go backward and then forward.

The absence of any academic affiliation may not necessarily be a disadvantage. We must never lose sight of the fact that Maimonides was no dry-as-dust ivory tower scholar, but a communal leader, judge and court physician. As regards Aquinas we have it on the very high authority of Professor Broad that there are very few cabinet posts which he could not have held with conspicuous success. His power of concentration was so great that he could dictate to three or four secretaries on different subjects at the same time, and we have been credibly informed that he had the ability to dictate coherently even in sleep. What multinational conglomerate would not be interested in hiring an executive or manager having such extraordinary abilities? The ingredients for success in the business world are not very different from those in the academic world. As John W. Gardner, the founder of Common Cause, observes in his *Excellence:* "An excellent plumber is infinitely more admirable than an incompetent philosopher. The society which scorns excellence in plumbing because plumbing is a humble activity and tolerates shoddiness in philosophy because it is an exalted activity will have neither good plumbing nor good philosophy. Neither its pipes nor its theories will hold water."

No man is an island unto himself. Gratitude is due my revered parents, whose blessed memory I cherish across the veil of years, for teaching me the language of Canaan and providing me with the education from which the present study draws its substance. Truly, "the days of the righteous die, but they themselves do not die." It is likewise a privilege for me to express my appreciation to my lamented and honored college teacher, the late Professor Alexander Brody. As a student at Yeshiva University I studied economics with him for two years, and took his courses in medieval history and American history . I had the pleasure of knowing him well outside the classroom, and it was he who first advised me to write a book on medieval philosophy. The independence and integrity of mind of my beloved mentor, and his devotion to excellence, were deep sources of inspiration to me. Yeshiva University and the City University of New York, where he also taught, are fortunate to have had his faithful service for such a long period of time. A special note of thanks is due to Professor Joseph Leon Blau, former Chairman of the Department of Philosophy of Religion at Columbia University, for writing the Foreword and encouraging me in my work. My measure of gratitude to him should not be belittled by the difficulty of expressing it in words. I am greatly beholden to Mr. Walter Schulze for reading the manuscript and correcting errors of style, and to my associate Dr. Arthur Morgan for relieving me from some of the burdens of my legal work and enabling me to devote myself to scholarly research. My sons, Sinclair Curtis and Brook Ariel, kindly helped me in the reading of the proofs. My debt to my wife is too great to be acknowledged.

The following have read various drafts of all or some of the manuscript, and have helped me greatly with criticism and comment: Professors W. Norris Clarke, S. J., Jacob I. Dienstag, Emil F. Fackenheim, David Fleisher, Thomas Aquinas Gallagher, Dom Aelred Graham, O.S.B., Leonard S. Kravitz, E. M. Macierowski, Leon Nemoy, Carol Ochs, and Bruce A. Williams, O.P. This is not to imply that these scholars have given my book their *imprimatur* and *nihil obstat,* or that they would necessarily wish to be associated with anything that I have written. In particular I wish to acknowledge with gratitude the immense debt that I owe to the great masters of scholastic thought to whom I have turned for help on particular obscure points. Whether I turned to a scholarly Benedictine for an exposition of Aquinas' view on the internal structure of the Holy Trinity, or whether I appealed to a learned Jesuit for an elucidation of the doctrine of the Real Presence in the Blessed Sacrament, or whether I inquired of an erudite member of St. Thomas' own Dominican order for the Saint's views regarding the personal union of the divine and human natures in the Incarnate Word, they have been uniformly generous in their response. Whatever merits or lack of merits this study may have, in its own small way it can serve to illustrate the spirit of applied ecumenism. The errors that remain are certainly not due to the lack of helpfulness of the living repositories of this learning, but rather to the fact that the author must have been born with a double dose of original sin.

"The last of the last is the dearest," in the words of the old rabbinic dictum. My father-in-law, Dr. William Korngold, placed his immense erudition in matters of Jewish learning at my disposal, and I owe more to him than I can possibly express. His luminous mind, so overflowing with rabbinical and philosophic learning, has served as a constant source of inspiration and encouragement to me. Ties of affinity disqualify me from testifying as to the full extent of his contribution. Were it not for his extreme reluctance, I should most certainly have placed his name on the title page where it rightfully belongs. It is a unique privilege to draw from this "running fount of erudition." Often, a mere suggestion or comment from him was more helpful to me than might have been a more pretentious and extended criticism from many a lesser man.

In conclusion, it goes without saying that despite the generous help of these scholars, I am painfully aware of the many shortcomings of these lucubrations, but I find solace in the sublime pleading attributed to St. Augustine, the meaning of which overflows the vessel of its words: *Domine, si error est, a te decepti sumus!* ("Lord, if there be error, it is by Thee that we are deceived!"). I hope that it will not be considered presumptuous of me to end this preface by quoting a few sentences from Maimonides' own preface to the *Guide*.

I implore every reader of this book not to rush into disproving me, for it may well be that he has misunderstood me. He thus would harm me in return for my having wanted to benefit him and would "repay evil for good" [cf. Ps. 38:21]. Nay, I ask everyone into whose hand my work falls to study it carefully. If he finds in it nothing of use to himself, he should think of it as not having been composed at all. Should he notice any opinions with which he does not agree, he should endeavor to find a suitable explanation, even if it seems a little far-fetched, and to give me the benefit of the doubt. Such a duty we owe to everyone.

JACOB HABERMAN

Long Beach, New York
June 1978

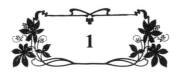

Introductory

The blending of Aristotelianism and Neoplatonism in the Middle Ages is thought to be the product of numerous false assumptions and attributions. To Aristotle were wrongly ascribed extracts from a paraphrase of books IV–VI of Plotinus' *Enneads* (the so-called *Theologica Aristotelis*) and an epitome of Proclus' "Elements of Theology" (*Liber De Causis*).[1] Among Muslim philosophers, the substantial identity of the thought of Plato and Aristotle became a standard belief.[2] This attitude was exemplified by Alfārābī's *Kitāb al-Jam' baina Ra'yai al-Ḥakīmain Aflāṭūn al-Ilāhī wa-Arisṭūṭālīs* (The Book of the Harmonization of the Opinions of the Two Sages, the Divine Plato and Aristotle).[3] Then, too, the Greek revival and the progressive rediscovery of the ancient classics came about slowly, and the medieval philosophers often had only a few Greek texts in translation with which to work.

These external circumstances were certainly significant for the fusion of Platonic and Aristotelian ideas, but there was also an inner evolution which should be of far greater interest to the student of the history of ideas. Medieval philosophers were attempting to devise a coherent system embracing reason and revelation, a task that had not confronted the Greek thinkers. To understand this, one must first consider the differences between ancient and medieval philosophy.

Aristotle said that wonder and disinterested intellectual curiosity are the first step toward true knowledge. It is through reflective thinking and the refusal to accept things as they seem that we arrive at a better understanding of their causes and a comprehension of reality. "It is through wonder that men now begin and originally began to philosophize; wondering in the first place at obvious perplexities, and then by gradual progression raising questions about greater matters too, for example about the changes of the moon

1

and of the sun, about the stars and about the origin of the universe."[4] This is characteristic of the pagan conception of the origin of truth. There is no mention of revealed and ready-made truths; all knowledge, for Aristotle, starts from experience. The doctrine that all knowledge is grounded in experience may almost be said to be the common property of all classical Greek thinkers. With the possible exception of the Platonic Ideas, a few logical and mathematical axioms, and certain historical information, all knowledge is thought to be the product of our own critical reflection, the fruit of our observation and experience.[5] The existence of God Himself is not an *a priori* truth but merely an inference arrived at by a process of demonstration.

Diametrically opposed to the Greek conception of the autonomy of reason is the biblical view of God and revelation. It never occurred to any prophet or biblical writer to prove the existence of God. God's existence is a matter of course, an absolute fact neither to be doubted nor proved.[6] The biblical prophets and writers operate with ideas that presuppose God's existence. In the words of Professor A. B. Davidson:

> The Hebrew thinker came down from his thought of God upon the world; he did not rise from the world up to his thought of God. . . . The thought of the Hebrew and his contemplation of providence and life were never of the nature of a search after God whom he did not know, but always of the nature of a recognition and observation of God whom he already knew.[7]

If men knew God, it is because He has made Himself known to them. He revealed Himself to His people and gave them an eternal Law, which was to make them live in accordance with His will, and He continued to guide them through His prophets and inspired teachers.[8]

While the Bible contains no proofs for the existence of God, we do find in it instances of what the scholastics referred to as arguments from convenience (*ex convenientia*). This type of theological argument cannot strictly prove a truth which is not already established; it aims rather at providing persuasive lines of thought to support the mind in accepting a revelation which transcends its powers. Given the fact of a divine revelation, the argument tends to show that this "fits in" and confirms an already established principle or fact by showing the congruity of its results (in terms of other revealed truths, the divine attributes, and so forth). Consider, for example, the Deuteronomist's account of the introductory discourse of Moses on the plains of Moab.

"For ask now of the days that are gone by, which were long before you, as far back as the time that God created man upon the earth, and ask from one end of the heaven to the other, whether such a thing as this has ever happened or was heard of. Has any people ever heard the voice of God speaking out of a fire, as you have, and survived? Or has any god ever attempted to go and take a nation for himself from the midst of another nation, by trials, by signs, by wonders, and by war, by a mighty hand and an outstretched arm, and by great deeds of terror, according to all the Lord your God did for you in Egypt before your very eyes. To you it was shown, that you might know that the Lord is God; there is none beside Him. . . . Therefore you must keep His laws and His commandments, which I command you this day, that it may go well with you, and with your children after you, and that you may prolong your days in the land which the Lord your God gives you for ever" (Deut. 4:32–35, 40).

We are not here dealing with a dry-as-dust proof of God's existence; this discourse is an argument not so much from history to God as from God to history. God, who is known to exist, has a special claim on Israel for its obedience to His laws and commandments because of the unparalleled revelations He has made to them, and the unparalleled deeds, the "trials, signs, and wonders," which He has performed for their deliverance.

The prophets and inspired poets have this same practical end in view when they turn from an appeal to history to the majesty and order of nature. "When psalmist or prophet," writes Sir George Adam Smith, "calls Israel to lift their eyes to the hills, or to behold how the heavens declare the glory of God, or to listen to that unbroken tradition which day passes to day and night to night, of the knowledge of the Creator, it is not proofs to doubting minds which he offers; it is spiritual nourishment to hungry souls. These are not arguments—they are sacraments."[9]

Perhaps the closest parallel to any of the classical proofs for the existence of God is to be found in one of the Psalms.

> They crush Thy people, O Lord,
>   and afflict Thy heritage.
> They slay the widow and the stranger,
>   and murder the fatherless.
> And they say, "The Lord does not see;
>   the God of Jacob does not perceive!"
> Understood, O brutish ones among the people—
>   Fools, when will you be wise?

> He who planted the ear, does He not
> hear?
> He who formed the eye, does He not
> see?
> He who chastens the nations, does He
> not chastise?
> He who teaches men knowledge,
> the Lord knows the thoughts of man. (Ps. 94:5–11)

At first blush it might seem that we have in this passage an approximation to the teleological argument, popularly known as the argument from design. But this is not the case. The argument here is that the Being Who gave others the endowment to hear and see, Who has the power to chasten the nations—all of which is *assumed* as being beyond question—that such a Being must surely be possessed of attributes which transcend those of any of His creatures. With the passage from the psalmist we may compare a genuine argument from design as succinctly stated by Aquinas (*S.T.* 1a, q. 2, art. 3, c., the fifth way).

> We see that things which lack consciousness, such as physical bodies, operate with a purpose, and this is evident from their acting always, or nearly always, in the same way, so as to obtain the best result. Hence it is plain that they achieve their end, not by chance, but designedly. Now whatever lacks consciousness cannot move towards an end, unless it be directed by some being endowed with consciousness and intelligence; as the arrow is directed by the archer. Therefore some intelligent being exists by whom all natural things are directed to their end; and this being we call God.

Just to juxtapose these two passages of approximately equal length makes it evident that we are dealing with a different literary genre, inspired by a different mentality, for an entirely different purpose. To the psalmist, who felt God as a living power, Aquinas' philosophical proof of His existence might well appear to be a strange fire on the altar of the Lord.

Medieval philosophy, which was the residuary legatee of both the Hebrew and Greek traditions, was grounded in the discipline of the grammar of assent and the belief that "the recognition of the authority of revelation is the presupposition of all true philosophy."[10] The Biblical Revelation is not indeed philosophy, but, as Archbishop William Temple has persuasively argued, the primary assurances of religion are the ultimate questions of philosophy.[11]

In this monograph I begin by considering the works of medieval philosopher-theologians, specifically Maimonides and Aquinas. By blending elements of different philosophical systems—(Neo-)Platonism and Aristotelianism in the case of Maimonides and Aquinas—they were, with some measure of success, able to work out a synthesis which left an organic place for a divine revelation. I shall then endeavor to show the following: (1) The medieval philosopher-theologians were less than successful in filling out the details of their respective systems, and they used improper procedures in trying to reconcile the teachings of reason and revelation and in attempting to ward off any potential conflict between them. (2) The best interests of both philosophy and theology are served if each of these disciplines goes its own way and pursues its own problems independently, without the subordination of one to the other.

If my critique at times seems harsh, it is because I have followed Kant's dictum that "it is only by criticism that metaphysicians (and, as such, theologians too) can be saved from . . . controversies and from the consequent perversions of their doctrines."[12] Though Kant may be considered to have been my guide as far as the critical *purpose* of my work is concerned, in the *methodological* details of my criticism I have followed the empiricism of David Hume and his contemporary followers. Thus I have sometimes employed methods and techniques associated with the movement broadly designated as "philosophical analysis." Philosophical analysis has so much currency in contemporary philosophy that most of my readers will presumably be acquainted with it and be able to follow my reasoning.

Though these philosophers and these movements have been my guides, I do not believe I am a true follower of any of them. If there is any position in philosophy and theology—particularly as regards their relation—which I hold, it would have to be called a form of fideism. It is, I trust, a moderate and not an extreme or irrational fideism.

A word may be in order regarding the somewhat copious notes. Notes are not very fashionable nowadays, but in this book they have the focal function of exploring alternate interpretations and explaining my preferences among these. For example, there has been much discussion recently on Aquinas' understanding of "necessary being"; in a long note in chapter 4 some of the diverse views propounded are examined.

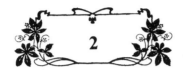

2

The Maimonidean Synthesis

The primary characteristic of Judaism is the performance and observance of the commandments of the Law (*Miṣwōth Ma'asiyyōth*) as the revealed will of God, rather than speculative thought about His essence and attributes.[1] In his farewell address, delivered on the plains of Moab on the eve of his death, Moses, the great lawgiver, his prophetic eye yet undimmed and his vigor unabated, declared: "The secret things belong to the Lord our God; but the things that are revealed belong to us and our children for ever, that we may do all the words of this Law" (Deut. 29:28). Judaism differs from other Western religions in that it is not a creed or a system of beliefs upon the acceptance of which redemption or future salvation depends.[2] It is, rather, a system of human conduct and a way of life.

The gap between this traditional Jewish world outlook and Aristotelianism seems too wide to be bridged. In an early essay, Professor Wolfson denies categorically that Maimonides achieved any sort of synthesis between these two views.

> Maimonides was not a rabbi employing Greek logic and categories of thought in order to interpret Jewish religion; he was rather a true medieval Aristotelian, using Jewish religion as an illustration of the Stagirite's metaphysical supremacy. Maimonides adheres staunchly to the Law, of course, but his adherence is not the logical consequence of his system. It has its basis in his heredity and practical interests; it is not the logical implication of his philosophy. Judaism designated the established social order of life, in which Maimonides lived and moved and had his being; and it was logically as remote from his intellectual interests as he was historically remote from Aristotle.[3]

With all due respect to Professor Wolfson, it seems that he has overlooked the possibility that the synthesis which Maimonides attempted to make has its foundation and starting point not in the field of theoretical philosophy, i.e., metaphysics and ontology, but in the field of "practical interests," in politics and ethics. Maimonides implies as much in a letter to one of his admirers, an excerpt from which we cite here in literal translation.

> I, Moses, inform his eminence, R. Jonathan ha-Kohen (may his Rock guard him!) and all the friends and sages who read my writings: Before I was formed in the womb the Torah (Law) had known me, and ere I was born she consecrated me[a] to her study and appointed me to scatter her springs abroad,[b] and she is my loving hind[c] and the wife of my youth[d] in whose love I have been ravished[c] since my adolescence. And yet for all that,[e] many foreign women[f] have become her rivals[g]—Moabites, Ammonites, Edomites, Sidonians, and Hittites.[f] God knows that these were taken in the first instance, solely to serve her as perfumers, cooks, and bakers,[h] in order to show the people and the princes her beauty, that she is exceedingly lovely to behold.[i] Nevertheless her conjugal rights[j] have thereby been diminished, since my heart has been partitioned into many sections in accordance with all types of wisdom.[4]

We must bear in mind that this letter was written to Jonathan of Lunel (Southern France), a recognized authority in talmudic scholarship, a man renowned for his piety, who had sent Maimonides an epistle raising twenty-four questions on points connected with his Code. Since philosophy as such was not cultivated by the Jews living in the Franco-German environment to the extent that it was in the Spanish peninsula, and since Maimonides had a natural desire to have his Code accepted as authoritative, we have every reason to suspect that he presented himself as being more strictly traditional than he really was and that he may have exaggerated his belief in the subservience of the various philosophical disciplines to the Law. But after due allowance is made for all this, as well as for the florid rabbinic style with its oriental hyperboles in which the letter is written, we cannot evade its plain implication that philosophy was auxiliary to the Law in the synthesis of the two which Maimonides attempted to achieve.

What was the nature of that synthesis, and how was it arrived at?[5] These are by no means easy questions to answer. In the light of Maimonides' acknowledgment that he would intentionally contradict himself in the body of the *Guide* in order to conceal his real views from all but a philosophically trained intellectual elite and prevent the masses from understanding certain of his doctrines, it is difficult to know ever what religious doctrines Maimonides did in fact affirm. As Leo Strauss says in order to unravel the esoteric teachings of the book the modern expositor would have to be "endowed with all the qualities of a Platonic philospher-king."[6] It is not surprising that widely conflicting intepretations of Maimonides' philosophy proliferate. Some have gone so far as to suggest that he was writing with tongue in cheek. Such a view betrays a lack of insight into human behavior and motivation. The human mind and soul are capable of accommodating simultaneously opinions which are not only inconsistent, but even mutually exclusive.[7] That Maimonides set out deliberately to deceive, seems unlikely to me. His other works, particularly his correspondence, make it difficult to picture him as a crafty schemer stooping to unworthy means even for the sake of a supposedly worthy end. Moreover, at least some of Maimonides' rationalist views appear undisguised in his Code, especially the opening part entitled *Sēfer ha-Madda'* (Book of Knowledge).[8]

Nevertheless, in the case of a deliberately esoteric writer like Maimonides, it is best, I believe, to divide the principal ideas advanced by him in his philosophical works into two classes (as suggested in *Guide* III:27–28): (1) those which he would defend on purely rational, philosophical grounds, and (2) those intended for the protection of the social order, that is, doctrines which he felt should be propagated whether they are in fact true or false, on the ground that they are valuable instruments for the promotion of good conduct on the part of the mass of the population. Although the separation of specific doctrines and tenets into one or the other of these two classes is difficult and at times perhaps arbitrary, methodologically it is perhaps soundest to deal with the matter in the following manner. We shall put into the first category and examine on their intrinsic merits, Maimonides' views on all major questions such as the existence and attributes of God, creation, the nature of prophecy, and Divine providence. In every instance we shall give Maimonides the benefit of the doubt, and assume that he advocated his views because he was convinced that they were true, and not merely an ideological cover for the protection of the established social order. Only when such an interpretation is precluded by the ordinary canons of literary criticism may recourse be had to the social utility and political usefulness of myths and fictions. A case in point is *The Treatise on Resurrection*. The views expressed in this work differ so radically from those expounded elsewhere by Maimonides that a distinguished Cambridge don came to the conclusions that this treatise is a thirteenth-century forgery.[9] For a number of reasons which would take us too far afield to consider here, I fail to be convinced by this argumentative thesis,[10] but the mere fact that it should have been propounded by a respectable authority indicates that the views expounded in that essay must be considered in a class apart. Indeed, Maimonides himself stressed the fact that in the *Treatise* he was speaking to the common man, and not to the philosophers, and that he strove to adapt himself to the mentality of "women and ignorant persons" in order that such simple-minded believers should understand him and be strengthened in their useful faith.

I cannot forbear quoting from one of the most acute philosophers of the recent past, the later Professor C. D. Broad, to help illuminate the motivation of Maimonides:

> It would probably be wise for the State to adopt the immortality of the soul as a fundamental "myth," and not allow it to be publicly questioned. I wholly agree with Plato in thinking that human society requires to be founded on certain "myths," which are not self-evident and cannot be proved; and that the State is within its rights in forbidding all public discussion of the truth of these "myths." And I think it is quite possible that the doctrine of human immortality (whether it be in fact true or false) is one of these socially valuable "myths" which the State ought to remove from the arena of public discussion. *This of course has no bearing whatever on the question whether the philosopher in his study ought to believe the doctrine of human immortality. He ought only to believe what is either self-evident, or capable of certain or probable proof, or verifiable by sensible or introspective perception.*[11]

Professor Shlomo Pines of the Hebrew University in Jerusalem, one of the leading authorities on Maimonides today, summarizes the purpose of the *Guide* in the long introduction (pp. lvii–cxxiv) which serves as a prolegomenon to his translation of that work (Moses Maimonides, *The Guide of the Perplexed,* translated from the Arabic with an Introduction and Notes by S. Pines [Chicago, 1963]). That purpose coincides precisely with Professor Broad's recommendation. If I were to summarize his complicated argument, there is always the possibility that the reader might think that I was unconsciously influenced to deftly choose and highlight those features which serve my end. To avoid this danger we shall quote the epitome of his argument as presented by Professor Marvin Fox in a review in the *Journal of the History of Philosophy* (vol. 3 [1965], p. 274).

> Maimonides sought to pursue philosophic inquiry in complete freedom, while at the same time preserving society from the destructive dangers of

philosophy. In Jewish law he saw the ideal instrument for achieving his double goal. Jewish law provided for the best kind of social order, in Maimonides' opinion, while leaving the pursuit of philosophy open to those who qualified. As legislator or interpreter of Jewish law Maimonides was rigorously orthodox; but as philosopher he rejected some of the very doctrines which he affirmed in his legal decisions. He believed that religious tradition is essential to provide for the masses the best life of which they are capable. It also provides for the philosopher conditions under which he can do his work freely. Therefore, the prudent philosopher will do his best to preserve those conditions both for himself and for society.

The failure to distinguish clearly between the two classes of ideas advanced by Maimonides vitiates many of the critical discussions of his theories. To attack the rational or logical basis of Maimonides' views on physical resurrection and immortality is to commit what linguist philosophers have referred to as "category mistake." It is like trying to blow out an electric light as though it were a candle. In the case of a deliberately esoteric writer like Maimonides, it seems to me that a two-pronged attack is necessary.

Regarding the social utility of religious doctrines, Professor Broad properly calls attention to Plato. According to Plato (*Republic* 485 C–D, 490 A–C) a ruler ought to have a passionate desire to know the truth and not to be in a state of error, but he may, and sometimes must, officially use lies, falsehoods, and deceptions on private citizens "for the benefit of the State" (389 B–D; cf. 414 and 459).

We see, then, that the political use of myth and fiction was advocated by eminent moral philosophers both in the fifth century before the common era and in our day. Against Plato and Broad, I believe, in common with a great number of thinkers, and especially John Stuart Mill (*On Liberty,* chap. 2), that the truth of an opinion is a necessary aspect of its utility and that no good ever comes from inculcated falsehood. There is something refreshing in the high regard the Victorians had for truth. "If a thing is true," said W. K. Clifford, "let us all believe it, rich and poor, men, women, and children. If a thing is untrue, let us all disbelieve it, rich and poor, men, women, and children. Truth is a thing to be shouted from the housetops."[12] Speaking for myself, I can only say that I opt with Clifford and against Maimonides. A modern critic has well said that in attempting to carry out his political program, Plato was "led to defend lying, political miracles, tabooistic superstition, the supression of the truth, and ultimately, brutal violence."[13]

However unpleasant it may be to acknowledge the truth, the fact remains that with the possible exception of superstition, every count in this indictment of Plato has its counterpart in the teachings of Maimonides, and all these charges can easily be documented in his writings, in certain pronouncements and if taken literally.[14]

This is all that we shall say about what Maimonides called "necessary beliefs," i.e., those necessary for political stability and the preservation of the social order. If it should be objected that this or that idea advanced by Maimonides and taken by us literally was meant as a useful and socially valuable myth, our basic objection would be the same.[15]

In our opinion, the best analysis of Maimonides' thought is the one worked out in detail in a number of significant and masterful studies by the late Leo Strauss, a brilliant German scholar who was Professor of Political Science at the University of Chicago.[16] In analyzing the Maimonidean synthesis, Strauss does not deny that Maimonides was an Aristotelian in his metaphysical views, but he contends that however much Maimonides was indebted to Aristotle, it was Plato's political philosophy that enabled him to justify the necessity of a divine revelation and to identify Scripture with that revelation.

Plato's theory of the ideal state is well known. He felt that the common man is not capable of working out his own salvation and that government of the ideal state must rest with philosophers—who should assume their rightful place as rulers and lawgivers—if it is to be guided wisely. "Until philosophers become kings . . . and political power and wisdom meet in one . . . cities will not cease from ill," said Plato (*Republic* 473 C–D). Thus, if there is to be justice, the philosopher must take upon himself the burdens of society, not resting in contemplation, but returning to instruct and guide the benighted dwellers in the Cave and ruling by a sense of social duty.

Strauss was the first to point out that Maimonides' prophetology was decidedly influenced by Plato's political writings. The authentic prophet, according to Maimonides, has at least all the knowledge of the philosopher. He also has an unusually developed imagination into which his knowledge flows abundantly. This enables him, under divine inspiration, to institute the Law, which alone can save mankind. This conception of the prophet is similar to Plato's view of the philosopher-king and the qualifications of the prophet resemble those of the Platonic guardians and the philosopher-king.[17] (Maimonides' professed exclusive reliance on the Bible and the talmudic-rabbinic literature for the qualifications of the prophet is somewhat of a pretense, as Strauss has shown.)[18]

According to Maimonides, therefore, the prophet is a philosopher-king; and the supreme prophet, Moses, "the man of God," was that charismatic prophet-lawgiver/philosopher-king all in one, who achieved intellectual superexcellence and was able to give the perfect and eternal law. Because of his unique power, Moses was able to do what no prophet had done before— he promulgated an ideal political code in which were expressed all the practices and beliefs essential for the physical and spiritual perfection of the individual and society.

The substitution in his system of Plato's *Republic* for Aristotle's *Politics* and the identification of Moses with the philosopher-king enabled Maimonides to come to terms with reason and revelation and incorporate the Jewish Scriptures in his synthesis.[19]

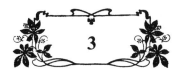

3

The Aquinian Synthesis

The essence of Pauline Christianity is salvation through faith in the person, mission, and saving work of Jesus and the attainment of fellowship with him. As the Apostle Paul puts it: "I have been crucified with Christ; it is no longer I who live, but Christ who lives in me; and the life I now live in the flesh I live by faith in the Son of God, who loved me and gave himself for me" (Gal. 2:20 RSV). We must bear in mind the Pauline doctrine of the Church as the Mystical Body of Christ (*corpus mysticum*) when we examine how and where Aquinas introduces Neoplatonic elements *ab extra* into the philosophical system of Aristotle.

Generally, Aquinas accepts the psychology, the physics, the politics, and to a certain extent the metaphysics of Aristotle,[1] and combines them with a Neoplatonic conception of human destiny. Epistemologically, he is an Aristotelian in his reliance on sense-data and abstraction from the empirical, as opposed to the Neoplatonic emphasis on illumination.

Aristotelian teleology, or belief in the purposiveness of nature, includes the principle that things can only be understood by considering the end at which they aim. The potential of the acorn can only be seen in the light of the oak. This principle, which in Aristotle is little more than the recognition of something in nature, more or less analogous to the "purposes" of man, is expanded by Aquinas in the doctrine that, since "all creatures, even those that are devoid of reason, are directed to God as their last end, and that all reach this end in so far as they have some share of a likeness to Him, the intellectual creature attains to Him in a special way, namely, through its proper operation, by understanding Him. Consequently, this must be the end of the intellectual creature, namely to understand God."[2]

We can now follow the line of thought which leads Aquinas to postulate revelation as an absolute necessity.[3] Beginning with the spiritual postulate that any fundamental, God-inspired yearning of man guarantees its own fulfillment, he argues in a series of beautiful and eloquent chapters in the third book of the *Contra Gentiles* that the beatific vision alone can fulfill man's demand for blessedness.[4] But human nature, according to Aquinas, has no power to apprehend immaterial things directly. The materials with which our minds work come to us through the senses. We can arrive at general truths through abstraction, but we are still dependent on sense impressions (*phantasmata*). We can never, he says, conceive of purely spiritual things that cannot be directly related to a universe of space and time.[5] Direct knowledge of God is beyond man on earth. God's creation of man's nature was not ordered to the natural world, but to the supernatural, and man's soul does not strive for perfection in the natural world but in the supernatural order. This perfection, however, is not capable of being reached by any human powers. We were never destined to lead purely natural lives, and therefore we were never destined in God's plan for a purely natural beatitude. But the Christian hope of blessedness is not vain or perverse, and therefore we have reason to expect a supernatural elevation and enlargement of our faculties in the hereafter, and the presentment of truths outside the sphere of reason through divine revelation for preparation here. Our nature, which is a free gift of God, was given to us to be perfected and enhanced by yet another free gift of God. This free gift is the grace of glory, with which we see not "through a glass darkly" but "face to face" (I Cor. 13:12). God's sanctifying grace perfects our nature with the gift of a life, an intellection, a love, and a mode of existence where our nature can achieve its true level, infinitely beyond that of our natural world.

We see, then, that Aquinas denies that the human intellect can attain the intuitive vision of the divine essence without the infused theological virtues, the gifts of the Holy Ghost, and the intervention of the *lumen gratiae* (prophetic or angelic illumination) which is absolutely supernatural, and to which must be added the divinely implanted *lumen gloriae* (beatified illumination). Aquinas agrees with the Neoplatonists that man's final goal is the acquisition of a mystic state that will unite him with God, but he also accepts the empiricist psychology of Aristotle, which allows no mystic faculty for entering into spiritual consciousness. Thus, while appearing to be both an Aristotelian and a Neoplatonist, he was neither. The Neoplatonists believed in a mystic goal, but they also believed they had a mystic sense that only needed discipline and development to help them reach that goal.[6] Aristotle recognized no such sense, but neither did he require it. To Aristotle, all that man needs to fulfill his desires is within his reach under favorable conditions. The essentials of the "good life" are material well-being, freedom from mental stress, human companionship, friendship, the search for truth, and above all the opportunity to contemplate such truths as have been found. In taking his theory of man's goal from the Neoplatonists and his account of man's nature from the Aristotelians, Aquinas left a convenient gap, which he neatly filled with the Christian revelation and its promises. Thus, the necessity and reality of a revelation finds its organic place in Aquinas' synthesis of Aristotelianism and Neoplatonism.[7]

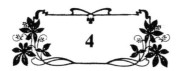

The Attempted Harmonization of Faith and Reason as Illustrated by the Doctrine of Creation

We have seen how the two foremost philosophical theologians of the Middle Ages were able to make room for revelation in their systems by combining elements of Platonism and Aristotelianism. The resultant philosophic structure in each case was not a *mixtum compositum* without rhyme or reason, or the eclecticism of a jackdaw, but a genuine synthesis showing true philosophic insight and the manifestation of creative power and genius. Arthur Koestler, in the *Act of Creation*,[1] explains the creative process as the result of the merging of two disparate contexts, of the putting together of two unconnected concepts or ideas to form a unified new intellectual synthesis. Using Koestler's analysis, we may refer to Platonism and Aristotelianism in the philosophy of Maimonides and Aquinas as the two autonomous subsystems which had to be fused into a new and creative synthesis by overcoming the "obstacle" of a supernatural revelation. The final synthesis worked out in each case may be judged to be work of the first order of genius, and there is no reason why either of these impressive philosophical systems, as presented in skeleton outline, is less likely to be true than pure and unadulterated Platonism or Aristotelianism. However, as we shall see in the later pages of this chapter, the two philosopher-theologians were not always able to fill in the details of their systems philosophically. When they are pressed, both Maimonides and Aquinas turn either to God's will or to faith in order to explain the phenomena. The Thomistic view is quite clear that reason is secondary to revelation: reason is called on when it is useful, but revelation is always there to fall back on.

We shall examine the doctrine of creation in both Maimonides' and

Aquinas' systems to understand how they attempted to harmonize faith and reason in this doctrine. Philosophy, as exemplified by Aristotle's arguments, holds that the world is eternal. Maimonides takes issue with Aristotle, saying that his arguments are (improperly) based on the nature of the world after it came into existence. Maimonides thinks that phenomena above the lunar sphere cannot be explained by mechanical laws, but require to be explained with the help of God's will. This then opens an intellectual place for prophecy, miracles, and revelation. We disagree with this point of view: it seems unworthy of God to create the world but to use another set of laws to keep it in being. This kind of doctrine could as easily be used to prove that the world was created last Friday. Still, as we shall see, some authorities agree with Maimonides, including some moderns.

Aquinas is indebted to Maimonides: We know from revelation that God created the world in time, but God's eternal act need not have an eternal effect; the effect can be whatever God wills it to be. Thus Aquinas refers the natural events of the world to God, whose existence is necessary and thus outside the world. Both Maimonides and Aquinas, therefore, leave the natural world behind in explaining it.

Another example of where philosophical explanations are left behind when faith demands it, is the doctrine of transubstantiation. In order to explain it, Aquinas abandons Aristotelian doctrine and maintains that accidents can inhere in accidents. Such basic concepts as substance and accidents are abandoned by Aquinas when Christian dogma demands it.

We now turn to a more detailed examination of how both Maimonides and Aquinas attempt to harmonize faith and reason in their systems.

I have used the expression "philosophical system" in connection with Maimonides and Aquinas with some hesitation. It may be something of an anachronism; we speak in these terms, but the medievals did not. Maimonides and Aquinas did not view themselves as system-builders. And even granting that the notion of a "system" is legitimate, the question can properly be raised whether one can say of Maimonides or Aquinas, who were professional theologians, that their system is philosophical rather than theological.

Such reservations seem to me by no means altogether unjustified, but after due consideration, I still believe that the overall designation of Maimonides' and Aquinas' philosophies as systems can be retained. In an extremely suggestive essay, Gilbert Ryle has noted that most philosophers at the present time would be far more inclined to liken their activities to the work of a cartographer than that of a detective.[2] They practice what Professor Strawson (in the introduction to his essay "Individuals") has aptly called "descriptive" rather than "reversionary" metaphysics, meaning to suggest thereby that they aim at describing and laying bare the latent actual structure of our thought about the world, and to make explicit the concepts fundamental to ordinary ways of thinking, rather than propose their replacement by an entirely different set of ideas.[3] But this is not the way the medieval thinkers viewed their task. Maimonides and Aquinas adhered to the detective rather than the cartographic nature of metaphysics. For them the metaphysician was like a detective trying to discover the true nature of the universe, and just as a detective frames a hypothesis to explain the facts, so too the philosopher-theologian frames his system to account for the nature of the world and reality. The simile likening the activities of the philosopher-theologian to the detective and his art is apt for one more reason. Medieval thinkers have not infrequently been accused of "knowing" the truth before they begin to philosophize. They did not, it is said, follow reason "whithersoever she may lead"; their conclusions are judged by something outside of reason—revelation. Now this criticism is justified to some extent; I certainly believe that there is a large element of truth in it. But we cannot know this without a specific study of the theories of the medieval thinkers; an attempt to characterize them in the abstract will not suffice. True the religious philosopher was convinced in advance of many things which he accepted on faith. But, like the detective already psychologically convinced of the identity of the murderer, he was seeking metaphysical proof that would stand up in a philosophical courtroom.

Bearing in mind, then, the dangers of exaggerating the systematic aspects of medieval thought, we can still, for the sake of convenience, speak in a general way of the system of Maimonides or Aquinas.[4] Now when it came to filling in the details of their systems, the medieval philosopher-theologians were not entirely successful. When there was no obvious danger of the clash of their hypotheses with the dogmas of revelation, they could and did take over whole theories of others and adapt them to their own purposes. Professor Wolfson maintains, for example, that St. Augustine's doctrine of grace is only a Christianization of the pagan Stoic doctrine of fate.[5] Again, one of the most fascinating parts of the system of Thomas Aquinas, where he allows himself considerable leeway and latitude, is to be found in his attempt to reconstruct on Aristotelian principles the psychology of man before the Fall, of the soul in the intermediate state after death and before the resurrection of the blessed, and of the angelic spirits (the so-called separables).[6]

But this type of assimilation is possible only in the case of peripheral or tangential matters. It leaves little room for the true philosophic spirit in attempting to solve the fundamental questions of metaphysics. In reality a considerable part of medieval philosophy is theology dressed up as pseudo-philosophy, an exercise in interested sophistication. I am glad to be able to claim some support for this view in the work of the distinguished historian of scholastic thought, M. Etienne Gilson. In the words of the *doyen* of contemporary Thomist scholars: "The most original part of the contribution made by Thomas Aquinas to philosophy has its origin in the *rational interpretation of the philosophies of the past in the light of theological truth.*" And again,

> Using the history of philosophy as a means to his own end, he seems to consider the successive efforts of various philosophers (or schools of philosophy) to answer a certain problem as a sort of collective philosophical undertaking whose conclusions are at the disposal of the theologian to criticize, to redress, to complete, and finally to incorporate within his own theological inquiry. This fundamental character of the theology of Saint Thomas is too often overlooked. Having always seen philosophical progress as cumulative, he often conceived his own function as that of a *theological arbiter of philosophical doctrines.* For this very reason, he often practiced a kind of *theological criticism* of the data provided by the history of philosophy. One can call this a *critical history of philosophy* conducted in the light of divine revelation.[7]

But if an extraphilosophical element, revelation, is the frame of reference, then the autonomy of philosophy is surrendered, and it becomes subordinate to theology and a form of apologetics (*ancilla theologiae*).

Thomists have sometimes wondered why other philosophers have frequently considered Thomism's appeal to reason fainthearted.[8] Far from being the enemy of reason, Thomism seems to grant reason a larger role than would be given it by most secular philosophies. G. K. Chesterton was a sound Thomist. His study *St. Thomas Aquinas* was described by Etienne Gilson (a most competent judge, surely), "as being without possible comparison the best book ever written on Aquinas." His Thomism even permeates Chesterton's fiction. On page 48 of his *Unity of Philosophical Experience,* Professor Gilson refers to Chesterton's intriguing detective story, "The Blue Cross." The plot deals with a lovable little rustic priest who exposes an imposter disguised as a priest as being, in reality, not a priest but a common thief. When the imposter asks him what made him so certain that he was not a priest, Father Brown simply answers: "You attacked reason. It's bad theology." Just so!

In contrast to modern crisis theologians and religious existentialists, who distrust reason and revolt against it, Thomism seems to be a true rationalism which is marked by an extensive appeal to reason. What, then, accounts for the suspicion and hostility against it? Very simply put, most philosophers, in the first place, resist the claim that Thomism has "all the answers," that the philosophy of St. Thomas contains the solution to all the major problems of philosophy. Secondly, they find the sharp line separating religion and philosophy too neat, the division between "revealed" knowledge and "natural" knowledge, between "the light of grace" and "the light of nature," too pat, especially since "the light of grace," that is, revealed faith, maintains its practical supremacy. The Thomist seems to be more in the position of an advocate. If he can justify the dogmas of his creed, so much the better; if not, he can always play the trump card of faith. One is reminded of John Locke's caustic remark: "I find every sect, as far as reason will help them, make use of it gladly; and, where it fails them, they cry out, 'It is a matter of faith and above reason.' "[9] The Thomist seems to feel that revelation is his "city of refuge" where he is immune from rational attack.

While respecting reason, Thomism appears to draw a line where dogmatic theology comes into play and says firmly to reason, "Thus far and no farther." For this reason Bertrand Russell, in his *History of Western Philosophy,* says there is little of the true philosophic spirit in Aquinas. Russell is aware, of course, that generally, when Aquinas judges a philosophical doctrine defective as a theologian, he gives two reasons: it is against the Christian faith *and* against reason, or sound philosophy. It is not his practice to pass a theological judgment against some philosophical doctrine without also giving a philosophical reason why he considers it unsound. But Russell's point is that since he can always take refuge in revelation, his appeal to reason is, in a sense, "insincere." Russell illustrates his criticism with Aquinas' arguments for the indissolubility of marriage as expounded in book III, part 2, chapter 123 of the *Contra Gentiles.* This is advocated, among other reasons, on the ground that the father as the head of the family is useful in the education of the children because (1) he excels in intelligence and is more rational than the mother, and (2) because, being stronger in physical power, he is better able to inflict punishment. To this Russell objects that (1) an advocate of women's liberation might retort that there is no evidence that men in general are more rational than women, and (2) a progressive educator might question the desirability of the sort of punishment that requires great physical strength. But no follower of St. Thomas, observes Russell, would on that account cease to believe in lifelong monogamy, because the real ground for this belief is the injunction of Jesus of Nazareth in the Sermon on the Mount quoted in the same chapter: "But I say unto you that everyone who divorces his wife, except on the ground of unchastity, makes her an adulteress; and anyone who marries a divorced woman commits adultery" (Matt. 5:32).

Before we dismiss Aquinas as a mere special pleader as Russell does, it is only fair to hear what the other side has to say. We have quoted Professor Gilson in support before, let us quote him once again. Our quotation is taken from the final paragraph of his *History of Christian Philosophy in the Middle Ages:* "It appears that objectivity in judgment and freedom from settled intellectual prejudices are not the exclusive property of the pagan philosophers, that reason is not always found at its best on the side of what is commonly called rationalism, and that, at any rate, the range of intelligibility is incomparably wider than that of reason."

A more balanced judgment may perhaps be obtained by considering a more central doctrine in Aquinas' philosophical system. Such a doctrine is creation *ex nihilo,* which plays such an important place in his thought and that of Maimonides. This doctrine is a test case for the following reasons. In the first place, as Aristotle pointed out in a passage we have already quoted, speculations about the origin of the universe first led men to philosophy. Secondly, the concept of creation was taken over by religious philosophers from theology; it is wholly foreign to Greek thought, which since Parmenides (Fr. 8, beginning) had rejected the notion that being could come out of nonbeing.[10] In the third place, the claim has been made by Julius Guttmann and others that the historical significance of Maimonides' achievement lies in his particular solution of the problem of creation. Says Guttmann: "Maimonides' theistic Aristotelianism established the place of the biblical Creator-God within the framework of philosophical cosmology, and thus achieved a true metaphysical synthesis between biblical religion and Aristotelianism."[11] Finally the learned British Jesuit, Fr. F. C. Copleston, contends that Aquinas' discussion of creation shows that he took seriously his distinction between philosophy and theology.

> St. Thomas was perfectly serious when he gave philosophy its "charter." To a superficial observer it might appear that when St. Thomas asserted a clear distinction between dogmatic theology and philosophy, he was merely asserting a formalistic distinction, which had no influence on his thought and which he did not take seriously in practice; but such a view would be far from the truth, as can be seen by one example. St. Thomas believed that revelation teaches the creation of the world in time, the world's non-eternity; but he

maintained and argued stoutly that the philosopher as such can prove neither that the world was created from eternity nor that it was created in time, although he can show that it depends on God as creator. In holding to this point of view, he was at variance with, for example, St. Bonaventure, and the fact that he maintained the point of view in question shows clearly that he seriously accepted in practice his theoretical delimitation of the provinces of philosophy and dogmatic theology.[12]

Let us now consider one of the arguments by which Aristotle establishes the eternity of the world (in chapter 1 of book VIII of the *Physics*). This argument is based on an analysis of the character of time.[13] Time taken in itself is continuous. It is impossible for time to exist or to be conceived without the "present now." But every instant "now" is an end as well as a beginning; time stretches from it in both directions. But, continues the argument, time is the measure of motion; it cannot exist if there is no regular or periodic movement that it can measure. That movement is the motion of the outermost sphere, from which we derive the division of time into periods; the movement of the sphere therefore had no beginning, and the world is eternal.

Of greater interest than the conclusion itself is the method of proof employed. This method is characteristic of the Greek spirit: it is based on an analysis of the nature, or fixed essence, of things. The world is eternal because time, which, by its very nature, has no beginning, cannot exist without it. In place of this reasoning, which proceeds from clear and definite concepts, the philosopher-theologian substitutes the arbitrary will of God. St. Thomas says (*S.T.* 1a, q. 46, a. 2): "God's will cannot be investigated by reason, except as regards those things which God must will of necessity; and what He wills about creatures is not among these, as was said above [q. 19, a. 3]. His will, however, can be manifested to man through Revelation, on which faith rests. That the world had a beginning, therefore, is an object of faith [*credibile*] but not of demonstration or science." Thus the issue is deftly shifted from the nature of the world to the inscrutable will of God, which is unknowable except by revelation.[14]

The shift is well brought out in the following illuminating passage in the *Guide*. Maimonides is discussing the tenth proposition of the Ash'arite Kalām, which concerns the theory of unlimited "possibility" (*at-tajwīz*). This theory states that whatever is imaginable (*mutakhayyil*) is also rationally possible (*jā'iz 'aqlī*) for God, with the exception of logical contradictions. Maimonides severely criticizes this theory and states that reason rather than imagination is the touchstone of judgment in deciding whether a thing is possible or not. Maimonides elaborates the points at issue in an imaginary dispute which he supposes to have taken place between a Mutakallim and an Aristotelian philosopher. The discussion between these two disputants is summarized by Maimonides as follows:

> When the philosopher, in his way of expressing himself, contends, "Reality is my evidence; by its guidance I examine whether a thing is necessary, possible, or impossible," the religionist replies, "This is exactly the difference between us; that which actually exists has, according to my view, been produced by the will of the Creator, not by necessity; just as it has been created with that special property, it might have been created with any other property, unless the impossibility which you postulate be proved by a logical demonstration."[15]

This is indeed an eminently fair characterization of two views which are diametrically opposed to each other, not only in their conclusions but also in the manner in which these conclusions are reached.

In only one respect, it seems to me, can Maimonides' analysis be improved upon. Maimonides contrasts the evidences of reason with the illusions of imagination as truth conditions for philosophical theories. This does not seem to be a very satisfactory criterion. Some people might contend, for example, that they cannot even *imagine* something being made from nothing. In fact, Maimonides seems to have realized the insufficiency of his criterion, for after having categorically rejected imagination as a test of whether a thing is possible or not in the first part of the *Guide* (chap. 73, 10th proposition), he again returns to the same problem in part 3 (chap. 15) and there leaves it undecided whether anything imaginable (without contradiction) is possible. But the contemporary school of logical analysis has offered us a more fruitful criterion in its distinction between meaningful and meaningless assertions and theories.[16] A factually meaningful theory or theoretical system is one which can be tested and which leaves itself open to possible refutation; any theory which no possible fact could disprove is altogether meaningless, vacuous, and worthless (unless it is a logical axiom). In other words, the criterion of the logical status of a factually significant theory is its falsifiability, or refutability, or testability. This criterion, as we shall now show, separates the cosmogenic theories of Aristotle not only from those of the Kalam, but also from those of all medieval philosopher-theologians, specifically including Maimonides and Aquinas.

Maimonides is of the opinion that the arguments advanced by the

Aristotelians for the eternity of the world (*a parte ante*) are inconclusive, because the laws by which the universe is regulated need not have been in force before the universe was in existence.

> We, the followers of Moses, our Teacher, and of Abraham, our Father, believe that the Universe has been produced and has developed in a certain manner, and that it has been created in a certain order. The Aristotelians oppose us, and found their objections on the properties which the things in the Universe possess when in actual existence and fully developed. We admit the existence of these properties, but hold that they are by no means the same as those which the things possessed in the moment of their production; and we hold that these properties themselves have come into existence from absolute non-existence. Their arguments are therefore no objection whatever to our theory; they have demonstrative force only against those who hold that the nature of things as at present in existence proves the Creation. But this is not my opinion.[17]

Maimonides illustrates his contention by an elaborate analogy between the human ovum and a mature person; it would be illegitimate to make an inference about the state of the fetus from a study of the nature of a fully developed person. If we did not know about the processes of pregnancy and birth, we would certainly scoff at anyone who told us that a person can live for months without light, without breathing, and without eating inside the body of another person. Obviously, then, one should not judge conditions before birth by conditions after birth; and the same thing holds true regarding creation, the birth of the world. No inference can be drawn in any respect from the nature which a thing possesses after having passed through all stages of its development to the state of that thing when this process commenced.

Under the misapprehension that Aristotle taught that the world emanated by necessity from God in all eternity,[18] Maimonides attempts to resolve the difference between eternity and creation into a more fundamental difference between an impersonal mechanical law as the explanation of the universe, and an intelligent personality acting with will, purpose and design. He is willing enough to admit that Aristotle was successful in tracing all motions below the lunar sphere in terms of mechanical laws, but in his opinion, a variety of phenomena in the outer spheres—principally the peculiarities of speed and direction of the heavenly bodies (*Guide,* II:19)—is not amenable to an impersonal mechanistic explanation and can best be explained as the result of the free and spontaneous character of God's will.[19]

But once we grant that the world is the work of an intelligent being, acting freely with particular design, we have established a place in our system for miracles, prophecy and revelation.[20]

What shall we make of this theory? It is Professor Guttmann's considered opinion that Maimonides can be our guide even today. "All modern attempts," he says, "to combine recognition of the laws of nature with belief in the dependence of the world on a divine creator follow in the main this line of thought originated by Maimonides, however much they may vary it in detail."[21] Granted that Maimonides based his theory on the conception of nature current in his time, his views would apply with equal force to the ideas of law in nature as held today. Scientific hypotheses and statements, it is urged, deal with relations between finite things in space and time. They assume that the process of events in space and time is already going on and inquire into their character and the laws of their relations within that empirically observable framework. In no way do they concern themselves about the origins of the whole system of finite things.

My own view differs radically. I think Maimonides' theory is neither religiously helpful nor intellectually satisfactory. It is an unnatural *ad hoc* hypothesis which indicates a lack of intellectual courage and faith and is not at all worthy of the "Great Eagle." The strange idea of God creating the world by *one* set of laws, and then keeping it going by an entirely *different* set degrades the idea of God to the level of a deceiving Cosmic Magician who uses a double standard to lead astray Aristotle and other humble seekers of truth in order to mock poor human reason into forming a conception of a changeless Deity.[22] Scientifically the theory is as sterile as religiously it is unsatisfactory. As concerns the scientific objections, it seems that we must either view all observable processes as amenable, to a greater or lesser degree, to the scientific method of explanation or to none.[23] There is no room for compromise here and no basis for a distinction between celestial and terrestrial phenomena. This matter has been settled once and for all by Hippocrates' study on *The Sacred Disease,* where he explains that all diseases are either equally "sacred" and fit to be dealt with by magic and incantation, or equally "profane" and fit to be dealt with by ordinary physical means, so that there is no ground for singling out one (epilepsy) because of its queer symptoms as "sacred."[24] Nor is Maimonides' drawn-out illustration from biology very illuminating. As if there is any valid comparison between the human organism at two stages of its life, with the attendant changes brought about by the natural processes of continuity and gradualness, and the instantaneous positing of the whole universe which is the heart of the supernatural notion of volitional creation *ex nihilo*. Maimonides' biological analogy is on a par with that other biological demonstration for the resurrection of the body that relies on the example of caterpillars becoming butterflies, of which proof Voltaire remarked that it was not more weighty than the wings of the insects from which it was borrowed.[25]

Maimonides' theory cannot indeed be strictly proved to be false, but there is not the slightest reason to suppose it to be true and it is difficult to take it seriously. Considered as an abstract logical possibility, it is irrefutable and no more and no less plausible than my own reconciliation of theology with the data of science which I submit herewith.

Know you, my faithful pupil, unto whom may God be gracious, that the universe and everything in it, all the choir of heaven and the furniture of earth [MS. Q here adds the obvious gloss "including the *Guide of the Perplexed*"] was created *ex nihilo* last Friday evening at twilight, at which time the Creator, may He be blessed and exalted beyond all blessings and praises, in the plenitude of His grace endowed the children of men with ready-made memories and presented them with neatly pressed Sabbath clothes to wear. In the Hebrew language the word *bārā'* means *ibdā'*, an absolute origination which makes something existent from vacuous nothing. David, in his prayer for pardon after being rebuked by Nathan the prophet for his sin with Bathsheba, exclaimed: "Create [*berā'*] for me a clean heart, O God, and put a new steadfast spirit within me" [Ps. 51:12]; here the parallelism shows that *bārā'* refers to an absolute creation. Note also that in the Torah and the prophetic books the verb *bārā'* in the simple conjugation can only have God as its subject, and the term is invariably employed to designate His creative activities and never takes the accusative of the material from which a thing is made, as do other verbs of making, but uses the accusative to designate only the thing made. Of course, I could equally well explain *bārā'* to mean creation out of a preexistent matter should the spirit so move me and strike my fancy, or should I become convinced of the Philosopher's arguments. You know what I mean when I say that I am not obacurantist and would not hesitate to interpret and explain away the words of Scripture if I thought that they contradicted established scientific theory. Recall the remarks about the figurative interpretation of texts in the *Guide* [Pt. II:25]. Truly truly, I say to you, the gates of interpretation are never shut. In fact, I confess to you, my son, that I have two prooftexts all prepared for that contingency: "God created [*wayyivra'*] the great sea monsters" [Gen. 1:21] and "male and female created He [*bārā'*] them" [*ibid.*, v. 28]. I cannot say more; *verbum sat sapienti*. Study this profound and recondite theory thoroughly until you understand it completely; it is a mighty fortress erected to protect the Law, and able to resist all attacks. Consider this well and reflect upon it; with this interpretation, all the objection brought against the biblical account of creation *ex nihilo* by the Aristotelians collapse.[26]

In rereading my somewhat harsh strictures on Maimonides' speculations regarding the limitations of a scientific account of the origin of the world, I find that possibly I was unfair to Maimonides. Perhaps constructive use can be made of his discussion along the following lines. In what follows I am largely indebted to the brilliant analysis of Professor A. E. Taylor, who does not, however, mention Maimonides.[27] Professor Taylor argues convincingly that it is impossible in science to resolve physical reality into a complex of rational laws without a remainder. Physical science will never succeed in eliminating chance or the "brute given" from its world picture. All scientific explanations must assume, to use J. S. Mill's terminology (*Logic* III, v. 8), both initial "collocations" as well as "laws of causation." There must be something to which the laws of nature apply, and the existence of this something is inexplicable by those laws themselves, but necessary before they could begin to operate.

The point can best be explained by a very simplified example. Suppose the world consists of just four objects, A, B, C, D. We can in part "explain" the behavior of A by the structure of B, C, and D, and the interaction of B, C, and D with A, and similarly with each of the other three constituents. Obviously enough, the behavior of A can be brought within the framework of a law and "explained" provided we are informed about its structure and the structures of B, C, and D. What has not been explained, however, is why A should be there at all, or why if there, it should have B, C, and D as its neighbors rather than others with a totally different structure of their own. This pattern must be accepted as a "brute" fact. To be sure, as science progresses, it succeeds in bringing an ever greater part of nature under the aegis of an ever diminishing number of laws. But however far science progresses, it can never dispense with the necessity of recognizing a "brute given" to which scientific laws are applicable. Professor Taylor makes it abundantly clear that we only get rid of the "brute given" at one point at the price of introducing it somewhere else. As Professor Taylor puts it:

We have to appeal in all our explanations of the actual not only to "laws" but to "collocations." Science, which hates to accept anything whatever as mere bare "given fact," is always trying, with much success, to reduce the "collocations" with which it starts as given to mere consequences of "laws." But every success in such reduction is achieved at the price of acquiescence in some assumption of an earlier and more ultimate "collocation." Without "collocations" which have to be taken as "brute fact," as there we do not know how or why, the functional dependences we call "laws" would reduce to functions without any arguments and would thus become as insignificant as the symbol f or ϕ before a blank. Here we clearly come upon an inevitable limit to the whole work of scientific explanation. As M. Emile Meyerson has argued in his recent brilliant work *l'Explication dans les Sciences,* the paradox of scientific explanation is that it gets rid of the unexplained and in that sense *irrational* in one place only on condition of reintroducing it somewhere else.[28]

These reflections show that no amount of knowledge of "natural laws" will explain the present actual state of nature unless we also assume as a brute fact that the distribution of "matter" and "energy" several hundred million years ago was such and such. With the same "laws" and a different "initial" distribution, the actual state of the world today would be very different. It follows that the primeval configuration must either remain a matter of chance, of unexplained "collocations," or else (always bearing in mind the contention of John Hick that the character of religious faith is noncoercive and optional in view of the fact that one need not refer to God in order to explain the workings of nature), as Maimonides and his modern followers contend, be referable to the Divine Will. I shall leave it to the reader to decide whether the above analysis is a legitimate exposition and development of Maimonides' views, or an eisegesis—an illegitimate reading into the text of what is not there.

Jewish authors have quite properly pointed out that Aquinas' treatment of the question of eternity versus the creation of the world was greatly indebted to Maimonides.[29] On closer examination, however, Aquinas' position turns out to be more subtle and philosophically sophisticated. By creation Aquinas understands the complete causation of the *whole* reality of that which is said to have been created (*S.T.* 1a, q. 45, a. 1, ad 3; q. 45, a. 2; *De Potentia,* q. 3, a. 1). Creation, because it produces something absolutely, requires the power of an infinite cause, and no creature could possibly be an instrument for creation (*De Pot.,* q. 3, a. 4; *S.T.* 1a, q. 45, a. 5c; q. 65, a. 3c). To say that God created the world "out of nothing" means that the physical world does not exist in its own right, but depends on a really self-existent Being, God, for its existence. Even a beginningless world ultimately depends on God for its existence. The metaphysical question why a thing exists is not answered by stating how long it has existed, or even by stating that it has always existed. "A thing which exists always," he says, "is not exempt in needing another in order to exist, insofar as it has its being not from itself" (*De Pot.,* q. 3, a. 13, ad 1). In Aristotelian language, creation means that the world was made and that it has an efficient cause, viz., the Mind of the Maker, but it does not have a material cause since it was not made out of anything. Aquinas clearly distinguishes the issue of the temporal origin of the universe from its ontological origin in creation *ex nihilo.* The distinction between a created thing and a thing which must necessarily have had a beginning was first made by Averroes,[30] but Aquinas elaborates on it and uses it as a powerful tool for his own purposes. His position is that (1) reason *can* demonstrate that the world was created *ex nihilo,* but at the same time he holds on philosophical grounds the *possibility* that (2) it should have been "created from all eternity," i.e., that it had no beginning, although he asserts on *faith* that (3) this possibility is contrary to fact and that the world's history had an absolute beginning *with* time (not *in* time, for time was created with the world).[31]

Briefly stated, Aquinas' view of creation boils down to this: If the world is eternal, it is simply because God willed freely from eternity that the world should come into existence from eternity; if, however, the world was created with time, it is because God willed freely from eternity to create the world in such a way that there is an ideally first moment of time. God *did* indeed reveal the absolute beginning of the world's history a finite period of time ago, but philosophically it is equally tenable that the world should have been created of eternal duration. The reason for this is that the question of whether the world had a beginning cannot be proved from the nature of things as they actually are, since no essence as such reveals anything about the duration of its act of existence (*S.T.* Ia, q. 46, a. 2). Here reason must confess its subordination to the infinitely higher realms of revelation and theology, because the duration of the universe depends upon God's inscrutable will, whose decisions cannot be investigated by reason but are recorded in Holy Scripture. Revelation alone can say with unfaltering accents, "In the beginning God created the heavens and the earth." Or, to state this "heads I win, tails you lose" argument more technically and philosophically, the creative act, as it exists in God, is certainly eternal and identical with the divine nature, but the external effect of that act, namely, the world, will follow in the way willed by God, and if God willed that the external effect should have *esse post non esse,* it will not have *esse ab aeterno,* even though the creative act, considered precisely as an act in God, is eternal. In other words, it does not necessarily follow from the fact that if the creation of the world happened at some fixed time, as a result of God's act of will, that God willed it at that time, or indeed at any other time; "from the eternal action of God an eternal effect does not follow, but only such an effect as God has willed, namely an effect which has being after non-being" (*S.T.* 1a, q. 46, a. 1. ad 10). In actual fact, therefore, theology resolves the issue with the revealed teaching that God eternally willed that, out of all possible worlds, this particular world should begin to exist in such a way that the temporal order is what it is.[32]

One cannot help feeling that the Saint was somewhat too accommodating in his explanation. *"Si dixeris 'aestuo' sudat."* What is the status of the divine will as the ultimate explanation of the world? Now it is not a *scientific* explanation for the origin of the world like (let us say) the now-discarded nebular hypothesis, and for a very obvious reason. A scientific explanation must explain why things are like this *and not like that.* It must be differential and specific. Newton's laws explain the movements of the earth; they would not be an explanation if they were true no matter how the earth moved. (Just what does a "scientific explanation" explicate if it is equally compatible with two mutually contradictory theories?) And for the same reason, the hypothesis that God exists can explain what happens on earth only if it explains why this happens and not that. Such an explanation would be valid only if there were some way of testing the Deity's intentions independently of the actual state of nature.[33] That is why Bacon said that in looking for the causes of things in nature, *Deum semper excipimus. Mutatis mutandis,* the same holds true for the universe-as-a-whole (if the universe can indeed ever be the subject of empirically justifiable propositions) unless it happens to be "just there" as a brute fact. As a physical explanation of this space-time universe and its nature, the will of God is, therefore, as fatuous as the coed's remark that God is always on the side of the team which has the best football coach.[34]

Professor A. E. Taylor admirably sums up Aquinas' arguments for viewing God as the ultimate *metaphysical* explanation of the world and why the world itself, or motion, cannot be the ultimate explanation.

Our knowledge of any event in Nature is not complete until we know the full reason for the event. So long as you only know that A is so because B is so, but cannot tell why B is so, your knowledge is incomplete. It only becomes complete when you are in a position to say that ultimately A is so because Z is so, Z being something which is its own *raison d'etre,* and therefore such that it would be senseless to ask *why* Z is so. This at once leads to the conclusion that since we always have the right to ask about any event in nature why that event is so, what are its conditions, the Z which is its own *raison d'etre* cannot itself belong to Nature.[35]

Should it be objected that Professor Taylor's argument operates within the framework of a modern epistemological context, and that the reference to "its own *raison d'etre*" is more reminiscent of Spinoza's *causa sui* than of anything in St. Thomas, we may point out that essentially the same critical observation is made in a study that is quite Thomistic in approach. Commenting on Aquinas' First Way, Professor Eric Mascall declares: "The point is not really that we cannot have an infinite regress in the order of nature, but that such an infinite regress in the series of moved movers would necessitate an unmoved First Mover not *in* the order of nature but *above* it."[36] The point of the reasoning is that each and every particular existing thing depends for its existence upon a pure Act of Being (*actus essendi*) which is absolute, self-sufficient, and free. Since this supreme cause creates not only being but order, it must be a knowing cause.[37] I find this whole line of reasoning unacceptable. I fail to see how a "self-sufficient" entity serves as an intellectually satisfactory metaphysical explanation of the world's existence and the present order of events. Why is it not perfectly proper to inquire into the reasons for the existence of the alleged pure Act of Being? It just will not do to say as Aquinas does (*S.T.* 1a, q. 3, a. 4) that God is a being Whose existence is His essence. Now the notion of such a unique Being takes for granted the twofold distinction between essence and existence, on the one hand, and necessary and possible, on the other, which was first clearly enunciated by Ibn Sīnā (Avicenna). In the *Treatise on the Soul* in the *Kitāb al-Shifa'*, Ibn Sīnā observes that we can imagine all beings to be nonexistent. He therefore argues that all beings in the world have the status of the merely possible. Ibn Sīnā then proceeds to argue that since everything *individually* may not have existed, and since the world is merely the totality or aggregate of individual existents, the world taken *as a whole* has the status of the merely possible. We shall not here inquire whether this is not an instance of the logical fallacy of composition, but consider his conclusion that the contingent nature of the world necessarily presupposes a Necessary Being (*wājib al-wujūd;* lit., Necessary of Existence) in Whom essence and existence are inseparably united. It took the efforts of Hume (*Dialogues Concerning Natural Religion* IX; *Treatise* I ii 6, I iii 7) and Kant (*Critique of Pure Reason,* A 592–603, B 620–630), not to mention many a lesser light, to analyze the fallacy of this argument. Hume pointed out that whatever we conceive as existent, we can conceive as nonexistent. That is to say, there is no being whose nonexistence implies a contradiction; and consequently no being whose existence is logically demonstrable. Kant reinforced the thrust of this argument by showing that existence is not an ordinary predicate or property whose addition enriches and whose removal impoverishes a concept. The predicate "exists" in the statement "God exists" has a status altogether different from the status of such a predicate as, say, "omnipotent" in the statement "God is omnipotent." The second can be denied in two ways, either because there is no God or because there is a God who is not omnipotent. The first can be denied in one way only, i.e., by the denial that there is a God. The upshot of these criticisms is that there is no self-explanatory being whose existence is necessitated by His nature. "Necessity" is a modal predicate which properly refers to propositions only and never to things or what is existent. A conclusion follows necessarily from its premises, but a being or thing simply exists or not. Period. "God is a Necessary Being" therefore means, "The proposition 'God exists' is logically necessary." But this is the principle of the ontological argument, and it justifies the comment of Kant that the causal proof of God's existence really involves the ontological one.[38] But Aquinas has already told us (q. 2, a. 1) that the ontological argument is unintelligible to man. God can understand it, but not we. In itself (*secundum se*), to be sure, the proposition "God exists" is self-evident because the predicate is identical with the subject; for God is His own being (*esse*) and in Him there is no separability between essence and existence, but the proposition is not itself evident for us (*quoad nos*). Hence Aquinas does not reveal to *our understanding* the ground for belief in a pure Act of Existence, and hence this supreme cause cannot be the ultimate answer to all metaphysical problems. The Necessary Being's self-existence (*esse per se subsistens*) remains a mystery, and the proof of God's existence is not rationally defended from the child's objection, "Who made God?", or more radically, "Why was there at some time a Necessary Being rather than nothing?" The biblical statement, "In the beginning God made the heavens and the earth," as Heidegger explicitly remarks, is not an answer to, and cannot even be brought into relation to, the fundamental question of philosophy. The believer who stops with a Necessary Being is not pushing his questioning "to the very end."[39] Writing specifically in reply to the Neo-Thomists, Professor Nagel states:

> It is obvious that anyone who invokes an "absolute cause" (or God) to explain "why" the world exists, merely postpones settling his accounts with the logic of his question: for the Being who has been postulated as the Creator of the

world is simply one more being into the reasons of whose existence it is possible to inquire. If those who invoke such a Being declare that such questions about His existence are not legitimate, they surmount a difficulty only by dogmatically cutting short a discussion when the intellectual current runs against them. If, on the other hand, the question is answered with the assertion that God is His own cause, the question is resolved only by falling back upon another mystery; and at best, such a "reason" is simply an unclear statement of the grounds upon which scientists regard as unintelligible the *initial* "why" as to the world's existence. But a mystery is no answer if the question to which it is a reply has a definite meaning; and in the end, nothing is gained in the way of intellectual illumination when the discussion terminates in such a manner.[40]

The "explanation" of Aquinas has this in common with that of Maimonides (whose work he studied), that both, instead of reflecting on the world and nature as they actually are, freely report allegedly revealed truths about the interior life of God, to which our intellect cannot rise by its unaided natural powers. But in doing this they have left behind the rational world and its laws and have entered a realm where all difficulties are solved by the introduction of a supernatural and inscrutable will that ontologically determines the existential process.[41] And not only have the philosopher-theologians signally failed to make the idea of creation explicable or "rational," but they were also unable to achieve a creative synthesis of the god (rather than God) of Aristotle, the unmoved mover aloof from the world in self-sufficient perfection, and the creative God of Genesis, the Maker of heaven and earth, who is personally and providentially concerned with temporal affairs and the welfare of His children. Thus, despite the exquisitely subtle logical devices employed by St. Thomas, there is an unbridgeable gulf that separates the God of the Sermon on the Mount, Who in His infinite tenderness cares even for the fall of the sparrow and of Whom it is written, *Sic Deus dilexit mundum,* and Aquinas' God in Whom there is (in the words of the occupant of the chair of theology at the Academy of St. Thomas in Rome and one of the most distinguished Dominican Thomists of the recent past) a "predominating indifference with regard to everything created."[42] Professor Lovejoy has summed up the matter well.

Perhaps the most extraordinary triumph of self-contradiction, among many such triumphs in the history of human thought, was the fusion of this conception of a self-absorbed and self-contained Perfection—of that Eternal Introvert who is the God of Aristotle—at once with the Jewish conception of a temporal Creator and busy interposing Power making for righteousness

through the hurly-burly of history, and with primitive Christianity's conception of a God whose essence is forthgoing love and who shares in all the griefs
of his creatures. When applied to the notion of creation . . . the dotrine of the
self-sufficiency of deity implied . . . that from the divine—that is, from the
final and absolute—point of view a created world is a groundless superfluity.[43]

The question may here be raised how such powerful and redoubtable
thinkers as Maimonides and Aquinas could be guilty of such flagrant
defects and flaws in their reasoning. Is it not presumptuous for modern
critics to assume a superior air toward the medieval philosopher-
theologians? Are we then intellectually superior to the medievals? To these
and related questions I would reply with a simile so beloved in medieval
literature. The medievals often viewed themselves as dwarfs seated on the
shoulders of the ancients, who are to be regarded as giants. From their van-
tage point, they maintained, they could see more things than the ancients
and things more distant, but this is due neither to the sharpness of their sight
nor to the greatness of their stature, but to the fact that they are raised and
borne aloft on the shoulders of the giants.[44] The medievals were so imbued
with ideas and concepts that seem strange and alien to us that they were
thrown off their guard and accepted them implicitly.

This becomes readily apparent if we study the medieval polemical
literature. Where two thinkers did not share the same common assumptions,
they were often keen in their criticism of each other. We shall illustrate the
point by an example taken from a Jewish thinker who lived at the end of the
medieval period and had some acquaintance with scholastic thought. In the
twenty-fifth chapter of book III of the *Sefer ha-'Iḳḳarim* (Book of Principles), Joseph Albo makes an attack on the doctrine of transubstantiation
which in its ill-mannered virulence and fury is in singularly bad taste. To be
sure, blunt and outspoken controversy, and occasionally even scathing attack, do lie at the very foundation of philosophical progress. But an attack
on a philosopher *qua* philosopher is one thing, and ridicule and mockery of
our neighbor's faith is quite another. Certainly there are extenuating circumstances; *tout comprendre, c'est tout pardonner.* Albo was persecuted by
an intolerant Church and forced to take part in a religious disputation at
Tortosa. This said, I for one would still like to think that Philo and Josephus
expressed the higher view of Judaism when they interpreted the scriptural
passage "You shall not revile the gods"[45] as teaching that one must not offend the religious sensibilities of the followers of other faiths or speak dis-
respectfully with scorn and ridicule of what others cherish as sacred. This is

not harking back to the days of the *odium theologicum* or replowing the barren sands of obsolete polemics. I shall deal exclusively with the philosophical analysis and buttressing of the dogma of transubstantiation —an antiquated Aristotelian notion of physics, as Fr. John McKenzie puts it in the new *Encyclopaedia Britannica*—with the theological or devotional aspects of the sacrament of the Eucharist I am not concerned. (Yet despite this caveat I confess that my lack of theological competence, which is so vital in such matters, vitiates what I shall have to say on the subject of transubstantiation, and I would have omitted this discussion had I not found ample medieval precedent for my undertaking it.) Before we begin our criticism, it behooves us to remember that Aquinas was well aware that the nature of the mystical change in the elements of the Eucharist cannot be strictly demonstrated. It eludes the grasp of human understanding and is known by revelation alone. Nevertheless Aquinas quite properly applied his mind to this strictly supernatural mystery and used Aristotelian concepts to show that what faith teaches is not impossible. These concepts, he held, lend clearness to some extent and help us to explore something of the intelligibility of this strictly supernatural mystery that can never be philosophically proved or justified. Against him Albo argues that this dogma not only transcends reason but flatly contradicts it; in the language of the Schoolmen it is not *praeter naturam*, but *contra naturam*. The significant part of Albo's criticism is the following (we shall not quote it in full, since being a homilist, he has the tendency to push an argument forward by mere pulpit rhetoric):

> [Transubstantiation] requires belief in the simultaneous presence of one body in two or more different places; for the body of the Messiah is present on different altars at the same time. . . . Again, they say that the substance of the bread and the wine changes into the body of the Messiah, while the accidents remain just as they were without any subject. The taste and the color and the odor and the feeling and the heaviness and the lightness and the softness and the hardness which we perceive in the bread are not in the bread at all, for the matter has disappeared and become the body of the Messiah.[46]

Now the body of Jesus was clearly not on the altar before the consecration. But a thing cannot be where it was not before, except either by its coming there itself or by something already there being changed into it. Obviously the body of Jesus does not come to the altar, for a body can only come to a place where it was not, and the impassable body of the Messiah, now glorious and immune from suffering change, does not leave heaven. But on the other hand, when one thing becomes another thing, that other thing begins to be; and therefore nothing can become a preexisting thing other than itself. Again, it is a basic thesis of Aquinas' philosophy that accidents cannot subsist apart from the substratum which sustains them, and the substratum must be a "substance." Now the substance of the Eucharist is the body of Jesus, and the accidents are not its accidents, but those of bread and wine. How, then, can the accidents, that is, the form or species, e.g., the color and taste of the bread and wine and their chemical and physical properties, persist apart from their subject?

How would Aquinas meet these difficulties? We need not speculate on this matter, since in his discussion of transubstantiation Aquinas gives us his reply to these and other objections to the doctrine. *Ab esse ad posse valet illatio!*

> Does an unbeliever profess that the changing of bread and wine into the body and blood of the Lord is impossible? Then let him consider God's omnipotence. Admit that Nature can transform one thing into another, then with greater reason should you admit that God's almighty power, which brings into existence the whole substance of things, can work, not as Nature does, by changing forms in the same matter, but by changing one whole thing into another whole thing.
>
> If he objects that such a change flies in the face of the appearance, since no change is observable, let him consider. . . . God is the creator of substance and accident; he can preserve accidents though their proper subject has been changed into something else, for his omnipotence can both produce and keep in being the effects of secondary causes without those causes.[47]

Considered externally and formally, the reasoning here shows an almost hallucinatory resemblance to Maimonides' attempt to reconcile creation with the Aristotelian philosophical system which he accepts. Yet the reasoning does not seem to be very convincing; Albo seems to have the better of the argument. Aquinas' proposed solution of the difficulties (cf. *S.T.* 3a, q. 77, a. 2), namely, that in the sacrament of the Eucharist the spatial dimension or dimensive quantity (*quantitas dimensiva*) of the bread and wine is the subject in which the other accidents inhere, is clearly unacceptable. Why? Because here, too, we are dealing with a desperate *ad hoc* theory. In any other connection, Aquinas would treat the concept of continued existence of accidents without any subject of inhesion as a Platonic philosophical heresy. He is emphatic on this point, and it is integral with his Aristotelian philosophic creed. The general principle is: "Dimensions can be considered to exist in matter only so far as matter is given substantial corporeal existence through a substantial form."[48] Dimensions, therefore, are accidents, and not substances; and neither they nor more specialized accidents can exist without a subject, as Aquinas categorically observes in his commentary on the *Sentences* of Peter Lombard.[49]

Aquinas gives his case away when he specifically refers to Plato in support of his theory that the spatial dimension—normally considered an "accident" and not a substance, and unable to subsist without a subject—of the bread and the wine takes the place of a subject and affords a support to the other accidents.[50] The substitution of a Platonic doctrine for a basic Aristotelian principle at a critical point shows to what curious straits a superior intelligence is driven in order to devise impossible reconcilements.

To summarize our criticism: the concepts of substance and accident, when applied in the context of Eucharistic theology, lead from orthodox premises to heretical conclusions, whose consequences Aquinas can avoid only by means of subtle or spurious distinctions and subdistinctions. Of course, Christian dogma does not stand or fall with the truth or falsity of Aristotelian concepts. Now had Aquinas at the very outset taken the position that substance is not a meaningful philosophical concept, we would have no quarrel with him.[51] But this is not the position taken by him. The twin concepts of substance and accident are the basic categories and foundation stones of his entire system. And no one—not even a saint—has the right to treat a philosophical concept (to borrow a metaphor from Schopenhauer) like a "hired cab" which one dismisses when one has no further use for it.[52]

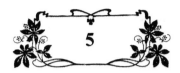

Devices to Bypass the Conflict
of Science and Religion

Let us now consider two other devices utilized by the medieval philosopher-theologian in order to reach conclusions already fixed in advance. The first of these I shall call the dialectical use of contradictory propositions, and the second, the sham solution of philosophical problems by mere verbalism. I shall illustrate these two devices from the works of Maimonides and Aquinas, respectively.

Maimonides explicitly states that in the *Guide* he may contradict himself in presenting his philosophic positions in order to veil some of his true views, which should not be disclosed to the undeserving. Maimonides went to great pains to camouflage his true teachings from the uninitiated. At the conclusion to the Introduction to the *Guide,* he speaks of the contradictions, apparent and real, which are to be found in every literary composition and divides them into seven classes or types. Of the two classes which he says are to be found in the *Guide,* the latter is the following.

> The seventh cause. In speaking about very obscure matters it is necessary to conceal some parts and to disclose others. Sometimes in the case of certain dicta this necessity requires that the discussion proceed on the basis of a certain premise, whereas in another place necessity requires that the discussion proceed on the basis of another premise contradicting the first one. In such cases the vulgar must in no way be aware of the contradiction; the author accordingly uses some device to conceal it by all means.[1]

Contradiction is one of three devices employed by Maimonides to conceal his "secret" (i.e., esoteric) teachings from the uninformed reader. The other two techniques are scattering (i.e., fragmentizing a subject into its constituent parts and then scattering them throughout the *Guide*), and the deliberate use of (inappropriate) technical terms "with great exactness and exceeding precision" so that they may catch the attention of the careful reader but will mislead a reader bent on being edified with restatements of what he already believes. But the most important of these three devices is contradiction. Its significance has been stressed by Leo Strauss in his important study, "The Literary Character of the *Guide for the Perplexed*."[2] "Contradictions," says Professor Strauss, "are the axis of the *Guide*. They show in the most convincing manner that the actual teaching of that book is sealed and at the same time reveal the way of unsealing it. While the other devices used by Maimonides compel the reader to guess the true teaching, the contradictions offer him the true teaching quite openly in either of two contradictory statements."[3] The objection is sometimes made that Strauss's criterion is too subjective and partially self-defeating: if pursued to its logical conclusion, his thesis would leave it entirely to the reader's discretion to decide between the true parts of the contradictions and those intended merely to conceal the truth.[4] I do not think that this objection is well taken. The critical canon for interpretation adopted by Strauss is the logical assumption that a seemingly casual contradiction of a conventional belief (or of a necessary presumption or consequence of such a belief) is what Maimonides really wishes to maintain, while repeated affirmations and reaffirmations of orthodox dogmas, if they are surreptitiously contradicted, are merely sops thrown to the "vulgar." Strauss quite properly concludes his analysis with the thesis that of two contradictory statements in the *Guide,* that which occurs least frequently (or which occurs only once) was considered by Maimonides to be true. Strauss's analysis has more recently been reinforced by a young Israeli scholar who points out that Maimonides' two favorite methods for calling attention to and communicating his esoteric teachings are frequently combined and interconnected. Abraham Nuriel, after a careful study of the methodological approach of Maimonides, comes to the conclusion that of two contradictory statements, the one which is formulated with a misplaced word is the one which Maimonides considers false. In the light of his theory, Nuriel examines the usage of the expression *ha-Bore'* (the Creator) in the *Guide*. He notes that this term (which rather surprisingly occurs only nineteen times in the entire work) never appears in those passages where Maimonides expresses his positive opinion on the creation of the world. Conversely, in each and every instance that this word appears, Nuriel finds that it serves to appease the censorious opinions of the vulgar. He therefore concludes that Maimonides explained the first verse of the Bible as referring to a primordial world.[5]

The more discerning and searching critics of the *Guide,* both medieval and modern, have noted that Maimonides became victimized by his methodology. From employing contradictions to conceal his positions, he passes on to using contradictory propositions as a dialectical means of reaching those positions. Maimonides at times uses contradictory premises in a completely arbitrary and cavalier manner to reach whatever conclusion he desires at the moment. We are reminded of the concept of "doublethink" in George Orwell's novel, *1984.* Doublethink means the keeping of two contradictory opinions in one's mind at the same time and the conscious disciplining of the mind to ignore the conflict between them. By the exercise of doublethink, one can, among other things, tell deliberate falsehoods while genuinely believing in them, to forget any fact that has become inconvenient, and then, when it becomes necessary again, to draw it back from oblivion for just so long as it is needed, and to deny the existence of objective reality and all the while to take account of the reality which one denies.[6] A good illustration of Maimonides' dialectical use of contradictory propositions is his proof of the existence of God. In his introduction to the second part of the *Guide,* he lists twenty-six "propositions" which summarize in compact and pithy form the main doctrine of Aristotle, by the aid of which the philosophers prove the existence, unity, and incorporeality of God. These propositions, Maimonides says, have all been proved in the *Physics* and the *Metaphysics* of Aristotle and his commentators without there being any doubt as to any point concerning them,[7] with the exception of the last one, which asserts that time and motion are eternal and therefore the world, too, is eternal. The truth of this last proposition he is willing to assume tentatively as a step in his proof, only to reject it later when he discusses the question of the eternity of the world. Shorn of embroidery, the proof is essentially Aristotle's cosmological argument of the Unmoved Mover.[8] Maimonides traces back all motion to the heavenly sphere. But this is not the end; the sphere must also have a mover. By a formally valid argument, Maimonides demonstrates that this ultimate astronomical body is moved either by (a) another body outside it; by (b) a separate immaterial entity; by (c) a corporeal force distributed in the latter; or by (d) an internal indivisible force. Of these four *prima facie* possible hypotheses regarding the nature of the mover of the sphere, (a), (c), and (d) are eliminated, leaving only alternative (b), namely, that the cause of the motion of the sphere is a separate immaterial entity which is God, the Prime Immobile Mover. But how are the other three possible alternatives eliminated? Alternative (a) is rejected because it leads to an infinite regress. But to eliminate alternatives (c) and (d) Maimonides has to assume the truth of the twenty-sixth proposition concerning the eternity of motion, which implies an infinite power. In other words, if it were not for the introduction at this critical point in the argument of what Maimonides himself in another context considers to be a false premise, viz., that motion is eternal, we would, according to him, be equally entitled to trace the primal cause of motion to a power immanent in the sphere like a human soul, or even to a corporeal force pervading the extension of the sphere as heat pervades an ordinary body, and we would have no cogent proof for the existence of God.[9]

The logical hiatus in Maimonides' argument did not escape the notice of his medieval commentators and critics. Shem-Ṭob Palquera 1225–1290), in his *Moreh ha-Moreh* (Guide of the Rebellious), asks sardonically: "How can such an important subject be demonstrated by a doubtful matter? All the more so, if it is not true! For if the premises of a proof are not true, how can the conclusion be true, and how can there be formed from them a demonstration which leaves no room for doubt?" Palquera concludes by damning Maimonides with faint praise: "Undoubtedly this did not escape the notice of our Master, of blessed memory, and all of his words are spoken with intelligence."[10]

All honor to Palquera for having detected the sophistry behind Maimonides' reasoning, but we are entitled to go much further in our criticism than he did. Allowing oneself the same latitude and conditions which Maimonides set for himself, one obtains a license to say anything and a *carte blanche* to "prove" everything. A little consideration of elementary logic will show that any arbitrary philosophical doctrine can be validly established by introducing contradictions into one's system of thought. Let us "prove" after the manner of Maimonides that Moses Mendelssohn (or, if you prefer, St. Thomas Aquinas) is the author of the *Guide*. We begin, like the Master, by affirming the contradiction "The world is eternal; the world is not eternal." Now let us treat the two halves of the contradiction as separate premises. From the former we infer that "either the world is eternal or Mendelssohn is the author of the *Guide*," for manifestly, *if* it is true that the world is eternal, then it is true that it is eternal or Mendelssohn is the author of the *Guide*. Next let us add the second half of the contradiction to the argument as a new premise, and we are now able to infer that "either the world is eternal or Mendelssohn is the author of the *Guide*, and the world is not eternal." But from this it clearly follows (by *modus tollendo ponens*) that "Mendelssohn is the author of the *Guide*." Similarly, *any* proposition whatsoever can be proved if we assume two contradictory propositions as premises.[11]

We are not here dealing with some minor point, but with the keystone of Maimonides' whole philosophical system, and it is worthwhile to examine his methodology more closely. Maimonides states that although he believes in creation *ex nihilo,* he will base his proofs for the existence, unity, and incorporeality of God on the assumption of the eternity of the world. He justifies this procedure on two counts. First, since the creation of the world is not amenable to demonstration, it cannot serve as a premise in any scientific proof. Second, on the assumption of the creation of the world, the existence of its creator is elementary, since whatever had a beginning must have been brought into existence by another being. *In utrumque paratus* could well be Maimonides' motto. If the world is not eternal, he has the proof of the Mutakallimūn. On the other hand, if the world is eternal, he has the Aristotelian proof based upon motion. He feels that the structure of his argument is above reproach and that the existence of God is assured. "You see," he says with evident self-satisfaction, "the proofs for the existence, unity and incorporeality of God must vary according to the propositions admitted by us, for only in this way can we succeed in obtaining a perfect proof, whether we assume the eternity or the creation of the universe" (*Guide* I:71; cf. II:2).

But can we? Most assuredly not. That the same identical conclusion could validly be reached by two independent arguments starting from contradictory premises ("the world is eternal—the world is not eternal") is an *impossibile per se,* a miracle which God Himself cannot perform. Take as a concrete example the most famous of all syllogisms: "All men are mortal; Socrates is a man; therefore, Socrates is mortal." The branch of philosophy known as logic has taken this syllogism as a paradigm of a valid deductive argument. The conclusion follows necessarily from the premises. Now if we substitute a counter-proposition for the major premise and change it to "No men are mortal," then the conclusion clearly is that Socrates is not mortal. Or change the major premise, substituting for it "All men are not mortal," meaning not all men are mortal, and there is no conclusion at all. If not all men are mortal, then Socrates' being a man does not prove that he is mortal or that he is not mortal. It is true, of course, that there may be more than one proof for the same thing, but the premises of these proofs cannot be contradictory. Thus Maimonides could quite properly have used a proof which prescinds from the question of temporal creation— the famous ontological argument of St. Anselm, for example. No exception could then be taken to his methodology. But this is not his procedure. He says expressly: "According to me the correct way, which is the method of demonstration about which there can be no doubt, is to establish the existence and the oneness of the deity and the negation of corporeality through the methods of the philosophers, which methods are founded upon the doctrine of the eternity of the world." And he adds: "For this reason you will always find that whenever, in what I have written in the books of jurisprudence, I happen to mention the foundations and start upon establishing the existence of the deity, I establish it by discourses that adopt the way of the doctrine of the eternity of the world. The reason is not that I believe in the eternity of the world, but that I wish to establish in our belief the existence of God, may He be exalted, through a demonstrative method as to which there is no disagreement in any respect."[12]

Someone at this point might object: "Maimonides is here criticized for demonstrating the existence of God on the double assumption that the world is both created and eternal. In fact, Maimonides undertook to demonstrate the existence of God first on the assumption that the world is created and then again on the alternative assumption that the world is eternal. His argument is a legitimate use of disjunction."[13] Let us examine this disjunctive argument more formally and see.

Either we know that the world had a beginning, or we know that the world did not have a beginning, or we do not know whether or not the world had a beginning.

@1. If we know that the world had a beginning, we must infer that it was brought into existence by a First Cause (the Kalāmist proof).

@2. If we know that the world did not have beginning, we must infer that the perpetuity of its motion requires a First Cause (the Aristotelian proof).

@3. If we do not know whether or not the world had a beginning, we must infer from what we do know of the actually existing world that it requires a First Cause.

Therefore, whether or not the world actually had a beginning, and whether or not we can know that fact, we must infer the existence of a First Cause.

Where, then, does the catch lie? Simply that the proofs do not prove the same thing. The term "First Cause" is equivocal. In @1 it means at least a maker and a mover, in @2 it means a mover but *not* a maker. What Maimonides has demonstrated is only what is common to the two different notions of a First Cause, not the God of theism and religion: a supreme personal Being, distinct from the world and creator of the world.[14] We have before us two different and incompatible conceptions of God. The unmoved mover of Aristotle—"an eternal paralytic" in Professor H. A. Wolfson's apt phrase—despite all the metaphysical compliments which Maimonides pays to Him, is not the God of Abraham, Isaac, and Jacob. On the one hand, we have the god of Aristotle, who, since his sole interest is in himself, is not a fitting object of worship, and who is postulated, as we had occasion to remark, in order to answer a problem set by metaphysics (and physics), namely, the ultimate source of motion, and on the other, we have the active Creator-God of the Bible, Who is providentially concerned with temporal affairs. Maimonides nowhere reconciles these two confused if not positively antagonistic conceptions of God; he merely incorporates both in his system. But once having proved to his satisfaction the existence of the unmoved mover of Aristotle, he expects his readers to respond to that being in the way they have traditionally responded to the loving, personal, and providential God of the Bible. In his Code (*Yad, Teshubah* 10:3) Maimonides raises the question, What is the love of God that is befitting? "It is to love God," he replies,

> with a great and exceeding love, so ardent that one's soul shall be bound up with the love of God, and one should be continually enraptured by it, like a lovesick individual, whose mind is never free from his passion for a particular woman, the thought of her filling his heart at all times, when sitting down or rising up, when he is eating or drinking. Greater even than this should be the love of God in the hearts of those who love Him. And this should continually possess them, even as He commanded us in the phrase, "with all your heart and all your soul" [Deut. 6:5]. This, Solomon expressed allegorically in the sentence, "for I am sick with love" [Cant. 2:5]. The entire Song of Songs is indeed an allegory descriptive of this love.

Yes, but one can no more adore a coldly impersonal unmoved mover than one can fall in love with a dynamo. Nor will it do to say, as Maimonides does say a few paragraphs further on: "One only loves God with the knowledge with which one knows Him. According to the knowledge will be the love. If the former be little or much, so will the latter be little or much" (*ibid.,* 10:6). No amount of knowledge will cause one to become ravished by the thought of Thought in aloof perfection any more than one can become infatuated with the second law of thermodynamics as formulated by Carnot-Clausius. When the prophet or psalmist, overcome by God's presence and providential care, like a loving Father who pities His children, exclaims: "O taste and see that the Lord is good! Happy is the man who takes refuge in Him!" (Ps. 34:8, Hebrew 34:9), we appreciate his sentiments and understand even if we do not share his religious experience. But the God of the Bible is not impassible; He has emotions and can experience sorrow, affection, and tenderness. "In all their affliction He was afflicted" (Isa. 63:9). "His tender mercies are over all His works" (Ps. 145:9)."I have loved you with an everlasting love; therefore with kindness I will draw you to Me" (Jer. 31:3). The prophet Hosea describes God as speaking in this way about Himself (11:8):

> How can I give you up, O Ephraim! . . .
> My heart recoils within Me, My compassion grows
>   warm and tender.

However, Maimonides expressly denies the qualities of affection and tenderness in God (*Guide* I:54), although some of the effects of His actions may appear, from the limited human viewpoint, to be merciful and others merciless. God is not affected by external influences, and therefore does not possess any qualities resulting from emotion (*Guide* I:52). It is therefore most difficult to perceive the religious availability of Maimonides' conception of God if we discount the emotions which the believer is likely to call up through association with the traditional concept of God as portrayed in the Bible. To anyone who would question this assertion, I propose a simple test. Let him read aloud the Twenty-third Psalm, substituting Maimonides' conception of God for that of the psalmist. The opening of the psalm would then run as follows:

> The Unknowable Negation of Privations is my shepherd;
>   I shall not want.
> It maketh me lie down in green pastures;
> It leadeth me beside the still waters.
> It restoreth my soul;
> It guideth me in straight paths for Its name's sake.
> Yea, though I walk through the valley of the shadow
>   of death,
> I will fear no evil,
> For the Unknowable is with me;
> Its rod and its staff—they comfort me.

And now, having seen the fallacies and the obvious holes in Maimonides' logic, we can recapitulate our conclusion. Maimonides (and his modern followers like Guttmann) attempt to fuse two conceptions of God which can no more be synthesized than oil and water. The unmoved mover of Aristotle and Maimonides is not really the same Being as the creative God of Genesis.

In criticizing Maimonides we are not unmindful of the problem faced by any authoritative spokesman of a great historical religion which must meet the needs of millions of adherents from every walk of life. These men and women possess different levels of understanding, and the presentment of truths must be adapted to their mental make-up. Maimonides, in his Code (*Yad, Yesode ha-Torah* 1:9), alludes to an ancient Midrash which calls attention to the variety of man's conceptions of the one God:

> God revealed Himself at the Red Sea as a mighty hero waging war [Exod. 15:3], and at Sinai [Exod. 24:10] as an old man full of compassion, even as it speaks in Daniel [7:9] of the Ancient of Days; but to the words, "The Lord is a man of war," [Exod. 15:3], the Scripture adds, "The Lord is His name" [i.e., His true essence]: it is the same God in Egypt, the same God at the Red Sea, the same God at Sinai, the same God in the past, the same God in the future, the same God in this world, the same God in the world to come.[15]

A great deal of latitude may rightfully be granted to a philosopher-theologian; latitude, yes, duplicity, no. The great critic of Maimonides, R. Abraham ben David of Posquières, for example, had to countenance reluctantly a certain mystical anthropomorphistic conception of the Deity. When Maimonides in his Code listed among the heretics and apostates (*minim*) "anyone who says that God is one but is a body and possesses a figure" (*Yad, Teshubah* 3:7), Rabad of Posquières sharply retorts: "Why does he call such a person a heretic? Many people greater and better than he have held this view in accordance with what they have seen in the verses of Scripture and even more by reason of what they had seen in those Agadot which confuse opinions."[16] Similarly, we can appreciate the remarks, undoubtedly occasioned by an actual experience, of Joseph Ya'beṣ, the fifteenth-century author of what Moritz Steinschneider has aptly described as an Apology of Theology Against Philosophy

> If there be by chance, God forbid, some ignorant woman who, barren of wisdom and understanding,is unable to conceive of God except in material

terms, but on the other hand scrupulously keeps all the commandments, and never transgressing, longs in her heart for her Creator, being ready to sacrifice her very life for God's law—and indeed, she did suffer greatly on its account—such a woman is kept in much higher regard by the Lord than all those self-styled wise intellectuals.[17]

Nor would one quarrel with St. Thomas when he wrote back as follows to an old woman who had asked him whether the names of all the blessed were written on a scroll exhibited in heaven: "So far as I can see this is not the case; but there is no harm in saying so." The same, however, cannot be said of the saint's analysis of the profound mystery of the Most Blessed Trinity for which he is known as the *princeps theologorum*. In elucidating St. Augustine's great treatise the *De Trinitate* in seventeen questions, *De Personis Divinis*, in the first part of the *Summa Theologiae*, questions 27–43, Aquinas presents his complex exposition of the metaphysics of the internal structure (i.e., the divine processions, relations and persons) of the Holy Trinity. The crux of the explanation revolves about the notion of a subsistent relation by means of which he tries to reconcile the diversity of Persons and the unity of nature in the Godhead. For example: the Father is distinct from the Son only by the relation of Fatherhood (*Paternitas*); similarly the Son is distinct from the Father only by his Sonship (*Filiatio*). So we have here literally a distinction without a difference—a "relatio cuius totum esse est *ad aliud* se habere." As Aquinas proceeds with his exposition—and any attempt to summarize his argument must necessarily be unsatisfactory and perhaps misleading—we observe a most powerful mind stunned—rendered unconscious, as it were—by the unbearable logical burden thrust upon it by Church dogma. A sympathetic but critical student makes the following comment on these cerebrations:

> The Scylla and Charybdis between which Aquinas has to sail are the conceptions that we can only distinguish the Persons as constituted by relations of origin, and are yet compelled to maintain that in God every relation is a *res,* or thing, and is the *same* thing in every case. So when we have "distinguished" between the intellective power, the thought or internal Word, and the love of God, we are to save these distinctions and relations from being regarded as merely conceptual by saying that the three Persons are *res,* realities existing in the Deity; but we must not insist in this connection, upon the truth (which we shall require, however, in other connections) that the three *res* are identically the same *res;* for so we should lose the "distinction." But again we must shrink even here from asserting that these "distinct" *res* are also "different," lest we

should directly impugn the divine unity. Nor, in insisting upon the supreme "simplicity" of the divine essence, admitting of no categorical distinction between substance and attributes, are we so to express ourselves as to imply that the distinctions, the relations, and the Persons are not real and "distinct" within that unity.... *If reason ... cannot hold either of two propositions without drawing from it inevitable conclusions that destroy the other, and is yet required to hold them both at once, and not to draw either of the mutually destructive conclusions, its submission has been pushed to the point of flat contradiction of its own nature.*[18]

It remains to show how Maimonides throws sand into the readers' eyes to prevent "the vulgar" from perceiving his juggling with contradictory premises. Numerous devices are employed by him to facilitate the movement from the premises to the conclusion, the favorite being to indulge in pious platitudes about the feebleness of the human intellect and the impossibility of knowing God's inscrutably transcendent will. Certainly, it must be conceded that the competence of human intelligence in matters of faith is very limited indeed, and that religious experience is incapable of description in wholly rational terms. When the French existentialist Gabriel Marcel makes the point (in *The Ontological Mystery*) that rationalist philosophy cannot deal with "mysteries," but only with "problems," and again, when Karl Barth and his followers aver that all rational thought is stunned and rendered unconscious, as it were, by the logical enormities thrust upon it by the Word of God, sympathy must be preferred to their religious revolt against a shallow rationalism, although I for one cannot share their extreme view that the only way into the kingdom of heaven lies through the crucifixion of the intelligence.[19] But these thinkers honestly and straightforwardly begin and continue their speculations by recognizing the limitations of reason; they do not fall back at their convenience on man's supposedly limited intelligence whenever their reasoning reaches an impasse. The situation is vastly different in the case of a professed rationalist like Maimonides. Maimonides takes into account the limitation and feebleness of the human intellect only when it serves his purpose; his on-and-off humility is sham and legerdemain to justify the smuggling of contradictory conceptions into his system. When it so suits him, human reason—his own reason—becomes most imperious and almost unlimited in its claims.

Consider Maimonides' doctrine of negative attributes. He maintains that the human intelligence is incapable of knowing anything about God's character—either in His absolute nonrelative essence or in terms of His relations to His effects—and that all predicates like "knowledge" and "goodness" are equivocal in theological usage. The correct interpretation of the biblical attributes is to regard them as denying their opposites. Every attributive expression predicated of God in the Bible either denotes the quality of a divine action, but not of the divine essence, or, although "intended for the apprehension of His essence and not of His action, it signifies the negation of the privation of the attribute in question" (*Guide* I:58, Pines trans.).[20] "All we understand is the fact that He exists, that there is an existent whom none of the existent things that He has brought into existence resembles, and who has nothing in common with them in any respect; in reference to whom there is no multiplicity or incapacity to bring into existence things other than He; whose relation to the world is that of a captain to his ship. Even this is not the true relation and a correct likeness, for this likeness has been used in order to lead the mind toward the view that He, may He be exalted, governs the existent things, the meaning of this being that He procures their existence and watches over their order as it ought to be watched over"(*loc. cit.*). (*Quaere,* is "governing" nothing positive? "Procuring"? "Watching"? It is surprising and most paradoxical that in the very passage where Maimonides categorically denies the possibility of knowing the character of God, he uses expressions such as "He governs," "He procures," and "He watches.") The upshot of this theory is that we are in a state of total ignorance in respect to God; we are left in the uncomfortable position of attributing unknowable properties to an unknowable Being, using an unknowable (equivocal) relation of attribution. But after stating that there is no relation possible between God and man (*Guide* I:52), and reducing the idea of God to an indescribable Thing that is worthless for any religious purpose (one cannot very well worship the "negation of privations"), Maimonides asserts with confidence, and repeats again and again in the third part of the *Guide,* that the goodness and wisdom of God demand that He give us a Law for our benefit, guidance, and perfection. On Maimonides' own showing that human knowledge is essentially limited, one should have thought that we could not know anything about God's infinite goodness; for all we know, His goodness or "goodness" (in quotation marks) may be entirely incompatible with our finite ideas of good and disappoint all expectations which they would lead us to entertain. Would Maimonides be prepared to maintain that God might not possibly have considered the development of self-reliance as the greatest good for man, and therefore purposely left him to his own resources in order to discover what is the good life and how to attain it without the crutch of a revealed Law? It has been said, and well said, that theological arrogance can also be a form of sinful pride. If Maimonides is so confident of what particular modes of conduct must be characteristic of God, he is in effect making himself equal with God in knowledge of the good, and is guilty of the sin of overweening pride in its most extreme form.[21] What has become, then, of man's feeble intellect? We seem to have traveled the full circle from the debasement of the individual to his deification.

Or consider the way Maimonides attempts to meet the arguments of the Arabic Aristotelians on the theme of the inconceivability of an act of creation by a perfect God. In part II of the *Guide,* chapters 14 and 18, Maimonides very fairly summarizes their arguments taken from the nature of God. Of the various arguments mentioned, we shall consider two. First, if God created the world *ex nihilo,* He must have been a potential agent before He was an actual one, and must have passed from potentiality to actuality. Consequently there was potentially in God, and there must be a cause which changed Him from a potential to an actual Creator. Again, assuming that God's action depends solely upon His own will, it would seem that His creating after not creating implies a change of will.[22] But there can be no circumstances or obstructive factors which might cause an omnipotent God to act at one time and not at another; therefore He cannot be assumed to have acted in creating the world after not having so acted.

The "error" of the Aristotelians, in Maimonides' view, comes from their failure to reflect on the absolute difference between the attributes of God and man. Purely intellectual beings, he says, are not subject to the same laws as bodies; that which necessitates a change in the latter or in the will of man need not produce a change in immaterial beings. He writes (II:18, second method):

The true essence of the will of a being is simply the faculty of conceiving a desire at one time and not conceiving it at another. In the case of corporeal beings, the will aims at certain external object changes according to obstacles and circumstances. But the will of an absolutely spiritual being which does not depend on external causes is unchangeable, and the fact that the being desires one thing one day and another thing another day, does not imply a change in the essence of that being, nor necessitate the existence of an external cause (for this change in the desire); similarly, the fact that it acts at one time and does not act at another does not constitute a change. . . . It is only by equivocation that our will and that of a being separate from matter are both designated as "will," for there is no likeness between the two wills.

Maimonides here plays a variation on his favorite theme: our total ignorance of the nature and essence of God. From the pure simplicity and absolute unity of God it follows that all His attributes are identical with His essence. Everything in God is one thing; there is no distinction of subject and
attribute, much less quantitative distinctions capable of being expressed by
predicates. What we call will in God is identical with what we call wisdom or
power or being in Him; these terms are identical with God's essence and
hence, like the essence of God, are unknowable in their meaning, and are
used only in an equivocal sense. Properly speaking, we have of the Super-
Being of God neither notion, definition, nor concept. (*Guide* II:18; cf. I:20,
50f., 53, 57, 68, III:20f., and *passim; Yad, Yesode* 2:10; *Eight Chs.*:8).

   In *Some Dogmas of Religion* (sec. 159), McTaggart has shown us with
the sure touch of a logician how to demolish effectively these sophistical and
perhaps piously insincere arguments which appeal to the limitations of
human reason. These considerations, he says, require us to be convinced,
not only that we do not know the nature of God, but that we do not know
the nature of a cause. Maimonides holds that God (or His will, which is
identical with God) is changeless and a cause. The Aristotelians argue that a
complete cause could not be changeless: if it were assumed that the universe
was created from nothing, it would imply that the First Cause had changed
from the condition of a potential Creator to that of an actual Creator, or
that His will had undergone a change. Maimonides rejects their argument
on the ground that the changelessness may be possible in some way which
we do not understand. But by the same token, what may be possible in this
mysterious way is not merely a changeless Creator but a changeless cause.
Hence a cause may be what our reason says it cannot be. But if we do not
understand the nature of a cause sufficiently to trust what our reason says
about it, the cosmological demonstration of a First Cause breaks down. "If
we are to be so skeptical about causes [says McTaggart], we shall have no
right to believe that every event must have a cause, or that an endless regress
of causes is impossible, since these conclusions rest on what our reason tells
us about causes." And his four cosmological arguments depend, as
Maimonides himself has shown in the introduction to part II of the *Guide,*
on the exclusion of the alternatives of an endless regress of causes, and of an
uncaused change.[23]

   Attention was called to some of these difficulties and contradictions by
the contemporaries of Maimonides. What is remarkable in this matter is
that this was done not only by the anti-Maimunists, which would be readily

understandable, but also by the followers and sympathizers of Maimonides. Anent the doctrine of Divine Providence, Samuel ibn Tibbon, translator of the *Guide* and staunch defender of Maimonides, pointed out flagrant contradictions between chapter 17 of part III and chapters 23 and 51 in the same part.[24] He wrote to Maimonides regarding the matter, but the Master chose to maintain a discreet silence and did not deign to reply.[25] Even more interesting are the contradictions to be found in Maimonides' doctrine of the divine attributes. Georges Vajda, in his readable *Introduction à la pensée juive du Moyen Age* (Paris, 1947), called attention to the glaring contradiction between *Guide* I:68, where Maimonides (following Ibn Sīnā) asserts the complete and permanent identity in God of the thinking subject, the act of thought, and the object of thought, and the negative theology developed previously in chapters 51–60.[26] What is most extraordinary is that the same inconsistency was noted and severely criticized by an anonymous medieval critic in a manuscript found in the Bodleian Library, entitled *The Treatise on the Unity of the Creator,* edited and published several years ago by Professor Alexander Altmann.[27]

It is not enough to criticize Maimonides' methodology from a theological viewpoint alone. One can legitimately question the morality of one who prides himself on deceiving the vulgar masses. Moral shortcomings of such a nature are bound to be reflected in one's philosophy, and one does not look for them in vain in the *Guide*. After "purifying" the concept of God to such a degree that this word lacks any ostensive reality referent (i.e., it cannot be pointed to in experience) and stands simply for the Unknowable, Maimonides makes a *volte-face* and speaks contumeliously of God's deceit, or guile. In the third part of the *Guide,* chapter 32, Maimonides speaks no less than half a dozen times of God's deceit (*al-talaṭṭuf al-ilāhi;* Ibn Tibbon, *'ormath ha-Shem*).[28] In explaining the purposes of the commandments and distinguishing between the different kinds of God's acts, he describes God's deceit as a moving force in nature and man's life. What great importance Maimonides ascribed to the idea of *'ormath ha-Shem* is evident from the fact that it serves as the keystone of his explanation of the Torah and its commandments.

Philosophers of religion have indeed frequently taught that God moves in mysterious ways His wonders to perform,[29] but hardly ever in recent times have they contended that God uses deceit to achieve his objects.[30] To this writer, it would appear preferable on moral grounds to inculcate literally all the anthropomorphisms of the *Shīʿūr Ḳōmāh* (Measure of the Divine

Body) than ascribe deceit to God.[31] Shaftesbury entertained a worthier notion of the Deity when he wrote to a young theologian: "Whilst you seek
truth you cannot offend the God of truth."[32]

In all fairness we must state that Maimonides was aware that it would be
difficult for his pupil or reader to acquiesce in the idea of deceit ascribed to
God; as if the Almighty could not achieve his ends in a direct and honest
way. He hesitates somewhat and trims badly. He imagines someone raising
the following objections to his theory of 'ormah and tries to meet them as
best he can. He says in brief:

> I know that you will recoil from the idea that the commandments were or-
> dained not for their own sake, but for the sake of something else, as if this were
> a ruse invented for our benefit by God in order to achieve His first intention.
> Nevertheless, the Torah itself tells us that God did not lead the Israelites to the
> Promised Land along the road in the direction of the Philistine country; but
> employed a roundabout route through the desert, thus inuring their bodies to
> the hardships they were to meet. Similarly, God employs a roundabout route
> for the soul to render it mature for its subsequent challenges, a way which
> necessitated that the divine command should obligate them to continue the
> practices to which they were accustomed.
>
> To the question: "What prevented God from giving a Law not employing
> such a devious way?" one may counter: "And what prevented Him from
> leading the Israelites by way of the land of the Philistines?" or "What
> prevented God from insuring obedience to His law without resort to
> punishments?"
>
> The answer to all such questions is: God does not change the nature of
> human beings by means of miracles. Though it is in His power to do so, He
> never wills it. Otherwise there would be no need at all for the Law and the ex-
> hortations of the Prophets.[33]

To this paltering we may reply in good rabbinic fashion: Your imaginary
opponent you have put off with a mere makeshift, but what will you tell us?
In human conduct, means often have no intrinsic worth but are employed so
that some end which has worth in itself can be attained. But there is nothing
which an omnipotent God cannot do—otherwise he would not be omnipotent. And therefore it would be inconsistent with his wisdom to use means
intrinsically worthless, since he can achieve their end as well without them.
Insofar, therefore, as any fact of nature or of man's moral life suggests that
it owes its existence to its utility as a means for a divine purpose, it suggests,
with just the same force, that God is not omnipotent. But this is not all.

Maimonides professes to believe in a God who is not only omnipotent, but all-good. Now, when we are dealing with human beings of limited power, the use of means to achieve some greater good may be completely justified. A surgeon, for example, is often justified in inflicting exquisite pain by an operation. But this is so because his end cannot be attained without the use of these means. To use an intrinsically evil thing—deceit—as a means when the end could be attained as well without it, would deprive the agent of all claim to goodness as well as to wisdom. And this would be the position of an omnipotent God who used such means. Obviously Maimonides' argument is not conclusive, because his premise that the Law as a whole is a means to an end is unacceptable. For normative Judaism the Law is the divinely appointed end in itself, as Professor Louis Ginzberg has correctly observed.[34] But if his premises were correct and his reasoning valid, the argument would establish not what Maimonides intended it to establish; rather it would be a proof positive that God is not all-good, all-powerful, and all-wise.[35]

Habent sua fata libelli. In Victorian England Dean Mansel, in his Bampton Lectures on *The Limits of Religious Thought*, delivered and published in 1858, championed a position on the nature and attributes of God not unlike that of Maimonides, namely that we can know *that* the infinite exists but not know *what* it is, and that God is perfectly good but that we cannot know the nature of that goodness, which is manifestly different from and superior to that of finite creatures. His theory, however, was given short shrift by John Stuart Mill, who, in a memorable discussion, exposed the disastrous and stultifying moral confusion which it entails.

> When we mean different things we have no right to call them by the same name, and to apply to them the same predicates, moral and intellectual. Language has no meaning for the words Just, Merciful, Benevolent, save that in which we predicate them of our fellow-creatures; and unless that is what we intend to express by them, we have no business to employ the words. If in affirming them of God we do not mean to affirm these very qualities, differing only as greater in degree, we are neither philosophically nor morally entitled to affirm them at all. . . . If in ascribing goodness to God I do not mean what I mean by goodness; if I do not mean the goodness of which I have some knowledge but an incomprehensible attribute of an incomprehensible substance, which for aught I know may be a totally different quality from that which I love and venerate . . . what do I mean by calling it goodness, and what reason have I for venerating it? If I know nothing about what the attribute is, I cannot tell that it is a proper object of veneration. To say that God's goodness may be different in kind from man's goodness, what is it but saying, with a

slight change of phraseology, that God may possibly not be good? To assert in words what we do not think in meaning, is as suitable a definition as can be given of a moral falsehood. . . .

If, instead of the "glad tidings" that there exists a Being in whom all the excellence which the highest human mind can conceive, exist in a degree inconceivable to us, I am informed that the world is ruled by a being whose attributes are infinite, but what they are we cannot learn, nor what are the principles of his government, except that "the highest human morality which we are capable of conceiving" does not sanction them; convince me of it, and I will bear my fate as I may. But when I am told that I must believe this, and at the same time call this being by the names which express and affirm the highest morality, I say in plain terms that I will not. Whatever such power such a being may have over me, there is one thing which he shall not do; he shall not compel me to worship him. I will call no being good, who is not what I mean when I apply that epithet to my fellow-creatures; and if such a being can sentence me to hell for not so calling him, to hell I will go.[36]

Aquinas tries to avoid the agnostic conclusion entailed by Maimonides' theory of negative attributes by his doctrine of analogical predication of being (*S.T.* Ia, q. 13, a. 5; *C.G.* I, chap. 34; *De Verit.* q. 2, a. 11 c). Professor A. E. Taylor has even attempted to show, in his excellent study, *St. Thomas Aquinas as a Philosopher* (cf. *Philosophical Studies* [London, 1934], esp. pp. 251 f.), that Aquinas' use of the principle of analogy stabilized the metaphysics of the Middle Ages, and reduced it from a chaotic and undisciplined play of opinions to a regulated system. It is quite true that Aquinas tries, by means of the notion of analogy, to escape from the pitfalls of anthropomorphism, on the one hand, and agnosticism, on the other. He recognizes quite clearly that if all predicates are assumed to be necessarily inapplicable, we would end in sheer agnosticism and could not think or speak of God at all, *non enim possumus nominare Deum, nisi ex creaturis.* On the other hand, if attributes are predicated "simply univocally" of God and of creatures, we land in the pit of anthropomorphism, for, as Aquinas quite properly points out, as applied to creatures every term implies limitations to which God is not subject. For example, when we call a man wise, "we signify that perfection as distinct from others"—from the essence "man" itself, from his power, his existence, and his other attributes, but in God, who is pure Being and, therefore, absolutely simple, all perfections are undivisibly united. St. Thomas wishes to break down this either/or dilemma by the affirmation of "analogy of being." By means of analogical reasoning we arrive at a kind of quasi-knowledge, which, although it cannot grasp the divine nature as it is in itself, yet does to some extent illumine us. Thomists place high hopes on analogical knowledge, which is so fundamental to their synthesis: "in our time it appears more and more that there lies the salvation of metaphysics."[37]

It is regrettable that Aquinas did not elaborate a theory of analogical predication. That task was left to his sixteenth-century follower and commentator, Thomas de Vio Cardinal Cajetan, known simply as Cajetan. His short treatise *On the Analogy of Names* (*De Nominum Analogia*) was until recently accepted by the vast majority of Thomists as a faithful interpretation of St. Thomas and became the classic opuscule on predication in general and on analogy in particular. This work was considered such a splendid and illuminating exposition of the subject that John of St. Thomas was led to remark that since the publication of Cajetan's work there is little left to be said on the subject.[38] Recently, however, Cajetan's version of analogy has been challenged both without (Lyttkens) and within (Klubertanz, McInerny, and Mondin) the scholastic tradition.[39] It is said that Cajetan was not entirely faithful to the thought of his master, and that he classified and interpreted Aquinas' teaching in a Procrustean manner. Cajetan has comparatively few followers now, though J. F. Anderson, in *Reflections on the Analogy of Being* (The Hague, 1967), still seems to follow the traditional interpretation of Cajetan as explained by John of St. Thomas and Penido. The correct interpretation of Aquinas may safely be left to the textual critics, but we shall briefly discuss a few problem areas in the theory of analogy.

We shall consider both the theory of Cajetan and some of the modern interpretations. But first a word of caution is in order. In *The Christian Philosophy of St. Thomas Aquinas,* Professor Gilson expresses surprise at the quantity of articles, papers, and volumes devoted to the subject of analogy in St. Thomas, in view of the relatively few texts directly devoted to this subject. Some of these studies, unfortunately, throw more heat than light on the subject. We find a Dominican Thomist violently accusing a fellow Dominican of perverting the sublime teaching of the Angelic Doctor on analogy, and both in turn denouncing a Jesuit for openly teaching Suarezianism in place of the perennial philosophy of the Common Doctor of the Church. A Neo-Thomist then enters the fray with the remark that he is very loath to attack a fellow Catholic theologian in these atheistic days when the faithful should unite for the defense of the faith and the good of souls, but . . . In such a situation an outsider can only shake his head and exclaim, "See how these Christians love one another!" I therefore ask for indulgence and a little Christian charity should I commit some ludicrous blunders on a very abstruse subject on which there is a diversity of opinions among the masters of the schools and which demands, according to Cajetan, a special elevation of the mind.

The explanation of the analogy of proper (intrinsic) proportionality as a four-term relation, the only true metaphysical analogy accepted by Cajetan (*De Nonimun Analogia,* chap. 3), was subjected to a devastating criticism at the beginning of this century by a professor of philosophy at the Catholic Institute of Paris, Fr. A.D. Sertillanges, O.P. (cf. "Agnosticisme ou anthropomorphisme?" in *Revue de Philosophie,* vol. 8 [1906], pp. 129–65, especially pp. 160 f.). The gist of his criticism is that the quasi-mathematical form of the alleged relations is deceiving and merely verbal. For instance, take the analogy: the goodness of man is to man as the goodness of God is to God. We note that two of the terms of this relation, namely God and His goodness, are strictly identical. Now St. Thomas generally, but by no means quite consistently, denied any real distinction of the absolute perfections in the divine essence, which is an undifferentiated unity and absolutely simple. Aquinas, in common with other Schoolmen, had to face the problem of how the unity and simplicity of God could be reconciled with a multiplicity of attributes which seem to be "superadded" to His essence. In order not to compromise the absolute simpleness of God, it was maintained that the Divine attributes are identical among themselves and with God's essence and existence. This is known as the doctrine of essential predication, i.e., that the predicates (Divine attributes) are identical with the essence of the subject (God) and with one another (by the transitivity of the identity relation). For Aquinas, God's goodness *is* God.[40] On one side of the proportion, then, we have an absolute identity. Furthermore, if there are no relations in God, then the relation of attribution is also ruled out.[41] At best any relations between God and His perfections can only be *in intellectu.* And even if—and this a big if— we were to grant that a purely logical distinction (i.e., one having no basis whatever in reality) is sufficient to found a similarity of proportions (having four terms related in a likeness of proportions) enabling us to establish ontological properties without falsifying reality, as some modern Thomists do indeed maintain,[42] we are still not out of the woods. Now in mathematical proportion it is possible to calculate the value of one term given the values of the other three. And even in ordinary analogical arguments, where the relation is not quantitative (A:B:C:D), at least three of the four terms are known and familiar, but in the analogy of proper proportionality *both* terms on the divine side are unknown. Thus in the illustration given, if we knew the nature of man and the nature of goodness in finite creatures, this would not enable us to discover anything about the essence of God or His goodness. This type of analogy, therefore, gets us nowhere.

Let us now consider the analogy of causal participation, which is favored by many contemporary Thomists, and see if it fares any better. According to Aquinas, the foundation of all analogy is the resemblance of creatures to God. The basis of analogical predication, says Professor Gilson, "is the resemblance which an effect always preserves in relation to its cause, however inferior to it it may be."[43] The ontological ground of the analogy between God and other beings is the principle that every agent, or cause, acts to produce its like (*omne agens agit simile sibi*), which St. Thomas takes to be self-evident.[44] Therefore, since every agent "acts in accord with its form, the effect must in some way resemble the form of the agent" (*S.T.* 1a, q. 4, a. 3 c). If the agent and the effect are in the same species, their like forms will be of the same specific type. If, however, the agent is outside the species but in the same genus, the forms will be alike, but not of the same specific type. But since God is not contained in any genus, His effects (creatures) can be said to "participate in the likeness of the agent's form . . . only according to some sort of analogy that holds between all things because they have existence in common" (*ibid.*). Thus it can be said, according to St. Thomas, that all created things are like God so far as they exist, since God is the "First and universal principle of all being" (*ibid.*). But in the absence of any specific or generic likeness, the resemblance of creatures to God may be affirmed "only *analogically* [*secundum analogiam*], viz., inasmuch as God exists in His own essence, and other things are beings by participation" (*ibid.*, ad 3, emphasis supplied). This seems to leave the Angelic Doctor in the embarrassing predicament of having to invoke one analogy to explain another and ending up in a vicious regress of analogical explanations. (Cf. Paul Hayner, "Analogical Predication," in *Journal of Philosophy*, vol. 55 [1958], pp. 855–62. This infinite regress argument is similar to the difficulty of the relation of the Platonic ideas to concrete objects that Aristotle refers to as "the third man" criticism.) This view of analogical predication with its grounding of analogy on analogy seems to be no great improvement over the classical exposition of Cardinal Cajetan.

I shall briefly state two other difficulties (among others) which I find in Aquinas' view of analogical predication.

1. The negative theology of the *via negationis* or *remotionis* (probably taken over from Maimonides and the pseudo-Dionysius), which would inhibit us from affirming *any* positive predicates of God—with the possible exception of "Being"—logically seems to be formally inconsistent with the analogical use of attributes in the *via affirmationis,* in which many analogical terms do have some positive elements of meaning predicable alike of creatures and God, "though in a more excellent manner." Thus in *Contra*

Gentiles 1:35 Aquinas sets out to prove that "the several names predicated of God are *not* synonymous." Furthermore, the distinction between the divine essence and its attributes is not merely "logical," but "real," as Aquinas makes clear in his Commentary on the *Sentences* of Peter Lombard (*In lib. I Sent.,* d. 2, q. 1, a. 3). But in discussing the method of remotion or negative differentiation in book I, chapter 14 of the *Summa Contra Gentiles,* Aquinas categorically states: "The divine substance, by its immensity, surpasses every form that our intellect reaches. Thus we are unable to apprehend it by knowing *what it is.* Yet we are able to have some knowledge of it by knowing *what it is not.* Furthermore, we approach nearer to a knowledge of God according as through our intellect we are able to remove more and more things from Him." Again, near the beginning of the *Summa Theologiae* (q. 3, proem.), before discussing the attributes of God, he says: "Because we cannot know what God is, but only what He is not, we must therefore consider the ways in which God is not, rather than the ways in which He is." Unless analogical predication can annul the Law of Contradiction, which traditional (but not modern) logic considers ontological or metaphysical,[45] I cannot see, with the best will in the world, how the affirmation and the negation of the same predicates of the same subject can be reconciled, or how it can consistently be maintained that we can only know what God is not, and also that we can know positively, though imperfectly, what He is, by arguments "proceeding to God from creatures." Aquinas' assertion (*S.T.* 1a, q. 13, a. 3) that affirmative predicates are excluded only with regard to their "mode of signification," but that with respect to "what is signified" by them only all imperfect limited realizations of the absolute perfections (all limited modes) are negated, and not the positive core of the affirmative way if it signifies absolute perfections, is based on an artificial distinction and is unconvincing. Neither do I think that it is quite accurate to say that the attribution of simple perfections to God gives us no real knowledge of His essence. Since according to Aquinas there are no accidents in God, it follows that any knowledge that we have of God *must* be knowledge of the divine essence, however imperfect. Even M. Maritain, in *The Degrees of Knowledge,* is forced to admit that we cannot claim to have knowledge of God without knowing anything of His essence.[46]

2. Some nonanalogical knowledge seems to be presupposed in Aquinas' account of God's attributes. Penido, with his usual clarity, states: "Analogy begins where the Five Ways end." Just so! This seems to me to put the matter admirably. There is no mention of analogy in the alleged proofs of God's existence. There God is not spoken of as something analogically resembling

a first unmoved mover, but as The First Unmoved Mover. If we had no univocal knowledge of God's properties, we could not even know which the appropriate attributes are to ascribe to God. If the proposition "God loves me" is not really true, but only "analogically" true *secundum modum altiorem,* how do we know that God's love might not appear as hate to us? A God who only possesses analogical perfections, in contrast to univocal ones, does not seem to be a fit object of worship or worth contending for. John Stuart Mill's criticism in the passage quoted on p. 57 hits the nail on the head. (Note: From the viewpoint of the *prima via,* I think that motion can be taken either univocally or analogically; and in the first case it is not necessary to speak of analogy. When one allows many different kinds of motion or change, then it is possible to speak of movers that are moved in one sense, unmoved in another; these may be referred to as "relatively unmoved movers," and they can pertain to many different categories of being. When one comes to a mover that is absolutely unmoved in all orders, then he has arrived at the FIRST Unmoved Mover. Nevertheless when pressed, the Thomist, it seems to me, would have to admit inconsistently that the description "The First Unmoved Mover," which can be applied to only one being, God, and is never used in any other predication of another being, is for Aquinas an analogical concept, although this is understood rather than explicitly stated by the Saint. Otherwise this unique combination of terms would be a true definition of God *per genus et differentiam,* which St. Thomas says cannot be given, since in question 3, article 5 of part I of the *Summa Theologiae* he denies that God is in any genus for several reasons, the chief being that God transcends all categories.)

The end is as the beginning. We began this discussion by pointing out that Aquinas utilized the method of analogy in order to avoid the opposite extremes of anthropomorphism, which results from the application of attributes in a univocal sense to God and creatures, and agnosticism, which results from applying them in a purely equivocal sense. While attempting to provide us with a genuine "middle way," the logic of analogy ends up in being a combination of—or a running back and forth between—the two extremes, oscillating between anthropomorphism and agnosticism as it tends toward one or the other of the unacceptable extremes.

St. Thomas was a much more systematic expositor of his views than Maimonides. Professor Gilson once described him as "the greatest arranger of ideas that ever lived." His system has been likened to a great "cathedral of ideas" where every concept is in its proper place. The Thomist philosophy gives us the conception of a rational world, of substance and act, of cause and effect, of potentiality and actuality. It affirms the hierarchy of being, the existence of God who is absolute being and pure actuality, and the world which He created not in order to increase His perfection, which is impossible, but as an act of selfless love, of infinite generosity, a diffusion of Himself which produced a universe graded from nothing to pure being—from chaos, through formed matter lacking life, through plant and animal and human life, through the pure spiritual life which is that of the angels, to the reality of God Himself, which transcends the created world. When one is confronted with the edifice which the Saint has constructed, one is tempted to exclaim, "Almost thou persuadest me to be a Christian" (Acts 26:28). Almost, but not quite. Upon a more precise consideration many scholastic theories turn out to be merely verbal; the arguments have validity only to a mind which accepts the scholastic terminology. Take, for example, the first of the Five Ways in the *Summa Theologiae* (Ia, q. 2, a. 3c), the proof *ex motu* for the existence of God. This seems to have been the favorite proof of Aquinas, who characterizes it as "the first and more obvious way" (*manifestior via*) and in the *Summa Contra Gentiles* (bk. I, chap. 13) devotes more space to it than to any of the other proofs. The senses (so the argument runs) observe something moving, and everything which moves must be moved by something else.[47] That which is moved must be in a state of potency, and that which moves in a state of act; thus fire, which is actually hot, makes wood, which is potentially hot, to be actually hot. A thing cannot be in potency and in act at the same time and in the same respect, it cannot move itself, and an infinite regress of causes is inconceivable. Therefore, there must be a First Mover, himself unmoved, who is the ultimate source of motion in the world. Otherwise there would be no actual production of motion and no motion could take place anywhere. Since we see that it does take place, it is necessary to posit such a First Mover.

The foregoing demonstration is valid only if one accepts the terminology of the Aristotelian-scholastic qualitative physics. According to Aristotle, the *qualitative* differences which our senses apprehend are fundamental. The world is made up of the following four elements (or mixtures of them in diverse proportions): fire, air, water, and earth. Furthermore, each element must have two of the following four sensible characteristics: hot, cold, dry, and moist. Thus fire is hot and dry; air, hot and moist; water, moist and cold; and earth, cold and dry. These are the qualities to which Aquinas refers when he says that when a body has one of them only in potency, it cannot acquire the quality unless it receives it from another body, which has it in act, or as we would say today, actually. On this analysis motion does not pass from the mover to the moved; it is already in the movable object, but in a state of potency; an agent (a mover) is needed to reduce the motion which is in potency to actual motion. By its action the agent arouses movement (i.e., change) in a movable object from the state of potency to the state of act.

Modern physics has discarded this type of analysis completely. It has abandoned qualitative distinctions, and it is built on a dynamic rather than static foundation. The problem of accounting for movement externally has no place in the mathematical physics of Galileo and Newton. They did away with the idea that motion (and hence other kinds of change) requires some explanation of its persistence. Newton's first law, frequently called the "law of inertia," states: "Every body continues in its state of rest, or of uniform motion in a straight line, unless it is compelled to change that state by forces impressed upon it."[48] Two points may be noted: (1) The law holds good for any kind of matter, and (2) motion as such does not need an explanation; it is only change in the direction or speed of motion that need be accounted for. Furthermore, differential motion and change in direction are fully explicable in terms of the interaction of forces communicated by one body to another by impact or gravitation. (To be sure, Newton's law does not by itself account for the origin and presence of motion in the universe, but at the very least, according to his principles, there would be no more difficulty about motion *ab aeterno* than about immobility *ab aeterno* of an unmoved mover.)[49] Thus the proof from motion is open to the objection that the Aristotelian-Thomistic principle "Whatever is in motion is put in motion by another" (*omne quod movetur ab alio movetur*), on which the whole argument depends, is irreconcilable with modern mathematical physics, and is therefore false.[50] Modern science, with its concepts of space-time, force and energy, radioactivity, relativity, process, etc., has created problems and difficulties of its own, but it has forestalled the problem of Aquinas, which was to account for motion externally. The point I am trying to make has been very well put by Alasdair MacIntyre.

Christianity does not and never has depended upon the truth of an Aristotelian physics in which the physical system requires a Prime Mover, and consequently many skeptics as well as many believers have treated the destruction of the Aristotelian argument in its Thomist form as something very little germane to the question whether or not Christianity is true. But in fact the replacement of a physics which requires a Prime Mover by a physics which does not secularizes a whole area of inquiry. It weakens the hold of the concept of God on our intellectual life by showing that in this area we can dispense with descriptions which have any connection with the concept.[51]

But my purpose is not so much to prove that there is bad science in Aquinas, which is admitted by everyone, nor even to point out the close bond that unites physics and metaphysics in his system, as to show that the chief categories in the Aristotelian-Thomist system have no explanatory value. The fundamental distinction between potency and act does not amount to anything more than the formulation in abstract terms of some half-refined common-sense notions. Add to this the law of identity, which forms the basis of all reasoning: A is A. Surely no one will question that this is a self-evident principle. How can anyone deny that A is A? It must be A, and everything left to itself is just itself, cannot be other than itself, and cannot change itself. If, then, it does change, the cause lies outside itself. Of course, whatever changes must have in itself the capacity or potentiality of being changed; but in and of itself it cannot realize this potentiality. Speaking philosophically we might say: another is needed to bestow otherness upon it. And that other must be actual, not mere capacity or potentiality, otherwise it could not give actuality to the potentiality in the changing thing, for obviously a thing cannot give what it has not got. Only being can generate, or cause, further being. And so, sooner or later, we must come to a first cause, and this we call God. All this sounds commonsensical and charming. But reflect for moment: To say that the acorn is potentially an oak and becomes the oak by maturation does not help us to understand why, or how, the oak develops out of the acorn. It it like saying that sleeping pills induce sleep because they have a soporific quality. In discussing the metaphysics of Sir Isaac Newton, Professor Burtt makes the pregnant observation: "Instead of treating things in terms of substance, accident, and causality, essence and idea, matter and form, potentiality and actuality, we now treat them in terms of forces, motions, and laws, changes of mass in space and time, and the like."[52] This shift in terminology has not so much refuted the Aquinian proof from motion as it has shown that this proof is largely verbal. That this is indeed so accounts for the fact that the scientific criticism of Aquinas' argument was anticipated by several hundred years by some of the Franciscan Schoolmen, especially William of Ockham. This also explains why at the dawn of the modern era, Dominic Bañes, whom Professor Gilson considers the most Thomistic of all the great commentators on the *Summa,* maintained that the attempt to demonstrate the existence of God by means of another philosophy and metaphysics, would be temerarious with respect to faith.[53]

Very instructive also is the reaction of some Neo-Thomists to the Newtonian difficulties. As modern science departs further and further from its medieval antecedents, it becomes increasingly laborious to reconcile the Thomistic metaphysic with modern science. Some attempted reconciliations sound like empty verbal abstractions. Some Thomists have said that the principle of inertia does not invalidate the First Way, but merely proves that local motion is not *motus* in the required sense. Local motion is merely an extrinsic variation, not a real transition from potentiality to actuality in a body, since one position in space is no more perfect than another. This is like arguing that if a man is traveling in a car on the highway and looks at the speedometer to check his speed and finds that the needle does not register, it does not follow that the speedometer is broken but rather that the car is not moving! Others maintain that the First Way depends upon a metaphysical analysis of phenomena of an exclusively metaphysical kind. Occult metaphysical transitions detectable only by the spiritual eye of the metaphysician are analyzed ultimately in terms of an existential act (*esse*) of the actual occurrence of a motion, this being taken to be something different from the motion occurring. Dr. Anthony Kenny, who was trained in scholastic philosophy at the Gregorian University in Rome, has done well to call nonsense by its name, and of course, I am not going to be more severe with the Thomists than he is. "The thesis," he says, "seems nonsensical in itself, and false as an interpretation of St. Thomas." And again: "The texts . . . from St. Thomas do not seem to support the nonsensical view that when you have explained a particular motion at a particular time you have to explain also the occurrence of that motion."[54]

Perhaps it will be said that these thinkers are atypical and that they do not do justice to the ideas of a philosopher whose influence is greater today than it was during the Middle Ages. The same cannot, however, be said of M. Maritain. This is how this thinker attempts to reconcile the doctrine of evolution with the notion of substantial form.[55] The difficulty is to see how, if a substantial form is fixed and definite, it can contain a principle that allows for its own transformation, not merely into another substantial form, but into a greater one.[56]

> No substantial form [says M. Maritain] can be transformed into another; when a substantial change occurs, the new substantial form is drawn out ("educed") from the potentiality of matter, according to the ultimate root dispositions introduced in matter by the activities of the substances which are in the process of "corruption," and which will cease to exist at the instant in which the new substance comes into being.

The new substance can be more "perfect"—imply a higher degree of integration and individuality—in the ontological scale of physical nature, not only because matter (prime matter) "aspires" to the full actualization of all the forms it contains in its potentiality, but because the new substance is just the integration, in a new formal and subsisting unity, of the activities brought about in matter by the antecedent substances, which "generates" it at the instant when they destroy each other (and whose forms remain virtually in the new substantial form then educed); and because the entire cosmos and the interaction of all its energies co-operate in the production of this substance, that is, in the "eduction" of this new substantial form. Now when it comes to the biological realm, the new living organism has of necessity the same specific substantial form as the organism or organisms from which it proceeds. How then is biological evolution to be conceived in terms of substantial forms? I see only two kinds of explanation. First, species (not the taxonomic but the ontological species) could be conceived, not only in a more extensive, but also in a more dynamic manner. And accordingly the substantial form, in the realm of life, would be regarded as protruding in its virtualities, beyond the capacities of the matter it informs in given conditions, and viewed as an ontological impulse realizing itself in various patterns along the line of a certain phylum. Yet such evolution could, of course, only take place within the limits of the phylum or the ontological species in question. Second, if now we take into account the transcendent action of the first cause, we may obviously conceive that, particularly in those formative ages when the world was in the state of its greatest plasticity, the existence-giving influx of God, passing through created beings, and using them as instrumental causes, enabled—and perhaps still enables—a substantial form to act on matter (by means of the vital energies which proceed from this form into the organism it informs) beyond the limits of its specificity, so that a new substantial form, specifically "greater" or more elevated in being, is educed from the potentiality of matter thus more perfectly disposed.[57]

To which I add a most fervent Amen! There is only one further comment that I should like to make on these "much too summarized considerations." "Non in dialectica," said St. Ambrose, "complacuit Deo salvum facere populum suum" (It has not pleased God to save his people with dialectics—*De Fide,* I, 5, sec. 42).

The well-ordered philosophical scheme of St. Thomas, which from the outside looks like the very citadel of truth, turns out to be, on closer examination, a mere house built on sand. All the quiddities, intelligible species, absolute essences, and oversubtle and artificial distinctions without differences between tweedledums and tweedledees, which are invisible even to a trained theological eye save under a scholastic microscope, do not offer an intelligible reconciliation of the discords in the universe, but only add new difficulties. As to creation: we have seen that why and how God created the world must remain a mystery. Aquinas has failed to tell us what possible reason, motive, or desire God, who is already complete and perfect existence, could have had to create the world. The most authoritative contemporary authority on Aquinas is forced to say:

> Why did God create the world when He did not have to do so? Why did he create this particular world when there were so many others [and better ones, *nota bene*—J.H.] He might have created? But such questions do not demand a reply unless one finds inadequate the simple statement that these things are so because God willed them. We know that the divine will has no cause. . . . He willed that there be men for the greater perfection of the universe and because He willed that such creatures should exist in order to enjoy Him. But it remains absolutely impossible to assign an ulterior cause to this last will. The existence of the universe and of creatures capable of enjoying their creator has no other cause than the pure and simple will of God.[58]

But if this is so, then the process of creation and the drama of salvation are meaningless. In the beginning, we are asked to suppose, there was God, and God was perfect in the closed circle of His own existence. There was no need for God to create the world, Aquinas maintained:"the divine goodness is perfect in itself, and would be so even if no creature existed" (*De Veritate,* q. 23, a. 4 c.). "The divine being contains in itself the whole perfection of being" (*S.T.* la, q. 19, a. 4 c.). The creation of the world and man was, then, a stupendous misfortune, for without it there existed only pure perfection, while with it there came into existence also innumerable degrees of imperfection and evil. Let us now suppose that all men will ultimately be redeemed and gain eternal life. But this was the condition at the beginning, when God reigned in self-contained perfection. What, then, is the meaning of a process which entails evil, pain, and suffering, and this, if all goes well (which, since there is free will, it may very well not do), has for its end a condition that is identical with its beginning?[59] On this point Maimonides for once is forthright, and his admission that the various theological explanations of the purpose of creation, when logically pressed, issue in a confession of ignorance is most significant. I quote from Friedländer's translation of the *Guide:*

But of those who accept our theory that the whole universe has been created from nothing, some hold that the inquiry after the purpose of creation is necessary, and assume that the universe was only created for the sake of man's existence, that he might serve God . . . The literal meanings of some passages in the books of the prophets greatly support this idea. Compare: "He formed it (viz., the earth) to be inhabited" (Isa. 45:18). . . . On examining this·opinion as intelligent persons ought to examine all different opinions, we shall discover the errors it includes. . . . Even if the universe existed for man's sake and man existed for the purpose of serving God . . . the question remains, "What is the end of serving God?" He does not become more perfect if all His creatures serve Him and comprehend Him as far as possible; nor would He lose anything if nothing existed beside Him. It might perhaps be replied that the service of God is not intended for God's perfection; it is intended for our own perfection,—it is good for us, it makes us perfect. But then the question might be repeated, "What is the object of our being perfect?" We must in continuing the inquiry as to the purpose of creation at last arrive at the answer, "It was the will of God" . . .[60]

Nor can we understand the secret of divine generation (as of the Son from the Father). "And Ambrose says, 'It is impossible to know the mystery of generation.'"[61] Add to this that the chief categories of the system have no explanatory value, and the whole synthesis becomes threadbare.[62]

What may be termed the half-hearted, rationalist theological explanations of the dealings of God with man, found in Maimonides, and to a much lesser extent in Aquinas, have a tendency to "turn off" both believers, who find them superfluous and fatiguing, and unbelievers to whom they appear unconvincing and useless.

This feature can be seen in Maimonides' view that one must accept some miracles but no more than necessary, and is even more prominent in his treatment of the phenomenon of prophecy.

Abraham Geiger, one of the pioneers of the Jewish new learning in the nineteenth century, makes an interesting observation in one of his early works. A certain talmudic sage once remarked in the Academy that although he was "like one seventy years old," he had never had the good fortune to comprehend the reason for a certain religious practice. What is the meaning of the phrase "like seventy years old"? Geiger says that there are three possible explanations.[63] The simplest, and the one that appeals to him most, is found in the Jerusalem Talmud. According to this interpretation, the phrase simply means "about, or nearly, seventy years old." We can call this the natural explanation. A second possible explanation is that the rabbi was a precocious young scholar, barely eighteen years old when he was elected to become the head of the Academy, and a miracle was wrought for him, whereby his hair turned white overnight, so that he could possess the dignity of office which white hair brings. The same idea seems to underlie the British custom of the wearing of a wig by a judge or attorney. Let us call this the miraculous or supernatural explanation. The third explanation is the pseudo-scientific rationalization offered by Maimonides, which Geiger finds unacceptable. According to Maimonides, hard study can make a teenager's hair turn white overnight, and this is exactly what happened. But, says Geiger, this picture of a college sophomore cramming for an examination just will not do. The "natural" gray beard serves no useful function. If the young man showed undue signs of mental development and had scholarly accomplishments to his credit, the gray beard is unnecessary, and if he was an ignoramus, the gray beard is of no avail, even if he were one hundred seventy years old.

Geiger has put his finger on a real weakness in Maimonides' thinking. A half-hearted rationalism is symptomatic of his philosophical views. At first glance his ideas sometimes seem very modern, but on closer analysis it will be found that they raise more difficulties than they solve.

His treatment of the phenomenon of prophecy is a case in point.[64] When Maimonides studied the biblical accounts of prophetical dreams and visions, he was struck by the fact that mention is usually made in the texts, expressly or implicitly, of an angel or of his discourse. Maimonides identifies the biblical angel with the creative imagination of the prophet and views the latter as an inspired genius. Thus prophetical revelations, whether in visions or in dreams (which differ from visions in degree but not in kind), are reduced to purely subjective experiences to which nothing corresponds in the external world. Prophetic visions and dreams do not reproduce real events taking place in the external world which are perceived by the prophet's sense, but rather events of his imagination generated by the Active Intellect under the influence of God's creative power.[65]

All this sounds very modern. The analysis of the prophetic experience into states, beginning with a preparatory stage of mental training followed by deep study and inspiration, closely parallels the stages of thought through which, according to a modern authority, every creative student must pass in his growth. If we examine a single achievement of thought, according to this authority, we can distinguish four stages: Preparation, Incubation, Illumination (and its accompaniments), and Verification.[66]

What is missing in Maimonides' analysis is the last stage, that of verifica-

tion and validation. There is no way of testing an alleged prophetic experience to determine whether it is veridical or delusive. As Hobbes says:

> For if any man pretend to me that God has spoken to him . . . immediate-
> ly, and I make doubt of it, I cannot easily perceive what argument he can
> produce to oblige me to believe it. . . . *When a man tells me that God spoke to*
> *him in a dream, all that I can be sure of is that he dreamed that God spoke to him.*
> . . . So that though God Almighty can speak to a man by dreams, visions,
> voice and inspiration; yet He obliges no man to believe that He hath done so
> to him that pretends it; who (being a man) may err, and (which is more) may
> lie.[67]

This criticism undermines completely all eleven grades of prophecy
enumerated by Maimonides.

It may be objected that the *Guide of the Perplexed* is not a work addressed to philosophical skeptics, but rather a systematic treatment of the
problem which must be solved if the principles of philosophy are to be
reconciled with the principles of the revealed law of Judaism (cf. *Guide* 11:2,
preface). But does Maimonides' treatment of prophecy succeed in achieving
such a reconciliation? Let us consider the objections raised against his
theory by the traditionalist Naḥmanides.[68] If the episode of Jacob wrestling
with an angel (Gen. 32:25–33) and sustaining an injury to his thigh occurred
in a dream apparition, then why, asks Naḥmanides, did Jacob walk with a
limp on the day following the vision? Surely a real injury cannot be
produced by an imaginary experience. This objection is not as formidable as
it might appear. The defenders of Maimonides did not fail to point out that
Naḥmanides has not taken into consideration the influence exercised by the
psyche on man's bodily functions. Very interesting, indeed, is the illustration offered by the saintly Don Isaac Abravanel. The concupiscent urge, he
says, may pollute the channels of the cerebral cortex during an erotic dream
and lead to an involuntary nocturnal emission. Similarly, he continues, the
intensity of Jacob's prophetic experience, albeit a phantasy, was so great
that he sustained a psychosomatic injury to his thigh, and this injury per-
sisted, although the vision had terminated.[69] The incident of Jacob and the
angel is therefore inconclusive as a refutation of Maimonides' argumentative thesis.

The story of the visit of the three angels (in the guise of men) to
Abraham (Gen. 18:1–16) offers greater difficulties. Here the subjective interpretation breaks the internal linkage of the biblical narrative. The angels

not only appeared to Abraham, they also rescued Lot (Gen. 19). If the three angels were not real beings but only existed in Abraham's mind as the products of his creative imagination, then as Naḥmanides astutely observed, Lot still remained in Sodom. One of the ablest recent students of Maimonides' philosophy considers this objection decisive and notes that Maimonides' method forces him to deny the historicity of the biblical narrative. The Bible becomes an unreliable and ambiguous source of factual information. "According to Maimonides' *philosophy,* Israel's *history* did not occur as reported in the Bible."[70]

I quite agree with this criticism, but I would express myself somewhat differently. In philosophical theology, I have yet to see a conclusive disproof of any theory, however nonsensical and ridiculous. The defenders of Maimonides in this instance also desperately attempt to plead the case of the master against the strictures of Naḥmanides. The biblical account of Sodom, they say, is etiological in character. The details of the narrative may not all be literally true, but the essential message of the story is timeless. The point of the vision of Sodom is that Lot's righteousness saved him from a city destroyed by God for its corruption. However, Lot was saved not by the miraculous intercession of supernatural beings, but by the forces of reason and piety within him, and—and this seems to come as an afterthought to restore coherence to the biblical narrative—on account of the virtue of Abraham, his uncle. These were the forces that Scripture refers to as "angels" who delivered Lot from the scene of God's most terrible judgment upon human sin.[71]

Thus what started out as a simple and straightforward theory is quietly abandoned and left to die slowly "the death by a thousand qualifications."[72] In fairness to the commentators who suggest this explanation, it should be noted that they make clear that they themselves do not accept this view. Obviously they devised it *ad hoc* in order to protect the "orthodoxy" of Maimonides. By rationalizations of this kind, any view can be read into the Bible. Abraham and Sarah can be, and were, made to represent matter and form; the twelve tribes of Israel can be, and were, made to stand for astral emblems or the twelve constellations; and the four kings who did battle against the five (Gen. 14:1–15) can be, and were, identified with the four elements and the five senses.[73] Miracles would present no difficulty to this view. Jonah swallowing the whale would be as readily understandable as the whale swallowing Jonah.

Perhaps it is better to expose the arbitrary nature of such theories than to attempt a strictly logical refutation of them.

The brilliant biochemist and geneticist, the late J.B.S. Haldane, once wrote a delightful and witty essay showing how this can be done. He was annoyed by popular preachers who constantly claimed that the latest findings of science support this or that dogma. To show the arbitrariness of their views, he composed a fantasy based on the supposition that Mithraism had survived to become the dominant religion of Europe. He imagines a modern churchman delivering a radio talk on "Science and Religion."

The clergyman says in part:

> Every advance of science has served to confirm the truths handed down to us by our Lord and his Apostles. To take a well-known example, every child asks his mother: "Why does the Sun let the clouds hide his face?"; and one of the dualistic heresies of the primitive Church was, of course, based on the idea that the clouds represented an evil power hostile to the Sun. Thanks to science, we know today that the Sun himself draws them up from the ocean by His own power. . . . No fact of religion has been more abundantly confirmed by science than that the Sun is "the Lord and Giver of Life." Not only has a study of photosynthesis shown that the energy for the lives of plants and animals is all derived from the Sun, but opinion is becoming stronger and stronger that life on our earth originated in organic matter formed by solar radiation in the primitive atmosphere. Finally, every year makes it more probably that our whole earth is only a detached fragment of His body. Zoroaster has been fully vindicated. . . . Light has properties like those of waves, others like those of particles; and matter also has properties of both kinds. By faith we have accepted the doctrine that the Sun, Mithras and the Holy Light are one. In every century there have been scoffers who asked how this was possible. In the nineteenth century, with the progress of astronomy and physics, the number of scoffers increased. "The Sun," they said, "consists of atoms, His light of vibrations—how can they be one?" Today, if still only incompletely, we see how. . . . There is not one of the central doctrines of our faith that has not been completely confirmed by science . . . [74]

We see, then, that the rationalizations of Maimonides, the "holy" the "perfect," the "light of the world," accomplish nothing. Attention may be called to a few more rationalizations in passing. The difficulties involved in the belief in the union of the soul with the active intellect—Judah ha-Levi had the courage to call it a pure myth (*Kuzari* v. 21)—are no less than those of the belief in the resurrection of the body for which this doctrine is substituted. Nor is the theory that sacrifices were ordained as a temporary measure and concession to wean away the Israelites from idolatry and lead them to the true spiritual worship of God (*Guide* III:22) necessarily an advance on the traditional view as expounded by Naḥmanides (Commentary on Lev. 1:9), among others.[75] From a philosophical point of view, as Maimonides himself came to realize, prayer no less than sacrifice implies anthropomorphism; as soon as we have a personal Being to be praised and supplicated, to whom we sacrifice, on whom we call and to whom we give thanks, we have ascribed human characteristics to the Eternal. Actually it does not affect the anthropomorphic conception whether we offer the body and blood of our bulls and goats in the form of a holocaust of "righteous sacrifices" or our inclinations in the form of "a broken spirit and a contrite heart" (Ps. 51).[76]

Finally, attention may be called to the fact that some of the pseudo-scientific rationalizations of Maimonides are not only unsound but positively harmful and dangerous. One example will suffice to make this clear. In part III, chapter 48 of the *Guide,* Maimonides asserts that all foods which are forbidden by the Law are unwholesome. But the very law which is declared to have known that certain food was noxious permits its sale to non-Jews (cf. Deut. 14:21), a license which would cast upon the Divine Legislator the just suspicion of having looked merely to the health of the Israelites and having allowed the poisoning of the non-Jew by not forewarning him of the injurious nature of the food given him by the forewarned Israelite.[77]

Nevertheless, credit should be given to Maimonides for stimulating the study of comparative religion as an aid to the study of biblical institutions. His contributions did not escape the attention of W. Robertson Smith, and were sometimes disregarded by other anthropologists and orientalists to their detriment.[78] Thus in the chapter just referred to, Maimonides explained the thrice-repeated biblical precept "not to boil a kid in its mother's milk" (Exod. 23:19, 34:26; Deut. 14:21) as directed against a Canaanite idolatrous rite which the Scriptures repudiated and wanted to suppress. Maimonides' hypothesis was rejected as unproved by so eminent an authority as Sir James G. Frazer,[79] but in the years between 1929 and 1939 clay tablets were discovered at Ras Shamra in Syria belonging to a Canaanite temple in ancient Ugarit, with inscriptions dating back to the thirteenth century before the common era, which corroborate the Canaanite practice of boiling a kid in its mother's milk as part of the worship of the pre-Israelite inhabitants of Syria.[80]

In this chapter we have dealt with two devices used by the medieval philosopher-theologians in order to reach their conclusions. What these conclusions were—as we saw in the previous chapter—had been predetermined by faith or revelation; reason was to be used merely to arrive at the same conclusions.

The two devices are contradiction and verbalism. Contradiction is the avowed method of Maimonides. He uses it to confuse the masses and hide his true meaning from them. In the end, however, Maimonides himself becomes victimized by the device of contradiction. He claims to be able to prove the existence of God from either of two contradictory propositions: that the world is eternal or that it is not. He ends up, however, by confusing the God of the Bible with the Unmoved Mover of Aristotle.

Maimonides also uses the argument that God's attributes are unknowable to us, so that we cannot judge what "good," for example, means as attributed to God from what it means when attributed to men. But this makes it questionable and even unreasonable to use the same word for God's attributes and man's.

A doctrine whose purpose it is to confuse and mislead the masses is fundamentally immoral. A sign of this immorality can be found in the fact that Maimonides even speaks of God's deceit.

Aquinas, like Maimonides, thinks that attributes do not mean the same thing when we speak of God as they mean when we speak of men. However, he does not hold God's attributes to be totally unknowable to us; rather he says that we can know them analogically, or that God's attributes are analogically the same as man's. But when we investigate this doctrine of analogical attribution, it turns out that either God's attributes are unknowable to us (as Maimonides was forced to say), or that we can know God but only through understanding Him anthropomorphically, i.e. as being like man. Either alternative is undesirable and wrong.

When Aquinas attempts to prove God's existence, in the First Way, by employing the Aristotelian notions of potency and act, he becomes embroiled in verbalisms, as can be seen by considering the views of such Neo-Thomists as Jacques Maritain.

Maimonides, too, falls into the trap of verbalism. This can be seen in the example of prophecy. Maimonides seems to be explaining it, but his pseudo-scientific explanation makes prophecy such a subjective activity that the whole Bible becomes unbelievable.

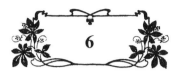

6

Autonomy of Religion and Philosophy Preferable to Their Synthesis

Jejune speculations and vague and hazy compromises of the type examined could never satisfy the boldest spirits either among the philosophers or the religionists. The mingling of rational and revealed truths and the spirit of harmonization at all cost did more harm than good. Consider a specific example. The Aristotelian logical scheme of the ten categories is well known. The categories are: substance, quantity, quality, relation, place, time, position, state, action, and passion. Later thinkers have speculated by what principles, if any, Aristotle was guided in composing his list and including only these ten categories and not others. They have not hesitated to criticize and exert efforts to improve upon Aristotle's classification of the ten predicates. This is as it should be and makes for progress in philosophical thought. It enables a Trendelenburg to point out that the imperfections in Aristotle's classification arise from his transference to thought and reality of grammatical distinctions between parts of speech in Greek syntax. It enables a John Stuart Mill to point out that Aristotle's crude enumeration exhibits defects of both redundance and omission. The list is redundant, because it is perfectly feasible to regard all other categories as forms of "relation"; it is defective, because the enumeration of relations is very incomplete, and the inclusion of those selected seems arbitrary. It is, Mill points out, like a division of animals into men, quadrupedes, horses, asses, and ponies.[1] If a theologian-philosopher, however, were to give the stamp of finality to the ten categories and assert that like the Ten Commandments, they were manifested in a divine revelation, how could the study of logic progress or develop? This is precisely what happened. When Abraham Ibn Dā'ūd asserts in the *Sublime Faith* that the ten categories were vouchsafed to King

David in a special revelation (recorded in Psalm 139), there is no way I know of to prove him wrong.[2]

The most original and daring philosophers fought for the independence of the philosophical disciplines from theological domination. Numerous illustrations from the history of philosophy present themselves, but we shall consider Kant's argument for the autonomy of ethics, since it played a significant role in modern Jewish thought.

Kant showed that moral obligation represents a factor in our spiritual nature which is ultimate and self-explanatory by drawing a very important distinction between hypothetical and categorial imperatives. A hypothetical imperative tells us to act in a certain way because it will tend to produce a certain result, and the need for the action is thus conditional on our desiring the result in question; but a categorical imperative commands us unconditionally, with no ifs, ands, and buts attached. For example, "If you would be rich, you must or should do such and such" is a hypothetical imperative. If you reply: "But I don't wish to be rich," all I can say is: "Very well then, you can leave this undone." But if I say: "It is your duty to do this," or "You ought to do such and such," you can only dispute it as *being* your duty or moral obligation. To say, "I don't want to do my duty" will in no way affect your obligation to do it. If it is your duty, it remains your duty nonetheless. To put the question not why this or that is one's duty, but instead why one should do one's duty is the same thing as to repudiate duty altogether, which is to be immoral. Therefore, Kant reasons, the obligation of the moral law is unconditional, ultimate, and absolute. No appeal to religion or theology is needed or indeed wanted.[3]

The more deeply committed religious thinkers also fought for the autonomy of religion freed from the shackles imposed upon it by alien systems.[4] When the Golden Age of Spanish Jewry began to wane, and suffering and persecution became the order of the day, the advanced thinkers and the philosophical "Ark-protectors" were the first to succumb and yield. The devotees of philosophy, who were only slightly attached to the religion of their fathers and on whom tradition had but a loose grip, were in the forefront of those who bent the knee in the house of Rimmon and abandoned Judaism.[5] Then the masses began to realize that they had been misled and betrayed, that the speculations of the "divine" Plato were but broken reeds, and the lucubrations of "the master of them that know" were strange fires on the altar of God. Then people recalled the warning against excessive tolerance and open-mindedness, and the going "a-whoring" after foreign gods, which they repeated twice daily in the *Shema*.[6]

In those turbulent times, there lived in Spain a most extraordinary personality, Don Isaac Abravanel. He was a scholar and a statesman who feared the Lord and served the King. When a conflict of loyalties arose, he did not hesitate, but chose to accompany his brethren into exile rather than remain as a convert in the comfortable position assured him by his wealth and his connection with the royal court. Here was no armchair metaphysician, but an exceptional man touched (*pace* Maimonides) by the finger of God. Not that he lacked philosophical ability. A contemporary relates that already in his youth people were astounded by his lectures on Maimonides' philosophy; his expositions were vastly superior to those of others, like wine compared to water or sunlight to moonlight. Yet even in those days he accepted Maimonides' philosophy only with many reservations. All his lectures ended the same way. When he was finished and about to leave the rostrum, he would pause for a moment, turn to his audience, and make the following disclaimer: "These are the opinions of our Master Moses [Maimonides], not of Moses our Master," that is to say, great as Maimonides was, his views are incompatible with the Law of Moses.[7]

The views of such a man deserve to be treated with the utmost respect, whatever our final judgment on them may be. Attention may particularly be called to one idea which he developed and which we cannot afford to ignore. This simple idea is of the utmost theoretical and practical importance, and if Abravanel had bequeathed to us nothing more, we would still be deeply indebted to him. His most important theological work, the *Rosh Amanah* (Pinnacle of Faith), is ostensibly devoted to defending the validity of Maimonides' Thirteen Principles of Faith against the attacks of Crescas, Albo, and others. But after having devoted twenty-two chapters to defending Maimonides' compilation, Abravanel rather abruptly explains in the two concluding chapters of his treatise that Maimonides compiled these principles merely in accordance with the fashion of other nations, which set up in every science fundamental axions and theorems, from which they deduce propositions which are less evident. But, thinks Abravanel, the Jewish religion has nothing in common with human science, and belief in principles of faith, or a creed as such, is incompatible with the character of Judaism as a divinely given law. For since any and every proposition of the Law, and any and every story, belief, or command contained in the Law, are revelations from God, all these propositions are of equal value, and none of them ought to be thought of as more fundamental than any other. Abravanel writes: "I believe that as far as the divine Law is concerned, it is improper to lay down principles or foundations in matters of faith, since we are obligated to believe in everything written in it and cannot place doubt even on the smallest detail." His conclusion is that "each sentence, word, and letter of the Law is a principle and root in itself."[8]

Abravanel has given clear expression to the view that the exposition of Judaism must flow from its own sources and that it cannot be fitted to the Procrustean bed of an alien philosophy. The importance of this view cannot be overestimated. If the acceptance of Judaism is made dependent on the validity of any external system of philosophy, then with the passing away of that system of philosophy, the rejection of Judaism should naturally and inevitably follow. This vitiates the whole theoretical basis and procedure followed by the medieval rationalist philosopher-theologians.

Practically, this view is no less significant. Religion conceived as a matter of creed is merely a way of talking, but religion conceived as the acceptance and observance of the commandments of the Law is a way of living. Words, if they are to be significant, must be reinforced by rituals and ceremonies; we must do our religious "thing." In fact, we *are* what we *do,* according to Erich Fromm, who points out that organized religion is under an impulsion to create the opportunities which will permit our learning to become a learning by the very genes, the muscle, the tissue of habit in our everyday existence. Nonspecific and nondemanding doctrines or articles of a creed have at best a very weak hold on the minds of their adherents. Such doctrines are interchangeable with other doctrines; they do not affect the course of life in any definite, recognizable way. Thus the transition from a unitarian to a trinitarian formula of belief demands only a change in the way of talking, not in the way of living. It is like changing from $1 \times 3 = 3$ to $2 + 1 = 3$. There is nothing sacrosanct about the number one; it is just a number like any other and no more holy than three, or forty-nine, or the square root of minus two. "Martyrdom," said Franz Rosenzweig, with his depth of spiritual penetration, "is not an arithmetical problem."[9] Just so! The foundation of Jewish monotheism is not God's numerical unity, but rather His absolute and undifferentiated uniqueness (cf. Ibn Ezra and Rashbam on Deut. 6:4) and His demands for ethical conduct: "You shall be careful to keep and do these laws" (Deut. 16:12). Now one does not stake one's life on the mysteries of the Law if its esoteric teachings, like the "Account of the Creation" and the "Account of the Chariot" (Ezek. 1), do no more than adumbrate the Aristotelian cosmography openly taught in all schools and known to the *cognoscenti* and savants of all religious communities.[10] It is the integral unity of Judaism and life that enabled the Jewish people to withstand the corrosive acids of assimilation and spiritual disintegraion and loss of identity. Judaism is coextensive with life not only because, to use the pregnant phrase of S. R. Hirsch, "the catechism of the Jew is his calendar," but because the Law governs the gamut of life from birth to death and even beyond the grave. It regulates the life of the Jew every day, every hour of every day, and every minute of every hour. It tells the individual Jew not only what are his religious and social duties and moral obligations, but also what food he may or may not eat and how this food should be prepared; what clothes he may or may not wear and of what materials the stuff thereof may or may not be made; how he shall build his house, sow his field, and even kindle his fire. The devout Jew was not even aware that he had a religion: he was a Jew. In times of persecution, a Sunday-school creed which demanded mere lip service was not enough; what was needed was the conception of a "fiery law" (Deut. 33:2) which demanded strict obedience in conduct. Such a philosophy Abravanel evolved out of his innermost being, and his views percolated down to the simple believers who may never have heard of his name. The young draftee in the Austro-Hungarian Army in World War I who upon being asked what was his religion, replied, "Wir haben keine Religion; wir sind doch Juden," may have been a greater philosopher than he realized.[11]

But to come back to Abravanel. His position is not necessarily obscurantist. We have pointed out that the Aristotelian-Thomist-Maimonidean division of reality into the celestial regions and the sublunar world is superficial; the deep line of cleavage is between those phenomena which are amenable to measurement and statistical analysis (the domain of the quantifiable) and those which are not. In other words, there are aspects of the world, to be taken into account in a comprehensive philosophy of it, in which the scientific method of exploration by observation, classification, experiment, analysis, reduction to law, and verification has a very limited application. An illustration will clarify this point. In the large Rabbinic Bibles, critical notes on the external form of the text are printed in the margins and at the end of each book. Among other things, these notes list the number of letters, words, and verses in that particular book as well as such other information as that ten passages in the Pentateuch are dotted, that a particular word is a *hapax legomenon,* or that a certain grammatical form is found so many times in Scripture. This information was painstakingly gathered by the Masoretes, although today, I suppose, this aspect of their activity, called the numerical Masorah, could readily be computed by a data-processing machine in a short time. But surely facts such as that the Book of Psalms contains so many letters, and that the number of its verses is a certain fraction of the number of verses in the Pentateuch, may be established without exhausting the spiritual truths or religious value of the Bible.

The point was well brought out by the late Sir Arthur Eddington in his parable of the learned ichthyologist who went out to catch marine life with a net of two-inch mesh and comes to the solemn conclusion that all fish are more than two inches long. The moral Sir Arthur would have us draw is that science fishes in the sea of reality with a particular kind of net—called the scientific method—and that there is much in the unfathomed sea which the meshes of the scientific net cannot catch. The naive notion that scientific truth is the only kind of truth and the unfounded and romantic belief in the omnicompetence of science in the solution of all human problems (i.e., scientism) is neither a conclusion from scientific data nor a necessary presupposition of scientific method. Thus scientific philosophy cannot represent an absolute and exclusive view of reality; it cannot be a bedrock of truth. It is an indispensable, progressively self-corrective, and public, but only partial, incomplete, and abstract kind of knowledge.[12]

In recent philosophy the implications of the above conception of the world for moral truths and spiritual insights have been best elucidated, in the opinion of this writer, by Nicolai Hartmann. In his *Aufbau der realen Welt* (Berlin: 1940, chaps. 55–61), he divides the structure of the world into four irreducible levels or realms: the inorganic, the organic, mind and spirit.[13] Each of these levels has its own laws and categories. There is no dependency "from above," only one "from below"; that is, while the lower levels reveal indifferences and greater strength in relation to the higher, these latter depend to a certain extent on the lower levels. But this dependency is never complete, for the dependence of the mind upon biological processes is merely a superconstruction without an embodiment of the lower in the higher. It is a grave mistake, therefore, and one to which philosophers in the past were prone, to interpret any of the levels in terms of categories used to characterize another sphere of being. Thus (to take an example not found in Hartmann), a starry-eyed pair of lovers who hold hands tenderly cannot be described in physiological terms as "quietly sweating palm to palm" (Aldous Huxley). The upshot of this dependence and autonomy in the hierarchy of strata is that "reductionism" must be avoided and that both idealism and materialism must be rejected. The everyday world which we perceive, the world of sense and touch which the various natural sciences explain, can in no way be dismissed as "mere" appearance or illusion. Religious intuition, or mystical illumination, or speculative imagination may disclose aspects of reality not otherwise accessible, but they can in no way negate or disparage the logico-empirical method of modern science for establishing cognitive claims. There may be more to reality than such a method can disclose, but there cannot be less, and unless this "more" can be interpreted in conformity with the established findings of modern science it will rightfully remain suspect.[14] Whether, indeed, there is more we shall examine in the next chapter.

Let us sum up the position we have reached so far. We have not got so far as a Supreme Being, much less the God of any actual religion. But we have tried to show that if we are to reach such a Being it must be *via* the natural sciences, that is, by building upon their findings and supplementing them, and not by negating them. In this respect, we are in basic agreement with the fundamental Thomistic thesis, "Grace does not destroy nature, but perfects it."[15]

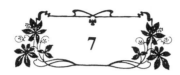

7

Conclusion and Evaluation

We have now examined some of the distinctive theories of the medieval philosopher-theologians. We have weighed them in the balance and found them wanting. We have tried to show that Maimonides' methodology leads to consequences which are so palpably absurd—that the world was created last Friday at twilight, or that Aquinas is the author of the *Guide of the Perplexed*—that no one but a philosopher needing to harmonize incompatible concepts would accept them. We have pointed out that there are internal inconsistencies and incoherences in Aquinas' system (in the notion of creation, for example, or in his analysis of transubstantiation). Finally, we have suggested that the whole bent of the scholastic mind is to make subtle but frivolous and spurious or irrelevant distinctions and subdistinctions that enable the inquirer to withdraw an issue at will from the possibility of a scientific or empirical determination. Our job is apparently done.[1] Only one task remains. Moritz Steinschneider, one of the pioneers of Jewish scholarship in the modern Western mode (*Wissenschaft des Judentums*), once pointed to a hoard of medieval manuscripts on his desk and said: "The sole remaining task of Jewish scholarship is to give a decent burial to the literary remains of the Jewish past."[2] David Hume had already prepared a short funeral address for the cremation ceremony. It read in part: "If we take in our hand any volume, of divinity or school metaphysics, for instance, let us ask: Does it contain any abstract reasoning concerning quantity or number? No. Does it contain any experimental reasoning concerning matter of fact and existence? No. Commit it then to flames; for it can contain nothing but sophistry and illusion."[3] But as the service is about to begin, some complications arise. M. Gilson is not willing to sign the death certificate. It seems that the patient has had a miraculous recovery. Indeed, the good doctor seems to feel that the patient will probably outlive his attendants. According to him, this is a phenomenon that happens once in every generation. The patient, philosophy, rises up and buries its undertakers.

In the concluding section of his work, *The Unity of Philosophical Experience,* Gilson presents some of the laws or conclusions he has inferred from his study of the history of philosophy. The first law that can be inferred is that despite mistakes which lead to skepticism, every instance of the death of philosophy has been accompanied by its resurrection: *"Philosophy always buries its undertakers."*[4] Man, though frequently disappointed with what he has been offered, returns to philosophy, for by his very nature he is a metaphysical animal. As St. Augustine says in his *Confessions* (bk. I, Chap. 1): "Thou hast made us unto Thyself, O Lord, and the heart of man is restless until it finds its rest in Thee." Many centuries later the philosopher Immanuel Kant, in the section of the *Critique of Pure Reason* devoted to the Transcendental Dialectic, observed that equally good arguments could be given in favor of opposing cosmological theses. Speaking of the first antinomy he points out that both the thesis that the world had a beginning in time and the opposite, that it had no beginning in time, can be proved as well as disproved, but that the first finds greater favor with mankind, for man flees the endless and desires a point where he can rest. "Thus there rises amid the miserable huts of men the cathedral with the everlasting peace of God."[5]

I think that Gilson's assessment of the philosophical situation is correct. While that philosophical excitement of the recent past known as "logical positivism" had the great merit of calling attention to various weaknesses in detail, the essential truth of the Platonic-Philonic view remains that in religion one comes upon things not to be expressed in human language or adequately conceived by the human mind. Robertson of Brighton, perhaps the most remarkable preacher of the nineteenth century, speaks for many, I suspect, when in his justly celebrated sermon on "Obedience," preached on March 2, 1851, he writes:

There are few more glorious moments of our humanity than those in which faith does battle against intellectual proof; when, for example, after reading a skeptical book or hearing a cold-blooded materialist's demonstration in which God, the soul, and life to come are proved impossible, up rises the heart in all the giant might of its immortality to do battle with the understanding, and with the simple argument, "I *feel* them in my best and highest moments to be true," annihilates the sophistries of logic.[6]

Perhaps such sentiments will be dismissed as mere pulpit rhetoric, and I will be accused of trying to smuggle in through the back door that which was previously rejected at the bar of rational evaluation. Perhaps; perhaps not. Let us see. Almost a hundred years to the day after Robertson spoke from his Brighton pulpit, a professor delivered a public lecture at the University of Adelaide in Australia. From the lecture itself it is apparent that the lecturer has no particular theological predilections or prejudices.

Professor J. J. C. Smart takes his point of departure from the outlook and use of techniques associated with contemporary linguistic philosophy. He admits that logic shows him that Leibniz's question, "Why is there something, rather than nothing?"[7] is absurd—yet he still wishes to ask the question and furthermore feels that it is a question of tremendous importance and significance. In the concluding paragraph of his lecture he writes:

> "Why should anything exist at all?" Logic seems to tell us that the only answer which is not absurd is to say, "Why shouldn't it?" Nevertheless, though I know how any answer along the lines of the cosmological argument can be pulled to pieces by a correct logic, I still feel I want to go on asking the question. Indeed, though logic has taught me to look at such a question with the gravest suspicion, my mind often seems to reel under the immense significance it seems to have for me. That anything should exist at all seems to me a matter for the deepest awe. But whether other people feel this sort of awe, and whether they or I ought to is another question. I think we ought to.[8]

But before we indulge our metaphysical and ontological anxieties, it might be best to point out the limitations of the method of conceptual analysis which we have found so useful. If we go back to consider once again Hume's Fork, as his rhetorical version of the Principles of Verifiability has been called by historians of philosophy, we note that it says that a piece of reasoning which does not express a formally true proposition or an empirical hypothesis is devoid of literal significance. Armed with Hume's Fork, we can indeed wreak havoc in our libraries. But before we throw all works of divinity and school metaphysics on a philosophical garbage dump for a huge funeral pyre, it might be appropriate to inquire into the status of his own principle, which itself is neither logical nor empirically verifiable. If we adhered to Hume's standard, we would have to reject emphatically many things besides divinity and school metaphysics, including Hume's *Enquiry* and the other works which he authored expounding the Humean philosophy.[9]

In this study I have attempted to dispel many half-truths and illusions. One final myth has been dispelled by a much more competent critic than I. I am referring to Arthur A. Cohen's recent work with the self-explanatory title, *The Myth of the Judeo-Christian Tradition* (New York, 1970).

The notion that there is a Judeo-Christian tradition has, in my opinion, done much harm in current religious thinking. It has led many contemporary Jewish theologians into the camp of the existentialists and the exponents of "dialectical theology." All this, I believe, is a mistake and based on the tacit assumption that the place of reason in the two traditions is the same. But this is not so. Judaism is more hospitable to the claims of reason than Christianity, which harbors latent anti-rationalist tendencies just below the surface.[10] "The preaching of the cross is foolishness to those who are perishing," says St. Paul, "but to us who are being saved it is the power of God. . . . Has not God made foolish the wisdom of the world? . . . For Jews insist upon miracles and Greeks demand philosophy, but we preach Christ crucified—an idea that is revolting to the Jews and absurd to the Gentiles" (I Cor. 1:18 ff.). Normative Judaism, however, respects the mind and does not ask its adherents to accept those things which are contrary to reason. To be sure, it recognizes that life is more than logic, and reality richer than thought and unexhausted by rational knowledge. Even from a purely logical point of view, an exclusively rational interpretation of the universe (one, that is, which interprets it in terms of what our reason can fully understand) cannot claim to fathom the true nature of reality; for all we know, the universe is not completely intelligible, but is built upon ultimate mysteries which our reason cannot explore. Aristotle long ago pointed out that all philosophies must start from some undemonstrable propositions for the sufficient reason that the validity of the rules of thought and logic must be assumed in all reasoning and cannot be validated because any would-be proof would have to presuppose and employ logic. (In order to give an account of logic, we must presuppose and employ logic.) We cannot even prove that grass is green,[11] or, for that matter, the very existence of the external world. Well did the great metaphysician F. H. Bradley speak of metaphysics as the finding of bad reasons for what we believe upon instinct.[12] The secularist no less than the religious thinker must allow his beliefs to exceed the cognitive grounds on which they may be said to rest. What immediately comes to mind is not only Anselm's "faith," Pascal's "wager," and James's "will to believe," but also Hume's doctrine of "natural belief," Santayana's "animal faith," and Moore's defense of common sense, as well as Broad's strictures on "silly theories" (i.e., those which may be held at the time when one is talking or writing professionally, but which only an inmate of a lunatic asylum would think of carrying into daily life). In his comparatively early essay "Reflex Action and Theism" (1881), William James puts the matter very clearly when he says in his own inimitable way:

> Certain of our positivists keep chiming to us that amid the wreck of every other god and idol, one divinity still stands upright—that his name is Scientific Truth, and that he has but one commandment, but that one supreme, saying, *Thou shalt not be a theist,* for that would be to satisfy thy subjective propensities, and the satisfaction of those is intellectual damnation. These most conscientious gentlemen think they have jumped off their own feet—emancipated their mental operations from the control of their subjective propensities at large and *in toto.* But they are deluded. They have simply chosen from among the entire set of propensities at their command those that were certain to construct, out of the materials given, the leanest, lowest, aridest result—namely, the bare molecular world—and they have sacrificed all the rest.[13]

The secularist has no right to prefer, for biological reasons presumably, the results of science, and deny the right of somebody else to supplement his practical faith by intellectual faith in a postulated existence of a Supreme Being which introduces more order into his intellectual household than any other alternative. There is in itself no ground for assuming that all of the phenomena of the universe can be explained rationally; there may be surds in experience which must be accepted as "brute" facts. Yet there is a tendency among Western thinkers to identify the real with the rational (Hegel), to reduce all our experiences to rational terms, and to ignore, or even deny, all those which resist such treatment. "Reason," said Spinoza, "is the light of the mind and without her all things are dreams and phantoms."[14] Nevertheless there may be, and probably is, as we have said, much more to "reality" than the rational interpretations offered by the various sciences are able to disclose; but there cannot be less.[15] Now the legal side of Judaism can be regarded as an application of reason to the concepts of faith, and behind this is the idea that these concepts are reasonable. The talmudic sages attached significance to human reasoning to the extent that the products of human reasoning often enjoyed authority comparable to that of the revealed law.[16]

This may seem like special pleading. There is a story by Philip Roth, "The Conversion of the Jews," in which the rabbi pontificates to his Hebrew-school class that Christianity is more irrational than Judaism, because it (Christianity) believes that Jesus was miraculously begotten of

God and born of a virgin mother. Little Ozzie then demands to know why an omnipotent God, who can divide the Red Sea and send plagues over Egypt, cannot make a woman become pregnant without sexual intercourse. This may be good material for a short story, but it is poor theology. Judaism does not stand or fall with the belief that Moses was a sorcerer armed with a magic wand, who could outsmart Pharaoh's magicians. Miracles are not prominent in Jewish theology; except for a stray reference, they are completely absent from the Jewish service and ritual.[17] Christian belief, on the other hand, is based on a series of miracles relating to the birth and resurrection of its founder, with which the whole apparatus of salvation and the entire body of faith is indissolubly connected. These alleged miracles are not only *evidence for* Christianity, they are *constitutive of* Christianity—that is to say, without them the Christian religion in its classical form is inconceivable. According to Paul, the Tarsian Pharisaic apostle of Christianity *in partibus infidelium* (Acts 23:6), the central fact in the Christian religion is a miracle: if Jesus did not rise from the dead, the Christian faith is a delusion, the preaching of the gospel is vain, and men's sins are not forgiven (I Cor. 15:14–17; cf. the Collect for Easter Day in the *Book of Common Prayer*). Christian worship, in its most solemn sacrament, rests on the daily recurrence of a miracle, wherein the sacrificial death of Jesus on Calvary is reenacted in the "unbloody sacrifice" of the Mass. Here the believer is permitted to eat the flesh and drink the blood of his Redeemer in the ritual form of bread and wine. From this it is but one step to Tertullian's crucifixion of reason (*sacrificium intellectus*), as expressed in chapter 5 of his *On the Flesh of Christ*. "The Son of God was born; I am not ashamed because men must needs be ashamed of it. And the Son of God died; it is by all means to be believed because it is absurd [*ineptum*]. He was resurrected from the grave. *Certum est quia impossibile est*—it is certain because it is impossible." Nor were the Protestant reformers any more hospitable to the claims of reason. Luther called reason a "beautiful whore," and "the most atrocious enemy of God [*Rationem atrocissimum Dei hostem*]."[18] And one of the most learned and profound contemporary Christian theologians has said that "the Person of Christ is the bankruptcy of human logic. . . . . ultimately we are driven back to Tertullian's famous dictum, and we must believe, because of the very *absurdity* of our faith."[19]

Normative Judaism does indeed include some elements totally impenetrable to the intellect, such as the ritual of the Red Heifer (Num. 19).[20] This ritual, now obsolete, involved an act, however, not a belief, as is the case, say, with transubstantiation. No Jew in the days of the Temple, even if we suppose him to be endowed with the latest scientific knowledge, would see in the observance of this "statute" (*hok,* i.e., a commandment or enactment of which the purpose is not patent) an offense against his reason. To perform on trust an act of worship, the reason for which God has not vouchsafed, is not a sacrifice of reason. We can only speak of such a sacrifice if we are asked to believe that which science teaches us is inherently impossible. The performance of the act may be blind obedience: the *credo quia impossibile* is blind faith and has no place in Judaism.[21] *Si manga licet componere parvis,* I will here illustrate this matter of unquestioning obedience to God's ritual commands from the relation of parents to their minor children. It is not possible for a parent to explain to a child of tender years the reason for many things which he orders, and which are necessary for the child's good. One cannot explain the properties of heat to an infant crawling in a playpen, but one can keep him away from matches. The gap between our powers of understanding and the intelligence of God is surely no less than that between the brains of adults and children. Surely, then, the same obedience may be reasonably expected by an infallible all-loving God.

Generalizing, we may say that Christianity restrains the mind, and Judaism the body. Thus a Jew is forbidden to eat oysters; a Christian is obligated to believe in transubstantiation. "The subtleties of the Rabbis," says Professor George Foot Moore, "were mainly in the sphere of observance, those of the theologians of the Church in that of correct beliefs, or to express it more accurately, of intellectual apprehension. The one is called 'legalism,' we might name the other 'creedalism.'"[22]

This, therefore, is not a modern distinction introduced for polemical or apologetic purposes. It is as old as the Creed of Nicaea, if not as old as the Epistles of St. Paul. It is significant that the pagan writers, from the time of Celsus on, attack Christianity for the incredibility of its dogmas: the Trinity within the unity of the Godhead, the substitutionary atonement of sin through vicarious suffering, the doctrine of the eternal punishment and the endless torments of the vast majority of mankind in hell (*massa perditionis*),[23] and the justification of one man and the damnation of another by predestination, though both are equally sinners.[24] A contemporary British critic, speaking of the lurid eschatology of the Church Fathers and the scholastics, writes: "The Christian God the Father, the God of Tertullian, Augustine and Aquinas, is the wickedest thing yet invented by the black heart of man."[25] But when similar critics shift their guns on Judaism, they attack its ritual and ceremonies: the Sabbath observance, which was equated with fondness for a life of idleness, the forbidden foods (especially swine's flesh), and—the unkindest cut of all—circumcision.[26]

In modern times, too, this difference between the two religions was clearly perceived by the famous criminal lawyer Clarence Darrow, a very able controversialist.

> Why, do you know [Darrow led off innocently when addressing a Jewish audience] there's a funny religion where they won't let a man eat meat on Fridays. Some other days in the spring they won't let him eat it either. Let him eat fish, oh yes, all he wants on Fridays and in springtime, too. Same protein in fish as in meat, but fish is O.K. and meat taboo on Fridays. Funny religion, ain't it? But I heard of another one [Darrow continued, with the air of revealing a great secret] where there's one kind of meat, good solid nutritious meat, full of strength for a man's work, if he has to work, but no. He just can't eat that meat. He not only can't eat it on Friday, or Thursday, or Wednesday, but not any day in the year, not even on his birthday or Fourth of July. Now there's seven days in a week, so this second religion is just seven times as funny as the other one, isn't it?[27]

This is the worst that can be said about Judaism. Its rituals may be attacked as outmoded taboos and as survivals of primitive rites. But the mind is given free rein in speculative matters; it is not trammeled or fettered in any way. There is nothing illogical or inconsistent about a Reconstructionist, or even a nonbelieving Jew, observing the dietary laws as expressions of Jewish religious folkways. The modern writer who refers to circumcision as a bloody, barbaric rite of physical mutilation has not advanced beyond the Roman writers on Judaism.[28]

Now it is readily understandable why Christian theologians should be attracted to existentialist thought. It is striking that difficulties referrred to by unbelievers as "contradictions," "mistakes," or some other uncomplimentary emotive appellation, are called "paradoxes" by the religious existentialists. In this way the wind is taken out of the sails of unfriendly critics. Once the initial leap of faith is taken, all other beliefs fall into shape and are invulnerable to further attack. In fact, Christian existentialists can claim with perfect justice that the type of objection raised by unbelievers actually accentuates and heightens the paradoxes of faith.[29]

"Once the initial leap of faith is taken"—there is the hitch. A story, probably apocryphal, relates that when Voltaire was told the story of St. Denis (the Patron Saint of France, who suffered martyrdom and who allegedly miraculously carried his head in his hands as he walked forty steps after it had been cut off), he said, "I have no problem with the thirty-nine steps—it is the first step that I do not believe, and this is what really counts." Precisely. The first step really counts. The whole foundation of existentialist theology is built on sand. It implies no external standard of truth and morality above individual decision. Thus rational discourse between exponents of contradictory claims is impossible; brute force and political power are the only possible standard of possession of existentialist truth. To an extent never dreamed of by the Reformers, the maxim *cuius regio, eius religio* holds.[30]

We see, then, that the existentialist's "leap of faith" is neither necessary nor helpful. It will be appropriate now to turn to a consideration of the several factors which, in our opinion, religious thinkers should bear in mind when engaging in philosophical reflection and inquiry.

First and foremost, religious thinkers must accept the conclusions of science on all questions which can be dealt with by the scientific method. Reality, as we have said, may have aspects that are not amenable to the scientific method of discovery, but mystery-mongering has no place in regard to matters which are, or may easily be, known to anyone having the requisite background and training. On this topic, it was Maimonides' glory to have made some observations which are of absolute, not relative, value. His words are all the more significant and remarkable since they are inconspicuously sandwiched in between ritual laws dealing with the sanctification of the New Moon, rather than in a work addressed to would-be philosophers.

> As regards the logic for all these calculations . . . all this is part of the science of astronomy and mathematics, about which many books have been composed by Greek sages,—books that are still available to the scholars of our time. But the books which had been composed by the Sages of Israel, of the tribe of Issachar, who lived in the time of the Prophets, have not come down to us. But since all these rules have been established by sound and clear proofs, free from any flaw and irrefutable, we need not be concerned about the identity of their authors, whether they were Hebrew Prophets or Gentile sages. For when we have to do with rules and propositions which have been demonstrated by good reasons and have been verified to be true by sound and flawless proofs, we do [not] rely upon the author who has discovered them or has transmitted them [but rather] on his demonstrated proofs and verified reasoning.[31]

If theologians had only heeded what Maimonides said, then Dr. Andrew D. White's two thick tomes, *The Warfare of Science with Theology,* could have been reduced to one-tenth their size. Among the things which can be investigated by the scientific method, I would specifically include the question of the literary composition of the various books comprising the Bible. The conclusions and results of biblical scholarship, arrived at with the help of the tools of philology, literary criticism, archaeology, and so on, must be respected. Thus, if we apply the techniques of computational linguistics to the Pentateuch, we may find traces of what can be interpreted as either documents or traditions emanating from different circles. It seems to me to be an anomalous, timid, and pitiful attitude for a religion to reject the tools of scientific discovery for its own domain. If it does this, it puts itself out of the realm of rational discussion and can no longer claim that its theological ideas are true, although they may be significant, to be sure. However that may be (and it would take us too far afield to discuss the matter at any length here), there is no logical inconsistency whatsoever in subjecting the scriptural text to criticism and simultaneously maintaining faith in it as the special and unrivaled source and norm of truth. To think otherwise is to commit what linguistic philosophers refer to as a "category mistake,"[32] which in the present instance would consist in confusing the theological problem of divine revelation and prophetic inspiration, with the literary problem of the evolution and transmission of the biblical text. Franz Rosenzweig clearly perceived that these two problems must be retained as quite separate. In a letter dated April 21, 1927, addressed to Jacob Rosenheim, the leader of separatist Orthodox Judaism (Agudath Israel), Rosenzweig observed:

> Where we differ from orthodoxy is in our reluctance to draw from our belief in the holiness or uniqueness of the Torah, and in its character of revelation, any conclusions as to its literary genesis and the philological value of the text as it has come down to us. If all of Wellhausen's theories were correct and the Samaritans really had the better text, our faith would not be shaken in the least. We too, translate the Torah as a single book. For us, too, it is the work of one spirit. . . . Among ourselves we call him by the symbol which critical science is accustomed to use to designate its assumed redactor: R. But this symbol R we expand not into Redactor but into Rabbenu. For he is our teacher; his theology is our teaching.[33]

Second, religious thinkers must avoid the use of "gimmicks" to solve real or apparent difficulties. Under this category I would include the pseudo-solution offered by Maimonides and his followers regarding the origin of the universe.[34] A modern thinker utilizing the Kantian distinction between the phenomenal and noumenal realms even tries to improve upon Maimonides.

Isaac Breuer relates a discussion he had with a natural scientist regarding the age of the earth. At one point in the discussion the scientist picked up a piece of coal, held it in his hand, and said in words or substance: "This fossil was formed in the earth's crust about 250 million years ago. It is composed of carbonized vegetable matter deposited in former epochs of the world's history; during the eras of geological time it has developed in accordance with physical and chemical laws." At this point, Breuer abruptly interrupted him and bumptiously said, "You are dead wrong. Stop!" The scientist was nonplussed, but when he regained his composure, he inquired where and how he fell into error. "The laws of nature," was the reply, "are only 5,686 years, minus six days, old. Period."[35]

This, Breuer feels, is a complete solution of the geology versus Genesis problem.

Under this heading I would include also the various theories of post-mortem or eschatological verification which aim to vindicate belief in God and immortality by maintaining that after death certain experiences will be available which should verify adequately for rational certainty the truth of religious assertions made in this life.

Post-mortem verification has indeed its use to expose the weakness of the claim of those dogmatic logical positivists who maintain that religious assertions are literally nonsensical or meaningless because not verifiable, but they are useless in meeting objections raised by skeptics. When trying to *prove* that we are created by a benevolent God and are immortal, we surely have no right to import considerations which depend on the very hypotheses we are trying to prove.

Third, religious thinkers must learn the lesson of humility. Speaking of our knowledge of God, the medievals themselves said, "If I knew Him, I would be He."[36] This principle was endorsed by both Maimonides and Aquinas. Maimonides stated that "human reason cannot fully conceive God in His true essence, because of the perfection of God's essence and the imperfection of our own reason, and because His essence is not due to causes through which it may be known." St. Thomas repeatedly declared that "to know God truly is to know that we do not know of Him what He is." And long before both, St. Augustine said: "It is impossible thoroughly to grasp and comprehend God, for couldst Thou comprehend Him, He would not be God."[37] Exactly! We are greater than anything we can fully understand. We will not worship a thing that we can understand completely, but will pass on and leave it in search of something more ultimate.

Yet how often have religious thinkers—very much including Maimonides and Aquinas—sinned against their own better understanding. They have God all figured out, and the rather disagreeable picture that emerges is that of a glorified theologian.[38]

But God, if there is a god, cannot be discovered as the conclusion of a syllogism, nor can the supernatural be *proved* to exist, for if it could, it would not be supernatural but natural.[39] It is hard to believe that anything short of a miracle could prove God's existence. And the evidence of miracles itself is very weak. For as Hegel observed—and he was not the first to do so—the Bible tells us (Exod. 7:14–8:11) that the Egyptian sorcerers were able to imitate the miracles performed by Moses and Aaron, and this very fact implies that no great value is to be placed on them.[40] The point is well brought out in a discourse by one of the Hasidic masters dealing with the question of why God did not choose to reveal himself by miracles beyond imitation. Said the Belzer Rabbi:

> We find that Pharaoh's magicians were able to perform by their secret arts the miracles of turning water into blood and bringing up frogs. The other miracles they were unable to duplicate. The question arises: Why did the Lord cause Moses to perform miracles that could be duplicated by magic? Could He not have enjoined that all the ten plagues be beyond imitation?
>
> The answer is as follows: the Lord knew that in later times unbelievers might arise and say: "The Egyptian soothsayers were possessed of little sagacity, and hence Moses was able to deceive them. We, however, would not have been victims of his chicanery." Then we believers might retort: "If you are wiser than the Egyptian sages, accomplish at least as much as they. Turn water into blood and bring up frogs. If you cannot do this, you must admit their superiority, and at the same time recognize that they acknowledged the divine power resident in the acts of Moses."[41]

Probably the most competent and illuminating analysis of the phenomenon of biblical religion and the concept of the holy is that of Rudolf Otto.[42] In his well-known work, *The Idea of the Holy*, Otto endeavors to describe the nonrational (nonconceptualistic) elements of religion in as rational and matter-of-fact manner as the subject matter permits. According to Otto, religion is rational in that it ascribes definable attributes to the deity; it is nonrational or suprarational in that the essence of the deity is not exhaustively defined in any such ascription. The latter element of religion is at its very core. For the nonrational feelings—the sense of the tremendous, the awesome, and the mysterious—the incommunicable, incomprehensible, and ineffable experience that is peculiarly religious, Otto has coined the word "numinous." The nature of the numinous, that aspect of the deity which transcends or eludes comprehension in rational or ethical terms, is most clearly portrayed in the prophet Isaiah's Temple experience. In the year that King Uzziah died, Isaiah the prophet beholds the sovereign figure of God: the train of His garments fills the *hekal* (in Sumerian *egal* = palace), that is, the Temple, in all its vastness, while the six-winged seraphim in solemn majesty surround the highly exalted divine throne and incessantly chant in chorus the Trisagion,

Holy, holy, holy is the Lord of hosts;
The whole earth is full of His glory. (Isa. 6:3)

At the sound of the chant, the celestial Temple is filled with smoke, and the foundations of the threshold shake. Soul-chilling terror seizes the prophet as he becomes conscious of his own insignificance and unworthiness as a man of unclean lips dwelling in the midst of a people of unclean lips. "'Holy' expresses the notion that He is high above any attribute of created beings," says Judah Halevi, the most Jewish of the medieval Jewish philosophers. "For this reason Isaiah heard an endless 'Holy, holy, holy,' which simply means that God is too high, too exalted, too holy, and too pure for any impurity of the people in whose midst His light dwells to touch Him. For the same reason Isaiah saw Him seated upon a high and exalted throne, by which is meant the spiritual sanctity which must not be represented in corporeal form and which nothing concrete can possibly resemble" (*Kuzari* IV:3; cf. also III:17).

In this moving representation of the sovereign might and awe-ful majesty of God, Otto finds a paradigm case of the holy in unsurpassable form. "If a man does not *feel* what the numinous is when he reads the sixth chapter of Isaiah, then no 'preaching, singing, telling,' in Luther's phrase, can avail him."[43] Around this passage, Otto's analysis of the religious consciousness as a whole revolves; to it he turns time and again to illustrate and verify his interpretation.[44]

The existence of intense religious experiences of the type described by Otto cannot be gainsaid. Again Otto is quite correct when he sees analogies to the numinous feeling in the spheres of art and music. It is, indeed, vain to suppose that, apart from more specifically religious experiences of a person, we can, in a manner of speaking, force religion upon his reluctant mind by means of intellectual arguments. It would be as idle to expect to do this as to expect to create by arguments of a quite general sort an appreciation of music or of poetry in a soul unsusceptible to aesthetic emotion. It is perfectly proper, therefore, for Otto to argue that we may as well expect the color-blind to appreciate the paintings of a Titian and a Raphael, or one whose ears are deaf to the harmonies of music to take delight in the symphonies of a Mozart or a Beethoven, as to convince a hardened agnostic or a determined skeptic of the existence and manifestations of the numinous.[45] But there is one vital difference between aesthetic experience and the religious experience of the numinous, viz., the cognitive value or epistemological worth of the experience. Now in the case of an artistic experience, the question of its being veridical or delusive cannot arise, but in the case of the alleged "sense of the numinous," we want very much to know if the feelings of religious rapture and exaltation, and the thrill of awe or reverence, are genuinely revelatory of an independently existing transcendent Being, and are not merely expressions of deeply felt human yearnings or the projections of human imagination and its myth-making propensities. The skeptic is quite willing to admit the existence of the mystical experience. What he wants to know is the conditions under which (how, when, and where) the numinous manifests itself, and what supporting public tests or independent criteria of corroboration there are, open to the scrutiny of friend or foe, by which we may distinguish the spurious claims of the bogus visionary from the authentic.

Despite his impressive erudition, the schematization of the idea of the holy by the use of purely *a priori* Kantian categories, and an excess of sesquipedalian Latin terms, Otto is unable to answer the skeptic's objections. At bottom, Otto's treatment of the "sense of the numinous" is vitiated by a confusion between logical and psychological issues; he confounds objective and subjective causes, or logical grounds with alogical and psychological motives. The distinguished Cambridge theologian, the late Professor F. R. Tennant, a penetrating and acute thinker, has pushed this point home with the utmost clarity in his analysis of the nature of belief. He distinguishes subjective psychological certitude, the convincedness of the believer (e.g., "I am certain that"), and logical objective certainty ascribed to propositions independently of whether or not they are believed (e.g., "it is certain that"). But, Tennant goes on to say, there is no necessary correlation between certitude and certainty. Whether a piece of reasoning is valid or not is a *logical,* not a *psychological,* question; logic, as the science of the weight of evidence, concerns itself with the grounds and criteria of validity. A hysterical dervish of the desert may be honestly convinced that he is guided from above, but we would do well to scrutinize and examine, to sift and test his private mental state of certitude to see whether there are reasonable objective grounds for his convictions, lest we become the blind followers of the blind. The mere feeling of certitude, even if coupled with an intensity of emotion and a depth of sincerity, is never a guarantee that what is believed is in fact certain, i.e., that that which is asserted is in conformity with certain objective states of fact (truth). Indeed, as Nietzsche remarked: "Strong faith proves only its strength, and not the truth of what is believed in."[46] Furthermore, while it can be rightly claimed that numinous cognition is psychologically immediate, it does not follow that it is epistemologically immediate; it may merely be the case that the subjects of numinous apprehension are unaware of its actual mediateness, as disclosed to reflection and analysis. A witness in court who can only assert the mere conclusion (as lawyers say), "*I am sure that the accused is guilty,*" is of no use. (This criticism does not apply to the validity of ordinary sense perceptions, where the testimony of one sense can be checked and supported by that of another, e.g., sight and touch. And statements about sense experience are, of course, psychologically more compelling and much easier to verify or falsify than propositions about disembodied spirits and God. If my companion expresses doubts about the table that separates him from me, I can simply ask him to walk toward me in a straight line.)[47] In other words, the psychological immediacy may not be a genuine immediacy, but rather a derived and mediated image or conception which is interpretatively read into perceptual or ideal objects as the case may be. Leuba and other psychologists have observed (undoubtedly with a great deal of exaggeration) that the mystics come from the intuitive contact with reality with the same truth that they took with them, namely, what they had accepted as true as a result of their training or racial heritage.[48] It must be admitted, it seems to me, that Tennant's clarification of several confusions, those, namely, of the mental state of efficacious certitude with logical or scientific certainty, of genuine with spurious immediacy, of psychological objectivity with reality or actuality, and of pure data with interpreted data, undermines the cogency of Otto's argument that "a numinous *object* objectively given must be posited as a primary immediate datum of consciousness."[49] And even if we were to grant that a given religious experience implies the existence of a supernatural being who produced it, the argument would in no way allow us to assign the experience to an Infinite God. We can here avail ourselves of the principle which Hume used so tellingly with regard to the occurrence of design in the universe: we must never suppose a cause which cannot be directly observed to be in any respect greater than the effect, but only exactly equal to it and no more. Now, since all human experience is finite, the attribution of any of it to an Infinite Cause must always go beyond the evidence; hence religious experience can in no way establish the existence of the Christian God of Aquinas, Who is a Being, underived, outside and above every genus, necessary, one, infinitely perfect, simple, immutable, immeasurable, eternal, intelligent, etc.

Despite the fact that Otto's theory of religious experience is not entirely acceptable, he has taken us a long way toward an understanding of religion. We can now see why it will just not do to say, as Havelock Ellis once did say, that the whole religious complexion of the modern world is due to the absence in Jerusalem of a lunatic asylum. This is so because in religion we come upon a unique feeling that cannot be defined conceptually. All theologies in a sense are self-defeating, because they attempt to translate into the conceptual language of reason that which is inexpressible in concepts. Otto has reminded us that there may be a genuine and important aspect of reality which is either ineffable, or if not, extremely hard to express in language, which was invented to serve the uses of the familiar world. It may even be possible, as Professor Broad has quite seriously suggested, that in order to have some peepholes into the supersensible world a man must be a little "cracked" in the head.[50] After all, "if there were such a thing as inspiration from a higher realm, it might well be that the neurotic temperament would furnish the chief condition of the requisite receptivity."[51] That there was a large element of eccentricity even in the great literary prophets does not seem to admit of question. If we would understand the prophet Isaiah, we must never forget that he was an exhibitionist who went about nude in the streets for three years (Isa. 20; *pace* Maimonides, *Guide* II:46).[52]

Even if Otto is not able to lead us into the promised land, he has taken us a long distance on the way. He has shown us why the assertions of the mystics cannot be rejected out of hand. Take the following utterance: "When you reach the stones of pure marble, do not say, Water, water!"[53] What are we to make of this? Is it the raving of a demented personality? Perhaps; perhaps not. But before we dismiss the utterance as unadulterated nonsense, we would do well to remember that its author, Rabbi Akiba, was also a man of great practical abilities, a distinguished jurist and statesman. Perhaps he was attempting, through inadequate symbols and hindered by linguistic inadequacy, to describe his spiritual vision and to communicate a religious experience to those who have never known anything of the kind themselves. We have no right to ignore the mystics' experiences, especially when they come from intellectually respectable sources. We must also be mindful of the fact that some of the great mystics were endowed with too˙ much psychological insight and critical and philosophical ability to be easily duped by extravagant claims. One voice out of many may be adduced. The philosopher-mystic St. John of the Cross, the Doctor of Night, went so far as to say of a nun who claimed to have had a conversation with God: "All this that she says, 'God spoke to me' or 'I spoke to God,' seems non-sense. She has only been speaking to herself."[54] Each alleged mystic experience must, therefore, be examined piecemeal on its own merits. As the Very Reverend Dean Inge once said, if a dozen honest men tell me that they have climbed the Matterhorn, it is reasonable to believe that the summit of that mountain is accessible, though I am not likely to get there myself. Similarly, when there is a nucleus of agreement between the experiences of men in different places, and when in spite of all differences of language, imagination, temperament, references, local conditioning, and historical setting, they all—from the ignorant peasant girl to the learned scholastic metaphysician—tend to put the same kind of interpretation on the cognitive content of these experiences, it is possible, if not probable, that they have come into contact with some aspects of reality which they may not have come into contact with in any other way.[55] Certainly, Dr. Johnson no more refuted the mysticism of Jacob Boehme with the remark that if Jacob saw the unutterable he should not have attempted to utter it, than he disproved Berkeley's idealist philosophy by kicking a large stone. In the final analysis, it may be more important, as the theologian Karl Rahner observed, to "stammer about God" than to "speak exactly about the world."

So far our position has not advanced beyond that of a respectful agnosticism. Are there no insights to be gained from medieval Jewish thought that can take us beyond such a position? In all sad sincerity, we have to answer in the negative. A modern writer on Jewish theology has indeed thought otherwise.

> Among all the Jewish religious philosophers, the highest rank must be accorded to Jehudah ha-Levi, the author of the *Kuzari,* who makes the historical fact of the divine revelation the foundation of the Jewish religion and the chief testimony of the existence of God. As a matter of fact, reason alone will not lead to God, except where religious intuition forms, so to speak, the ladder of heaven, leading to the realm of the unknowable. Philosophy, at best, can only

demonstrate the existence of a final cause, or of a supreme Intelligence working toward sublime purposes; possibly also a moral government of the world, in both the physical and the spiritual life. Religion alone, founded upon divine revelation, can teach man to find a God, to whom he can appeal in trust in his moments of trouble or woe, and whose will he can see in the dictates of conscience and the destiny of nations. Reason must serve as a *corrective* for the contents of revelation, scrutinizing and purifying, deepening and spiritualizing ever anew the truths received through intuition, but it can never be the final source of truth.[56]

While I agree with this authority that Judah Halevi has more to teach us than Maimonides—in general, the works of those medieval thinkers in which the pure philosophic element, whether Neoplatonic or Aristotelian, is smaller are of greater value for the thinking of the Jew today and can be used with greater confidence by him in the resolution of his own perplexities—and also with his assessment of the functions of reason and revelation, I feel that what he says about the *Kuzari* represents the ideal or aim of the author of that work rather than his accomplishment, and the work certainly does not satisfy the needs and requirements of today.

The truth or falsity of religion being thought to be inaccessible to philosophic inquiry, some have sought to find the answer in a psychological approach. Reviving the view popularized by Voltaire in his *Essay sur les moeurs* that divination originated when the first knave met a fool, certain psychologists attempt to account for the birth and development of religion by considering the general laziness of mankind. J. B. Watson, the founder of behaviorism, sees the origin of religion in the laziness of certain men who wanted to gain their living without hard work and so invented such superstitions as belief in God and the supernatural. The successors of these medicine men are the priests and preachers of today, and their views are as baseless as the grossest superstitions of savages.[57]

This cynical theory seems to me to be too ridiculous to be worth a moment's consideration. Psychological explanations cannot even enter into the picture, much less be used to discredit religious belief, unless the unbeliever has first established his case on *independent* grounds. But this is well-nigh impossible for the unbeliever to do. He would have to be in a position to say that if God existed and there were providential control of the course of events, certain events would have to occur which in fact do not occur. But this is precisely what he cannot say. (The factual suffering of the "good" and the prosperity of the "wicked" would be such an event only on the added assumption that God is a benevolent "grandfather in heaven," to use C. S. Lewis's phrase, whose only purpose is to make man happy in this life.) In the absence of this, psychological explanations are always reversible. Repudiation of the religious hypothesis by psychology alone, therefore, cannot succeed. The theist and the atheist (or agnostic) can each explain the reasons for the allegedly false position taken by the other without abandoning the premises of his own belief or lack thereof. Thus there can be no clear victory for either side on the level of psychological explanation. If, as Freud says, religion is a rationalization of the father ideal and the infantile wish for protection from the terrors of nature, then by the same token atheism and unbelief may be construed as the projection of ambivalence or outright hatred of one's physical father.[58] If, unlike the characters in Philip Roth's novels, I happen to love and cherish my parents, why should this condemn me? It is significant that psychologists always make an exception in favor of their pet theories; their own views are *hors concours*. Thus a Freudian will not explain (as Jung did) the psychoanalytic interpretation of religion as being the result of the personal complexes of Sigmund Freud, but will attribute logical validity to it. Psychological explanations of religion are, therefore, self-defeating theories; to the extent that they succeed, they refute their own assumptions. When combined with sinister economic motives and factors, such psychological explanations result in theories like the one propounded by Watson in his *Behaviorism*. If such a theory is applied to the rise of normative Judaism—with which we are concerned here—it reaches the height of absurdity. The Pharisees and their rabbinic successors did not have any material interests for the sake of which they may have been tempted to suppress the truth. For many centuries, down to the end of the Middle Ages and beyond, the rabbis earned their living in other professions—their religious work was unpaid. Consequently their thoughts were completely independent and their motives untarnished. Maimonides sums up the evidence well. "Among the greatest rabbis," he says, "were hewers of wood, and porters, drawers of water, iron workers, and smiths; and they asked nothing of the community, nor would they take anything when it was offered to them."[59]

Since we see that metaphysical issues cannot be resolved by appealing to any other discipline, we are apparently back where we started from. We cannot even fall back on the dictum of Bishop Butler that probability is the guide of life and attempt to demonstrate that the theistic position is on the whole the more reasonable one. As long ago as 1913, Professor W. E. Hocking observed: "The world would be consistent without God; it would also be consistent with God; whichever hypothesis a man adopts will fit experience equally well; neither one, so far as accounting for visible facts is concerned, works better than the others."[60]

To get out of this impasse, let us avail ourselves of a line of argument which Professor A. E. Taylor so forcefully used in the concluding chapter of his Gifford Lectures, entitled *The Faith of a Moralist.*[61]

Professor Taylor observes that the division between believers and unbelievers is not peculiar to any class or social grade or level of culture, but exists everywhere and at all levels. If modern society were viewed as the image of a mountain or a pyramid, with the different levels representing degrees of education and knowledge, we should see the division between the believers and unbelievers not as a horizontal one, dividing off the higher part of the pyramid from the base below, but as a vertical or lateral one running through the pyramid from apex to base. On the very highest level, among the academicians and the original workers and thinkers in the various departments of knowledge and thought, believers and unbelievers are found side by side. At the bottom, among the most ignorant and uncultured, one will find both the devoutly orthodox and the scornfully antireligious, and one will meet the same situation at any intervening level of the pyramid.

This state of affairs may appear at first blush to be equally favorable and unfavorable to the claims of both the believer and the unbeliever. In reality, as Professor Taylor has urged, it is more unfavorable to the "scientific humanist," and for a plain reason. Believers do not have to assert that their belief is arrived at as a scientific inference from universally recognized data, in such a wise that they are able to demonstrate the truth of their convictions as one may demonstrate a proposition in mathematics. The believer does not have to assert that with sufficient native intelligence and adequate education, every man must necessarily become a believer, for he realizes that the grace and help of God must be sought above all. He believes in an actual historical revelation, and he realizes that God's love is an unconditioned love which comes independently of the particular individual's amount of knowledge and culture. So he prays: "Our God and God of our fathers . . . Sanctify us with Thy commandments; . . . satisfy us with Thy goodness and gladden us with Thy help and purify our hearts to serve Thee in truth."[62] If the believer's view of the nature and destiny of man is correct, it is understandable that there should be men of the highest intelligence and the best education who are irreligious. But it is part of the case of the "scientific humanist" that theistic beliefs can be proved to be false or unfounded to anyone of high intelligence and good education. The militant unbeliever does claim that his objections to theism are based upon scientific knowledge (e.g., the Darwinian theory of evolution and Freudian psychology); he does contend that a man has only to be learned enough in order to be logically bound to deny the truth of theism. For him, therefore, it is a really awkward fact—a paradox, if you will—that there should be believers at the highest levels of intelligence. He cannot account for this by appealing to the Idols of the Tribe and of the Cave (by showing how the sentiments and desires, especially those inbred by childhood associations, early training, and the prevalent tradition may enter to corrupt the process of inference; how prejudice and obstinacy vitiate human judgment, etc.), because, as we have seen, all such *ad hominem* arguments can be met by *tu quoque* replies, and cancel each other out.

Of course, the foregoing argument does not prove the truth of theism or of the tenets of any one sect, but it does show that the appearances are very strongly against the humanists who regard religion as a mere widespread popular delusion, and it should make one wonder whether the reports of God's death, like the initial reports of Mark Twain's, have not been greatly exaggerated.[63]

Our final conclusion is rather modest. I believe that the distinctive element in the theistic hypothesis is not that of belief, but that of a fundamental and pervasive attitude toward the world which permeates and transforms all of man's activities and interests, what Professor R. M. Hare calls a "blik."[64] The religious view cannot logically be shown to be the only right or sane blik. But the same is true of any philosophical position or perspective. As the late Professor F. Waismann, who himself was an Oxford philosopher who distinguished himself in the philosophy of mathematics and logic, once put it: "No philosophic argument ends with a Q.E.D. However forceful it never forces. There is no bullying in a philosophy, neither with the stick of logic nor with the stick of language."[65] Waismann concludes that "at the heart of any philosophy worth the name is vision. . . . what is decisive is a new way of seeing and, what goes with it, the will to transform the whole intellectual scene."

The impossibility of "knock-down" proofs in religion should not be considered upsetting. A geometrically rigorous proof of God's existence would reduce men to puppets without the opportunity freely to commit themselves to Him in religious faith and trust. But God wants the heart; He wants to enter into a personal relationship of love and trust with His human creatures. Faith is the existential response, beyond further analysis, of the whole being to Truth, and not a mere estimate of probabilities at an intellectual level. For the true believer, as Cardinal Newman pointed out, "ten thousand difficulties do not make one doubt" (*Apologia,* beginning pt. V). If we could produce logically cogent proofs for the existence of God, we would be unable to make a free decision to love God; at most we could have a notional assent (in Cardinal Newman's terminology as developed in chap. 4 of *A Grammar of Assent*) to the proposition "God exists," as opposed to a real assent to a Supreme Being to whom men can freely commit themselves in religious faith and trust. As Alasdair MacIntyre said at a time when he was a Christian apologist: "We do not decide to accept Euclid's conclusions; we merely look to the rigor of his arguments. If the existence of God were demonstrable we should be as bereft of the possibility of making free decisions to love God as we should be if every utterance of doubt or unbelief was answered by thunder-bolts from heaven."[66] Well did one of the ancient rabbis say, "Everything is in the hands of Heaven except the fear of Heaven."[67] Too much certitude is as fatal to religious belief as too little; the one takes away the merit of believing, the other reduces faith to credulity. "Faith," St. Thomas quotes with approval from Pope St. Gregory the Great, "faith has no merit where human reason presents actual proof from experience."[68] "According to its very definition, faith implies assent of the intellect to that which the intellect does not see to be true. . . . Consequently, an act of faith cannot be caused by rational evidence, but entails an intervention of the will."[69] Faith is a free and unmerited gift from God, as is the grace necessary to attain the supernatural goal which faith apprehends. "We are moved to believe divine revelation," says St. Thomas in *De Veritate* (14, a.l.c.), "because we are promised eternal life as a reward if we believe. And this reward moves the will to assent to what is said, although the intellect is not moved by anything which it understands." The primarily volitional character of faith and its origin in the human soul has been perceptively described in the manual of scholastic philosophy edited by the late Cardinal Mercier:

> If it be asked how it is that the will acts upon the intellect so as to constrain it to assent to what, if left to itself, it would not assent to, we should say that the part played by the will is both that of withdrawing the reason from a close scrutiny of difficulties which naturally arise from the obscurity of the material object and also that of concentrating attention on the consideration of motives which makes the proposition certain: that a revealed truth can be believed by a

prudent man and ought to be believed. When firmness of our assents surpasses the cogency of the rational motives, this bespeaks within us some action above ourselves, of an action called by theologians the effect of supernatural grace.[70]

Nor can one deduce specific moral principles from theological foundations or religious dogmas. In his *Treatise* (bk. III, pt. 1, sec. 8) Hume makes it clear that nonmoral premises cannot logically entail a moral conclusion. It is a fallacy in the strict sense to derive a conclusion containing the term "ought" or "right" from premises which do not contain this term. Now the Thomist account of the moral life as the fruition of human nature runs diametrically counter to Hume's analysis. The starting point in Aquinas' teleological moral theory is the quest for the ultimate end of man, and once having established it to find the means necessary for its attainment. These means are the foundation stones of the Thomist ethic in the form of the natural and theological virtues, and morally good and obligatory actions. Hume's moral theory, to be sure, is far from being the last word of ethics, but it has the merit of showing the inadequacy of the Thomistic theory of morals by pointing out that no sense of obligation can be deduced from the actual constitution of mankind without some logical sharp practice. The specific modes of conduct prescribed by the great religions are either based on reflections of a nonmetaphysical kind or on revelation.[71] The fact of revelation can indeed never be proved—otherwise it would cease to be supernatural—but philosophical theology is under the burden of demonstrating the possibility of revelation and, by "withdrawing the reason from a too close scrutiny of difficulties," gaining our assent to the historical revelation recorded in the Bible.

The modest mold of this conclusion should not be upsetting. In some ways the results of linguistic philosophy are closer to the biblical faith than the elaborate Neoplatonic and Aristotelian systems worked out by the medieval thinkers. Archbishop William Temple once remarked that the Bible says very little about atheism but a great deal about idolatry. To clear the ground of useless intellectual rubbish so that positive reconstruction can begin is itself no mean task. We may remember that the cleaning of the Augean stables from filth was a Herculean task which was all but impossible. The philosopher, said John Locke, is usually merely an "under-laborer . . . clearing the ground a little, and removing some of the rubbish that lies in the way of knowledge."[72]

A distinguished contemporary religious thinker in the camp of linguistic analysis has acutely observed:

> In spite of immense intellectual investment which has gone and is still going into the various attempts to demonstrate the existence of God, the conclusion ... that this is indemonstrable is in agreement both with the contemporary philosophical understanding of the nature and limits of logical proof and with the biblical understanding of man's knowledge of God.[73]

The biblical writers, as we have mentioned,[74] assume the existence of God and are not concerned with metaphysical speculations as to His nature and being. It was as an experienced living personal force, and not as an inferred metaphysical entity, that God was adored by Israel. The prophets and sages of Israel would have agreed with the distinguished Oxford philosopher who said: "We don't want merely inferred friends. Could we possibly be satisfied with an inferred God?"[75] "Knowledge of God" is not the mere assent of the intellect to the statement that God is, or even to the statement that God is good (as indeed He is). Rather, it is the vivid realization of God and His love, and the consciousness of His demands for righteous living. "Wherever Scripture speaks of 'knowledge of God,'" says Professor Kohler, "it always means the moral and spiritual recognition of the Deity as life's inmost power, determining human conduct, and by no means refers to mere intellectual perception of the truth of Jewish monotheism. ... It is man's moral nature rather than his intellectual capacity, that leads him 'to know God and walk in His ways.'"[76] "Knowledge of God" is the inner conviction of the heart that God loves us and cares for us, that our times are in His hands, that He is our refuge, and that underneath are the everlasting arms.

> As a deer longs for flowing streams,
> So longs my soul for You, O God.
> My soul thirsts for God,
> For the living God. (Ps. 42:1–2; Hebrew 42:2–3)

This abiding and increasing sense of God's presence and love brings with it an inner security and an absolute repose. Not that the religious man feels himself protected in a sense in which others are not protected from physical danger, but rather he is ready to face whatever may befall him of good report and ill report, because nothing can happen to him without the will of God, who loves him. "Nevertheless I am continually with Thee; Thou dost hold my right hand. Thou dost guide me with Thy counsel, and afterward Thou wilt receive me with glory. Whom Have I in heaven but Thee? And there is nothing upon earth that I desire besides Thee. My flesh and my heart fail, but God is the rock of my heart and my portion for ever" (Ps. 73:23–26). The believer has attained that inner serenity and peace of soul which neither worldly success nor worldly failure, neither the love of life nor the fear of death, can disturb.[77]

> When you pass through the waters I will be with you;
> And through rivers, they shall not overwhelm you;
> When you walk through fire you shall not be burned,
> And the flame shall not consume you. (Isa. 43:2)[78]

This religious perspective and attitude unifies, transforms, and gives direction to the believer's whole life and thought and action.

Consider the problem of justifying the goodness of God in the face of evil, sin, and suffering. This problem is more primary than that of proving rationally the existence of God. For the theologian can readily admit that the criticisms of Kant and other philosophers have invalidated all the traditional proofs of God's existence, and can still maintain that his position is unshaken, since the divine may be known in some other, nonrational way. But the criticism made by way of the classic problem of evil is much more radical. Here it can be shown not only that religious beliefs lack rational support, but that they are positively irrational and inconsistent with each other. For the theologian theodicy is, in the words of M. Windelband, the squaring of the circle in the field of religious thought. When the great luminaries, Maimonides and Aquinas, make the observation that evil is privation, we wonder why the privation is not evil,[79] but when the biblical Book of Job treats the why of the suffering of the innocent, we sit up and listen. Apart from all questions of religious and theological import, this is because Job does not attempt to provide an intellectual answer to the problems of evil.[80] The climax of the book comes when the voice of God answers out of the whirlwind (chaps. 38–41). God comes in at the end not to answer riddles but to propound them. Instead of comforting Job with easy solutions, He propounds universal and overwhelming puzzles. G. K. Chesterton, expert in paradox, has elaborated on this paradoxical situation.

> A more trivial poet would have made God enter in some sense or other in order to answer the questions. By a touch truly to be called inspired, when God enters, it is to ask a number of more questions on His own account. In

this drama of skepticism, God Himself takes up the role of skeptic. . . . He seems to say that if it comes to asking questions, He can ask some questions which will fling down and flatten out all conceivable human questioners. The poet, by an exquisite intuition, has made God ironically accept a kind of controversial equality with His accusers. He is willing to regard it as if it were a fair intellectual duel: "Gird up now thy loins like a man; for I will demand of thee, and answer thou me." The Everlasting adopts an enormous and sardonic humility. He is quite willing to be prosecuted. He only asks for the right which every prosecuted person possesses; He asks to be allowed to cross-examine the witness for the prosecution. And He carries yet further the correctness of the legal parallel. For the first question, essentially speaking, which He asks of Job is the question that any criminal accused by Job would be most entitled to ask. He asks Job who he is. And Job, being a man of candid intellect, takes a little time to consider and comes to the conclusion that he does not know.[81]

Thus, as Chesterton implies, human doubt is rebuked by a cosmic skepticism, and the doubter is confronted by enigmas beyond his penetration. Job suddenly becomes satisfied with a new blik, or pervasive attitude, toward the world. "He has been told nothing, but he feels the terrible and tingling atmosphere of something which is too good to be told. The riddles of God," concludes Chesterton, "are more satisfying than the solutions of man."

In my judgment, Chesterton had a profounder understanding of the biblical view of God and man than Maimonides, who in the preface to a discussion of the insoluble problem of suffering as posed by the experience of Job, makes the presumptuous claim: "I will now resolve all the difficulties!" (*Guide* III:24).

In a famous passage in the Book of Exodus, God is reported to have revealed Himself to Moses at the burning bush. Moses, overcome by awe, asks God to disclose His name to him and straight away the divine Voice from the burning bush identifies itself as the I-AM-WHO-I-AM, and then continues to say to Moses: "Tell the Israelites I-Am (*Ehyeh*) has sent me to you" (3:14). This key text from Exodus plays a prominent part in scholastic philosophy, and on it Etienne Gilson builds up so much of his thought. In *The Spirit of Medieval Philosophy* he calls the name of God given in this text "the cornerstone of all Christian philosophy," and in his *Philosophy of St. Thomas Aquinas* he devotes the entire fourth chapter to the "sublime truth" conveyed by this name.[82] Furthermore, in a true ecumenical spirit he devotes a special study to the meaning of this name in the philosophy of Maimonides.[83]

What, then, is the significance of this name in the thought of Maimonides and Aquinas? For Maimonides it means "the Existent Being which is the Existent Being, i.e., the Necessary Being" (*Guide* 1:63). This is the core of Maimonides' doctrine of God: We know *that* God is but not *what* He is. Over one hundred years ago a recognized authority composed a definitive study on the meaning of God as conceived by the medieval rationalist Jewish philosophers which has never been replaced. More than a hundred closely reasoned pages in that study are devoted to the thought of Maimonides. His considered conclusion as regards the outcome of Maimonides' speculation on the nature of God is: "All that we know of God is the mere fact of His absolutely necessary existence—this constitutes the beginning and end of Maimonides' theology."[84]

According to Professor Gilson it was the supreme achievement of the Angelic Doctor to grasp with full understanding the truth that in God, and only in God, being (*esse*) and essence (*essentia*) are identical. St. Thomas considers QUI EST (HE WHO IS)[85] the most proper name for God for three reasons: (1) for denotation, because it signifies God according to His essence, that is, as Being itself; (2) for universality, because HE WHO IS does not more closely determine the divine essence which is inaccessible to the human intellect in this life. "Therefore the less determinate the names are, and the more universal and absolute they are, the more properly are they applied to God"; and (3) for connotation, because it signifies being in the present which is appropriate to God, Whose being transcends past and future (*S.T.* 1a, q. 13, a. 11c).

The sublime truth that was revealed to Moses, according to these philosophers, is that the HE-WHO-IS of Exodus means *Ipsum Esse Per Se Subsistens,* the pure Act-of-Subsistent-Being-Itself. Professor Gilson believes that the medieval philosophers were correct in their interpretation of this text. "There is but one God and this God is Being, that is the cornerstone of all Christian philosophy, and it was not Plato, it was not even Aristotle, it was Moses who put it in position."[86] It is no objection to this thesis to say that the Exodus passage is not a metaphysical proposition, that a homily on God's aseity would have no meaning to a group of oppressed and despondent slaves. "Of course," says M. Gilson, "We do not maintain that the text of Exodus is a revealed metaphysical definition of God. But if there is no metaphysic *in* Exodus, there is nevertheless a metaphysic *of* Exodus."[87] While the Exodus passage is not a philosophical propostion, it contains in its compactness an inexhaustible metaphysical fecundity. The scholastics, like the rabbis before them, believed that Moses and other divinely inspired writers may have been permitted by God to understand several different truths under one single set of words, so that each and every one of these different truths was the meaning of the inspired author. This possibility suggests that the meaning differentiated by the medieval philosophers may be a justifiable interpretation of the text. The fundamental question is rather this: Is this interpretation of Scripture true in itself?

The exponents of philosophical analysis have not always been very gentle with the claims of scholastic and neoscholastic philosophers. In one of his seminars, the famous Oxford teacher, the late Professor J. L. Austin, jeered at the scholastic doctrine that God's essence is "Subsistent Being Itself," or the notion that "what subsists in God is His being." He is reputed to have referred to the episode of the burning bush and to have made the following profound or clever remark (I forget which): When the voice from the thornbush said to Moses, "I am," the only proper and sensible reply should have been the question "You are *what*?" Technically, of course, Professor Austin is right: "I am." and "God is." are incomplete sentences. In the fifth chapter of his book *The Five Ways,* Anthony Kenny elaborates on this criticism in a more pedestrian manner. The predicate "being" is too thin and uninformative to be of any use in describing the nature of God (in the sense that this predicate is common to every substance), or, if it belongs in a very special sense to God since in Him (and in Him alone) essence and existence are identical, this predicate is no predicate at all. It is a variable expression which permits of no substitution; it is to equate "God is" with "God is F," and then deny that any genuine predicate can take the place of "F". "So interpreted, the incommunicable name seems to be just an ill-formed formula." Under logical analysis the notion of God as the very Act-of-Subsistent-Being "so far from being a profound metaphysical analysis of the divine nature, turns out to be the Platonic Idea of a predicate which is at best uninformative and at worst unintelligible."[88]

I speak regretfully, because one does not like to see so much enthusiasm, learning, and acuteness wasted over metaphysical moonshine, but the whole scholastic effort seems to me to be misguided, one-sided, and incorrect. What man longs for is not an abstract and obscure metaphysical formula on the identity of essence and existence in an indescribable blur, but a Friend behind phenomena, to use Edwyn Bevan's apt phrase: man yearns for the Living God with Whom one can establish a genuinely personal relationship. We need a Supreme Person of perfect moral love to Whom we feel akin and to Whom we are drawn by bonds of affinity; we need an all-loving and all-providing Father[89] to trust in and to commune with in prayer. I cannot help feeling that the ancient rabbis, despite their lack of philosophical discipline, had a truer conception of the majesty and holiness of God than the scholastics, Jewish and Gentile, with all their logic-chopping. They saw in the name I-AM-WHO-I-AM the assurance that God is the ever-present, ever-ready Helper in all times of need ("I am with you"). He can help us in our trouble and affliction, and solve the abysmal and impenetrable mystery of our own being.[90] This is not the God of the "philosophers," but the God of Abraham, Isaac, and Jacob, the God who says, "Walk before Me, and be perfect!" (Gen. 17:1); "Be holy, for I, the Lord your God, am holy" (Lev. 19:2). This point has been admirably made by Martin Buber:

> Not "I am that I am" as alleged by the metaphysicians—God does not make theological statements—but the answer which his creatures need, and which benefits them: "I shall be there as I there shall be" (Exod. 3:14). That is: you need not conjure me, for I am here, I am with you; but you cannot conjure me, for I am with you time and again in the form in which I choose to be with you time and again; I myself do not anticipate any of my manifestations; you cannot learn to meeet me; you meet me, when *you* meet me: "It is not in heaven; that thou shouldst say: 'Who shall go up for us to heaven, and bring it unto us, and make us to hear it that we may do it . . . ' Yea, the word is very nigh unto thee, in thy mouth, and in thy heart, that thou mayest do it" (cf. Deut 30:12, 14).[91]

God manifests His dynamic moral vitality in His righteous will. But beyond God's holy will is His character; beyond His deed, His strong and tender love (*ḥesed*). If we make our will conform to God's will, He will fill our soul with peace, joy, and love, and supply our life with new meaning and moral power. "Our wills are ours to make them thine,"[92] cries the poet. Only in such a richly personal conception of God may we find our peace in His will.

In *Two Types of Faith* (London, 1951), Martin Buber contrasts the "faith of Abraham" with the "faith of Paul." In biblical and Pharisaic Judaism, faith (*emunah*) means unconditional trust and confidence in God, as opposed to the Pauline belief in the truth of a proposition (*pistis*) about God. This distinction between trust and belief is not as clear as it might be. It fails to distinguish between true and false beliefs and confuses credulity with faith. What of the child who "believes" in Mother Goose in the "trusting" sense? Much more fruitful is the distinction made by philosophers between "beliefs that" and "beliefs in." In his Gifford Lectures, H. H. Price has discussed at length the question whether in all cases "belief-in" a thing or person is in one way or another reducible to a "belief-that" it or he exists and has certain properties.[93] As instances of reducible "beliefs-in" he mentions factual beliefs in fairies (or in King Arthur) which can be reduced to the "belief-that" they exist (or he existed). Even certain evaluative kinds of "belief-in" can be reduced to the "belief-that" a certain proposition is true, provided that suitable value concepts are introduced into the conceptions believed. For example, my belief in my doctor is reducible to "I believe not only that my doctor has been and is good, that is, efficient and effective at curing diseases (or a specific disease), but also that he will continue to be so and that it is a good thing that he is and will continue to be a good doctor." It is Price's contention, however that not all matters of "belief-in" are reducible *prima facie* to straightforward and obvious matters of "belief-that." He maintains that there is at least one class of "belief-in" statements that is simply irreducible, namely, belief in someone because one trusts him. Now the trusting aspect of such a "belief-in" cannot be reduced to the belief that one's friend is good at this or that skill or activity. This is because "trusting" is not merely a cognitive but an "affective" attitude and hence has a "warmth" or "heart-felt" character. In the final analysis we can only know what it is to trust someone by actually being in the mental attitude which the word "trusting" denotes. This particular attitude is best characterized as a disinterested valuing or "believing-in" someone for his own sake. It amounts to believing that it just is a good thing that he exists, and still would be if I got nothing out of it. Disinterested belief in a friend is really a matter of "the heart" whereby we simply trust him as the individual, unique human being that he is. Our friend's efficiency, or lack of it, is irrelevant to our belief in him, if we do believe in him as a friend. It is this latter "belief-in," or trust, in a friend which Price maintains is irreducible to any "belief-that."

Belief in God, like belief in a friend, is clearly an attitude of this kind. At its highest level in the three great monotheistic faiths, Judaism, Christianity, and Islam, it is disinterested as well as interested, i.e., one trusts God not only for the benefits which have been bestowed on oneself or on one's fellows by the plenitude of His love and compassion, but for His own sake. The psalmist's verse, "Blessed is the man who fears the Lord, and in His commandments delights greatly" (Ps. 112:1), led an ancient rabbi to remark, "in His commandments, and not *in the reward* of His commandments" (Abodah Zarah 19a). All three traditions mention the touching story of the saint carrying a chafing dish of fire in his right hand and a cruse of water in his left, so that he could burn up heaven with the fire and make a clean end of it, and put out hell with the water and make a clean end of it too, in order that mankind may henceforth worship God out of pure love.[94] Guillaume de Tocco, in his *Life of St. Thomas Aquinas* (chap. 34), records the following naive but moving incident which brings out this point very clearly. Friar Dominic of Caserta once concealed himself in a chapel to observe Thomas in prayer. Thomas prayed fervently and then spoke to the crucifix hanging on the wall. The figure on the cross said in a clear voice, "Thomas you have written well about me. What reward will you have for your labors?" And Thomas replied, "Nothing but yourself, O Lord!"

Price's analysis is superior to that of Buber because he shows that there are two elements involved in faith: the first, cognitive, and the second, volitional. The trusting attitude is indeed an essential ingredient in faith, but it can come into play only *after* reason has shown that the existence of God in whom to believe is possible. Price makes it painstakingly clear that "belief-in" God always presupposes the cognitive belief that He exists. To put one's trust and confidence in a nonexistent being would obviously mean to have faith in a figment of one's own imagination and to worship an idol. Since the time of Kant—the "Alleszermalmer" Kant—the metaphysical "proofs" for God's existence have been considered philosophically inconclusive. The proper conclusion to be drawn from this state of affairs, as we have already indicated, is not that agnosticism is the correct position to adopt, but that religious faith need not be dependent on philosophical arguments. Once philosophical theology has shown that theism, though beyond rational proof, does not, or need not, conflict with scientific knowledge, and does not turn out upon examination to be self-contradictory or devoid of content, its task is accomplished. The existence of God and other fundamental religious beliefs are exactly in the same boat, in not being strictly provable, as are the belief in scientific laws (induction), the trustworthiness of memory, the existence of other people, and the ultimate justification of moral principles, to name just a few. If this is indeed the case, should we not return to the biblical standpoint and try to be receptive to its insights? We have indicated that to the biblical writers the nonexistence of God was inconceivable. They lived, and moved, and had their being in an environment where such belief was taken for granted. We can learn absolutely nothing from the biblical authors regarding the "belief-that" God exists. But we can learn a very great deal from these religious geniuses about the "belief-in" God, the trusting attitude and the awareness of God's constant Presence which is also an essential ingredient in faith. The great personalities of the Bible had an immediate experience of God. The vast majority of people today, including the most religious of them, do not have this vivid "sense" of being in personal intercourse with the Supreme Power ruling the universe. Here we can sit at the feet of the ancients. It may be a disturbing idea and uncomfortable to our ego, but I think it must be admitted that in the sphere of religion the ancient Hebrews were the masters and we are dependent on them. In the words of the book of Genesis (6:4): "There were giants on the earth in those days." That is perhaps why the religious mind is essentially conservative and does not like to tamper with ancient rituals. Truly, in the realm of religion "if our ancestors were angels, we are human beings; and if our ancestors were human beings, we are like asses" (Shabbath 112b). Because the school of philosophical analysis has helped to clear away the cobwebs of scholasticism which had obscured the biblical insight into God and man, theists should view that movement not as an antagonist, but as an ally which can help modern man find a faith grounded in intellectual integrity.

The metaphysician Francis Herbert Bradley once declared that he would not "rest tranquilly" in a theory which, however logical, was "hateful" to him. He went on to say that "rightly or wrongly" he would insist that the inquiry was not yet closed and that the result was at best but partial.[95] What Bradley meant was that a really satisfactory philosophy must do more than satisfy the demand for logical cohesion; it must take account of and satisfy all sides of our being, including the demands of our ethical, aesthetic, aspirational, and religious natures. If the question should be raised why I prefer the theistic world outlook to a humanist frame or view of the secular manufactured religions, the answer that I would give is that the humanist viewpoint does not satisfy my innermost being. The humanist view is too thin and meager to appeal to anyone outside a small coterie of devotees. "Most men," remarks C. E. M. Joad, "need a creed and there is nothing in the empirical world upon which a creed can be based. For the empirical world contains nothing but the movements of matter and these, though they can be observed, cannot be believed."[96] Naturalistic humanism with its idolatrous exaltation of an idealized and unreal humanity is unable to touch the sources of human motivation. As Charles Bennett says: "One does not need to be a pessimist or a cynic to feel that man is one of the poorest substitutes for God that ingenuity can propose. It is better to repudiate religion and all its works than to chatter about worshipping or adoring humanity."[97] Unlike some modern secular religions like communism, materialistic naturalism or scientific humanism, as this ideology is variously called, is not a movement for which men bleed and die. It is too hopelessly cerebral and too sicklied over, perhaps, with the pale cast of thought. Nature, however, abhors a vacuum in the spiritual no less than in physical realm. "When the gods go, the half-gods arrive" is still a true picture of the human condition. When man's ineradicable quest for God finds no fulfillment; when he sees the spring sun shine out of an empty heaven to light up a soulless earth; when he views himself as a mere bundle of cellular matter performing the mechanical operations involved in turning good, healthy nourishment into rather inefficient manure—when these things happen, man will fall prey to various irrational beliefs and substitute religious ideologies. It is as if when he cannot find God in heaven, he must fall down before a half-god on earth or deify some idol made of wood, or of gold, or of ideas, as Dostoevsky pointed out with profound insight in *A Raw Youth.*[98] When I contemplate the history of the world since 1912—that whole Dantesque inferno of atomic warfare, concentration camps, crematoriums, massacres, tortures, persecution, rape, arson—and the nearly successful genocidal murder of the Jewish people, I feel that the prophetic message to the pagan world is more imperative than ever: "The gods who did not make the heavens and the earth must vanish from the earth and from under the heavens!" (Jer. 10:11).

To assert more than the foregoing would be to go beyond the evidence. It would also fail to take into account the extent to which our belief or absence of belief is conditioned, though not wholly determined, by the accidents of birth and upbringing.

But there comes a point where the question "What can I know?" glides into "What may I hope for?" I trust that the day will come when the theistic viewpoint will become universal, "and no longer shall each man teach his neighbor and each man his brother, saying 'Know the Lord!' for they shall all know Me" (Jer. 31:34). But when that day comes, if it ever does come, there will be no longer any need for philosopher-theologians or their finely spun systems.

The Reverend Professor Bruce A. Williams, O. P., who made many helpful comments on the incomplete first draft of this book, jotted the following charming marginal note opposite my concluding observation to the effect that, whatever uses philosopher-theologians may or may not have in this world, they will not be needed in the hereafter: "Even then there will be a need for them." My knowledge of the hereafter is microscopic and on this point I defer to Fr. Williams's greater wisdom, all the more so since he is on the side of the angels. Indeed, the uses that Fr. Williams finds for philosopher-theologians among the blessed in heaven are particularly refreshing in these days when philosophy has a bad image, many believing that it is "dead" and a useless discipline, and when even Wittgenstein asserts, "Philosophy leaves everything as it is" (Die Philosophie lässt alles wie es ist).[99]

8

Epilogue

Herbert Loewe's Apologia for Traditional Judaism:
An Unorthodox Defense of Orthodoxy
Raba' de'amēh, medabrana' de'umatēh, bōṣīna dinehōra'
(Ket. 17a)

Several of the readers to whom my manuscript was submitted have remarked on its largely negative and destructive character. To this charge I must plead guilty. In extenuation I can only assert that I have honestly examined the arguments employed by two outstanding philosopher-theologians and have found them wanting. Limiting himself to the recent past, the Reverend Dr. Keith Ward of Trinity Hall, Cambridge, not long ago lamented in the pages of the *Expository Times* that "it seems to be the case that all the clearest and best arguments belong to the atheists," which is but small comfort to theologians.[1] Now one can expose the weakness in a philosophical system without constructing a more acceptable one to take its place. Nevertheless, as a committed theist and an Orthodox Jew, I feel somewhat uneasy, and I think it might be best if I were to redress the balance to some extent by indicating what positive lines of approach I find most promising. But rather than foist my own inexpert reflections on the reader, I should like to call attention to a seminal scholar whose work has been much neglected. Herbert Loewe was Reader in Rabbinics at Cambridge University in the decade before the Second World War. It is a sad commentary on the sorry state of contemporary Jewish theology that one can find more substance in the parerga and paralipomena of a biblical and rabbinical scholar than in the theologies of contemporary Jewish thinkers. I have long been acquainted with Loewe's writings, but their contemporary relevance was brought to my attention when reading J. V. L. Casserley's *The Retreat from Christianity in the Modern World* (London, 1952). Certain of the arguments in that work had a strangely familiar ring to them, and it seemed to me that I had seen them before. The following passage (which appears on pp. 61–62) in particular caught my attention.

> The Western seeker for light among the non-Christian religions is apt, rather unfairly but no doubt inevitably, to contrast the great spiritual treasures of the Eastern religious world with the day-to-day life of the Western Church, the Upanishads, shall we say, with the local Vicar's Sunday sermon. But this is hardly a just way of proceeding. The great Eastern religions have also, in those parts of the world in which they flourish, their own characteristic popular life, wherein the Western seeker after truth in the rich mines of Oriental spirituality would discover all the failings and limitations of the day-to-day life of the Western Church, and many far more grievous and terrible ones besides, not only the relatively harmless dogmatism of some simple man of God talking as simply as he can to people perhaps simpler than himself, but also a wallowing in degrading superstition, an immense gap between the mass religious life and the rich spiritual treasures which lie, almost wholly unknown to the multitude, at the very heart of the religion itself, such as nothing in the Western Church even faintly approaches. We cannot escape from the many human defects in our practice of the religion which we know simply by reading about and meditating upon a form of spirituality of whose popular practice we know nothing, unless we travel to the East, and which would almost certainly shock our consciences to the depths if we did.

Before long I solved the mystery. Casserley's defense of Christianity against the vigorous challenge of the Eastern religions is strongly reminiscent of Loewe's apologia for the traditional Judaism of the Pharisees against the strictures of certain Christian critics. Loewe had pointed out that it is unfair to compare the actual life of the Jew in the first centuries of the Christian era with the theoretical counsels of perfection of the gospel Jesus. He urges that the Sermon on the Mount marks the highest level, reached only by Jesus himself, and it is not to be regarded as representative of average Christianity.

> To measure the standards upheld in such ethical but purely theoretical declarations with those prevalent in everyday Jewish life contemporary with Jesus is uncritical. Instead one must look to the primitive Church. Weighed against Paul's converts in Romans i, for example, the average Jewish congregation would emerge with credit. One cannot fail to be astonished that

when Paul or James reproach their Churches with grave moral lapses, the obvious conclusion does not seem to occur to them. The Jew could fling the *Tu quoque* at Paul. "Through the Law sin came to us, you say. But has your Christianity brought your converts to a higher life? You lash your Churches for shameless immorality such as has never disgraced the Synagogue; in your attacks on the Law have you been able to find things as bad with us? What, then, has your breach with the Law achieved save Bolshevik lawlessness?" . . . One must always remember that Jesus was a free-lance, he had no responsibility. . . . He was in a position to pick and choose, to select a particular topic and ignore others, not out of indifference necessarily, but because other teachers were concerned with them. The difference is that between the rector of a parish, to whom the work of the church is the primary consideration, and the itinerant Salvationist. The rector must urge parents to observe the Mitzvoth, e.g., to baptize their children, to be regular in church attendance, to support charities, and to take part in all the duties of a member of the congregation. The Salvationist can confine himself to popular preachings on the Atonement, "the blood of Jesus washes away sins," "only believe in the Cross and you will be saved." But does the rector believe in faith any less because he is apparently the more interested in fasting, communion or the colour of vestments? . . . What did Jesus propose? For him it was easy enough to denounce. He had no responsibility; he was not called upon to be constructive; he was in opposition. But what would he have done had he been in power? We have seen the stoutest opponents of the Government, the boldest, most uncompromising Radicals become docile and conventional when office falls to their lot. The Keir Hardies and John Burns become changed indeed when they have to act and not merely to speak.[2]

Since in today's post-modern society, Christians within the total world picture represent the kind of minority that the Jews used to represent within the Christian world, I wonder whether some considerations raised by Loewe and some of his insights are not bound to strike a more responsive chord today than when they were first advanced more than half a century ago.

In 1966, the editors of *Commentary* magazine compiled a symposium on the present state of contemporary Jewish thought which was later published in book form under the title, *The Condition of Jewish Belief* (New York, 1967). Among the topics which the contributors to the symposium were asked to discuss are the following: the sense in which the Torah is a divine revelation; whether Judaism is the one true religion, and if so what the status of Christianity is in relation to Judaism; the challenge of modern thought to traditional Jewish beliefs. In his introduction to the symposium, Milton Himmelfarb, a contributing editor of *Commentary*, observes that the single

greatest influence on American Jewry is Franz Rosenzweig, a German
Jewish layman who died before Hitler took power and came to Judaism
from the very portals of the Church.[3] It might be interesting to consider
what Loewe had to say on some of the topics considered in the *Commentary*
symposium, and on occasion to contrast his views with those of
Rosenzweig.

Writing before Rudolf Bultmann made "demythologizing" popular,
Loewe deals somewhat differently with the antiquated world-view with its
demonology, miraculous intervention, cosmic catastrophe, and so on, which
the biblical authors seem to presuppose. Now the belief was common in ancient times that all diseases, sicknesses, and infirmities were inflictions of
demons. Thus in Jewish demonology, we find a special demon of blindness,
of catalepsy, of headache, of epilepsy, of nightmare, of fear, of madness, of
leprosy, of melancholy, of croup. This last disease was caused by a special
evil spirit called *shibta,* a female demon, who was especially dangerous to
those who ate food touched with unwashed hands (Yoma 77b, Ḥullin 107b,
see the *Tosafot* on these passages: Ta'anit 20b). Now Loewe suggests that
there are good reasons for supposing that it is not really a demon that is
meant. He calls attention to something similar in the *Shulḥan 'Aruk* (the
Code of Jewish Law accepted as authoritative by Orthodox Jews), where
there is a reference to the evil spirit "which clings to a man's unwashed
fingertips," and where the necessity of washing them is urged. "It is scarcely
conceivable," he writes, "that the evil spirt in this case can have any other
meaning than dirt, a word for which the Hebrew language does not contain
an appropriate equivalent." Generalizing, on the basis of instances of this
kind, he concludes:

> One of the peculiarities of the Hebrew language as compared with Greek, is its
> paucity of abstract nouns. Although Aramaic, especially that dialect in which
> the Talmud is composed, has a far larger vocabulary than Mishnic Hebrew,
> yet it cannot be denied that the mind of the Jew preferred nouns of a concrete
> meaning. This fact deserves recognition when considering demonology. The
> vocabulary contains no word which could adequately render such terms as
> "dirt" "infection" "hygiene," etc., and in dealing with scientific terms it was
> and still is, a matter of extreme difficulty to find suitable translations. This fact
> will be evident to anyone who attempts to render into classical or even
> Mishnic Hebrew a piece of philosophical prose which could be turned into
> classical Greek with facility. Consequently the personification of a quality is
> sometimes to be disregarded, and the underlying principle must be extracted.

It might be urged that the Greek no less than the Hebrew people had its
demons; but other circumstances, which will readily suggest themselves, have
to be taken into account.[4]

We come now to a second point. Many religious beliefs and archaic
customs are said to have their basis and origin in primitive superstitions and
in supposedly pre-logical ways of thinking. A fallacy common among people having no clear knowledge of cause and effect is that of *Post hoc ergo
propter hoc* (this came *after* that, and therefore it must have happened
because of that). This is the fallacy of arguing that, simply because one thing
occurred after another, therefore, the second must have occurred on account of the first. One who commits this fallacy argues from a premise of the
form "A preceded B" to the conclusion of the form "A caused B." This fallacy has been termed "The Whatever-follows-must-be-the-consequence"
fallacy. The logical mistake is well illustrated by Bacon from an old Greek
story. It was the custom in times of trouble to call on one of the Olympian
deities for help, vowing that if help were forthcoming the person benefited
would dedicate a commemorative tablet in a temple. Once upon a time
Diagoras, surnamed the atheist, was shown in a temple the votive tablets
suspended by those who had escaped the peril of shipwreck, and was
triumphantly asked by the priest in charge whether he would now recognize
the power of the gods. He replied with the question: "At ubi sint illi depicti
qui post vota nuncupta perierint?" (But where are the portraits of those who
have perished in spite of their vow).[5] By a brilliant *retorsio argumenti,* or
turning of the tables, Loewe called attention to this device and was able to
elucidate and solve not a few of the moral problems of the Bible. He readily
admitted that the Israelites had but a rudimentary idea of causes, but he
used this fact against the detractors of the Bible and Judaism. Hebrew, he
points out, contains many words that identify cause and effect. *Pe'ullah*
means both "reward" and the "work" which merits the reward. *Het* means
"punishment" as well as "sin." *Dam* means "blood" and, in the plural,
"blood-guilt, fine."[6] Sequence in time was equaled with sequence in cause.
The compiler of the Second Book of Kings has Elisha the prophet kill forty-
two children for making fun of his bald head (II Kings 2:23 ff.): "He went
up from there to Bethel; and while he was going up on the way, some small
boys came out of the city and jeered at him, saying, 'Go up, you baldhead!
Go up, you baldhead!' And he turned around, and when he saw them, he
cursed them in the name of the Lord. Then two she-bears came out of the

woods and mangled forty-two of the lads. From there he went on to Mount Carmel, and thence he returned to Samaria." Norman H. Snaith (in his comment on the passage in the popular *Interpreter's Bible*) says:

> This story of the small boys who were rude to the prophet has been sub-
> jected to various explanations in commentators who have hoped to make it ac-
> ceptable to proper standards of justice and fairness. It is merely an example of
> premoral exhortation to respect the prophets as the holy men of God. The
> story compares most unfavorably with N.T. teaching (Matt. 5:44; Luke 23:31),
> and indeed will not stand examination from any moral point of view.

This is not fair. Such texts as Matthew 25:41, Luke 19:27, John 17:9, Acts 8:20, 23:3, I John 2:23, II John vv. 10–11, and II Thessalonians 3:6 should make expositors careful of drawing beloved contrasts between the so-called Old Testament and the New. A careful reading of the text will show that Elisha did not incite the bears. At worst the story is in full accord with the teachings and practice of St. Paul: "Alexander the coppersmith did me much evil; the Lord reward him according to his works" (II Tim. 4:14). The real explanation is that the narrator draws the irresistible conclusion *post hoc ergo propter hoc.* Two events which happened on the same day, Elisha's journey to Carmel and the death of the children at Bethel who were eaten by bears, are connected by the compiler of the narrative. But, Loewe skillfully continues, Elisha, who had a tender heart and healed the widow's son, would not have cursed little children. The historian merely enlarged what was probably a playful rebuke, to add artistic verisimilitude to his vivid description and characterization. "His theology forbade him to regard the intrusion of the bears as an accident due to natural causes, and therefore he was bound to seek the divine intervention. Thus, mere chronological sequence becomes an active factor." "The writer of the Book of Kings views history purely from the standpoint of morals; happiness and misfortune, health and disease, are the result of previous misconduct; and insistence on this theory was the sole justification for the study of history."[7]

We shall now consider the subject of the relation of Judaism to other religions. Franz Rosenzweig introduced a new "theological" notion into Jewish thought by interpreting the coming of Jesus as having a messianic significance for the Gentile nations, but not for the Jewish people. Rosenzweig based himself on a *logion* of the Johannine Jesus, which sums up the central message, or *kerygma,* of the fourth gospel: "I am the way and the truth and the life; no one comes to the Father but by me" (14:6). This, Rosenzweig interpreted to mean that no man "comes" into the divine covenant save through the "Son of God"; but he claims "the situation is quite different for one who does not have to reach the Father because he is already with him."[8] The people of Israel, defined as a *Blutgemeinschaft,* or community of blood, was elected by God from the very beginning to make a covenant with. Thus, according to Rosenzweig, Christianity in its relationship to Judaism has a special status granted to no other religion. Both are equally "true" and valid paths to the one God. Symbolically, Judaism is the "eternal flame" and Christianity the "eternal rays" issuing from the fiery "star" of redemption.

> The truth, the whole truth, thus belongs neither to them [the Christians] nor to us [Jews]. For we too, though we must bear it within us, must for that very reason first immerse our glance into our own interior if we would see it, and there, while we see the Star, we do not see—the rays. And the whole truth would demand not only seeing its light but also what was illuminated by it. They (the Christians), however, are in any event already destined for all time to see what is illuminated, and not the light.[9]

There is no need to dwell on Rosenzweig's blood-and-race theory. His works swarm with references to the biological and racial bond of the Jewish people. "We possess what the Christian will one day; we have it from the time of our birth and through our birth, it is in our blood." "Only a community based on common blood feels the warranty of eternity in its veins." "Other peoples not content with bonds of blood sink their roots in the night of the earth." "The blood-community does not have to resort to such measures . . ." "Natural propagation of body guarantees it eternity." Nazi ideologists were not slow to seize upon such utterances and to viciously distort and twist them for their propaganda purposes. On this subject Loewe has expressed himself clearly and unequivocally:

> Between any sort of Judaism and Nationalism I see an immense difference, a cleavage which can never be repaired. I am not speaking now of the question of Palestine but of the so-called "National Idea" which maintains that a Jew is a Jew by blood, whether he believes in God or not, whether he has adopted the Christian faith or not; that it is impossible for a Gentile to become a proselyte since he cannot change his blood, and that a belief in God—though no doubt harmless, nay, even desirable, for those who care to hold it—is not an essential

in the definition of Judaism. . . . Nationalism is the declaration that racial descent is equal to a belief in God as a test of Judaism. But Judaism teaches "Thou shalt have no other gods."

Here then we have a gulf which is not to be bridged. . . . Is the Jew to be separated from his God or not? On this point there can be no compromise; for this Jews have died, and for this, Jews must live. But the declaration that blood prevails over ideals is the very antithesis of Judaism. It is the motto of the swastika.[10]

Neither can one take seriously Rosenzweig's tortured and far-fetched exegesis of the text from the Gospel of John. This gospel is the most anti-Jewish book in the New Testament. It indicts "the Jews" indiscriminately and unqualifiedly and denies them any knowledge of God. All the nice, pseudo-eloquent talk about Christianity being the "eternal way" and Judaism the "eternal life" (which is the basis of Rosenzweig's speculation) clashes head-on with the very *logion* on which it is allegedly based, since that very text also refers to the Jesus of faith as "the life."[11]

What is rather more surprising is Rosenzweig's lack of insight into the mentality of the true believer. No true believer can dispense with the assumption that his religion comes closer to the truth than any other. A much more helpful figure than fire with its flame which sends out rays of light (the Christian missions) to account for the relationship between, and the truth-claims of, different religions is that of a Jacob's ladder of innumerable steps, set up on the earth and whose top reaches into heaven. The differences among religions are comparable to differences of rungs on the ladder. This is precisely how Loewe views Judaism vis-à-vis Christianity. In discussing the gospel conception of faith, he finds a certain primitiveness in Jesus' teachings, rather than a novelty, which to him is unacceptable for two reasons: (1) the stress on the miraculous and its inextricable association with faith, and (2) the emphasis on the personality of Jesus. "Believe in me" seems to be the gist of his message. The gospel Jesus is represented as constantly demanding faith in himself and declaring it a sin not to believe in him. Loewe elaborates on the first point by indicating that for the rabbis, miracles—excluding the Bible miracles, which were common property of both sides—don't matter, in the gospels they do.

Now in the Gospel, faith and miracles seem inseparable. All passages more or less link the two. Of course, the question arises how far are the miracles claimed for Jesus by a later age and projected backwards, and how far are they authentic. I feel that if you cut away miracles, what remains? Where is your lesson on faith, on trust in God, amid the ordinary events and dangers of life? A Jew can derive this lesson without the superstructure of the miraculous; can the Christian do so? Suppose he says (1) "I do not believe that Peter walked on the sea by faith," (2) "all that Jesus did in the way of faith-healing can be explained psychologically—why then do you ask me to have faith?"[12]

Jesus' conception of faith was something old and even superseded. His audience was "less advanced theologically than the audience of the Rabbis teaching in Judea, from whom something more than mere passive acceptance of the belief in God was to be expected. Jesus' view was 'unless you become as little children'; it was a kindergarten teaching, needed for a kindergarten class. The Rabbis did not wish this to be given to those who had grown older, and had passed to a higher stage."[13] The picture which emerges from Loewe's delineation of the personality of Jesus and his mission is as follows. Like his older contemporary Hillel, Jesus was a pious artisan, but unlike Hillel he did not study and consequently took no part in Halakah. He was a free-lancer and had no responsibility. He was free to devote himself to popular evangelistic work and preaching to the masses. Essentially his preaching was a watered-down version of the preaching of the rabbis, often pushed to an excess by his highly eschatological outlook. Jesus' teachings were an "interim ethic" (*Interimsethik*) inspired by the illusion that the end of the world was imminent. Hence, the ascetic exaggerations of his teachings and his belief that people should abandon the ordinary conditions of settled social life and concentrate on the approaching change in the order of things. Jesus said: "If anyone comes to me and does not hate his own father and mother and wife and children . . . he cannot be my disciple" (Luke 14:26); and to a would-be disciple who wanted first to bury his father, he laid down the hard condition, "Follow me, and leave the dead bury their own dead" (Matt. 8:22). Judaism, however, did not consider family ties as an impediment to the service of God. Elijah, in less urgent circumstances than the need to bury a father, sent Elisha back to kiss his father and mother before following his call (I Kings 19:20–21). Judaism, then, represents a higher rung on the ladder of religious truth. To be sure, each religion can provide its adherents with the same emotional satisfactions, but they cannot be equally true. Loewe quotes an ancient Midrash to the effect that the babe and handmaid at the Red Sea had a surer vision of God than did the greatest prophets, but when that vision was translated into a way of life and a creed, as it inevitably had to be, it led to reciprocally incompatible faiths with mutually contradictory dogmas, which could not all be equally true.[14] As Boswell once said in another context, in his *Life of Samuel Johnson:* "A small drinking cup and a large one may be equally full; but, of course, they do not hold an equal quantity of water." The image seems applicable here.

In the introduction to the *Rabbinic Anthology,* Loewe's collaborator, C. G. Montefiore, quotes Ernest Renan's remark in the *Life of Jesus* to the effect that if one wants to understand a religion he should have once believed it, but then to have ceased to believe in it. Dean Inge says that this remark of Renan's proves the fundamental frivolity of his outlook upon life, and I would not want to quarrel with his judgment. What Renan probably had in mind is that the student of a religion must possess two qualifications which appear mutually exclusive if not contradictory: (1) The ability of detaching himself from his subject and viewing the facts impartially and in just proportion. Husserl and the phenomenologists would say that one must "bracket out" all emotional involvement with the religion being analyzed. (2) The capacity to enter with a sympathetic intelligence and an appreciative understanding into the attitudes of men of faith. This quality of sympathetic understanding has always been a rare one, and today it is rarer than ever. Now while the rabbinic literature as it bears upon the New Testament is familiar to Jew and Gentile, to believers and agnostics, to men of different faiths and none, I cannot help feeling that Loewe, because of his "unswerving loyalty to traditional Jewish life and practice" (as he characterized it), sometimes saw things in a different and illuminating perspective. Take, for example, the story in the gospels where Jesus proves the resurrection of the dead and allegedly exposes the ignorance of the Sadducees. Loewe was able to shed light on this narrative, I believe, because of certain association of ideas ingrained by the habit of daily devotions. The matter is of some importance since it has long passed from the sphere of New Testament exegesis to the philosophy of religion. In his *Philosophical Theology,* Loewe's Cambridge colleague Dr. F. R. Tennant remarks, speaking of the belief in immortality, that "a God who can be worshipped by moral beings must be a respector of the persons whom he has moulded in his own image. Hence theists generally regard the Supreme Being as God, not of the dead, but of the living."[15] The allusion here, of course, is to the method employed by Jesus to demonstrate the future life; "God of Abraham, God of Isaac, and God of Jacob. He is not the God of the dead but of the living!" (Matt. 22:32, Mark 12:25 f., Luke 20:37 f.). These words have become so familiar and ingrained to our ears that we may not pause to consider the reasoning. When we do so we must surely find it very odd. Why is the God of the Patriarchs of yore the

God of the living? Strack and Billerbeck, in their commentary, call attention to the following passage in the Talmud. "It was taught: R. Simlai said: Where is resurrection intimated in the Torah? From the verse, 'I also established my covenant with them [*sc.* the Patriarchs], to give them the land of Canaan' [Exod. 6:4]: not, to give 'you', but to give 'them'; here the Torah intimates resurrection" (Sanhedrin 90b). There is a certain logic to this exposition, i.e., since the Patriarchs died long before the land belonged to their descendents, the biblical promise could be literally fulfilled only by their resurrection and subsequent personal enjoyment of its possession. But the key element of the exposition is missing in the gospel parallels. Loewe, however, is able to illuminate the thought process of Jesus from the standpoint of its formulation. According to him, Jesus uses the daily *'Amidah* (the Eighteen Benedictions) to demonstrate the resurrection of the dead. Now the first two blessings of this prayer are called in the Mishnah (Rosh ha-Shanah 4:5) respectively *Aboth* (Patriarchs) and *Geburoth* (powers).

> These two blessings deal with three themes which are closely associated. Not only their association but their logical sequence is discussed in the Mishnah and Gemara (Berakoth), and the fixing of the order is ascribed to the Men of the Great Synagogue. This fixing of the order implies that one idea is intended to link and support the other. The three themes are:
>   (1) May the God of the Patriarchs (Aboth) redeem their posterity.
>   (2) May the God of power, who sends the rain to revive the earth,
>   (3) Quicken the dead. . . .
> Thrice a day, then, was a Jew reminded of the future life by recalling the God of the Patriarchs and by avowing the eternal endurance of his lovingkindness. That is the reason why Jesus says, "Ye err, not knowing the Scriptures (i.e., Moses and the burning bush), nor *Aboth* and the power of God (i.e., Geburoth)." In other words, the reply is, "How can you ask such a question! Think of the Bible and also of the *'Amidah,* which is said thrice each day!"[16]

The foregoing is a good example of the happy combination of the scholar's quest with genuine religious feeling.

Space does not permit us to examine in detail all the weapons in Loewe's arsenal, but a few more may briefly be mentioned. At a time when archaeological discoveries of ancient Semitic codes made it fashionable in some circles to deny the originality of the Bible and to disprove the belief in revelation, Loewe pointed out that the Code of Hammurabi contains laws which are closer and have more affinity to those found in rabbinic literature than to those in the Torah. Many of the legal ramifications of the Pentateuchal laws found in the Talmud are ancient Semitic usages. These discoveries, therefore, tend to support the traditional dogma of the unity of the Written and Oral Laws. This was his answer to the *Babel und Bible*—to cite the title of a popular work by Franz Delitzsch—school of thought.

Loewe's knowledge of Semitic philology stood him in good stead in helping shed light on the age-old question as to whether the Jews are a nation, a race, or a religion. After pointing out that the modern idea of a unifying element is consanguinity, while the link between Semites was solely that of common worship, Loewe argues that

> to translate the words *'am* and *goi* by "nation" is to beg the question and to presuppose an idea of "nationality" akin to that which the word now conveys. The term *'am* implied an essentially religious kinship, because in primitive times the god was of the same kin as his servants. . . . While religion to a Semite—Jew or Muslim—includes . . . much more than is now ordinarily understood by the word, a kinship on the basis of blood or language or any other but a religious tie is conceivable neither to the prophets of old nor to the Semitic ethnologist or historian of today. Monotheism, not some physiological inheritance, is the *raison d'être* of Judaism.[17]

There is no need to dwell on Loewe's assertion that every recrudescence of nationalism has brought misfortune to the Jews and Judaism, because it is subjective in nature and will be accepted or not depending whether one is a Zionist or not. However his conclusion cannot be gainsaid, namely, that the "return" of Israel to Zion, to which Judaism looks forward and which is so ingrained in traditional Jewish thought, is essentially spiritual and non-nationalistic in nature and nearly always associated with religion. "May our eyes behold *Thy* return in mercy to Zion, and there we will worship Thee in awe as in the days of old, and as in the ancient years" (*Musaf 'Amidah* for the Festivals).[18]

As regards the moral dilemma between the unforgiven sinner and the unforgivable sin, there is value in Loewe's observation that "the Rabbis aimed (1) at keeping the door open as widely as possible; (2) at enforcing respect for law and order also. The idea of an unforgivable sin seems abhorrent; they solved the problem by retaining the hypothetically unforgivable sin and by finding excuses or extenuating circumstances for the unforgivable sinner, so that in fact, he was forgiven."[19]

Critique of Loewe. Since Loewe was primarily a biblical and rabbinic scholar and not a professional theologian, his contributions in the latter area have been largely neglected. It is the great merit of Dr. Mordecai

Kaplan, the founder of Reconstructionism, to have called attention to and publicized some of Loewe's ideas. Since I believe that his criticism is completely off the mark and a total fiasco, all the more is it necessary to give credit where due.

As early as 1915, Kaplan viewed with disfavor Loewe's book-length article on Judaism in James Hastings's *Encyclopaedia of Religion and Ethics*. He quoted the following passage from the opening paragraph:

> Judaism may be defined as the strictest form of monotheistic belief. But it is something more than a bare mental belief. It is the effect which such a belief, with all its logical consequences, exerts on life, that is to say on thought and conduct. . . . A formal and precise definition of Judaism is a matter of some difficulty, because it raises the question, What is the absolute and irreducible minimum of conformity? . . . Judaism denounces idolatry and polytheism. It believes in a universal God but it is not exclusive. It believes that this world is good, and that man is capable of perfection. He possesses free will and is responsible for his actions. Man is free; he is not subject to Satan; nor are the material gifts of life inherently bad; wealth may be a blessing as well as a curse.

Kaplan's criticism of the above runs as follows.

> In the instance quoted, it is both amusing and painful to follow the author's vacillating description of Judaism. At first Judaism is a form of belief. Then it becomes the effect of that belief upon thought and conduct. From that it evolves into some irreducible minimum of conformity, if we can only get hold of it. This being difficult, it gets to be a series of colorless platitudes. Such a definition calls up the image of a streamlet, now leaping over rocks and boulders, now meandering upon level ground, and finally losing itself in the marshes. The fitfulness and inconsistency of the formulation, the picking up of different threads of thought without following out any one of them to its conclusion, are characteristic of this type of definition. . . . The merest tyro can see that one can profess the principles they embody without being a Jew. There are many sects that would heartily subscribe to all of them. Universalists, Deists, Theists, Unitarians, and even Ethical Culturists hold these doctrines. As matters stand at present, these sects engage more actively in spreading them than we do.[20]

Two points may be noted. In the first place, Loewe may quite properly have felt that the true character of Jewish thought is unstructured and cannot be put into the straitjacket of a narrow logical definition. We would consider it an egregious error if a botanist were to confuse a tropical jungle with a neatly arranged nursery garden. Secondly, the marks of ellipsis cut out the following key sentence from the paragraph noted: "On the other hand, it may be said, more widely, that the foundation of Judaism rests on two principles—the unity of God and the choice of Israel." Who ever heard of a Universalist, Deist, Theist, Unitarian, or even an Ethical Culturist who subscribed to the doctrine of the election of Israel? By means of dishonest editing, then, Kaplan was able to score a cheap point. Apparently, Kaplan used Loewe merely as a foil to advance his own ideas. He must have felt guilty since, rather sheepishly, he never mentions Loewe by name in the article.

Kaplan returned to the attack almost a half-century later—this time mentioning Loewe by name.[21] His opening remark that Loewe really belonged to the Conservative school in Judaism does not augur well for what is to come. Since Loewe was the successor but one to Solomon Schechter, the father of the Conservative movement in England and America, in the chair of Jewish studies at Cambridge University, he was presumably familiar with his predecessor's views. Since he nevertheless described himself as Orthodox, he must have differed from Schechter in his views on Judaism. In point of fact he rejected outright most of the things which the Conservatives stand for. "Each individual *Mitzvah,*" he says,

> represents a separate but integral brick in a building. Everyone who starts whittling away will ultimately lose all. There is only one logical conclusion to the whittling away process, and that is the Christian one. Either *all* of the *Mitzvoth* or *none.* If you believe in the founder of Christianity, you do not need the *Mitzvoth;* that is Christian doctrine. The converse is true in the case of Judaism, but the converse means EVERY *Mitzvah.* . . . We must look at the *Mitzvoth* as a whole; we must ask ourselves not, What is the result of *Sha'atnez* [the prohibition of wearing clothing made of wool and linen mixed together]? but, What is the result achieved by living the Jewish life, "*bechol perateha uvechol dikdukeha*? (in every detail)."[22]

These are hardly the sentiments of a Conservative Jew. When we come to concrete practical questions, we find the same disparity between Loewe's views and those of representative spokesmen of the Conservative movement. For example the Conservatives have modified the laws of Sabbath observance and permitted traveling to accommodate those who live far from the synagogue. Loewe anticipated this argument and rejected it categorically.

It is sometimes said "I live too far away from the Synagogue to walk there on Sabbath, therefore I must either ride or not attend." Jewish law answers uncompromisingly that riding is in every contingency forbidden. No commandment can be fulfilled by the breach of a prohibition (*Mitzvah haba'a ba'avera*). . . . One of the consequences of the prohibition is that Jews tend to live near a place of worship, near a religious school, near a *Kosher* butcher, and among their co-religionists. Jews who do not associate exclusively in non-Jewish society, are saved from the danger of their children intermarrying with non-Jewish friends. . . . The simple prohibition of riding on Sabbath thus gives him security, and safeguards the whole basis of Jewish life.[23]

In point of fact, in the United States, I suppose, his position would be described as modern Orthodox. But Loewe eschewed party labels. What he said of his predecessor and friend Israel Abrahams is equally true of him: "He was, first and last, a great Jew, a fervent Jew, an unhyphenated Jew."[24]

The purpose of Kaplan's tactic was to box his opponent into an indefensible position by means of what logicians call a persuasive definition. A textbook example of this procedure is Salomon Reinach's remarkable definition of religion as "a sum of scruples which impede the free exercise of our faculties."[25] But, adds M. Reinach, not *any* scruples are meant, but a special kind of scruples called taboos. The sanction of such scruples is not a practical sanction, such as the fear of injuring oneself; nor is it the fear of a legal penalty. It is the fear of "a calamity such as death or blindness falling upon the guilty individual." But M. Reinach would not, I take it, call the fear of death which prevents one from touching a high tension wire, or the fear of nuclear fallout which might cause blindness, an instance of the sort of scruple which he means. In point of fact he means a *religious* scruple, and so the word "scruple" in his obtuse definition, coupled with the pseudo-explanatory jargon label "taboo," tacitly begs the question. Similarly, if "fundamentalist" is made part of the definition of "Orthodox Jew," Loewe could not have been, as he described himself, "an Orthodox Jew, but . . . not a fundamentalist."[26] But such a question-begging procedure, which *excludes by definition,* tells us nothing about Orthodox Jews in general, or Loewe in particular. Such a procedure is no more defensible than arguing that all Orthodox Jews lead exemplary moral lives, and then, on being confronted with the example of X, who goes to synagogue regularly and makes great profession of Orthodoxy and devotion, but is a scoundrel and a cheat, replying that X is not "really" an Orthodox Jew.

We come now to a more fundamental issue, the Torah and its manner of revelation. Loewe had stated that the manner in which God manifested His will to us is strictly incomprehensible and called attention to the diversity of viewpoints in the classical Jewish sources. He then continued: "Maimonides, who finally decides in favor of an audible voice on Sinai, mentions that others held that Revelation was subjective. But though the method of Revelation be hidden from us, and though we cannot think of it save in metaphor, each according to his own way of thought, of the central, unalterable fact of Revelation, none has any doubt. This is what we term *Torah min ha-Shamayim.*"[27] Commenting on this Kaplan says sharply: "How a metaphor which everyone is at liberty to interpret as he chooses can be of any help in identifying a 'central fact,' and be set up as a dogma is, indeed, baffling."[28] This criticism can be met *ad rem* and *ad hominem.* I shall begin with the latter. Dr. Kaplan is hardly the person to demand greater precision in thinking. He repeatedly refers to God as "the Power that makes for salvation."[29] What is this but an empty, hypostatized abstraction? The habit of washing ourselves might just as well be termed "the Power that makes for cleanliness," or "Early to bed and early to rise," the "Power that makes for longevity," and so on. This seems to be a case of the pot calling the kettle black.[30]

This brings me to the second, and more important, criticism. The difficulty felt by Kaplan can be clarified by an illustration. Consider, for example, a familiar physical object such as the sun. There is a vast difference in the way it is perceived by different people as it moves with the seasons from pole to pole. In different climes, and at different times, it has been viewed as a benign, heavenly blessing; a destructive, evil force; unpredictable, disturbing to some; dependable and regular as a timepiece to others. From the torrid equator to the arctic region of perpetual night and perpetual day, its impact on life is radically different. In extreme climates, the nature of life on earth is changed in a manner never experienced by the inhabitants of the temperate zones. And the theories by which its workings have been interpreted, from primitive man to astrophysical scientists, have been even more varied. The sun has meant a burning rock or a pile of nebular dust; the center of our solar system and an incessant source of light; the generator of unlimited energy with the advent of atomic fission. Future scientists are sure in the coming centuries to discover wonders of solar energy beyond man's capacity to imagine today. In all this speculation, there is not the slightest hint that there is no sun or that this central, unalterable object is a mere feeling engendered by warmth and light. The sun exists as an objective fact. If it did not, our feelings and perceptions about it would long ago have been exposed as nothing more than fantasy. Analogously, the exact manner in which the Torah was communicated to Moses will be conceived differently by different people, but all exponents of authentic Judaism would agree on the centrality of the fact of revelation. We know that God cannot be conceived by the organ of physical vision. We comprehend Him only through spiritual perception, with the eyes of faith instead of physical eyes. God appears to man under different forms (His various self-manifestations), but the object of the vision nevertheless remains unchanged. It is a fixed point of reference. God appeared "on the Red Sea as a hero making war, at Sinai as a scribe teaching the Law, in the days of Solomon as a young man, and in the days of Daniel as an old man full of compassion."[31] Every prophet, every sage, received at Sinai his share of the revelation, which in the course of history was announced by them to mankind. All heard indeed the same words, but the same voice, corresponding to the individuality of each, was God's way of speaking to them. And as the same voice sounded differently to each one, so did the Divine vision appear differently to each. "Why," asked Rabbi Simḥa Bunem of Przysucha (Pshiskhe), "does the Prayer Book call Pentecost 'The Time of the Giving of the Torah' and not 'The Time of the Receiving of the Torah'?" "The reason," he said, answering his own question, "is that the giving of the Torah took place in the month of Sivan, but the receiving of the Torah takes place every day." To which his disciple, Reb Menaḥem Mendel of Kotsk, added: "What was given was the same for everyone, but it was not received by everyone in equal proportion, since what is received varies according to each person's capacity."[31a] We are not so much concerned with the "Mosaic authorship" of the Pentateuch as with the momentum of a revelation, which in a profound sense, enables us to say: "The Law which Moses commanded us is the heritage of the congregation of Jacob" (Deut. 33:4). This, perhaps, is how Loewe would have answered Kapan.[32]

The question may be raised as to what the basis in Jewish tradition is for Loewe's (re)interpretation of the concept of revelation? Is his conception of Orthodox Judaism merely a case of Orthodoxy or My-doxy and Heterodoxy or Thy-doxy, as Bishop William Warburton once remarked? Loewe himself calls attention to two precedents. First, Maimonides' treatment of the eternity of the world. "We can be fairly safe in asserting that had the question of biblical criticism presented itself to Maimonides," says Loewe, "he would have treated it as rationally and as sympathetically as he treated the question of the eternity of matter."[33] The reference is to part II of the *Guide,* chapter 25, where Maimonides asserts that if creation *ex nihilo* could be shown to be unreasonable, he would not hesitate to reinterpret the words of the Bible so as to reconcile them with the requirements of reason and science. We have seen in chapters 4 and 5, above, that Maimonides' position is not as clear and unambiguous as it might be. But granting that Maimonides' method of "interpretation" is indefensible,[34] nevertheless his attitude and his implicit trust in the light of reason is essentially sound, and, in the long run, surely the only possible one.

Loewe is on stronger grounds when he appeals to Naḥmanides' approach to the Haggadah in the famous disputation of Barcelona. "Naḥmanides in 1263, did not hesitate to proclaim that a Jew was at liberty to reject haggadic interpretations, though, naturally, he allowed to Haggadah great ethical value."[35] Elsewhere he says:

> Naḥmanides boldly threw overboard and abandoned the whole Haggadah, declaring that fables were no theology and that the private opinion of any individual Rabbi lacked corporate authority. Although it is more than doubtful whether some of our present-day friends would follow Naḥmanides, his examples are good enough for many Orthodox Jews. Naḥmanides is in this respect a surer guide. In the seven centuries that intervene between us and Naḥmanides, we have learnt to go farther. We may pass from Haggadah into the field of Halakah.[36]

It would appear that Loewe disagreed with most modern scholars, who maintain that Naḥmanides argued against his own convictions for the sake of expediency and that what he said was merely formal and outward and did not really represent his true views. In the transparent spiritual sincerity of Naḥmanides, Loewe saw a kindred spirit, and he evidently felt that a saint and a man of faith would not misrepresent his true views even in the context of a forced disputation. This position has now received strong support from the outstanding rabbinic scholar Professor Saul Lieberman, who has examined the question anew. After demonstrating that Naḥmanides expressed the same opinion regarding the Haggadah in a work written exclusively for Jewish consumption, and citing many Gaonic and medieval authorities—the most interesting of which is, perhaps, Judah Halevi (*Kuzari* III:73, end)—who expressed similar views, Rabbi Lieberman comes to the following conclusion: "The words of Naḥmanides are firm and established literally and according to their ordinary sense."[37] The innovation of Loewe, if there is any, lies in the extension of the precedent in a limited way from the realm of Haggadah to that of Halakah.

In one respect, it must be admitted, Loewe is out of step with the temper of the times. He was a rationalist and there is a sweet reasonableness that permeates all his work. He carefully avoids the tactic of many apologists who present their readers with forced either/or choices which ignore possible alternatives. Loewe never pushes an argument too far or tries to browbeat his audience. He would never have argued concerning the inspiration of the Bible in the manner of a spokesman of the Conservative movement: "To deny the divine origin of the Bible is to brand the entire history of spiritual efforts and attainments in Judaism, Christianity and Islam as the outgrowth of a colossal lie, the triumph of a deception which captured the finest souls for more than two thousand years. . . . The Bible has either originated in a lie or in an act of God."[38] Not only was this type of bullying alien to him, but he was too well acquainted with Christian theology not to know that some of its apologists used a very similar argument to prove the divinity of their founder: *Aut Deus aut malus homo* ("Either God or a bad man"). Speaking of the doctrine of the Incarnation, C. S. Lewis argues: "A man who had merely said the things that Jesus said would not be a great moral teacher. He would either be a lunatic—on a level with the man who says he is a poached egg—or else he would be the Devil of Hell. You must make your choice. Either this man was, and is, the Son of God; or else a madman or something worse."[39]

We live in an age which glorifies the irrational whether it be in philosophy (existentialism), religion, or art. I have always considered it a great privilege to have been able to study the Talmud and rabbinic texts under the guidance of Rabbi Joseph B. Soloveitchik, not because of my worthiness, but on account of *zekut 'aboth* (the merit of my sainted parents), but his stance in the field of philosophy of religion has never appealed to me. My revered master and teacher once began a lecture by saying that he would merely tell about his own personal experiences and the listener could either accept them or not.[40] This puts him in the same camp as Karl Barth, the most outstanding Protestant theologian of the twentieth century, who is alleged to have said: "Belief cannot argue with unbelief; it can only preach to it." But is not this a renunciation of the biblical promise and mandate? Speaking of God's laws and statutes, the Deuteronomist says: "Observe them faithfully; for that will be your wisdom and your understanding, in the sight of the people, who on hearing all these laws will say, 'Surely this great nation is a wise and understanding people!'" (4:6).

In my opinion the popularity of the various irrationalist movements in modern theology is due to the belief that the position which they espouse is impregnable to rational criticism. This, I believe, is a mistake. To be sure, insofar as the irrationalist is not supporting his beliefs with logical arguments, they are immune from direct attack. But this does not prevent a critic from collaterally attacking the conclusions of the dogmatic irrationalist. Let me illustrate this point with an illustration from another field. Suppose that someone claims that Abraham Lincoln was a Jew, supporting his claim with the contention that his given name is Jewish, and his surname a corruption of Lincohen. It would not be difficult to expose the flaws and weaknesses of this argument. Non-Jews frequently have biblical forenames (more frequently than Jews, indeed), and the form Lincoln is attested in the oldest records and seems to be derived from an old English place-name (cf. Hugh of Lincoln). But suppose now that the person who maintains that Lincoln was a Jew admits from the outset that he has no evidence for this belief, that it is based only on "intuition." Since no proof is offered, there is no evidence that can be attacked. But the *conclusion* itself can be disproved in any number of ways, e.g., by checking baptismal records, entries in the family Bible, etc. For another thing, irrationalism of this type is a two-edged sword: It can lead to the Athanasian Creed of Karl Barth, or to the discipline of Zen Buddhism, just as readily as to the cabbalistic typology of Soloveitchik. Granted that faith transcends, and is an extension beyond, knowledge, but it does not fly in the face of facts or turn its back on them. There may be more to life than logic, but there can be no justification for beliefs for which there is no evidence. Faith agrees with the evidence as far as it goes, but goes further.

Loewe "saw life steadily and saw it whole"; which is not to say, of course, that he saw the whole of life, but rather that what came within the range of his vision he saw integrally. He was practical as well as critical, and he would never sacrifice life to logic, and he by no means disregards the emotional appeal of religion with its ceremonials. In one place he compares the Jewish religious year to a Wagnerian cycle at the opera.

Take the period from the first solemn call to repentance on the Sabbath eve, when the penitential season opens, until, after *Sukkoth,* the gaiety dies away peacefully on Sabbath Bereshith, a sober prelude to the coming of winter. In this period how wonderfully does each day fit into the general scheme, how the note of penitence rises in intensity until the consciousness of full pardon is reached in the grand diapason of Kippur, how the relief from the burden of sin gives way to rejoicing, until Tabernacles ends in the merry-making of *Simchath Torah* and the lengthening evenings invite us to recommence our study of the Law. Just as each sentiment, during these great days has its musical "Leitmotif"—its canonical colour, so to speak—so is the whole range of human feeling covered by the complex body of customs, precepts, prayers and poems which make up what we call the Jewish life. The value of this life has never been questioned. It has preserved Jewry and Judaism throughout the ages amid the cramping walls of Ghettos and slums. It has created Jewish family life with its virtues of chastity, charity, love and righteousness, nowhere surpassed, and rarely equalled. For all this is simply due to the *Mitzvoth* by which, if a man do them, he shall live. The *Mitzvoth* are the abiding proof that it is not by bread alone that man lives. Nothing is "trivial." Life is made up of the "common round and trivial task," which the *Mitzvah* brightens and hallows.[41]

This is not the place to review the scholarly work of Loewe. Since, however, we have grounded our appeal to his thought on his mastery of the classic sources of Judaism—which by no means can be presupposed in Jewish thinkers in the modern period—it is worthwhile to consider whether his ideas have stood the test of time. We shall limit ourselves to considering three works: a lecture, a monograph, and an article contributed to a *Festschrift*. We have purposely omitted from consideration his most famous work, *A Rabbinic Anthology,* which he compiled and edited in collaboration with Claude G. Montefiore, and to a new edition of which his learned son, Professor Raphael Loewe of the University of London, has added a prolegomenon. Although written from a different standpoint and with a different audience in mind, that work compares favorably to Bialik and Rawnitzki's *Sefer ha-Aggadah,* which went through many editions. A word of caution is in order here; those who are allergic to a technical discussion of topics of Jewish scholarship can safely skip the next few pages.

We shall first consider an abstract of his unpublished lecture on the vocalization of the unpointed Talmud text. On this subject much misleading information has emanated even from eminent scholars at the Hebrew University in Jerusalem. The abstract is so brief and to the point that it deserves to be quoted in full.

How the Gemara should be "pointed" is a matter of considerable uncertainty and various views prevail among scholars. The "Talmud Babli" is written in a dialect of Aramaic—or as it used incorrectly to be termed, Chaldee—and Aramaic was a language of many dialects extending over many countries and centuries. Thus Laban spoke Aramaic (Gen. xxxi.47); the books of Ezra and Nehemiah, the Targumim, the Liturgy (i.e., Kaddish), all represent dif-

ferent forms of Aramaic. The "Zohar" is in Aramaic and there was too a
revival of this tongue in the sixteenth century at Safed. Then there is Christian
Aramaic, known as Syriac. The case of the Gemara is further complicated
because it is largely affected by Hebrew. So when we come to "point" the text,
we are at once confronted with the problem, to which period and to which
dialect are we to conform? The Gemara represents gradual development and if
we wished to be accurate, we ought really not to follow the fashion of speech
prevailing when the Gemara was finally edited—if we were certain of this—
but to point the remarks of each Amora according to his era and country,
reproducing his speech as uttered. But this would be a task beyond our
powers. Take a parallel from England. "Hansard" contains the discussions of
the House of Commons. Suppose you desired, at some time in the dim future
when all knowledge of our English phonetics was lost, to edit some six centuries of "Hansard" and then read out your product aloud. Think how many
changes English has undergone. Take four names, Chaucer, Shakespeare,
Pope and Kipling, to typify four periods. Think again of the varieties of
locality. Your Parliament includes many members. Cockney, Welshmen,
Devonians, Northumbrians and numerous others. What would you do? The
answer is that you would do your best and be conscious that a conventional
tradition, weakened by wanderings in many lands, might not always adequately sustain the onslaught of scientific research and to-day there is not much fear
that a student will be rebuked by a Professor of Aramaic for misusing a Lamed
or Nun imperfect, and so he may rely, for all practical purposes on the conventional "pointing" in use in some modern handbooks for teaching Talmud.

"Render Unto Caesar" (Cambridge, 1940), Loewe's last work, was, as its
subtitle indicates, a study of religious and political loyalty in Palestine in the
talmudic period. It deals with the question of the relation of Church and
State. The monograph was originally prompted by the marriage and abdica-
tion of Edward VIII, but many contemporary analogies will readily suggest
themselves (e.g., the status of the Gush Emunim settlements in the light of
the Halakah according to some authorities). The following questions are
discussed: What are the limits of loyalty to an earthly government? When is
it right to refuse obedience? Who is to judge whether a command is
legitimate or whether obedience to it involves apostasy? More specifically,
the question of Jewish loyalty to Rome is treated. Both the teaching and the
actual practice are examined in detail. As summarized by Loewe himself, his
key findings are: The action and teaching of Jesus on the matter of loyalty to
the State would seem sometimes to be misinterpreted. It is frequently asserted that Jesus, by inculcating loyalty to the State, broke with Jewish
tradition. This is incorrect on the basis of the evidence. Jesus' standpoint

was not an innovation, proclaiming to the Jews for the first time that man's fealty to his human king is correlative to his fealty to God, and opposing a theory that a truly God-fearing man must, of necessity, be a rebellious subject, or at least a passive resister. His declaration "Render unto Caesar" is in complete harmony with rabbinic teaching, both antedating Jesus and extending after his time: it was a repudiation of the opposing view, possibly put forward by *agents provocateurs*—such a view was Zealot, not Pharisaic. Disloyalty was a rejection of biblical and rabbinic teaching, and, in practice, the Jews were neither more nor less disloyal to Rome than others. References to the "wickedness" of Rome in no way invalidate this argument: a distinction was made between the "wickedness" of individuals and the conception of imperial government. Only when that system of government involved idolatry was opposition justified. The great mass of the people, as well as the larger part, by far, of their teachers, rose against their rulers only when religion was threatened. They asked but quiet and freedom to serve their God. When this was refused, they were ready to face death.

In an important public lecture delivered at the Hebrew University, Professor Louis Ginzberg, one of the greatest talmudic scholars of the recent past, reached a diametrically opposite and contradictory conclusion.

There is a well-known answer of Jesus, son of Miriam, to the question as to whether it is permissible to pay taxes to the Roman government. He exhibited a coin stamped with the image of the emperor and said: Render unto Caesar that which is Caesar's and unto God that which is God's. The New Testament commentators maintain that this response by Jesus is in accord with the teaching of the Pharisees, that the law of the land is to be obeyed. This assertion is completely wrong, . . . the view of Jesus is poles apart from that of the Pharisees. . . . The Mishnah states: "It is permissible to make a vow . . . to tax-collectors that they (cattle) belong to the royal domain even though they are not of the royal domain. (Ned. III,4)." . . . This ancient discussion in the Mishnah Nedarim. . . . shows that in Temple times the Pharisees regarded taxes as robbery by the government, for otherwise they would not have permitted the taking of a vow . . . to the tax-collector in order to be rid of him. . . .
It is certainly true that our sages stated that the law of the land was to be obeyed; but this enactment, which was transmitted to us in the name of Samuel of Babylonia, was decreed only for Babylonia and other lands of the diaspora. Our sages, as true disciples of the prophets, followed the teaching of their predecessors; just as Jeremiah had instructed the elders of the Exile of his time, "and seek the peace of the city whither I have caused you to be carried away captive" (Jer. 29.7), so they taught that Jews should accept the rule of

those gentile nations which opened the gates of their countries to them. However, this is completely different from the relationship of our sages to the gentile rulers who held sway over the Holy Land, whom the sages regarded as robbers and extortioners without any rights whatsoever either in the land or over its inhabitants.[42]

Despite the sweeping and categorical character of these assertions, there is not even the shadow of evidence to sustain them.[43] On the Mishnah cited by Ginzberg, the Gemara (Nedarim 28a) comments: "But Samuel said, The law of the country is law?—R. Hinena said in the name of R. Kahana in the name of Samuel: The Mishnah refers to a publican who is not limited to a legal due." The distinction is, therefore, not between Palestine and other countries, but between a fixed tax and plain extortion. This distinction is supported by the traditional commentators and by the modern form criticism of the talmudic text. Since *both* the principle "the law of the land is law" *and* the differentiation between a fixed and an unfixed tax are attributed to Mar Samuel in Nedarim, there is no basis whatever for the proposed distinction which Ginzberg makes between the Holy Land and the Diaspora.[44] If Ginzberg were correct, we should have expected the reply in the Talmud to run as follows: "Rabbi X said in the name of Rabbi Y, Samuel's rule applies to the Diaspora, but our Mishnah refers to the Holy Land." The conclusion of Loewe, therefore, remains intact and unshaken.

It is fitting that the final contribution of Loewe which we shall consider is devoted to the theme of peace, scholarship, and religion. It is an elucidation of the closing passage of several talmudic tractates (*viz.*, Berakoth, Keritoth, Yabmuth, Nazir, and Tamid), which has been incorporated into the traditional *Siddur* (prayer-book). It runs as follows: "Rabbi Eleazar said in the name of R. Hanina, 'Scholars increase peace throughout the world,' as it is said, 'And all your children shall be taught of the Lord; and great shall be the peace of thy children' [Isa. 54:13]. Read not here *banayikh*, 'thy children,' but *bonayikh*, 'thy builders.'" The logical incongruity of "builders" and "peace" is evident: the argument seems to be a *non-sequitur*. The difficulty is solved by Loewe with his suggestion that *bonayikh* was understood by R. Hanina (Berakoth 64a and parallels), not as "your sons," but as the *Qal* participle of the verb *bin,* "understand." "I venture to remark," says Loewe,

that Hanina made no mention of "builders" at all. What he proposed to do was to take the second *Banayikh* not as a plural of *Ben,* "a son," but as the plural of *Ban,* the participle *Qal* of *Bin,* "to understand ." The two words, "thy sons" and "thy scholars," are homonyms, *banayikh,* and neither in writing nor in speech can they be differentiated. What Ḥanina said was this: "Scholars spread peace in the world, as it is said 'all thy sons are taught of the Lord and great is the peace of thy sons': Read not 'thy sons' but 'thy scholars'!"[45]

Subsequent to Loewe's essay, his interpretation was not confirmed by the Isaiah scroll from Qumran, which was discovered in 1947, where the second *bonayikh* is spelled plene with a *waw* (i.e., "your builders"). Finally, forty years after the original essay appeared, a different author substantially repeated the same argument, but the caliber of Loewe's scholarship is evident from his more thorough analysis and finer elaboration.[46] In the first place, Loewe quite properly calls attention to Jeremiah 49:7: "Is wisdom no more in Teman? Has counsel perished from the *banim?*" Now, as Loewe points out, R. David Kimḥi (acronym RaDaK), in his Commentary *ad loc.,* interprets *banim* as the present-participle *Qal* plural of the root *bin,* and he is followed by most modern translators of the Bible, who render the word "prudent." However, already in ancient times this rare form was liable to misinterpretation, and the Targum (pseudo-) Jonathan renders it by "sons," and Rashi, who has "generation," seems to agree with this. This shows that already in ancient times the verbs *bin* and *banah* were confused. Secondly, in this age of women's liberation, the analogy which Loewe cites from the Midrash about "daughters" as a counterpart to R. Ḥanina's "sons" deserves to be quoted, especially as it helps to clinch the argument. In Midrash Exodus Rabbah 23:10 we read: "'O ye daughters of Jerusalem' Cant. 1:5. The Rabbis say, read not *benoth* (daughters) but *bonoth* Jerusalem, that is, the great Sanhedrin whose members sit and build up Jerusalem (*mebhannim,* i.e., the *pi'el* of the root *banah,* 'to build')." Again we note the *non-sequitur.* Why are daughters the builders? Here, however, we have a parallel passage which is most enlightening. In Canticles Rabbah I. 5, 3, the conclusion runs as follows: "By this is meant the great Sanhedrin of Israel, who sit and instruct them [*mebhinim,* from the root *bin* 'making to understand'] in every difficulty and point of law." Hence we may eliminate the "builders," male and female, completely, and reintroduce, we hope, the "scholars" of both sexes.

Herbert Loewe was a master builder of bridges of understanding. He edited *Judaism and Christianity:* volume 2, *The Contact of Pharisaism with Other Cultures* (London, 1937), to which he contributed a valuable essay summarizing the specifically Pharisaic conceptions and ideals which have passed over into Christianity. This essay, as well as the monograph in defense of the Pharisees in volume 1 of the same series, is as valuable today as when it was first published. Loewe's consciousness of current Christian "assumptions" and/or "prejudices" lends his presentation a rare distinction and significance. He gave unstintingly of his knowledge to other scholars. James Parkes, in the preface of his magisterial study, *The Conflict of the Church and the Snagogue* (1934), acknowledges the immense debt which he owes to Loewe and lamentfully adds that "his departure for Cambridge has left Oxford without a Rabbinic scholar." Again, in the introduction to his edition of Ta'anit, Henry Malter expresses his deep gratitude "to Mr. Herbert Loewe, who has taken great pains in copying and practically editing" a Genizah fragment for his use.

Finally, Loewe was a man of peace and good will. Professor Raphael Loewe has recently reminded us that his late illustrious father befriended many Continental scholars who were sent into exile as a result of Nazi persecution. In the opening paragraph of his Presidential Address delivered to the Society of Old Testament Study in January 1939, he said:

> When human lives are at stake, study seems futile, the pen must be laid down. The mind cannot be focused on literary problems when letters and telephones unceasingly call for instant effort and whole-hearted endeavour, in order to snatch from torture or murder some unknown fellow-creature who appeals for aid. . . . I can truthfully say that, while preparing this paper, I have on no single day had fifteen consecutive minutes free from interruption.

He used to lead a select study-group which met regularly on Saturday afternoons to read and discuss Midrashic texts. On the table in front of them would lie, alongside the copies of the text concerned, the usual *sefarim,* and the regular apparatus of Jewish scholarship, also Liddel and Scott's *Greek-English Lexicon,* Lewis and Short's *Latin Dictionary,* and Samuel Krauss's *Griechische und Lateinische Lehnwoerter im Talmud,* etc. (After 1938 the last-mentioned author personally participated in these seminars.) And so this most unusual group would study for an hour or two on *Shabbes* (Saturday) afternoon in Cambridge and then adjourn for tea to Mrs. Loewe's drawing room or garden. What one would not give to have been able to sit at the feet of these scholars as they discussed the Midrash, "and drink their words with thirst" as the Sage counsels (Aboth 1:4). To that highly select study circle the words of R. Samuel b. David ha-Levi in *Naḥalath Shib'ah* seem applicable:

Why are they called *Talmide Ḥakhamim* [disciples of the wise] and not *Ḥakhamim* [scholars]? Because they are disciples in relation to each other, each needs the other's stimulus. Only when there is humility in learning, is peace produced in the world. Further, it says "Taught of the Lord," i.e., those who recognize that learning is of God: without this recognition learning is of no avail.

But Loewe's influence was not limited to his peers. In the period between the two World Wars he served as a spiritual advisor to many of the Jewish undergraduates at Oxford and Cambridge. Loewe once remarked that when, as an undergraduate at Cambridge, he turned to his mentors for guidance on the subject of biblical criticism, they failed to even comprehend his difficulties. So he had to work out an acceptable position all by himself. And, because he had done so, he could, in turn, sympathize with the sincere perplexities of undergraduates as they came in contact at the university with the new learning which seemed to clash with the Orthodox Jewish faith in which they had been reared. He patiently showed them the path which he had trod, helped them in their efforts to resolve their difficulties, and he brought them peace of mind and peace of soul. But, above all, there was the inspiration of his own life. We hear much in certain circles of the "synthesis" of traditional Judaism and modern Western thought. But the concept has largely remained an empty catchword and shibboleth. Loewe, however, was a living proof of the possibility of such a "synthesis." He demonstrated that staunch adherence to Judaism does not demand obscurantism; that one can be a professor at Cambridge and an Orthodox Jew; and that one can be a president of the Society of Old Testament Studies and put on *tefillin* daily. For this we may all be grateful to him. Reverence, sincerity, high character, scholarship, walking with God and one's fellowman in peace and uprightness—these are the qualities which caused the young to seek instruction from his mouth. And they did not seek in vain. Truly, "the lips of the priest have safeguarded knowledge and many have they brought back" from loss of faith (Mal. 2:6–7).

I was born in the wrong place, and too late, to have had the privilege of having known Mr. Loewe personally, but I nevertheless count him as a formative influence in my life. In my youth I was an avid reader and literally devoured many articles in the old *Jewish Encyclopedia*. The format of the biblical articles in that work is well known. First, the biblical information is given accurately enough, but then it is immediately followed by the "Critical

View," which mercilessly tears the traditional account into shreds. I still remember vividly reading the article on Solomon by Emil G. Hirsch, which came to the ponderous conclusion that "a critical sifting of the sources leaves the picture of a petty Asiatic despot, remarkable, perhaps, only for a love of luxury and for polygamous inclinations." It is easy to appreciate how unsettling to traditional beliefs such views can be to an immature mind which is overawed by the authority of an encyclopedia article. (I must confess that this kind of awe never left me until much later, when I began writing encyclopedia articles myself.) How refreshing and restorative it was, then, to read Loewe's article on Judaism in Hastings's *Encyclopaedia of Religion and Ethics,* which begins with the frank aknowledgment: "The present article on Judaism is avowedly written from the orthodox standpoint." To be sure, knowledge has not stood still in the last sixty years, but, in the writer's opinion, the articles which Loewe contributed to that encyclopedia, as well as to the fourteenth edition of the *Encyclopaedia Britannica,* are still accurate in their essential outline. It would be most instructive to compare some of the articles written by Emil G. Hirsch for the *Jewish Encyclopedia* with those authored by Loewe and to make inquiry as to which have better stood the passage of time. I honestly do think that, if such an investigation were made by someone, no matter what school or party in Judaism he belongs to, or none, Loewe would come out ahead. Speaking for myself, I can only say that Loewe was my "Guide for the Perplexed." His essay "The Orthodox Position" (Cambridge, 1915) is still the best vindication of traditional Judaism that the writer is acquainted with.[47]

The Jewish scholar in the modern world is often a lonely man. Of Loewe's predecessor, Israel Abrahams, an Anglo-Jewish paper remarked that he was neglected throughout the greater part of his active life, that his books were mostly unread, and that he gave lectures to small audiences for no fees. In his biography of Abrahams, Loewe disputed the accuracy of this verdict, claiming that Abrahams's influence was far wider than that journal was able to appreciate. Perhaps the same can be said to be true of Loewe. Professor Gilson says in the foreword to his magisterial study, *The Christian Philosophy of St. Thomas Aquinas:* "Personally, I do not say of St. Thomas that he was right, but that he *is* right." I venture to say the same of Herbert Loewe and his apologia for traditional Judaism.

"And Benaiah the son of Jehoiada was the son of a living man from Kabzeel, a doer of great deeds" (II Sam. 23:20, *Ketib*). The rabbis remark that the righteous even in his death can be called "alive" for his influence for good persists, and therefore Scripture refers to Benaiah as "the son of a living man"; from "Kabzeel," that is, he was very active in behalf of the Torah (*Kabaṣ* he collected; *e-l,* for God). There was no one like him in the time of either the first or the second Temple (Berakhoth 18a–b; Tanḥuma, Deut., *ad fin.*). So it was said of Benaiah of old, and so we can say of Herbert Martin James Loewe, a true scholar, a master builder who labored untiringly "to make the Torah great and glorious" (M. Makkoth 3:16, Isa. 42:21), and a man of peace in its biblical connotation—of harmony, completeness, and the untrammeled growth of the soul. "The memory of the righteous is indeed a blessing" (Prov. 10:7).

Appendix A

RaMBam or Maimonides

We are here concerned only with the place of the Law (halakhic corpus) as such in the Maimonidean system; for the inconsistencies and discrepancies between Maimonides' philosophical and legal writings as regards individual *halakhoth,* see the interesting study of A. Klein with the suggestive title "Rambam oder Maimonides," in *Festschrift Jacob Rosenheim* (Frankfurt a/M, 1931), pp. 212–26. Some of Klein's attempted reconciliations are farfetched and pilpulistic in nature. See also the remarks (which bear careful examination) of the nineteenth-century French talmudic scholar Chief Rabbi Klein of Colmar, which are quoted by Munk, *Le Guide,* pt. II, "Additions et Rectifications," pp. 375 f. At first glance it would appear that Munk (*ibid.*) and some of the medieval commentators on the *Guide* are correct when they maintain that in his philosophical works Maimonides at times disregards rabbinic exegesis; see *ibid.,* vol. 3, chap. 41, p. 313 n. 1; chap. 46, p. 372 n. 2; chap. 48, p. 400 n. 2, and the citation in the references given of pertinent passages. The renowned German talmudist R. Jacob Emden (d. 1776) went so far as to maintain that the *Guide* could not have been written by Maimonides, the great rabbinic decisor, who was not capable of authoring such a heretical and jejune philosophy (see *Mitpaḥath Sefarim* [Lemberg, 1870], p.56; cf. pp. 3 and 64 f.). Shem-Ṭob, in his commentary on the *Guide,* III:51, quotes the opinion of some medieval rabbinic scholars to the effect that some parts of the *Guide* are spurious, and in the alternative, if genuine they should be expunged or burnt because of their heresies. Soon after the death of Maimonides the rumor was spread that he had recanted his rationalist views and adopted the standpoint of the Cabbalists. The first to mention this report is Shem-Ṭob ben Abraham ibn Gaon (b. 1283), in his commentary *Migdal 'Oz, Yad, De'oth* 1:10, who states that he found this written "in a very old, smoke-damaged parchment scroll." For details, see Gershom Scholem, "From Philosopher to Cabbalist (a Legend of the Cabbalists on Maimonides)," in Hebrew, *Tarbiz,* vol. 3 (1935), pp. 334–42, and the references given in *Talmudic Encyclopedia,* ed. S. J. Zevin, vol. 15 (1976), p. 78, n. 261.

The whole subject of the relation of Maimonides' legal and philosophical works is a very difficult topic calling for continued further study. See the present writer's remarks in *Tradition,* vol. 10, no. 3 (1969), pp. 107 f. Unfortunately most commentators on the *Guide* were not trained rabbinic scholars like Maimonides. It was rare in the Middle Ages to find philosophers who were also outstanding talmudists, and it is even more rare today. One example will illustrate what work can be done in this area.

In chapter 41 of part III, the *Guide* discusses the biblical *lex talionis,* which states that one who mutilates someone else's limb shall himself be deprived of a similar limb in accordance with Leviticus 24:20: "As he has disfigured a man, so shall he be disfigured." In the course of his discussion Maimonides makes the following enigmatic comment: "You must not raise an objection from our practice of imposing a fine in such cases. My purpose is to give the reasons for the biblical texts and not for the pronouncements of the Talmud [lit., legal science—*fiqh*]. I have, however, an explanation for the interpretation given in the Talmud, but it will be communicated *viva voce.*" Opinions among the commentators differ as to what Maimonides intended by his remark, but they have this in common—they assume that Maimonides rejected the traditional interpretation mitigating the biblical *lex talionis.* Narboni suggests that Maimonides' opinion was that the Talmud itself requires the infliction upon a wrongdoer of the same injury which he has caused another if there is no danger of inflicting death. Shem-Ṭob interprets Maimonides' position to be that monetary compensation is acceptable only in the case of an accidental injury without premeditation, whereas an intentional tort is punishable by mutilation. However, Shem-Ṭob does not approve of such explanations and remarks in anguish:

> I am exceedingly amazed at the words of the Master. . . . after all, the verses are not true, be it in toto or in part, but in the light of the tradition which our Sages received, and according to what our Sages explained in the Talmud; and this Master himself has taught us that if the Messianic King should come and state that the explanation of the scriptural passage is according to the verbatim reading, "an eye for an eye" [Exod. 21:24], literally he would be punishable by death, since he would be contradicting the Talmud [cf. Baba Kamma 84a]. I know not whither our Master and our Teacher has turned, for not so has he taught us. And may the Lord pardon him and us.

We may note in passing that the remark about the death penalty anent the literal interpretation of the *lex talionis* attributed to Maimonides is nowhere to be found in his writings and could not have been made by him. The death penalty would apply only in two instances: (1) an elder rebelling against the decision of the Jewish Supreme Court who also states his ruling to others so that they may act thereon (*Yad, Mamrim* 3:4), or (2) a false prophet who claims divine inspiration for the erroneous interpretation (*Yad, Abodah Zarah* 5:8; cf. Maimonides' Introduction to the Mishnah [ed. Kafiḥ p. 6], concerning the *lex talionis,* or law of retaliation, in the case of indecent assault mentioned in Deut. 25:12). Most modern savants of the *Wissenschaft des Judentums* type who are not trained talmudists or rabbinic scholars have generally followed Shem-Ṭob in smelling heresy in Maimonides' remarks. One is reminded of Mark Twain's observation, "The researches of many antiquarians have already thrown much darkness on the subject, and it is probable, if they continue, that we shall soon know nothing at all."

The question was treated anew by Jacob Levinger in "The Oral Law in Maimonides' Thought" (Hebrew), *Tarbiz,* vol. 38 (March 1968), pp. 282–93. Levinger's theory, as summarized by himself, is that Maimonides viewed the commandments according to the simple meaning of the biblical text, thus representing the original interpretation of these laws in the Mosaic period. Maimonides' claim that the accepted interpretation offered by talmudic tradition was also revealed at Sinai appears in his rabbinic writings to serve as a popular dogma for the masses, but does not express his true theoretical-philosophical outlook. Since in the *Guide,* Maimonides allegedly attempted to give reasons for all the precepts according to the cultural atmosphere which reigned among the Jews and the pagans during the period when they were first given (i.e., the Mosaic period), he interpreted them according to their literal meaning. The talmudic interpretation of these passages was, according to Levinger, considered by Maimonides to be of later vintage. We are most grateful to Professor Levinger for reconstructing the social milieu and the historical background of the biblical legislation, and should we ever desire to know what brand of snuff Maimonides used, we would certainly turn to him for enlightenment, but for a deeper understanding of Maimonides' legal views we must look elsewhere.

The true explanation of Maimonides' remarks, it seems to me, is the one suggested by Professor Samuel Atlas, who was outstanding both as a talmudist *and* as a student of philosophy. In the illuminating notes to his edition of the commentary of Rabad of Posquières on the tractate Baba Kamma, he makes it abundantly clear that according to the rabbinic interpretation of the biblical law, the indemnity paid by the tortfeasor for the felony of mayhem does not constitute a mere monetary liability, but is a punishment (fine) to serve as a propitiation and atonement (*kofer*). The true intention of the Divine Lawgiver was that the injury inflicted by the tortfeasor on another shall be inflicted on him. As Maimonides puts it in his Code, the offender "fittingly deserves to be deprived of a limb" (*Yad, Ḥobel u-Mazzik* 1:3), but this mutilation is commuted to a monetary compensation so that the judicial process may be safely carried out. But even after this commutation of punishment a certain penal quality remains. This may very well be the explanation which Maimonides wanted to give to his devoted pupil by word of mouth, and Maimonides, far from rejecting the traditional explanation of the rabbis, actually wanted to show the rationale of that explanation (see S. Atlas, *Novellae on Tractate Baba Kamma by Abraham ben David* [London, 1940], p. 364, n. 3; cf. also the Commentary of Asher Crescas on *Guide* III:41 and Ibn Ezra *ad* Exod. 21:24).

Not long ago, I had occasion to visit a former teacher of mine, Rabbi Samuel E. Volk, for many years one of the outstanding talmudic scholars on the faculty of Yeshiva University. In discussion with him, I called attention to some of the discrepancies between Maimonides' philosophical and legal writings, and with his usual depth of penetration he was able to shed much light on the subject. He has since published some of his findings in volume 6 of *Shaarey Tohar* (New York, 1978), pp. 411–19. His extremely suggestive treatment of this subject shows great learning and acuteness, and I cannot do better than refer the interested reader to that work. See further the masterly analysis of S. J. Zevin, "The Judgment of Shylock" (Hebrew), in *Le'or ha-Halakah* [By the light of the Halakah], 2nd ed. (Tel-Aviv, 1957), pp. 325 f. and the references there given to other talmudic-rabbinic authorities.

If on rare occasions Maimonides does deviate from normative (halakic) interpretation of Scripture, he is by no means unique in this respect among medieval authorities. R. Samuel ben Meir (RaSHBaM), in his commentary on Exodus 13:9 (ed. D. Rosin, p. 98), interprets this verse ("It shall be a sign upon your hand . . ."), from which the Talmud derives the obligation of wearing *tefillin,* in a figurative and symbolical manner; i.e., it shall be an everlasting memorial, as if written on your hand. ("According to the essence of its literal significance it means, 'it shall ever be a memorial as though it were written upon your hand' as in the verse: 'Set me as a seal upon your heart, as a seal upon your arm'"—Song 8:6). Interpretations contrary to the accepted halakah are frequently found in Rashi's biblical commentaries. See, *inter alia,* his commentary on Exod. 23:2; Deut. 22:1, 26 and the examples enumerated by Elijah Mizraḥi in his supercommentary on Rashi *ad* Exod. 22:8 (where an instance from Naḥmanides is also cited). But the practice of interpreting the Bible even in contradiction to the accepted halakah antedates medieval authorities, being found in the Palestinian Targums on the Pentateuch, as was first demonstrated by Abraham Geiger last century in his monumental *Urschrift und Uebersetzungen der Bibel* (1857). The most outstanding example of this is a Palestinian Targum on Exod. 22:4 (Hebrew) to which Paul Kahle first called attention in his *Masoreten des Westens,* vol. 2, (Stuttgart, 1930), pp. 1 ff., Ms. A = the Genizah fragment found in the Cambridge University Library, T-S., 20.155 (cf. Kahle, *The Cairo Geniza,* 2nd ed. [New York, 1960], pp. 205 ff.). This Targum interprets the wrongdoing envisaged by this verse as due to fire and not depasturization (literally, "tooth", i.e., damage done by an animal grazing) in opposition to the Mishnah and the Talmud, M. Baba Kamma 1:1 and Tal. Bab. 2b (bottom), 3b. This exegesis not merely contradicts a detail of tannaitic halakah, but undermines one of the central pillars of the classification of the various torts, the general outline of which was accepted by all authorities in the Talmuds. Rabbi Dr. Jechiel J. Weinberg, the Dean of the Orthodox Rabbinical Seminary in Berlin before World War II, devoted the greater part of his *Investigations in the Talmud* (Hebrew) (Berlin, 1938) to the elucidation and analysis of this verse and the halakic ramifications of the Genizah targum. (This monograph was reprinted in Jerusalem in 1969, and forms the first section of the fourth volume of his *Seridei Esh.* See especially, pp. 48–62, and cf. M. Kasher, *Torah Shelemah,* vol. 18 [1958], pp. 182–185.) His "explanation" that the text of the Targum is corrupt and based on a scribal error is no longer tenable in the light of Professor A. Diez-Macho's discovery, and subsequent edition, of Ms. Neofiti I in the Vatican Library which preserves the same reading as the Genizah fragment.

In his recently published *Maimonides: Torah and Philosophic Quest* (Philadelphia, 1976), Dr. David Hartman puts forward his own interpretation, the main trend of which is an investigation of the unified character of Maimonidean thought. We have already called attention to the important and perceptive study of Isadore Twersky, "Some Non-Halakic Aspects of the *Mishneh Torah,"* in *Jewish Medieval and Renaissance Studies,* edited by Alexander Altmann (Cambridge, Mass., 1967), pp. 95–118. Dr. Isadore Twersky, who has shown himself to be a fit successor to Harry A. Wolfson as Professor of Jewish Studies at Harvard University, is presently engaged in writing an introduction to the *Mishneh Torah* for the Yale Judaica Series, in which I assume he will discuss in detail the problems of Maimonides the philosopher and scientist versus Maimonides the halakist. We eagerly look forward to his conclusions in this matter.

While this book was in press, the American Academy of Jewish Research issued the volume *Pathways in Hebrew Law* (New York, 1978, in Hebrew) by the late Dr. Samuel Atlas who at the time of his death was Emeritus Professor of Talmud and Jewish philosophy at the Hebrew Union College-Jewish Institute of Religion. This posthumous publication contains an important essay entitled "An Eye For An Eye" (pp. 83–129, and cf. p. 2). In it the author elaborates his views and offers a more extensive and comprehensive analysis of Maimonides' statement regarding the biblical *talio* ("an eye for an eye"). Atlas demonstrates that Maimonides did not disassociate himself from the traditional Rabbinic view and he supports his conclusion with a masterful analysis of numerous passages and themes (*sugyot*) in Talmudic literature. The author's recent death is a great loss in the field of Jewish learning and his essay is worthy of careful study. Dr. Atlas was the product of the East European *Yeshivot* (rabbinic schools) where he was considered a youthful prodigy and to him we can apply the rabbinic saying, Happy and blessed is he whose youth has not disgraced his old age.

That the interpretation of Atlas is correct is evident from the following consideration. In the talmudic-rabbinic literature compensation, or monetary damages, was substituted for retaliation only insofar as the earthly judicial system is concerned because it was considered impossible for human judges to administer the *talio* fairly and safely. But such considerations do not apply to divine retribution; here the principle of the *talio* governs. The divine law by which the world is ruled is the principle of retaliation or "measure for measure" (cf. M. Sotah I, 7–9, and the references given by Ch. Albeck in his edition of the Mishnah, particularly Sifre Num. #18, on 5:27, ed. Horovitz p. 22). This shows that from the divine—that is from the final and absolute point of view—retribution, and not compensation, is the ideal remedy.

In an earlier study, "Maimonides ueber das biblische 'jus talionis'," in the *Jubilee Volume in Honour of Edward Mahler* (Budapest, 1937), pp. 415– 426, the late Professor Michael Guttmann discussed the views of Maimonides and his commentators on the law of retaliation. *Inter alia,* he compares Maimonides' remarks concerning the *lex talionis* to the interesting deviation from the traditional halakah found in Josephus' discussion of the law in *Antiquities,* IV. 280 (35). The law, as expounded by Josephus, permits the injured person himself to fix the amount of money he would accept instead of inflicting like punishment on his assailant, and the plaintiff's word is considered final "unless he shows himself too severe," that is asks for an exorbitant sum. This would tend to confirm the view of some of the commentaries on the *Guide* who maintain that traces and residues of the biblical *talio* survived into later times. See also the discussion of Josephus' views in Heinrich Weyl, *Die Juedischen Strafgesetze bei Flavius Josephus* (Berlin, 1900), pp. 98ff. and 156. In this connection I should like to call attention to the gloss in the scholion to *Megillat Ta'anit,* ch. 4 (ed. Lichtenstein in the *Hebrew Union College Annual,* VIII-IX, 1931–32, p. 331), where it is stated that the Sadducees (Boethusians) interpreted the *talio* literally. While scholars rightly consider the passage late, it at any rate shows that retaliation was still recognized as a form of legal punishment in post-biblical times and that the old law was not entirely obsolete.

Appendix B

The Historians of Medieval Jewish Thought

Niels Bohr, the Nobel Prize-winning Danish physicist, had a wonderful knack of expressing and criticizing ideas by means of humorous stories. One of his favorite stories was about a rabbi. As told by Aage Peterson, assistant to Bohr, the story runs as follows:

> In an isolated village there was a small Jewish community. A famous rabbi once came to the neighboring city to speak, and as the people of the village were eager to learn what the great teacher would say, they sent a young man to listen. When he returned, he said, "The rabbi spoke three times. The first talk was brilliant—clear and simple. I understood every word. The second was even better—deep and subtle. I didn't understand much, but the rabbi understood all of it. The third was by far the finest—a great and unforgettable experience. I understood nothing, and the rabbi himself didn't understand much either."[1]

The three talks of the rabbi in the story can perhaps illustrate the relative merits of the three outstanding historians of medieval Jewish philosophy: Husik, Wolfson, and Guttmann.

Husik's *History of Mediaeval Jewish Philosophy,* like the first talk of the rabbi, is clear and simple; the author wears his learning lightly and with much grace. He presents a good summary of the various thinkers with critical evaluations, not hesitating to call nonsense by its name. (For a detailed discussion of Husik's work in medieval Jewish philosophy, see L. Strauss, in the preface, pp. vii–xxxii, to Husik's *Philosophical Essays,* posthumously edited in 1952 by Milton L. Nahm and L. Strauss.)

Professor Wolfson's studies are deep and subtle. He traces the various philosophical ideas to their sources, and he seeks to identify the anonymous quotations so frequently encountered in medieval works. This requires not

only an enormous amount of erudition and what the Germans call
Belesenheit in philosophical literature written in several languages, but also
a rare critical acumen. (M. Gilson somewhere remarks that one of the most
demanding tasks in Thomist research is the identification of the anonymous
quotations introduced by "quidam" and "aliqui," which are found in
almost every article of the *Summa*.) Professor Wolfson was preeminent in
this type of scholarship in our day, as was Solomon Munk in the nineteenth
century, and his place is securely established as a historian of philosophical
ideas. Now it is true that the trained eye of the dry-as-dust scholar may often
see what is invisible to the uninitiated. But it is also true that scholars, being
human, can overdo a good thing and fall prey to uncritical imagination.
Anent Wolfson's interpretation of Spinoza a critic has penetratingly
observed: "Obsession with the 'Jewish literature' has hindered the commentator from perceiving the words of the text, and has made him read others in
it, put there by his prejudice" (Martial Gueroult, *Spinoza, Tome I: Dieu*
[Paris, 1968], p. 445).

If the analogy were true to form, Guttmann, the third historian of the
Jewish philosophical tradition, would occupy the highest rank. Many indeed have given him this place of honor. I must confess that I do not share
their view. To be sure, if profundity is measured by obscurity, then he
deserves first place. But as Nietzsche once observed, it does not follow that a
stream is deep because one cannot see the bottom; it might be muddy. This
observation seems pertinent here.

I believe it was Josh Billings who once said, "It is better to know nothing
than to know what ain't so." Guttmann "knows" many things which are
not so, and his attempts to solve intricate problems of historical re-
lationships between ideas by *ex cathedra* pronouncements are particularly
disconcerting. He dismisses offhand, for example, the possibility of
scholastic influence, notably of John Scotus Eriugena, on Ibn Gabirol
(*Philosophies of Judaism*, p. 424, n. 65). But this question bears careful consideration, and recent scholarship favors the probability of a Latin influence
on Gabirol. See the important study of Alexander Altmann, "Problems of
Research in Jewish Neoplatonism" (Hebrew), in *Tarbiz*, vol. 27 (1958), p.
506.

The one good feature of Guttmann's *Philosophies of Judaism*, viz., the
grouping of medieval thinkers into the three successive schools of
Kalamists, Neoplatonists, and Aristotelians, is not original with him. It is
already found in Husik's earlier article on Jewish philosophy in the *Encyclopaedia Britannica* (14th ed. [1929], vol. 13, pp. 37–42; reprinted in

Philosophical Essays, pp. 47–67), which antedates Guttmann's work by several years, and in Henry Malter's article "Philosophy, Jewish" in volume 9 of the *Encyclopaedia of Religion and Ethics,* which preceded them both (1917).

One last point. Guttmann fancied himself to be an original thinker and philosopher in his own right, but the fabric of his thought is comparable to the nonexistent clothes of Anderson's fairy-tale emperor. His most original ideas have reference to his own superiority as a historian of medieval Jewish thought over such scholars as Duhem, Strauss, and Wolfson, who are obviously greater than he. His discussion of the notion of creation—the point here under consideration—shows how effeminate, thin, and acidulous his mind is. He does not even hesitate to defend palpable nonsense recognized as such by the better medieval commentators on the *Guide.* Evidently this "defender of the faith" felt it incumbent upon him to justify all the "arguments from reason" which the medievals devised.

Appendix C

Kant and Judaism

The Kantian analysis of moral obligation has created special difficulties for modern Jewish thinkers. It is impossible for Kant to allow that moral laws derive their binding character or sanction from the fact that they are laid down in the Torah or other collections of revealed precepts. Obligation can never be reduced to a divine imperative or to acting in conformity with the revealed will of God, for that would be to convert the *categorical* imperative of morality into a *hypothetical* one. What then happens to the status of the *Miṣvoth* (divine commandments or statutory laws)? Moritz Lazarus, in his pretentious *Ethik des Judenthums,* attempts to solve this thorny problem. But although Lazarus has full confidence in himself as a mastermind, Hermann Cohen devastatingly exposed his encyclopedic ignorance of the historical development of the morals of Judaism according to the primary sources ("Das Problem der Juedischen Sittenlehre, eine Kritik von Lazarus' *Ethik des Judenthums,*" in *MGWJ,* vol. 43 [1899], pp. 385–400, 433–49; reprinted in *Gesammelte Schriften,* vol. 3, pp. 1–35). As for his excursions into the Kantian metaphysics, the redoubtable head of the Marburg school of Neo-Kantianism says that Lazarus does not know Kant, that he does not begin to know Kant, and worst of all, he does not know that he does not know Kant. But rudeness aside, we have here a perfect illustration of the dangers of putting the Jewish *Weltanschauung* into the straitjacket of an alien system. Interestingly enough, an older brother of Moritz, Leser Lazarus, wrote a small essay entitled "Zur Charakteristik der talmudischen Ethik," which does the subject much more justice than the long and ambitious tome of Moritz. And it does this not only because Leser Lazarus had a better mastery of the sources than his brother—he was the successor of Zacharias Frankel as director of the Jewish Theological Seminary in Breslau, and in his youth he had sat at the feet of the great Akiba Eger—but also because he did not attempt to impose a foreign philosophical system on

Jewish ethics. Cf. F. Perles, *Bousset's Religion des Judentums Kritisch Unter-
sucht* (Berlin, 1903), p. 6, n. 2 (for a contrary view as to the merits of
Lazarus's essay on talmudic ethics, see Steinschneider, *H.B.,* vol. 27, p. 31).
For a recent attempt to grapple with the problem of how one can *morally*
obey a law which is, and never ceases to be, *essentially revealed,* see Emil F.
Fackenheim, "The Revealed Morality of Judaism and Modern Thought: A
Confrontation with Kant," in *Rediscovering Judaism,* ed. Arnold Jacob
Wolf (Chicago, 1965), pp. 51–75 (reprinted under the same title in
Fackenheim, *Quest for Past and Future* [Bloomington, 1968], pp. 204–28).
Fackenheim claims that Judaism escapes from this dilemma because, on the
one hand, the law is given in love, and on the other, it is freely appropriated
by those to whom it is given, who thereby make the content of the divine will
their own and so freely will the law. But as J. A. Isaacson points out
(*Conservative Judaism,* vol. 20, no. 2 [Winter 1966], p. 88), this proposed
solution does not deal effectively with Kant's criticism, for in freely accepting the law, one freely replaces the autonomy of conscience (or of a will
determined rationally by the moral law) with the heteronomy of another's
will. Neither the love with which the law is given nor the faith with which it
is accepted affect this in the least.

In the age-old controversy as to whether, if something is good, it is so
because God wills it, or whether God wills what is logically antecedent and
intrinsically good, most medieval Jewish philosophers hold with the Platonic
Socrates (*Euthyphro*) that the divine will is not arbitrary and despotic, but
rational. Goodness is an *independent* value, being prior to, and not
derivative from, the idea of deity, and we are bound to observe the commandments not only because God commands them, but also because they
are right. In the Kantian terminology, the proposition that God wills what is
good, or right, is a synthetic, and not an analytic, proposition. This seems to
be the opinion of Maimonides (see *Guide* III:26 and 31). This view finds support in the Bible. "Shall not the Judge of all the earth do right?" demands
Abraham (Gen. 18:25; cf. Isa. 5:16). But the question would be meaningless
if by the term "right" were *meant* only what the Judge of all the earth
decrees, and if we had no clear independent understanding of the meaning
of the term. Again, when Joseph exclaims: "How then can I commit this
great wickedness, and sin against God?" (Gen. 39:9), the clear implication is
that wickedness is intrinsic and *therefore* a sin. See also Gen. 13:13, Lev.
5:21, Num. 5:6. Some Jewish thinkers, however, regard the moral law as
dependent on the revealed will of God, or as modifiable by it. They hold
that things are good and right only because God decreed them; and that if

He were to command us to steal, then stealing would be good and right, because ultimately all morality is dependent on the absolute divine will. See, for example, Abraham ben Meir ibn Ezra, *Commentary on Exodus* (standard version), 3:22. (Although the Israelites would "borrow" all they could from the Egyptians with the intention of not repaying, they would be free from moral censure since they fulfilled God's wish. That is, God is reported to have commanded them to lie and steal.) In a brief discussion (*S.T.* 1a, 2ae, q. 94, art. 5, ad. 2) of the immoralities of the Patriarchs and other biblical heroes, Aquinas has to some extent given his adhesion and guarded endorsement of this view. But in general his opinion is that the rightness or wrongness of actions is independent of the fact of God's having commanded them (see the classic text *De Veritate,* 23, 6, and cf. *C.G.* II, 24). Much more extreme is the view espoused by Gabriel Biel and his more famous master, William of Ockham. "God could command that a man deceive another through a lie," wrote Biel, "and he would not sin" (*Epithoma,* II, 38, q. 1, G; cf. Ockham, *In II Sent.,* q. 19, 0). With this compare the very puzzling injunction of the gospel Jesus, who bids his disciples to "make friends for yourself with unrighteous mammon" (= tainted money dishonestly acquired, Luke 16:9), which has by no means been explained by all commentators and interpreters as harmless or morally innocuous.

Archbishop Whately, with his customary acumen, succinctly and devastatingly exposed the emptiness of this amoral view, which would make the divine imperative the foundation of ethics. "If one attaches no meaning to the words 'good,'' and 'just,' and 'right,'" he says, "except that such is the divine command, then to say that God is good, and His commands just, is only saying in a circuitous way that He is what He is, and that what He wills, He wills, which might equally be said of any being in the universe" (Richard Whately, critical annotation to William Paley, *Principles of Moral and Political Philosophy* [London, 1859], p. 24, on vol. 1, chap. 5; cf. Richard Price, *Review of the Principal Questions in Morals,* ed. David Raphael [Oxford, 1948], p. 16). Aquinas' teleological moral theory, according to which morality consists of the perfection of one's nature, is exposed to Whately's objection, namely, that in terms of it, it is meaningless to speak of God as morally good, in a slightly different form. If morality involves the perfection of men's nature, then if God in the plenitude of His wisdom had chosen to create us with different natures, the principles of moral conduct would have been different, or there would have been no such thing as morality. Since it is impossible to assign an ulterior cause to God's autocratic will, His decision to make us as He made us is therefore (from the human standpoint) a purely arbitrary decision, beyond good and evil, about which no moral judgment can be made. (Note: the Thomist use of "good" to mean perfection of being is a nonmoral use of the term.)

While I am very strongly convinced by the cogency of Archbishop Whately's reasoning, it is only fair to state that on this question, as on most philosophical questions, philosophers are by no means in agreement. (William James once facetiously defined a philosopher as one who contradicts other philosophers.) On page 15 of the January 1965 issue of the *Philosophical Review,* the philosopher Friedrich Waismann relates that he had a conversation with Wittgenstein in 1930 in which the latter thinker espoused "the deeper view" of Ibn Ezra and some of the Franciscan Schoolmen like Ockham that good is good solely because God wills it.

> Good is what God orders. For this cuts off the path to any and every explanation "why" it is good, while the [other] conception is precisely the superficial, the rationalistic one, which proceeds as if what is good could still be given some foundation.
>
> The first conception says clearly that the essence of the Good has nothing to do with facts and therefore cannot be explained by any proposition. If any proposition expresses just what I mean, it is: Good is what God orders.

Appendix D

The Keystone in S. R. Hirsch's Philosophy of Judaism

Medieval apologetics are no longer acceptable today because the belief in the verbal inspiration ("dictation theory") of Scripture and the factuality of the Sinaitic Revelation as recorded in Exodus, which was considered almost axiomatic in the Middle Ages and was accepted by *all* philosophic parties, is no longer shared today even by "religious" Jews. [1] Maimonides here, as usual, is among the most moderate of all medieval Jewish thinkers, yet even he insists that the Pentateuch in its entirety is the direct utterance of God, every verse and letter being consequently inspired;[2] hence the genealogy of Esau and his descendants in Genesis (chap. 36) is no less inspired than the Ten Commandments or the principle of the unity of God. "In handing down the Torah," says Maimonides, with regard to the question of the divine origin of the Pentateuch, "Moses was like a scribe writing from dictation the whole of it, its chronicles, its narratives and its commandments. It is in this sense that he is termed *meḥoqeq* (i.e. "copyist"). There is no difference between verses like 'The sons of Ham were Cush, Mizraim, Put and Canaan' (Gen. 10:6), or 'And his wife's name was Mehetabel, the daughter of Matred' (Gen. 36:39), or 'Timna was a concubine' (Gen. 36:12), and verses like 'I am the Lord your God' (Exod. 20:2), and *'Shema' Yisrael!—*Hear, O Israel: the Lord is our God, the Lord is one' (Deut. 6:4). They are all equally of divine origin and all belong to the Torah of God which is perfect, pure, holy, and true."[3]

The brilliant attempt of S. R. Hirsch to buttress the belief in the revelation on Mount Sinai with an elaborate analogy between Torah and Nature must be judged to be a failure. In a lengthy note appended to the Eighteenth

Letter of his epoch-making *Nineteen Letters on Judaism* (1836), he expatiates on this analogy.[4]

> Two revelations are given to us, Nature and the Torah. For the investigation of either only one method of research exists. In Nature all phenomena stand before us as indisputable facts, and we can only endeavor *a posteriori* to ascertain the law of each and the connection of all. The proof of the truth, or rather of the probability of our assumptions is again Nature itself. The right method is to verify our assumptions by the known facts so as to reach the highest degree of certainty ever attainable, namely, to be able to say: "The facts agree with our assumption"; or in other words, all phenomena brought under our observation can be explained by our theory. One single opposing phenomenon therefore makes our theory untenable. . . . Whenever and as long as we have not been able yet to discover the law and the connection of any phenomenon which exists as a fact, the phenomenon itself remains, nevertheless, undeniable, and cannot be reasoned away. Exactly the same principles must be applied to the investigation of the Torah. The Torah is a fact like heaven and earth. The Torah, like Nature, has God for its ultimate cause. A fact can be ignored in neither, even if cause and connection are not discovered. . . . In Nature, the phenomenon remains a fact, although we have not comprehended it yet as to its cause and connection, and its existence is not dependent on our investigation but vice versa. So, too, the components of the Torah remain the law for us, even if we do not comprehend the reason and purpose of a single one.

This analogy between the laws of nature and the laws (commandments) of the Torah is the keystone and distinctive feature in the whole philosophy of Judaism as expounded by Hirsch. It is a theme to which he returns again and again. In his philosophy of Jewish laws and observances entitled *Horeb,* which was first published in 1837, Hirsch completes section 454 on the dietary laws by once again dwelling on this analogy.

> One thing is certain: high above all human speculation stands the Torah, the law of Israel's life, eternal and immutable like the laws by which the planets move in the sky and the grain of seed grows in the soil. The same God Who laid down the law which Nature of necessity follows, also pronounced the law which Israel is asked to follow of its own free will. And just as the laws of Nature are unchangeable—despite any opinion man may hold—so all speculations on the laws of the Torah can only be an enlightenment of our own minds, but never the cause of their validity; for the *causa causarum* of the laws of Nature as well as the laws of the Torah is. . . . God.[5]

In all humility and without offense, one must suggest that Hirsch took a concept (now outmoded) from the nineteenth-century philosophy of science and tried to hitch it to the timeless Torah and Judaism eternal. Not the Nineteenth Psalm, but the nineteenth-century rigidly deterministic concept of a law of nature, was the ultimate source of Hirsch's inspiration. Far from building a system of Judaism autochthonously, i.e. organically, out of its own sources ("aus sich selbst heraus") by sound scientific method, his whole philosophy stands or falls with a preconceived notion concerning the laws of nature. The elaborate analogy between legal and natural facts is based on a trick of terminology, a logical equivocation of the word "law." The confusion in the use of the term "law" to express both the regularity of natural phenomena and principles of morality and conduct ("law and order") decreed and enforced by a sovereign power ultimately goes back to the theory developed by the Roman Stoics, and more especially by Philo, that the physical world is run like a legal system under "laws of nature."[6]

Today physicists are pretty generally agreed that scientific laws are statistical averages or descriptive generalizations of phenomena, not normative prescripts or juridical behests of what events should or ought to happen. Moritz Schlick's observation is very pertinent: "The laws of celestial mechanics do not prescribe to the planets how they have to move, as though the planets would actually like to move otherwise, and they are only forced by these burdensome laws of Kepler to move in ordinary paths; no, these laws do not in any way 'compel' the planets, but only express what in fact planets actually do."[7] A scientific law is obtained through abstraction from a total situation of a certain type, and merely formulates how specific factors in such total situations may be expected to work. Scientific laws take the form of "if-then" sequences or relations. *If* certain particular conditions prevail, *then* certain particular effects will take place. Thus the laws of falling bodies state certain constant relations between the factors involved, but these laws do not reveal the actual paths or velocities of specific falling bodies, much less can they tell us if anybody will or should drop a weight from the Leaning Tower of Pisa tomorrow. On his own showing, therefore, Hirsch is only entitled to argue that the "components of the Torah remain," like the phenomena of nature, indubitable facts, whatever explanation we may suggest, or fail to suggest, with respect to their composition and value. That, however, is a far cry from sustaining the logical inference that these "components of the Torah remain *the law* for us." For the actual facts constituting "the components of the Torah" are also amenable to the diverse explanations offered by the Bible critics: the Graf-Wellhausen *Quellenkritik,*

for example, or the more extreme theories of radical critics such as Friedrich
Delitzsch of *Babel und Bibel* and *Die Grosse Täuschung* fame, or, to give a
more recent example, the flights of fancy of John M. Allegro and his school
of thought. I am not suggesting for a moment—perish the thought!—that
the views of these higher critics—"higher anti-Semites," Schechter aptly
dubbed them[8]—are correct, but I merely want to point out that Hirsch has
gone a long distance beyond the bare facts and has surreptitiously introduced a particular explanation of those facts as his starting point. Nor
can it be urged, in charitable mitigation, that the explanation of the Torah
as consisting of 613 commandments binding as law is really included among
"the components of the Torah," for, as Geiger pointed out at the time in a
review of Hirsch's work, it is a cavalier and unhistorical procedure to
"prove" the authority and binding force of a revelation by assuming the accuracy of the narratives through which it is conveyed to us. In this way all
religions could equally attribute absolute authority to the "sacred" Scriptures on which they base their ideas. As Geiger says further, and in ex-
asperation: "For goodness sake, what an error we have here! May God save
Israel from such 'a warped spirit of dizziness and confusion' (Isa. 19:14)."[9]
Or, to put the same criticism more technically, evidence must be kept distinct from explanatory theory. The fact of a particular explanation is one
thing, its validity another, and to assume its validity is only one—not *the*
only—explanation of that explanation regarded as a fact, that is, as a
record.[10]

One word more is in order regarding the strong and lasting appeal of
Hirsch's philosophy in certain circles. Professor Joseph L. Blau, in a recent
particularly illuminating study of modern movements in Judaism, has
thrown out the suggestion that religious ideologies, to be successful, must
change while both seeming changeless and protesting their changelessness.
The religious ideology of an age must serve as a link with the past; it must
convince its adherents that they are following the way of their forefathers
and that the sanctions of the past are theirs. However, in order to remain
viable and to continue to have relevance to the lives of those who accept it, it
must change with the changing cultural situation, all the while appearing
not to change if it is to be influential.[11] The philosophy of Samson R. Hirsch
is a perfect illustration of Professor Blau's thesis. Despite all of his vigorous
disclaimers of external contemporaneous influences, despite his contention
that all his interpretations are based purely on the Bible, the Talmud, and
the Midrash, and despite his insistence that he is bringing the wisdom of immemorial antiquity to bear upon the solution of contemporary problems,

Hirsch was essentially a typical nineteenth-century German-Jewish intellectual who to a large extent—unconsciously and in good faith—repeated and
adapted the ideas and modes of thought of popular contemporary German
thinkers like Hegel, Fichte, Herder, and others.[12] (It could not be otherwise,
else how would his views of Judaism differ from those of the despised
"Polish *rebbe*" who was as much at home, if not more so, in the various
primary sources of the Jewish tradition?) Herein lies the strength—and the
weakness—of Hirsch's philosophy of Judaism.

After the present excursus was completed, Noah H. Rosenbloom's
study, *Tradition in an Age of Reform: The Religious Philosophy of Samson
Raphael Hirsch* (Philadelphia, 1976), appeared. My confidence in the essential soundness of my analysis of the Hirsch mystique is increased by the fact
that it turns out to resemble Professor Rosenbloom's excellent and detailed
analysis of it in a number of important aspects.

Appendix E

The Fatherhood of God as the Foundation of Morality

The basic truth that one cannot derive moral notions from exclusively non-moral premises ("No Ought from an Is") can be seen by considering the argument so popular in certain theological circles that the relation of one human being to another may be inferred from their relation to God. Thus, if God is the Father of all, all men are His children and equal, brothers who ought to love one another. This view of the human condition is summed up in the popular slogan, "The brotherhood of man under the Fatherhood of God."

This argument simply will not hold water. The great religious teachers of mankind have taught that human inequalities are trivial in view of man's supernatural destiny, but that they were ordained by God, and must, therefore, be maintained. Mrs. C. Frances Alexander (d. 1895), a prominent hymn-writer, gave expression to this belief in the third stanza of "All Things Bright":

> The rich man in his castle,
> The poor man at his gate,
> God made them, high or lowly,
> And ordered their estate.

This belief has been characteristic of the Christian "ethos." When the German peasants demanded that villeinage should end because "Christ has delivered and redeemed us all, the lowly as well as the great, without exception, by the shedding of his precious blood," Luther indignantly declared that such a proposition "would make all equal and so change the spiritual Kingdom of Christ into an external worldly one. Impossible! An earthly Kingdom cannot exist without inequality of persons. Some must be free, others serfs, some rulers, others subjects" (quoted by R. H Tawney, *Religion and the Rise of Capitalism* [New York: Mentor, 1948], p. 84). The famous German theologian and social scientist Ernst Troeltsch well sums up the gist of Christian social philosophy as follows: "It [the Christian ethos] recognizes differences in social position, power and capacity, as a condition which has been established by the inscrutable Will of God; and then transforms this condition by the inner upbuilding of personality and the development of the mutual sense of obligation into an ethical cosmos" (E. Troeltsch, *The Social Teachings of the Christian Churches,* trans. O. Wyon [New York, 1931], vol. 2, p. 1005; cf. vol. 1, pp. 39 ff.).

What is frequently overlooked in discussions of the divine Fatherhood is that the doctrine is nowhere taught in the classic texts of Judaism or Christianity, not excluding the Sermon on the Mount. "Neither Judaism nor Christianity has ever," says the great Unitarian scholar R. Travers Herford, "unless in recent times, taken up the position that all human beings are God's children, Torah or no Torah, Christ or no Christ" (*The Teachings of the Pharisees* [London, 1924], p. 159).

The pertinent New Testament passages concerning the Fatherhood of God have been examined by Archdeacon H. E. Guillebaud in chapter 2 of his work on the atonement, *Why the Cross* (2nd ed. [London, 1946], pp. 45–56). His conclusion is that if we carefully study every instance in the gospels where Jesus uses the expression "your Father," either in the singular or the plural, it will be found without exception that it is expressly stated that he is addressing his own disciples. Those passages in which Jesus speaks of God as "my Father" need not even be considered, since it is clear that no doctrine of the universal Fatherhood of God can be derived from this mode of speaking. He calls himself the "only-begotten" son (John 3:16), and carefully guards against confounding his special and unique sonship with that of other men (cf. Matt. 11:27). More typical is the Sermon on the Mount, where the expression "your Father" occurs some fourteen times, but that sermon is said (Matt. 5:1) to have been addressed, at least primarily, to "disciples." It is true that we read that there were "crowds" present, and at the close of the sermon it is said that "the crowds were astonished at his teaching, for he taught them as one having authority." But this does not neutralize the explicit declaration that the sermon was addressed to the "disciples," as distinguished from the "crowds." A lawyer in a courtroom *addresses* the jury. He is *heard* by the crowds who come as spectators. What he has to say to the jury cannot be understood as necessarily applicable to the general audience. Moreover, the sermon itself contains abundant internal evidence that it was addressed to disciples, or at the very least, to would-be disciples. "Blessed are you when men revile you and persecute you and utter all kinds of evil against you falsely on my account" (Matt. 5:11). Still less can this doctrine be derived from the parable of the Prodigal Son. Archdeacon Guillebaud does well to remind us (*op. cit.*, Appendix B, "The Interpretation of Parables," pp. 189 ff.; cf. pp. 52 ff.) that parables are comparisons and must not be made to run on all fours. God's love to man is in this parable illustrated by the love of a good father for a wayward son. But in the same chapter (Luke 14) it is also illustrated by a shepherd's care for a lost sheep and by a woman's care for a lost coin. The chapter no more proves that God is a universal Father than it proves that He is a universal shepherd or a universal loser of money.

It would take us too far afield to examine all the other passages in the gospels referring to the divine Fatherhood, but it is safe to generalize and say that in none of them is there a declaration to the effect that God is the Father of all mankind. When addressing his disciples, Jesus speaks of God as "your Father"; but he never uses this phrase when addressing the Pharisees or others who are not in sympathy with him. So far from this, we read in John 8:42 f. that when certain of the Jews, in their encounter with Jesus, said to him in terms of ordinary courtesy, "We were not born of fornication; we have one Father, even God," he replied, "If God were your Father you would love me." And in verse 44 he adds, "You are of your father the devil." Here is a distinct assertion that the Fatherhood of God is not universal. It would be difficult to find a more explicit declaration that God is *not* the Father of all men than this dialogue.

Nor do the gospels teach the universal brotherhood of man. Jesus is reported to have said (Matt. 12:50): "Whoever does the will of my Father in heaven is my brother and sister and mother." The Johannine Jesus enjoins on his disciples brotherly love of a very narrow compass: "A new commandment I give to you, that you love one another; even as I have loved you, that you also love one another. By this all men will know that you are my disciples, if you have love for one another" (John 13:34–35). Christian scholars have been at a loss to explain in what sense this is a "*new* commandment." The golden rule, "Love your neighbor as yourself," is after all found in the Torah (Lev. 19:18), and the context (v. 34) makes it abundantly clear that the injunction is not limited to fellow Israelites, but includes the non-Israelite stranger (*ger*). The startling answer to this difficulty, which I can only outline in a very summary and tentative fashion, is that the rabbis tended to universalize moral obligations and extend their application to wider groups, whereas Jesus sought to limit them and narrow down their pertinency. For the exclusiveness of the gospel message as a whole, attention may be called to Matthew 10:5–6 and the disagreeable way in which Jesus treated the Syrophoenician woman, Matthew 15:21–28, and parallels. I hope to discuss this thesis in a more extended and comprehensive manner in a forthcoming paper; suffice it to state here that the gospels themselves, especially John, as we have seen, make it abundantly clear that the Pharisaic Jews were the defenders of the concepts of the moral unity of mankind and the Fatherhood of God. If one of the criteria of ethical advance and moral progress is the extension of the area or range of the common good, as the philosopher T. H. Green maintained (*Prolegomena to Ethics* [Oxford, 1883], pp. 217 ff.), then it cannot be gainsaid that "the righteousness of the scribes and the Pharisees" was superior to that of Jesus.

It has always seemed to me that Jesus' denunciation of those who did not believe in him or who wanted evidence for his messianic claims, and in particular his savagely vindictive and unrestrained attacks on the Pharisees, are not only inconsistent with his teachings, but are a flaw and blemish in the character of one who is looked up to by millions as the unique religious exemplar of every age. His denunciation and excoriation of the Pharisees is all the more shocking if we realize that the Pharisees, for all their possible shortcomings, were, as a group, far superior to the apostles and early Christians in religious earnestness and moral seriousness. In Matthew 23, for example, this stream of invective comes in one verse after another, until it almost appears as if the gospel Jesus enjoyed this torrent of wrath and assault, or else it would not go on and on. "Scribes and Pharisees, hypocrites!" reverberates again and again. "Woe unto you scribes and Pharisees, hypocrites! for ye are like unto whited sepulchres, which, indeed, appear beautiful outward, but are within full of dead men's bones, and of all uncleanness. . . . Ye serpents, ye generation of vipers, how can ye escape the damnation of hell?" If these are terms of endearment expressive of love of one's enemies and of Christian charity and forgiveness, or even if they are an example of lofty and dignified rebuke, it is hard to see what resources of language are left to provide a vehicle for condemnation.

On the other hand, I cannot agree with the late Chief Rabbi of the British Empire, Dr. Joseph H. Hertz (Commentary on Exodus), that the universal Fatherhood of God is taught in Exodus 4:22, where Israel is called the "first-born son" of God, implying that all human beings are also His children. It must be said to be a poor case that is considered to need the support of such forced exegesis and strained interpretations. Indeed, bearing in mind the biblical right of primogeniture, the phrase itself contains an important difference between Israel, the elder brother, and the other nations, the younger brothers of Israel. A better example of the universalism and deep compassion of the Bible is the Book of Jonah, which is read in the synagogue on the solemn Day of Atonement. The Book of Jonah teaches that God, who created the whole earth, must also be the God and Father of all peoples. In His loving, kind, and fatherly heart all men are equal, and before Him there is no difference of nation and creed, but only individual souls which He has created in His own image. God's love is not limited to the Jews alone, nor is His concern confined to the Holy Land, but it extends to the Gentiles as well. The people of Nineveh do not become Jews, neither are they circumcised. They simply repent and that is enough. God's impartial concern for all His creatures is summed up in the final verse of the book: "Should I not pity Nineveh, that great city, in which there are more than a hundred and twenty thousand infants who do not yet know their right hand from their left, and also much cattle?!" (4:11). An acute student of the history and philosophies of religions has well summarized the notion of universal love and all-embracing compassion found in biblical and postbiblical Judaism.

The Hebrew Bible relates that when God told Abraham that he was about to destroy Sodom and Gomorrah, Abraham raised his voice against God to say that it would be shameful for God if there would be a few decent people in those cities and he killed them along with the wicked (Genesis 18). Job also argued with God and insisted that his ways were not just. Jeremiah, without claiming that Jerusalem had been innocent, still mourned over her destruction. The author of the Book of Jonah insisted that even the people of Nineveh, the archenemy, should be forgiven all of their outrages as soon as they repented. The Pharisees made allowance for the just among the Gentiles and in any case did not revel in dreams of hell.[1]

While not specifically discussing the divine Fatherhood, Professor Harry M. Orlinsky, in an essay on "Nationalism—Universalism and Internationalism in Ancient Israel" (in *Translating and Understanding the Old Testament: Essays in Honor of Herbert Gordon May,* ed. Harry T. Frank and William L. Reed [Nashville, 1970], pp. 106–26), carefully analyzes the landmark passages in the Jewish Bible that delineate the biblical view of God in relation to Israel and the rest of the world. His conclusion is that the biblical writers view the God of Israel at one and the same time as their national God and as the only Deity in the world, but they did not consider Him the God of any other nation. This also seems to have been the attitude of the talmudic sages. The rabbis taught (to paraphrase George Orwell) that all men are equal, but that some men, the Jews, are more equal than others. Typical is the sentence of Rabbi Akiba (Abot 3:14):

> Beloved is man, for he was created in the image [of God]; still more beloved in that it was made known to him that he was created in the image, as it is said, "In the image of God made He man" [Gen. 9:6]. Beloved are the Israelites, because they are called the children of God; still greater love that it was made known to them that they are called children of God, as it is said, "You are the children of the Lord your God" [Deut. 14:1].

But in rabbinic Judaism at its highest, national limitations are clearly and on principle broken through. A well-known passage in the *Sifra* (Kedoshim IV.12 on Lev. 19:18) discusses the most comprehensive principle in the Torah. "'You shall love your neighbor as yourself.' Rabbi Akiba said: 'This is the greatest principle in the Torah.' Ben Azzai said: 'This is the book of the generations of man' [Gen. 5:1] is even a greater principle than the other." The Commentaries (see especially *Korban Aaron* by R. Aaron Ibn Hayyim, a Moroccan rabbi who died in 1632) explain that there is no difference between these sages on the question itself: love of one's fellowman is fundamental. But while Rabbi Akiba wants to derive this basic teaching from the golden rule in Leviticus, Ben Azzai points out that the expression "your neighbor" is open to a narrow nationalist interpretation, as meaning only a fellow Israelite. He therefore preferred a more unambiguous text. This he found in Genesis: "This is the book of the generations of Adam [man]," which concludes with the words, "In the day that God created man, in the likeness of God He made him; male and female He created them." Thus right at the beginning of the Bible, in the story of creation in Genesis, he found the basic principle of the Torah, which is the brotherhood and unity of man, and the consequent obligation that accrues to every man to love his fellow. The correct interpretation of this passage in the *Sifra* was perceived by the late Professor Gerhard Kittel, of unlovely memory, in *Die Probleme des palästinischen Spätjudentum und des Urchristentums* (Leipzig, 1926), p. 116. Kittel says: "For Ben Azzai the concept of 'man' is bigger than the concept of 'fellow-countryman,' and humanity is greater than an exclusive nationalism." See also the parallel passages in Jerusalem Talmud, Nedarim 9:3, 41c and Genesis Rabbah 24:7 (p. 236, ed. Theodor-Albeck).

Perhaps the finest rabbinic thought on our subject is found in an ancient

Mishnah, Sanhedrin 4:5, in the solemn admonition to witnesses testifying in a capital case. I quote from Canon Herbert Danby's translation:

> Only one single man was created in the world, to teach that, if any man has caused a single soul to perish, Scripture imputes it to him as though he had caused a whole world to perish, and if any man saves a single soul, Scripture imputes it to him as though he had saved a whole world. Again, but a single man was created for the sake of peace among mankind, that none should say to his fellow, "My father was greater than your father"; also that the heretics [*minim*] should not say, "There are many ruling powers in heaven." Again, but a single man was created to proclaim the greatness of God, for man stamps many coins with one die, and they are all like to one another; but God has stamped every man with the die of the first man, yet not one of them is like his fellow. Therefore every one must say, "For my sake was the world created."

LIST OF ABBREVIATIONS

AHDL	Archives d'histoire doctr. et litt. du moyen age.
C. G.	Summa Contra Gentiles.
CCAR	Journal of the Central Conference of American Rabbis.
HB	Hebräische Bibliographie.
HTR	Harvard Theological Review.
HUCA	Hebrew Union College Annual.
JQR	Jewish Quarterly Review.
MGWJ	Monatsschrift fur Geschichte und Wissenschaft des Judentums.
PAAJR	Proceedings of the American Academy of Jewish Research.
P. G.	Migne, *Patrologiae cursus completus,* Series Graeca.
P. L.	Migne, *Patrologiae cursus completus,* Series Latina.
REJ	Revue des Etudes Juives.
S. T.	Summa Theologica.

Titles which are seldom referred to are quoted in full.

Notes

PREFACE

1. See, for example, the prayer-book *Siddur Tehillath ha-Shem* (New York, 1974). The rite of "the divine Rabbi Isaac" (*Nusaḥ ha-'Ari*) is followed by the Ḥabad (Lubavitch) school in Hasidism, which is by far the largest and most intellectual of all Hasidic groups in the world today. For Ḥayyim Vital's statement, see his *Peri 'Eṣ Ḥayyim* 1:1 (ed. Jerusalem [1965–66], p. 15) and the truncated version thereof in *Magen Abraham*, the commentary of R. Abraham Abele Gumbiner, on the *Shulḥan 'Aruk, 'Oraḥ Ḥayyim* 68:1; cf. also Master Luria's "Manner of Life and Devotion" (*Hanhagoth*), in *Sefer Toledoth ha-'Ari* (Hebrew), ed. Meir Benayahu (Jerusalem, 1967), p. 537, no. 19. The objection to the Thirteen Principles was justified to the extent that they were formulated in conscious imitation of Muslim prototypes, and that, whether or not Judaism has any formal dogmas in the strict sense, the recital of a creed as a confession of faith is certainly un-Jewish and was completely unknown until the time of Maimonides. See S. D. Luzzatto, *Meḥkere ha-Yahaduth* [Studies in Judaism], vol. 2 (Jerusalem, 1970), p. 168; D. Neumark, *History of Dogmas in Judaism* (Hebrew), (Odessa, 1919), vol. 2, p. 161; J. D. Eisenstein in the Hebrew encyclopedia *Oẓar Israel*, s.v. "'Ikkarim," vol. 8 (1912), p. 127. Despite Maimonides' declaration in the epilogue to his Thirteen Principles that membership in the religious body of Israel rests upon assent to the Thirteen Principles in their entirety, and that anyone who rejects even one of its articles is considered a heretic and it is obligatory upon the faithful (according to Maimonides) "to hate him and to cause him to perish," it may confidently be stated that no proceedings were ever instituted before a Jewish court on the ground of refusal to accept the Maimonidean principles. On the contrary, by a true irony of history Maimonides was himself charged with heresy and his books burned. See J. Saracheck, *Faith and Reason: The Conflict Over the Rationalism of Maimonides* (Williamsport, 1935), and Daniel J. Silver, *Maimonidean Criticism and the Maimonidean Controversy: 1180–1240* (Leiden, 1965).

INTRODUCTORY

1. See A. R. Badawī, *Aflāṭūn 'ind al-'Arab* (Cairo, 1955, in Arabic). A study of pseudographic and misattributed works in the Middle Ages is a prime desideratum long overdue. M. Steinschneider's *Zur Pseudographischenliteratur des Mitteralters* (Berlin, 1862) is limited in scope and outdated.

2. They followed Porphyry, Simplicius, and the later Neoplatonists. Boethius announced a grandiose scheme—never completed—of translating into Latin the complete works of both Plato and Aristotle and establishing a complete harmony between them. See the introduction to the second book of the *De Interpretatione* ii (Migne, *P.L.*, vol. 64, col. 433 C, D).

3. Arabic text edited by F. Dieterici (Leiden, 1890), and trans. into German by him under the title *Alfarabis Philosophische Abhandlungen* (Leiden, 1892); a new edition prepared by A. N. Nadir appeared in Beirut in 1960. On this topic see M. Fakhry, "Reconciliation of Plato and Aristotle," *Journal of the History of Ideas,* 36 (1965): 469–78. Many conspicuously (Neo-) Platonic elements and features entered the Thomistic synthesis by way of Pseudo-Dionysius, who was thought to have been a companion of St. Paul (Acts 17:34), and whose works Aquinas, in company with other medieval philosophers and theologians, regarded as authentic. With the exception of Aristotle, Pseudo-Dionysius is quoted or cited as an authority by Aquinas more often than any other philosopher, and his mystical theology exerted a deep influence on the Saint. All in all there are some seventeen hundred quotations from this dubious character in the works of Aquinas, in addition to the *Commentary on Dionysius' Divine Names* which Aquinas wrote in the last decade of his life. See J. Durantel, *Saint Thomas et le Pseudo-Denis* (Paris, 1919); M. D. Chenu, *A Guide to the Study of Thomas Aquinas* (New York, 1965), p. 226, n. 44. Edwyn Bevan is greatly dismayed by this fifth-century impostor and his fraudulent writings, and in his Gifford Lectures he cites Professor Dodds, who in his edition of Proclus' *Elements of Theology* calls the writings of the Pseudo-Dionysius outright a "fraud," and adds in a footnote: "It is for some reason customary to use a kinder term; but it is quite clear that the deception was deliberate" (p. xxvii). The fraudulent author, for example, claims that he witnessed the death of the Virgin Mary. "It is strange to think," continues Professor Bevan, "what an immense influence has been exerted upon Catholic doctrine in two different fields by two bodies of writing which were definite impostures. The Catholic doctrine regarding the temporal rights of the Sovereign Pontiff rested largely for many centuries upon the forged Decretals—a forgery which the Roman Church has now long recognized as such, and repudiated. It is perhaps unfortunate that it has not yet repudiated with equal decision the other imposture, whose influence has been no less in the field of metaphysical theology than that of the forged Decretals was in the field of the Pontiff's temporal claims—the works of the false Dionysius" (*Symbolism and Belief* [Boston, 1959], pp. 347 f.). For the Renaissance attempt to fuse the thought of Plato and Aristotle, see N. A. Robb, *Neoplatonism of the Italian Renaissance* (London, 1935). More recently, John Wild attempted to amalgamate or synthesize the theories of Plato and Aristotle in his *Plato's Theory of Man: An Introduction to the Realistic Philosophy of Culture* (Cambridge: Harvard University Press, 1946).

4. Aristotle, *Metaphysics,* 1 (A), chap. 2, 982b 12–17 (Loeb Classical Library trans.). See also the remarks of the Platonic Socrates, *Theaetetus* 155D; *Republic*

475C, if rightly interpreted. This characteristic note is already struck by Xenophanes in his famous couplet (written perhaps at the end of the sixth century): "The gods did not reveal all things to men from the beginning / But, as time goes on, by searching men discover more and more" (Xenophanes *apud* Stobaeus, *Anth.* I, 8, 2, quoted in Diels, *Fragmente der Vorsokratiker*⁵, fragment 18, vol. 1, p. 133). In the nineteenth century this theme was developed and given a characteristically pessimistic turn by Arthur Schopenhauer in the chapter "On Man's Need of Metaphysics" in *The World as Will and Idea* (Supplements to the first book, chap. 17).

5. I say possible because: (1) many modern interpreters (e.g., the Marburg school of Cohen and Natorp) give a purely conceptualist interpretation of the Platonic Ideas. According to these thinkers the Ideas, viewed from their ontological aspect, are not metaphysical principles existing in and for themselves apart from the sensible world, but rather logical essences which are enacted nowhere save in the particular objects exemplifying them. See Paul Natorp, *Platons Ideenlehre* (Leipzig, 1903, rev. ed. 1921), J. A. Stewart, *Plato's Doctrine of Ideas* (1909; reissued, New York, 1964); (2) the axioms of mathematics and logic can be empirically tested by the method of "concomitant variation": e.g., the more nearly our magnitudes approach equality the more nearly do the axioms fit the facts observed; (3) historical knowledge has been thought to be amenable to the empiricist approach by many logical positivists; see A. J. Ayer, *Language, Truth and Logic,* 2nd ed. (London, 1946), pp. 18 f. and 101 f. More recently Professor Ayer has modified his views; see *The Central Questions of Philosophy* (New York, 1973), pp. 24 f.

6. As Professor Whitehead has put the contrast (*Adventure of Ideas* [Cambridge, Mass., 1933], p. 132), the question "Canst thou by searching find out God?" is good Hebrew, but bad Greek.

7. A. B. Davidson, *The Theology of the Old Testament* (Edinburgh, 1904), pp. 32 f. This observation had already been made by Pascal, in his *Pensées,* ed. Brunschvicg, iv, para. 243: "C'est une chose admirable que jamais auteur canonique ne s'est servi de la nature pour prouver Dieu." See also H. Malter, *Saadia Gaon,* pp. 174 f., of which use is here made. David Neumark's criticism of Malter is not well taken ("Saadya's Philosophy," in *Essays in Jewish Philosophy* [1929], pp. 152–155 [pp. 145–218]). Neumark attempts to reduce such passages as Isaiah 40:25–26 and Jeremiah 31:35–36 to a syllogistic form and find in them the cosmological argument for God's existence. But his attempt lacks even the shadow of a foundation; in each case the major premise of the syllogism is supplied by Neumark and not found in the biblical writer. All that the passages in question imply is that false ideas of what God is may be corrected, or at least brought home to men's consciousness, by the observation of natural phenomena and the events of providence in life. The rabbinic doctrine of God does not differ essentially from the biblical in this respect. The judicious remarks of A. Cohen deserve quotation: "As in the Bible, so throughout the literature of the Rabbis, the existence of God is regarded as an axiomatic truth. No proofs are offered to convince the Jew that there must be a God. To avoid the

profane use of the sacred Name, in accordance with the third commandment, various designations were devised, common among them being 'the Creator' and 'He Who spake and the world came into being.' They indicate the view that the existence of God follows inevitably from the existence of the Universe." See *Everyman's Talmud,* rev. ed. (New York, 1949), p. 1. It may be noted that Josephus (*Antiquities* I, 7. 1, par. 156) and Philo (*De migrat. Abr.,* 32, I, 464M), writing in a Greco-Roman milieu, put a rudimentary form of the cosmological proof for the existence of God into the mouth of the patriarch Abraham, and that Jewish legend stresses the fact that Abraham came to know God through his own reasoning about the universe and its ruler who must necessarily exist (Genesis Rabbah 38:13 and 39:1 and the literature cited by Ginzberg in *Legends,* vol. 5, p. 210, n. 16; p. 217, n. 49; p. 227, n. 108, but none of these sources antedate the contact of Judaism with Greek culture).

8. What is said in the text about the Jewish Scriptures and Law applies to the Gospels and Epistles if we consider the teacher of Nazareth as the incarnate Son of God (cf. Heb. 1:1 ff.).

9. George Adam Smith, *The Book of Isaiah,* vol. 2, rev. ed. (New York, 1927), p. 91.

10. L. Strauss, *Philosophie und Gesetz* (Berlin: Schocken, 1936), p. 47. Cf. M. Etienne Gilson's definition of Christian philosophy: "Every philosophy which, although keeping the two orders [of faith and reason] formally distinct, nevertheless considers the Christian revelation as an indispensible auxiliary to reason" (*The Spirit of Medieval Philosophy* [New York, 1936], p. 37). For a more personal account, see the same writer's *The Philosopher and Theology,* (New York, 1962), pp. 175–99. *Mutatis mutandis,* this definition holds good for medieval Jewish and Muslim philosophy. See also H. A. Wolfson's outline of the common elements of medieval Christian, Jewish, and Muslim philosophy in the last chapter of his two-volume study of Philo (*Philo: Foundations of Religious Philosophy in Judaism, Christianity, and Islam* [Cambridge, Mass., 1947]. They consist, according to Wolfson, of these principles: (1) *Belief in a twofold source of truth.* Divine revelation as recorded in Scripture is the one infallible source of truth; but God has also equipped man with reason. (2) *The belief that there is no conflict between these two sources of truth.* Since God is the author of revelation and reason, there can be no conflict between them: Scripture must be interpreted in the light of what is most evidently true in reason, and reason must be corrected in the light of what are most evidently the true teachings of Scripture. (3) *The basic teachings of Scripture.* Scripture teaches the existence and unity of God, the creation of the world, divine providence, and the divine origin of the rules of conduct. (4) *The aptitude of reason to discover these truths.* Reason has led philosophers to some of the above-mentioned truths, but it has failed to prove the unity of God as implying his uniqueness and simplicity, the impossibility of knowing His essence, the creation of the world, God's power to change the laws of nature by performing miracles, individual providence, and freedom of will.

These principles, according to Wolfson, were the bequest of Philo to European thought, a bequest that turned out to be a *damnosa hereditas.*

11. William Temple, *Nature, Man and God* (London, 1934), chap. 1, especially p. 35.

12. *Critique of Pure Reason,* Preface to 2nd edition.

2. THE MAIMONIDEAN SYNTHESIS

1. It has often been pointed out, and rightly so, that "Law" is an inadequate rendering of Torah, which is a larger concept meaning "teaching" or "instruction," but this does not affect our consideration. Jewish philosophy, we must remember, is not indigenous to Palestinian Judaism, but a product of the *Galuth* (diaspora); from Philo of Alexandria to Martin Buber in our own day, Judaism never produced a single philosopher on its own soil. Now, when interpreting Judaism to alien cultures, its own spokesmen—one need think only of the Septuagint, Josephus (especially in *Contra Apionem*), and Philo—*did* equate the concept of Torah with *nomos,* Law, and insofar as the main characteristic of Jewish religion is that it is not creedal or dogmatic but preceptive and halakic, they were correct in so translating Torah by Law.

The Hebrew Bible is marked by the absence of technical philosophy or anything approaching it. The ancient Israelites neither asked the questions that philosophers ask nor did they answer the questions that they did ask as philosophers do. This needs emphasizing because from time to time modern scholars have attempted to expound the philosophical ideas and teachings allegedly contained in the Hebrew Bible in such works as *The Philosophy of the Bible* by David Neumark (Cincinnati, 1918) and *The Hebrew Philosophical Genius* by Duncan B. MacDonald (Princeton, 1936). But there is no agreement among these scholars as to what the fundamental ideas were and how they were arrived at. These writers seem to confuse implicitly held beliefs with logical analysis of them, probing with demonstration, and questions with the reasoning procedures of philosophers. It is a distinguishing character of technical philosophy that it submits beliefs—however self-evident—to rational criticism. Admittedly, the ancient Hebrews grappled with many of the basic problems of humanity which the great philosophers throughout the ages have sought to answer, but it does not follow because a man, or a book, states ideas which can be constructed into a philosophy, that he, or it, has any philosophy. Émile Meyeson, the great philosopher of science, somewhere suggests that a dog snapping at a piece of meat tossed to him by his master, implies a belief in the external and independent existence of "things." But it is Meyerson, not the dog, who develops the canine philosophy. Similarly, modern scholars can to their own satisfaction construct a philosophy out of the implied beliefs of the ancient Hebrews. But the success of the enterprise is that of the modern scholars and not that of the biblical writers. It was only when the Jews were "emancipated" (in Salo W. Baron's words) from the shackles of statehood and territory and came into contact with other nations and other cultures, first with the Greeks, and then with their disciples, the Arabs, that the Jewish genius for abstract speculative thought began to assert itself, and not until then did the philosophical movement among the Jews take root and begin to flourish. (Cf. L. Strauss, *Natural Right and History* [New York, 1955], p. 81; H. Malter, s.v. "Jewish Philosophy," in Hastings's *Encyclopaedia of Religion and Ethics,* vol. 9, p. 1873; Abraham S. Halkin, "The Attitude of Normative Judaism to Philosophy," in *Perspectives in Jewish Learning,* vol. 4, ed. M. A. Friedman [Chicago, 1972], p. 1 [pp. 1–10].)

As in other times and in other countries, Jews in the Muslim empire insisted on participating in the local culture as completely as they were permitted to. So there was a public outcry, "Give us a Jewish philosophy—reconcile Judaism with reason and logic." To such public outcries the rabbis gave in, however reluctantly. We shall find much to take exception to in Julius Guttmann's *Philosophies of Judaism* (New York: Holt, Rinehart & Winston, 1964), but on this point credit should be given where due. Right at the beginning of his work (pp. 3 f.) Guttmann says: "The Jewish people did not begin to philosophize because of an irresistible urge to do so. They received philosophy from outside sources, and the history of Jewish philosophy is the history of the successive absorptions of foreign ideas which were then transformed and adapted according to specific Jewish points of view. . . . The character of the Jewish community in the Diaspora precluded these appropriations from ever leading to the formation of a Jewish philosophy in the national sense." (The last sentence is completely garbled in the English translation of Guttmann's work. We have translated it verbatim from the German original and the Hebrew version. On the poor quality of the English translation of Guttmann's work, see the review of Professor Alexander Altmann in *Conservative Judaism,* vol. 19, no. 1 [Fall 1964], pp. 73–77.) Again at the conclusion of his work (p. 397) Guttmann says: "With the Nazi destruction of European—and especially German—Jewry (which since the days of Mendelssohn had been the focal point of Jewish religious philosophy), no new generation remained to work out the philosophy [of Judaism]. There are some thinkers of the past generation who are occupied with it, but they have no disciples. Jewish philosophy, which had been renewed in the last decades of the nineteenth century, has now reached its nadir. If it once more arises to continue its work, it will develop under entirely new conditions."

It would be interesting to write the history of the philosophical movement in Jewry by viewing the thinkers as secondary figures revolving as satellites in the orbit of their Gentile prototypes. The relations of Philo to Plato, of Maimonides to Aristotle, of Judah Halevi to al-Ghazzālī, and of Hermann Cohen to Kant immediately come to mind. Cf. Shlomo Pines, "Scholasticism After Thomas Aquinas and the Teachings of Ḥasdai Crescas and His Predecessors," in *Proceedings of the Israel Academy of Sciences and Humanities* 1, no. 10 (1967): 1 ff.

2. We must never lose sight of the fact that the division of certain sentiments into "political" and "religious" is an arbitrary one of Western or European origin, as the language of the terms indicates. It is foreign to the thought-forms implicit in Semitic linguistics, and an ancient Hebrew would not have understood these terms. Speaking of the nature of the Semitic religious community—Jewish or Muslim—Robertson Smith correctly says: "Broadly speaking, religion was made up of a series of acts and observances, the correct performance of which was necessary or desirable to secure the favor of the gods or to avert their anger; and in these observances every member of society had a share, marked out for him either in virtue of his being born within a certain family and community, or in virtue of the station, within the family and community, that he had come to hold in the course of his life. . . . Religion did not exist for the saving of souls but for the preservation and welfare of society, and in all that was necessary to this end every man had to take his part, or break with the domestic and political community to which he belonged. . . . There was no separation between the spheres of religion and of ordinary life. . . . it was impossible for an individual to change his religion without changing his nationality, and a whole community could hardly change its religion at all without being absorbed into another stock or nation" (W. Robertson Smith, *The Religion of the Semites,* 2nd ed. [New York: Meridian Books, 1956], pp. 28, 29, 30, 37).

3. H. A. Wolfson, "Maimonides and Halevi," in *JQR,* n.s. vol. 2 (1911), pp. 314 f. (pp. 297–337). It is not certain that Wolfson adhered to this viewpoint without modifications. A not dissimilar view was surprisingly expressed by the saintly S. R. Hirsch, who castigates Maimonides as "the product of uncomprehended Judaism and Arabic science," who "was obliged to reconcile the strife which raged in his own breast" (*The Nineteen Letters of Ben Uziel,* trans. B. Drachman [New York, 1942], Letter XVIII, p. 181). Cf. H. A. Wolfson, "Hallevi and Maimonides on Design," etc., *PAAJR* 11 (1941): 136, n. (pp. 105–163). In his definitive study of Philo, Professor Wolfson has modified his earlier opinion regarding the rationalism of Maimonides and has to some extent given his assent to the view that Maimonides considered philosophy as ancillary in its relation to Scripture (*Philo,* vol. 1, p. 157). See also the interesting study of Ben Zion Bokser, who reaches a similar conclusion: "Reason and Revelation in the Theology of Maimonides," *HUCA* 20 (1947): 541–84 ("in all the crucial issues where philosophy and the Torah clashed, he upheld the Torah," p. 582). These conclusions can only be justified by giving undue weight to Maimonides' popular, mass-oriented writings in contradistinction to the *Guide,* which is addressed to would-be philosophers.

We are more inclined to agree with the conclusion of Professor Chaim Tchernowitz (Rav Tzair):

With respect to every matter of Jewish law with which he [Maimonides] dealt, if there was a definite opposition to it from the standpoint of science, he generally decided in favor of the latter. In this matter he followed the same usage as in the *Guide of the Perplexed* with respect to questions of beliefs and doctrines contradicting philosophy. Even regarding the opinion of the eternity of the world, "which fundamentally contradicts the Law," he states that if a compelling proof were found for it he would fit the scriptural texts to it, as he did with the negation of corporeality because "His not being a body can be demonstrated; from this it follows necessarily that everything that in its literal sense runs counter to this logical proof needs further interpretation" (*Guide* II:25). He followed the same method in regard to Halakah. . . . His sworn defender, the author of *Migdal 'Oz* [Shem-Tob ben Abraham (ibn) Gaon], who said about him [in his commentary on Maimonides' *Yad, Hilkot 'Erubin* 5:9, *et passim*] that "he wrote in his work only what is explicitly stated in the Talmud, and did not add anything new of his own," grossly exaggerated. The truth is that Maimonides added much that is new on the basis of his knowledge of science and philosophy. Maimonides, the philosopher, can be clearly recognized behind the walls of his own structure of traditional Jewish law.

Chaim Tchernowitz, *Toledoth ha-Poskim* [History of Jewish Codes], vol. 1 (New York, 1948), pp. 254 f. See also Tchernowitz's article, "If a Second Moses Had Not Arisen" (Hebrew), *Moznaim* 3 (1935): 385–401.

This view has the support of no less an authority than R. Elijah Wilna, the Gaon *par excellence*. In his notes on the *Shulḥan 'Aruk* (*Yoreh De'ah* 179:13) he attacks Maimonides for allowing himself to be guided by "the accursed philosophy" of Aristotle and refusing to believe in the efficacy of cabalistic formulas for the conjuring up of demons. See Jacob I. Dienstag, "Did the Gaon R. Elijah Oppose Maimonides' Philosophical Teachings?" (Hebrew), *Talpiyot* 4 (1949): 253–68, and W. S. Wurzburger, "Meta-Halakhic Propositions," in *Leo Jung Jubilee Volume*, ed. M. Kasher *et al.* (New York, 1962), pp. 211–22.

4. Maimonides, *Responsa*, ed. Alfred Freimann (Jerusalem [Mekiṣe Nirdamim], 1934), p. LX. (a) Jer. 1:5; (b) Prov. 5:16; (c) Prov. 5:19; (d) Prov. 5:18; Mal. 2:14; Isa. 54:6; (e) Lev. 26:44; (f) I Kings 11:1; (g) Sanhedrin 103b and Rashi *in loc.*; also Saadiah's version of Lev. 18:18; (h) I Sam. 8:13; (i) Esther 1:11; (j) translator's euphemism for esthetic reasons. Maimonides' pious declaration achieved its intended purpose. In the conflict aroused by his philosophy, the traditionalists underlined the importance of this epistle. See, among others, Moses Alashkar, *Responsa* (Jerusalem, 1961), no. 117; Ibn Adret, *Responsa* vol. 1 (Bnei Brak, 1958), no. 414; Joseph Ya'bes, *Or ha-Ḥayyim* (Ferrara, 1554), chap. 10. For modern interpretations of the passage, see I. Elbogen "Moses ben Maimons Persoenlichkeit, *MGWJ* 79 (1935): 70 (pp. 65–80) and H. A. Wolfson, *Philo*, 1, p. 157.

5. Strictly speaking, Maimonides did not claim to be presenting a synthesis. In *Guide* I:71, which might be called his outline of the history of philosophy, Maimonides asserts that the Jews and not the Greeks were the original cultivators of philosophy, and that the other nations owed their progress in that study to the Jews.

For Maimonides Greek thought is contained in the Torah and is essentially nothing other than its true meaning (i.e., "the secrets of the Law"). This view, so flattering to the pride of the Jews, is found not only in Jewish authors, but repeatedly among pagan Christian and Muslim writers as well. Eusebius (*Praep. evang.*, bk. X), for example, accuses the Greeks of being plagiarists who tacitly borrowed their lore from the Jews. There is, of course, no historical basis for these claims, which were probably fabricated by the Alexandrian Jews as early as the second century B.C.E. (being found in Aristobule of Paneas, an author quoted by Josephus and Eusebius). The purpose of this propaganda was to explain the presumed harmony existing between the teachings revealed in the Bible and the doctrines taught by pagan philosophy. See Munk, *Guide* I:71, n. 3, p. 332, and the literature there cited; Steinschneider, *Hebr. Ueber.*, p. xvi; particularly David Kaufmann, *Die Sinne* (Budapest, 1884), pp. 5 ff., and *Studien über Salomon Ibn Gabirol* (Budapest, 1899), p. 14; Henry Malter, in *JQR*, n.s. 1 (1910): 166 f. The nature of this ingenious theory becomes transparent when we reflect on the double and concurrent tendency found in medieval writers in their attitude toward Aristotle: (1) Aristotle's philosophy is true, therefore he borrowed it from Moses; (2) Aristotle's philosophy is false, therefore he retracted it and became a convert (*ger ṣedeḳ*) to Judaism. See Louis Ginzberg's article, "Aristotle in Jewish Legend," in vol. 2 of the old *Jewish Encyclopedia.* Professor Abraham S. Halkin characterizes claims of this sort, namely, that all culture and philosophy is in reality Jewish in origin, as "defensive arguments" and asserts that it may be maintained with a considerable degree of confidence that the advocates of philosophic study knew very well that they were engaged in something which was both new and generally unaccepted. "They realized that they were occupying themselves with problems and with solutions which did not constitute the normal activity of Jewish scholars . . . " A. S. Halkin, "The Attitude of Normative Judaism to Philosophy," in *Perspectives in Jewish Learning,* vol. 4, ed. M. A. Friedman (Chicago, 1972), p. 7 (pp. 1–10). Similarly Professor Pines concludes: "In spite of the convenient fiction, which he [Maimonides] repeats, that the philosophic sciences flourished among the Jews of antiquity, he evidently considered that philosophy transcended religious or national distinction" (Translator's Introduction to *Guide,* pp. cxxxiii f.).

6. Leo Strauss, *Persecution and the Art of Writing* (Glencoe, 1952), p. 58. In the same essay Professor Strauss remarks quite seriously: "An adequate interpretation of the *Guide* would . . . have to take the form of an esoteric interpretation of an esoteric interpretation of an esoteric teaching" (p. 56). See also Arthur Hyman, "Interpreting Maimonides," in *Gesher* (New York, 1976), pp. 46–59.

7. Perhaps I may illustrate this with an example, happily no longer embarrassing to anybody. As a graduate student, I was greatly disturbed by Professor Louis Finkelstein's work, *The Pharisees: The Sociological Background of their Faith.* What troubled me was that Dr. Finkelstein, the Chancellor of the Jewish Theological Seminary of America, in this work seemed to follow the Marxian view of the

economic determinism of history, while at the same time in his popular addresses
and writings he inveighed against social and economic materialism. As I understood
him, Finkelstein's thesis was that Israelite traditions (prophetic, Pharisaic, and rabbinic) were the products of a consistent cultural battle between the submerged, un-
landed groups and their oppressors, the great landowners. In my studies I chanced to
read Joachim Wach's *Sociology of Religion* (University of Chicago Press, 1948), and
I saw that this author had articulated many of the difficulties which I felt (pp. 12 f.). I
wrote to Dr. Finkelstein, and he sent me a very nice reply wherein he conceded the
justice of Professor Wach's criticism of his discussion of the Pharisees. He promised
that in a future edition of *The Pharisees* he would "stress what is referred to only in
passing in the present work, namely, that while many of the Pharisaic views are
related to particular sociological backgrounds, their main concepts were unique and
cannot be interpreted as outgrowths of purely human situations. Struggles between
town and country are universal, but the Pharisees, like the Prophets, were unique. In
this book I tried to indicate the elements in the Pharisees' position which are
analogous to those of similar groups in other communities. However, it is significant
that the Pharisees concentrated on the interpretation of religion and the spiritual life
which is, of course, what no similar group did" (personal communication, dated
March 8, 1954). Professor Finkelstein is a man of his word; in 1962 he brought out a
new edition of his work in the introduction to which he retracts the basic thesis enunciated in the former edition. Whereas in 1938 he was cocksure that "customs create
exegesis, not exegesis customs" (p. 131; see also pp. 43–53, 101, 145, 216, 261, and
344), maturer thought brought him grave doubt that the rabbis "could possibly have
been motivated in their judgments, even unconsciously, by hedonistic needs, or
would dare to interpret Scripture 'to adjust the Law to life.' They might consider
comfort or convenience, even in the interpretation of the ritual law, where the Torah
was really ambiguous or silent. But how could these God-fearing men, their
predecessors, and their followers possibly be accused of 'changing' the ritual Law,
through pseudo-interpretation and pseudo-exegesis, when its meaning was clear and
beyond doubt?" (Introductory Note to the third edition, pp. ix f.).

8. See the perceptive essay of Isadore Twersky, "Some Non-Halakic Aspects of
the *Mishneh Torah,*" in *Jewish Medieval and Renaissance Studies,* ed. A. Altmann
(Cambridge, Mass, 1967), pp. 95–118. At the same time it cannot be gainsaid that
there is some esotericism in the *Guide* and that Maimonides held at least some un-
conventional, radical, or heterodox views; otherwise his calculated obscurity would
be without rhyme or reason.

9. J. L. Teicher, "Maimonides' Treatise on Resurrection: A Thirteenth Century
Forgery" (Hebrew), *Melilah,* vol. 1 (Manchester University Press, 1944), pp. 81–92.
Although Maimonides, in his popular, mass-oriented writings, stresses the belief in
personal immortality, he does not discuss the matter *ex professo* in his speculative
work, the *Guide;* the logical upshot of his theories, however, is a denial of individual
immortality. See *Guide* I:74, seventh method, where Maimonides adopts Avempace's

doctrine of the numerical unity of souls in the hereafter, which amounts to a denial of individual immortality (cf. Shem-Ṭob's commentary *in loc.*); Asher Crescas, Commentary on *Guide* I, 70 (5); I. Euchel, scholium on *Guide*, II, Intr., prop. 16. This view is shared by numerous modern expositors; see Munk's note on *Guide* I:74, p. 434, n. 4; Husik, *Mediaeval Jewish Philosophy,* Intr. pp. xlvii and 313; S. Pines, Translator's Introduction to *Guide,* pp. cii–civ, and p. 221, n. 11.

10. See I. Sonne "A Scrutiny of the Charges of Forgery Against Maimonides' Letter on Resurrection," *PAAJR* 21 (1952): 101–19.

11. C. D. Broad, *The Mind and Its Place in Nature* (London, 1925), pp. 511 f. (emphasis supplied). A closer parallel in time would be the Muslim philosopher Averroes, who was very highly regarded by Maimonides although it is doubtful if he was acquainted with his writings at the time that he composed the *Guide.* The theory of the twofold truth—the esoteric for the philosophers, and the exoteric for the masses—attributed to him by the scholastics, exists potentially if not explicitly in his writings. Cf. S. Pines's Introduction to his translation of the *Guide,* pp. cviii ff.; H. A. Wolfson, *Crescas Critique of Aristotle* (Cambridge, Mass., 1929), p. 323; A. Altmann, *Studies in Religious Philosophy* (Ithaca, 1969), p. 109, n. 3.

12. W. K. Clifford, in *Lectures and Essays,* ed. Stephen and Pollock, (London, 1879), vol. 2, p. 161. For contemporary restatements of this view see Bertrand Russell, *Human Society in Ethics and Politics* (New York, 1954), pt. 2, chap. 7; Mentor Books ed., pp. 183 f., and J. Bronowski, *Science and Human Values* (New York: Harper Torchbooks, 1965), pp. 65 f.

13. Karl R. Popper, *The Open Society and Its Enemies,* vol. 1 (Princeton, 1950), p. 100. On the reactionary nature of Plato's doctrines, see also R. H. S. Crossman, *Plato Today,* 2nd ed. rev. (London, 1959).

14. Anent superstition Morris R. Cohen remarks: "Maimonides was not free from superstition. He believed that the stars have souls or angels to guide them and that these influence the course of human events. He also believed in various forms of supernatural divination" (*Reflections of a Wondering Jew* [Boston, 1950], p. 88). But see *contra* Alexander Marx, "The Correspondence between the Rabbis of Southern France and Maimonides about Astrology," *HUCA* 3 (1926): 311–42. Among others, the following modern students of Maimonides' thought have defended the political interpretation of his philosophical system: Jacob Becker, *Maimonides Philosophical Doctrine* (Hebrew) (Tel Aviv, 1955)—written in a somewhat sensational style, but valuable for his references to the medieval commentators on the *Guide*); L. V. Berman, "Ibn Bajjah and Maimonides" (Ph. D. diss., Hebrew University, Jerusalem, 1959); Alvin J. Reines, *Maimonides and Abravanel on Prophecy* (Cincinnati, 1970)—the *Guide* contains two significantly different religious systems: a naive theistic supernaturalism for the uninformed masses, and a sophisticated theistic naturalism, intended for the intellectual elite (p. lvi); Leonard S. Kravitz, "Maimonides on Job: An Inquiry into the Method of the *Moreh*," *HUCA* 38 (1967): 149–58. Kravitz is the most convincing of all these writers; his pregnant thesis is that

Maimonides' treatment of Job and his comforters in the *Guide* provides us with an insight into his philosophical system. In a subsequent article Kravitz elaborates on his earlier study and attempts to unravel the esoteric and exoteric views of Maimonides on providence, prophecy, miracles, and creation. See "The Revealed and the Concealed," *CCAR* 16, no. 4 (October 1969): 2–30, 78.

15. Since it is our aim to confine ourselves as far as possible to purely philosophical considerations, and since the problem of meaning and intention does not arise in the interpretation of Aquinas as it does in the case of Maimonides, we shall have little to say of Aquinas' socio-political theories. But his views, if anything, were even more reactionary than those of Maimonides. E. Crahay, a distinguished Belgian Catholic lawyer, shows ("more in sorrow than in anger"), with ample supporting documentation, in *La Politique de S. Thomas d'Aquin* (published in 1896 by the Pontifical Institut Superieur de Philosophie at Louvain), that, among other things, according to the socio-political doctrine of Aquinas, absolute monarchy is the ideal regime (p. 114); that slavery and serfdom are both economically and morally justified (he condemns the Jews wholesale as slaves of the Christian Church, which has the right of confiscating their goods, *ST.*, 2a, 2ae, q. 10, art. 10; *ibid.*, q. 12 ad. 3; 3a, q. 68, art. 10, ad. 2); that the State and its rulers are and should be in perpetual subordination to the Church and its hierarchy (123); and that we must refuse freedom of conscience and execute heretics (129), because faith is an act of the will, and murderers of the soul are worse than murderers of the body. *"Tantum religio!* To such evils could superstition urge mankind!" Aquinas' views on the "Jewish question" are elaborated in a letter which he wrote to the duchess of Brabant (Belgium), who had consulted him about the morality of confiscating the property of the Jews, which was done everywhere. In his reply St. Thomas says: "It would be licit, according to law, to hold the Jews, because of their crime [deicide], in perpetual slavery, and therefore the princes may regard the possessions of the Jews as belonging to the state; nonetheless, they should use them with a certain moderation and not deprive the Jews of those things necessary to life." And after this sublime concession the Saint continues: "I consider that the punishment must be greater for a Jew and for any usurer than for another culprit, particularly since it is known that the money taken from him does not belong to him. One can also add to the fine another penalty, lest it not appear to suffice for his punishment that he be deprived of the money owed by him to another" ("De Regimine Judaeorum," sec. 2, *Opuscula omnia*, ed. J. Perrier, Paris, vol. 1, pp. 213–14, see also A. P. D'Entreves, *Aquinas, Selected Political Writings* [Oxford, 1959], pp. 84 ff.). How evangelical! It is well to recall that Xavier Vallat, the infamous minister in charge of Jewish affairs under the Vichy regime during World War II, sought supporting authority for his anti-Jewish measures in the teachings of the Common Doctor of the Church, and at his trial after the war stated that he acted "in the light of the teaching of St. Thomas" and on his own Thomist upbringing. (See *La procès de Xavier Vallat* [Paris, 1948], pp. 67–77).

The Austrian Catholic historian Friedrich Heer, in the foreword to his book *God's First Love,* reminds us with brutal frankness that once, in a conversation with Cardinal Faulhaber, Hitler pointed out—apparently without being contradicted—that he was doing only what the church itself had been preaching for centuries and also practicing against the Jews.

16. L. Strauss, "Maimunis Lehre von der Prophetie und ihre Quellen," in *Le Monde Oriental* 28 (1933): 99–139 (reprinted with minor changes in *Philosophie und Gesetz,* pp. 87–122); *idem,* "Quelques remarques sur la science politique de Maimonide et de Farabi," in *REJ* 100 bis (1936): 1–37; *idem, Persecution and the Art of Writing* (New York, 1952), chaps. 1 and 3. Strauss himself has given the best summary of his views in English in the opening pages of his essay "On Abravanel's Philosophical Tendency and Political Teaching," in *Isaac Abravanel,* ed. Trend and Loewe (Cambridge, 1937), pp. 95–102 (pp. 95–129). E. I. J. Rosenthal, "Maimonides' Conception of State and Society," in *Moses Maimonides* (VIII Centenary Volume), ed. I. Epstein (London, 1936), pp. 191–206, worked out a similar thesis independently of Strauss, but the latter shows the deeper and profounder analysis and the finer elaboration. For an assessment of Strauss's work in Jewish philosophy and political science, see Milton Himmelfarb, "On Leo Strauss," *Commentary* 58, no. 2 (August 1974): 60–66, Alexander Altmann in *PAAJR* 41–42 (1975): xxxii–xxxvi, and Ralph Lerner in *American Jewish Yearbook,* vol. 76 (Philadelphia, 1975), pp. 91–97.

17. Compare Maimonides' *Guide,* pt. II, chaps. 38–40, with Plato's *Republic* 374E, 376C, 485A–487A. The immediate source of Maimonides is probably Al-Fārābīs, *Al-Madīnat, al-Fādilah,* ed. F. Dieterici (Leiden, 1895), pp. 46, 55–60.

18. *REJ* 100 (1936): 20, n. 1; *Philosophie und Gesetz,* p. 115, n. 4. Strauss, in the studies cited in n. 16 *supra,* has shown that Maimonides was greatly influenced in his interpretation of Plato by the Arabian Aristotelians, especially al-Fārābī and ibn Sīnā (Avicenna), who adapted Plato's doctrines to their own requirements. See also R. Walzer's study, "Al-Fārābī's Theory of Prophecy and Divination," *Journal of Hellenic Studies* 77 (1957): 142–48, and E. I. J. Rosenthal, *Political Thought in Medieval Islam* (Cambridge University Press, 1958), pp. 128 ff. See, further, M. E. Marmura, "Avicenna's Theory of Prophecy in the Light of Ash'arite Theology," in *The Seed of Wisdom: Essays in Honor of T. J. Meek,* ed. W. S. McCullough (Toronto, 1964), pp. 159–78. The transformation of the philosopher-king into the lawgiver-prophet was possible in medieval Islam and Judaism, because in both of these religious civilizations revelation had the character of divine Law rather than of Faith. (Cf. L. Gardet and M. M. Anawati, *Introduction à la theologie musulmane* [Paris, 1948], pp. 332, 335, 407, and *passim.*) The very phrase in Hebrew for describing apostasy is to speak of one as having "changed his Law," not his faith. Muslim thinkers taught that the caliph, the vicar of the Prophet as a political and religious leader, must conform to the qualifications set for the philosopher-king. See Sir Thomas W. Arnold, *The*

Caliphate (Oxford, 1924), pp. 121 ff. Maimonides similarly conceives of the Messiah as a philosopher-king and minimizes the supernatural elements usually associated with the Messianic Age (*Yad, Melakim,* chaps. 11–12).

19. It is true that the *Politics* was never translated into Arabic, and into Hebrew only in the post-Maimonidean period (Steinschneider, *Heb. Übersetzungen,* pp. 219 ff.), but this may have been the result of a deliberate choice made at the beginning of the medieval period. Cf. R. Walzer's remarks in *Entretiens,* vol. 3, p. 213 (Fondation Hardt, Vandoeuvres-Geneve, 1957). Hermann Cohen, "Charakteristik der Ethik Maimunis," in *Moses ben Maimon, sein Leben, seine Lehre und sein Einfluss* (Leipzig, 1908), vol. 1, pp. 63–134, has already shown that the ethics of Maimonides was Platonic, but he largely touched on peripheral matters. Abraham Heschel has credibly shown that Maimonides viewed himself as a "second Moses" who wrote a code entitled *Deuteronomy* or *Repetition of the Law* (*Mishneh Torah,* after Deut. 17:18, cf. the introduction which Maimonides prefixed to his Code). See A. J. Heschel's monograph, "Did Maimonides Believe That He Had Attained the Prophetic State?" (Hebrew), in *Louis Ginzberg Jubilee Volume* (New York, 1945), Hebrew sec. pp. 159–88; cf. A. S. Halkin, in his (Hebrew) introduction to the *Epistle to Yemen* (New York, 1952), pp. xii f. See also the commentaries of Efodi and Shem-Ṭob to the conclusion of the *Guide.* These commentaries intimate that the contrast drawn at the end of the *Guide* between light and darkness refers to the period after and before the composition of the *Guide,* and that Maimonides considered his work as the fulfillment of Isaiah's prophecies (Isa. 35:5 and 9:1). It is significant that the rabbis of the old school never cite Maimonides' Code under the title *Mishneh Torah,* which the author himself had given it, but in their oral discourses as well as in their novellae (*ḥiddushim*) and responsa invariably refer to it as the RaMBaM (an acronym for R. Moses ben Maimon), although the usual rabbinic custom is to refer to authors by the title of the *magnum opus* which they wrote, e.g., "the Sha'aghath Aryeh tried to reconcile the views of the *Tosefoth Yom Tov* and the *Beth Joseph.*" Maimonides' pretensions may have given rise to the opposition to him in traditional circles during his lifetime and after his death, although it must be conceded that some of the opposition was fanatically motivated. The Cabbalists went so far as to desecrate Maimonides' tombstone and deface it with the following inscription: "Here lies buried Moses the son of Maimon, the excommunicated heretic" (Gedaliah ben Joseph [ibn] Yahya, *Shalsheleth ha-Kabbalah* [The chain of tradition], Amsterdam ed., p. 33b). In his readable study of traditional Judaism, the late Principal of Jews College, Rabbi Isidore Epstein, in the course of an argument appeals to Maimonides "whose Orthodoxy no one at the present day will venture to impugn" (*The Faith of Judaism* [London, 1960], p. 184). Just so! Thus the heterodoxy of one age becomes the orthodoxy of another. It is worthy of note that Maimonides held an extremely low opinion of his contemporaries; he considered them hopelessly corrupt and their culture completely decadent, and he advised his followers to shun all contact with civilization and to live in seclusion in the desert as hermits (*Yad, De'oth* 6:1;

cf. Maimonides' letter to the scholars of Lunel [Southern France], *Kobeṣ Teshubot ha-RaMBaM we-Iggerotaw,* ed. A. L. Lichtenberg [Leipzig, 1859], II, p. 44). (See Appendix A, "RaMBaM or Maimonides.") Curiously enough, according to Karl Popper (*The Open Society and Its Enemies,* vol. 1, chap. 8, sec. 8), we have strong reason to believe that Plato fancied himself to be the divine philosopher-king and that the *Republic* is his own claim for royal power.

3. THE AQUINIAN SYNTHESIS

1. See the qualifications regarding this matter made by E. Gilson in chaps. 3 and 4 of *The Spirit of Medieval Philosophy* (New York, 1936).

2. *Contra Gentiles* iii, 25 (trans. by the Fathers of the English Dominican Province).

3. In the technical scholastic terminology the necessity is *ad melius esse* (not *ad esse simpliciter*).

4. See the detailed exposition of this argument in the *Contra Gentiles,* bk. iii, chaps. 25–37, culminating in the demonstration, "that man's ultimate happiness consists in contemplating God" ("Quod ultima hominis felicitas consistit in contemplatione Dei"). In chaps. 52–53, he demonstrates that this rational vision of God as He truly is can only be attained in the life beyond with the help of supernatural grace. Cf. also *S.T.,* Ia, q. 12, a. 1, and *ibid.,* Ia–IIae q. 3, a. 8, and q. 5, a. 1. A good critical analysis of Aquinas' position may be found in Philip H. Wicksteed, *Reactions Between Dogma and Philosophy,* Hibbert Lectures, Second Series (London, 1920), Lectures 2 and 3, and in H. O. Taylor, *The Medieval Mind,* 5th ed. (1949), vol. 2, chap. 41, especially pp. 466–81.

5. Aquinas, *In Boet. de Trinit.,* q. 1 a. 2 (Eng. trans., *The Trinity and the Unicity of the Intellect,* by R. Brennan [St. Louis, 1946], p. 26); cf. *S.T.,* Ia, q. 12, *ibid.,* q. 83, a. 7; *C.G.* I, 3. For the source of the doctrine cf. Aristotle, *De Anima,* Schütz, *Thomas Lexikon* (2nd ed.; photoreprint, New York, 1957), pp. 451 f., s.v. "intelligere" (a) 16, and Fredrick D. Wilhelmsen, *Man's Knowledge of Reality: An Introduction to Thomistic Epistemology* (Englewood Cliffs, 1956), p. 132. St. Thomas, following Augustine, makes an exception in the cases of Moses and St. Paul, probably out of deference to Scripture, and incautiously admits that they saw God face to face in ecstatic vision in this life when rapt out of their corporeal senses . *S.T.* Ia, q. 12, a. 11, ad. 2; 2a, 2ae, q. 175, a. 3, 4, 5 and 6.

6. Cf. for example, Plotinus, *Enneads,* I, 6, 8–9; V, 5, 12 and VI, 7, 34. On the desire for God and its realization in Plotinus, see the excellent study of René Arnou, *Le désir de Dieu dans la philosophie de Plotin* (Paris, 1921). Plotinus did not believe in that fake mysticism achieved in irrational outbursts of emotion. He puts his insight to metaphysical and rational test and forces it upon us as a logical conclusion. He tells us in a strictly reasoned account of his ontological theory why God *must* be inef-

fable, apart from the fact that he finds him so. Plotinus himself is reported by his disciple Porphyry (*Vita Plotini* 23) to have achieved, on four separate occasions within a six-year period, a mystic self-identification and ecstatic union with "the One." I have been unable to understand or conceive his alternating subsidence into, and numerical identity with, the One and re-emergence from It with *memory* of his lapse. Cf. *Enneads* VI, 9, 10–11; IV, 8, 1.

7. Father A. G. Hebert, the distinguished Anglican theologian, has summarized the point we are trying to make very perceptively: "The idea of God which is built up in the opening Quaestiones of the *Summa,* is mainly taken from Aristotle. The process of salvation is conceived in Aristotelian terms as 'the movement of the rational creature towards God.' The idea of Beatitude is closely related to the Neoplatonic idea of the Vision of the One, and bears little relation to the Beatitudes of the Gospel" (translator's preface to Anders Nygren, *Agape and Eros* [London: 1932], pt. 1, pp. xi f.).

Neo-Thomist scholars who fail or refuse to recognize the composite background of St. Thomas's discussion of the end of man have suffered traumas in trying to explain how there can be a natural desire for the beatific vision which is wholly supernatural. Some of the better contributions on the subject in English are: P. K. Bastable, *Desire for God* (London, 1947); J. Buckley, *Man's Last End* (St. Louis, 1949); W. R. O'Conner, *The Eternal Quest* (New York, 1947, with a thorough bibliography); *idem, The Natural Desire for God,* Aquinas Lecture (Milwaukee, 1949) (for a critical study of the last two works, see Donald A. Gallagher in *Modern Schoolman* 26 [1949]: 159–73); James E. O'Mahony, *The Desire of God* (Dublin, 1929). Most recently M. Gilson has attempted to tackle the problem in his study, "Sur la problematique thomiste de la vision beatifique," in *ADHL* 31 (1964): 67–88. For a Catholic view of the incoherence of the philosophical system of Thomas Aquinas, see Pierre Duhem, *Le Système du monde,* vol. 5, chap. 12, especially pp. 565–70.

4. THE ATTEMPTED HARMONIZATION OF FAITH AND REASON AS ILLUSTRATED BY THE DOCTRINE OF CREATION

1. Arthur Koestler, *The Act of Creation* (New York, 1964).

2. Gilbert Ryle, "The Theory of Meaning," in *British Philosophy in the Mid-Century,* ed. C. A. Mace, 2nd ed. rev. (London, 1966), p. 264 (pp. 239–64).

3. Professor Strawson's division of metaphysics into reversionary and descriptive can be related to C. D. Broad's distinction between critical and speculative philosophy. See his introduction to *Scientific Thought* (London, 1923), and his essay, "Two Lectures on the Nature of Philosophy," originally published in the Norwegian

journal *Inquiry* and reprinted as chap. 2 in *Clarity Is Not Enough,* ed. H. D. Lewis (New York, 1963).

4. I note that G. K. Chesterton, in his study *St. Thomas Aquinas* (New York, 1933), which Professors Gilson and Maritain have both hailed as the best book ever written on Aquinas, speaks throughout of "the system of St. Thomas"; cf. pp. 184, 231, 236, and *passim.*

5. H. A. Wolfson, "St. Augustine and the Pelagian Controversy," in *Religious Philosophy: A Group of Essays* (Cambridge, Mass., 1961), pp. 158–76.

6. On the last topic see the excellent study of James Collins, *Thomistic Philosophy of the Angels* (Washington, 1947). Professor Gilson writes: "St. Thomas's study of the angels is not entirely or specifically a theological inquiry. Angels are creatures whose existence can be demonstrated. In certain exceptional cases they have even been seen. To disregard them destroys the balance of the universe considered as a whole. Finally, the nature and operation of inferior creatures, men, for example, can only be well understood by comparison and contrast with angels" (*The Christian Philosophy of St. Thomas Aquinas* [New York, 1956], p. 160). Against the prevailing attitude of the Doctors of the Church and his own contemporaries, Aquinas maintained that the pleasurable sensation in the male-female sex act felt by unfallen men would have been more intense and greater, not less, than that felt by fallen men (*S.T.* 1a, Q. 98, a. 2, ad 3). According to St. Augustine, before the Fall, Adam had his "membrum virile" directly under the control of his will, as we even now have such volitional control over our arms and legs. As a result of sin, however, this "member" defied the control of the will and begins to rise and fall of its own accord and not, like the other organs, at the dictates of the "owner's" will. But in Eden the unfallen sexual activity of man was different: "Even if there had been no sin in the Garden, there would still have been marriages worthy of that blessed place and . . . lovely babies would have flowered from a love uncankered by lust" (*De Civitate Dei,* bk. XIV, chap. 15, 24, and 26). Sometimes Aquinas' reconstructions are so daring that they seem to undermine his justification of the Church's teachings in other parts of his work. Thus he asserts that the blessed in heaven who have attained their final beatitude exercise freedom of the will yet can never will evil (*beata necessitas non peccandi*). Further beatified angels who possess greater or more perfect freedom than human beings, who are naturally peccable, cannot choose aught but what is truly good (*S.T.* 1a, Q. 62, a. 8, ad 3). It is hard to square these assertions with the contention made elsewhere that moral evil is a necessary concomitant of free will, i.e., that after the Fall all human beings will sin to some extent or other, and that most must ultimately fail. The question suggests itself: Why could not God in His infinite mercy have so ordered our circumstances that we should have an inbuilt desire to achieve the good while retaining our freedom? Why could not things have been so disposed that man would be biased to achieve that Vision which is his supreme good and be ordained to it by grace and that charity by which he becomes, under grace, freely the friend of God? It is difficult to see how it can be an *imposibile per se* for a

human being to be in the natural order who should be free and at the same time in-capable of sinning, if we have such a situation in the case of the blessed in heaven. Surely an omnipotent Being could have created them in that fortunate condition, without the previous existence of evil. Elsewhere (*C.G.* bk. II, chap. 25) Aquinas makes a whole catalog of things which God "cannot" do, as for example, to an-nihilate Himself or commit suicide. In general the concept of "omnipotence" (under-stood in the strict theological sense) is utilized by philosopher-theologians only when it suits their needs. "With God everything is possible, even that He should exist," said Ernest Renan. The following medieval Jewish thinkers among others discuss the question of the "impossible" for God: Saadiah, *Amānāt*, p. 110; Maimonides, *Moreh* III:15; Crescas *Or ha-Shem* V, 2, 3; Albo, *'Ikkarim* 1, 22.

    7. M. Etienne Gilson, *Elements of Christian Philosophy* (New York, 1960), pp. 41, 90 (emphasis supplied); cf. *idem, History of Christian Philosophy in the Middle Ages* (New York, 1955), pp. 365 ff. Elsewhere Gilson refers to Aquinas as a "sleight-of-hand artist" and a veritable "magician" who read undreamt meanings into the words of the Greek philosophers whose ideas he metamorphosed in the light of Christian revelation (E. Gilson, *The Christian Philosophy of St. Thomas Aquinas* [New York, 1956], p. 136). See also the detailed study of the blending of theology and philosophy in two works by Anton C. Pegis: *The Middle Ages and Philosophy,* (Chicago, 1960) and *St. Thomas and Philosophy* (Milwaukee, 1964). The learned author, who was President of the Pontifical Institute of Medieval Studies in Toronto, reaches essentially the same conclusions as Gilson. For a Thomistic critique of the Gilsonian view, particularly in relation to the question of the existence of God, see the monograph by T. C. O'Brien, O.P., *Metaphysics and the Existence of God* (Washington: Thomist Press, 1962). See also George P. Klubertanz, "Metaphysics and Theistic Convictions," in *Teaching Thomism Today,* ed. George McLean (Washington, 1963), pp. 271–306, and Germain Grisez, "Etienne Gilson: Elements of Christian Philosophy," *Thomist* 23 (1960): 448–76.

    8. See the comments found in the dated, but still useful, volume edited by J. S. Zybura, *Present-day Thinkers and the New Scholasticism* (St. Louis, 1927). Cf. also James Collins, "For Self-Examination of Neo-Scholastics," *Modern Schoolman* 21 (1944): 225–34.

    9. John Locke, *An Essay Concerning Human Understanding,* bk. IV, chap. xviii, sec. 2.

    10. See *S.T.,* Ia, q. 44, a. 2. W. D. Ross has noted that "Aristotle has no theory either of divine creation or of divine providence." *Aristotle,* 2nd ed. (London, 1930), p. 184.

    11. Julius Guttmann, *Philosophies of Judaism* (New York, 1964), p. 182; cf. p. 153.

    12. F. C. Copleston, *A History of Philosophy,* vol. 2, *Medieval Philosophy,* pt. 1 (New York: Image Books, 1962), p. 19. An excellent exposition of Aquinas' doctrine

of creation is to be found in the same author's *Aquinas* (London: Penguin Books, 1955), pp. 136 ff., of which use is made in the following discussion.

13. Aristotle lays greater stress on the correlative argument proving the nonincipiency of motion, but the argument from the nature of time is less bound up with an outdated system of physics.

14. Gersonides (d. 1344) does use empirical arguments in support of creation, but he postulates an unorthodox dualistic belief in a preexistent matter upon which God exercised his creative act (*Milḥamot* VI, 1, chaps. 1–16); cf. Seymour Feldman, "Gersonides' Proofs for the Creation of the Universe," *PAAJR* 35 (1967): 113–39. For Albalag's heterodox views, see G. Vajda, *Isaac Albalag* (Paris, 1960), pp. 130–67.

15. *Guide* I:73, 10th proposition, end (ed. Munk, pp. 115b–116a), Friedlander's trans. For quotations from the *Guide* in English, we use the new translation of Pines when a literal translation is called for; otherwise we avail ourselves of Friedlander's more literary rendition.

16. This is not to say that linguistic analysis has eliminated all appeals to imagination and conceivability. Its exponents speak of analytic propositions as "self-evident" or "self-explanatory" or "intuitively true," and even Hume's famous attempt to explain away causality (*Treatise,* bk. I, pt. III, sec. iii) relies heavily on psychological criteria.

17. *Guide* II:17 (ed. Munk, p. 35b), Friedlander trans. Query whether the view here expressed by Maimonides is consistent with the position taken in his polemic against the Mutakallimun, where he maintains that "the universe must be examined as it is and premises must be derived from what is perceived of its nature" (I:71, p. 98b). Julius Guttmann, unmindful of Occam's law of parsimony, distinguishes three states: that which preceded the creation of the world, that of creation, and that in which the world has been since its creation. The laws valid in the world since the conclusion of the creative process have no validity either for the stage before its creation or for the process of creation itself. (Maimonides, *Guide,* abridged edition, with an introduction and commentary by Julius Guttmann [London, East and West Library: 1952], p. 215, n. 44).

18. Guide II:21-22; cf. H. A. Wolfson, "The Platonic, Aristotelian and Stoic Theories of Creation in Hallevi and Maimonides," in *Essays Presented to the Very Rev. Dr. J. H. Hertz,* ed. I. Epstein *et al:* (London; 1942), p. 428 (pp. 427–42; reprinted in H. A. Wolfson, *Studies in the History of Philosophy and Religion* [Cambridge, Mass. 1973], p. 235 [pp. 234–49]). This misinterpretation was taken over from the Arabic Aristotelians, among others al-Fārābī and Ibn Sīnā.

19. The celebrated reply of Pierre-Simon Laplace to Napoleon Bonaparte's query about the absence of God the Creator from the astronomical theory of his *Mecanique celeste* is well known; Laplace said, "Sire, I had no need for that hypothesis." What is not so well known is the wry comment of the great mathemati-

cian Joseph Louis Lagrange upon being told of this reply. "Ah!" he exclaimed, "but the theistic hypothesis is a fine hypothesis: it explains so many things." See E. T. Bell, *Men of Mathematics* (New York, 1937), p. 181.

A very charitable interpreter might argue that Maimonides' comparison of the "coming-into-being" of the universe with the biological processes of growth and development shows an adumbration of, or groping toward, the notion of creative or emergent evolution, although, of course, he did not use these terms.

20. We have limited ourselves to giving a brief summary of Maimonides' views on creation. In the *Guide* (pt. II, chaps. 13–25), Maimonides expatiates freely on this subject and presents his views with such a smug, self-complacent vanity that one feels he was of the opinion that had he been present at the creation he might have offered some valuable advice. The whole rigmarole of Maimonides' argument, as well as that of Aquinas, can be conveniently followed in A. Rohner O.P., *Das Schöpfungsproblem bei Moses Maimonides, Albertus Magnus u. Thomas von Aquin* (Münster i. W., 1913) (*Beiträge zur Geschichte der Philosophie des Mittelalters*, XI, pt. 5).

Maimonides admits that the creation of the world *ex nihilo* cannot be demonstrated and is known only by revelation, but he does differentiate between the Platonic and Aristotelian theories of the eternal existence of the world. In a valuable essay in German, Rabbi Isidore Epstein argues plausibly that while Maimonides would not countenance any departure from the doctrine of *creatio ex nihilo,* in favor of a notion of a preexistent matter that would imply the existence of some other eternal and uncreated being, in independence of God, he would not rule out altogether the idea of the eternity of matter as long as its existence is attributed to the free activity of the Divine will. See I. Epstein, "Das Problem des goettlichen Willens in der Schöpfung nach Maimonides, Gersonides and Crescas," *MGWJ* 75 (1931): 335–48, and for an English restatement of his views see his *The Faith of Judaism* (London, 1954), pp. 169–93.

21. *Guide* (ed. East and West Library), Introduction, p. 15.

22. The immutability or unchangeableness of God is insisted upon in such scriptural passages as Mal. 3:6, Num. 23:19, and I Sam. 15:29. The principle of divine immutability was supported by the Greek philosophers with rational arguments. At the end of the second book of the *Republic* (381B), Plato argued that since a perfect being is a supremely excellent being, any change in such a being would constitute corruption, deterioration, and loss of perfection. According to Aristotle, God or the gods (it makes no difference which is used) are conceived as perfect beings whose capacities for development are fully realized. Now if God were subject to change, he would in that respect and to that extent be a being with an unrealized capacity for development, a being merely potential and not fully actualized, and hence not perfect (*Metaphysics* XII, chap. 9, 1074b 26).

23. My remarks must not be construed as implying that mechanical (causal) and teleological explanations are mutually exclusive alternatives.

24. Hippocrates, in W. H. Jones's edition in the Loeb Classical Library, vol. 2, pp. 132–183, especially pp. 138 ff. Cf. also Husik's penetrating criticism on pages 274–76 of his *History of Mediaeval Jewish Philosophy* (New York, 1916), which cannot be quoted in full for lack of space (to quote less would be to mutilate). (See Appendix B, "The Historians of Medieval Jewish Thought.")

25. The parable of the boy on the island may have been suggested to Maimonides by Ibn Ṭufayl's philosophical romance, called after its hero, *Ḥayy ibn Yaqẓān*. It is the story of a sort of metaphysical Robinson Crusoe, who grows up alone on a desert island and comes to develop out of his own head the essentials of Aristotelian philosophy and Islamic religion. But the use to which the parable is put is original with Maimonides.

In our day, an Israeli rabbinic authority has embellished Maimonides' illustration with pulpit rhetoric to make it support the belief in immortality; see Y. M. Tucatzinsky, *Bridge of Life* (Hebrew) (Jerusalem, 1960), pt. 3, pp. 5 ff.; cf. also I. Jakobovits, *Journal of a Rabbi* (New York, 1966), pp. 293 ff. Some medieval Jewish thinkers to the contrary notwithstanding (e.g., Judah Halevi, *Kuzari* I, 95, 103; II, 12 ff.; Abravanel, *'Atereth Zeḳenim,* chap. 13; Naḥmanides, *Commentary* on Deut. 18:15; Albo, *'Iḳḳarim* III, 11), revelation is not an arbitrary, local, limited, and mechanical process of communicating divine truth to Israel; the white spotlight of divine inspiration does not seem to shine exclusively on the Holy Land. The prophetic cry is still true: "The Lord is great far beyond the borders of Israel!" (Mal. 1:5). The Eternal in His omnibenevolence vouchsafed this same "proof" several decades earlier to the liberal Protestant modernist preacher, the late Rev. Dr. Harry Emerson Fosdick. See his *As I See Religion* (New York, 1932), pp. 58 ff., which in turn shows the influence of the first chapter of pt. 1 of Joseph Butler's *Analogy of Religion* (1736).

26. That Maimonides' thesis is sophistical and piously insincere did not escape the notice of the medieval commentators of the *Guide.* When, in chap. 27 of the second part of the *Guide,* Maimonides asserts that the world, though created, is indestructible, Moses Narboni (ed. J. Goldenthal, p. 37) sardonically remarks that the Master has met Aristotle halfway, apparently being of the opinion that philosophical questions, like litigations in court, can be settled by a compromise (cf. Joseph ibn Kaspi, *Maskiyyot Kesef,* ed. Werbluner, pp. 99–101, and Pines, *op. cit.,* pp. cxxvii ff.). There is a Mephistophelian irony in the fact that the modern conception of natural law is much more akin to the view of the Mutakallimūn than to that of Maimonides, who views the laws of nature as behests or decrees of the divine will. If we take the view of the Mutakallimūn and leave out Allah, we have the modern conception, which views natural laws as purely descriptive, or as statistical averages. Maimonides' assertion that the views of the Mutakallimūn undermine science is therefore a gratuitous libel and, as the scholastic saying goes, *quod gratis asseritur gratis negatur.*

27. A. E. Taylor, "The Vindication of Religion," chap. 2 in *Essays Catholic and*

Critical, ed. E. G. Selwyn, 3rd ed. (New York, 1950), pp. 53 f., 37 (pp. 29–81).

28. *Contemporary British Philosophy,* ed. J. H. Muirhead, vol. 2 (London, 1925), p. 298.

29. Jakob Guttmann, *Das Verhaeltnis des Thomas von Aquino zum Judenthum und juedischen Literatur* (Goettingen, 1891), pp. 58–72; E. S. Koplowitz, *Über die Abhängigkeit Thomas von Aquinos vom Boethius und R. Mose b. Maimon* (Kallmuenz, 1935), pp. 71–81.

30. See Averroes, *Tahafut al-Tahafut,* ed. Maurice Bouyges, S.J. (Beirut, 1930), p. 162.

31. Cf. Fr. Rohner, *op. cit.,* especially pp. 136 f., and the very important study of M. Fakhry, "The Antinomy of the Eternity of the World in Averroes, Maimonides and Aquinas," in *Le Museon* (1953), pp. 139–55. That the above does indeed represent the true thought of Aquinas is shown by the chapter sequence in the *Summa Contra Gentiles.* Bk. II, chap. 16, endeavors to demonstrate that God has brought things into being out of nothing. The question whether the created world has *always* existed is discussed separately in chaps. 31–37, and the conclusion reached in chap. 37, which contains an excellent summary of Aquinas' views, is simply that "there is nothing to forbid the assumption made by the Catholic Faith that the world has not always existed." Finally, in chap. 38, the arguments produced by "some" (notably his contemporary, St. Bonaventure) to *prove* that the world must have had a beginning are reviewed and rejected.

32. For Aquinas on creation see: *S.T.,* Ia, q. 46, a. 1; *C.G.* II, 31–38; *Qu. disp. De Pot.* q. 3, a. 17; *In Lib. II Sent.,* d. 1, q. 1, a.5 *De Aeternitate Mundi, Concerning the Eternity of the World: Against the Murmurers* (the "murmurers" against whom this tract is directed were those of his contemporaries who did not have the foresight to realize that Aquinas was destined to become the Common Doctor of the Church— which was to adopt his doctrine as her own—and had the temerity to accuse him openly of heresy). For a detailed study of this subject, see Th. Esser, *Die Lehre des heil. Thomas von Aquin über die Moeglichkeit einer Anfangslosen Schöpfung* (Münster i. W., 1895), and the work cited in n. 20 *supra.* Crescas, *Or ha-Shem,* III, 1, 5, follows the views of Aquinas on creation; cf. Guttmann, *Philosophies of Judaism,* p. 438, n. 267, and the literature there cited.

33. Cf. J. S. Mill, *System of Logic,* bk. III, chap. XIV, 4; M. R. Cohen, *Reason and Nature* (New York, 1931), pp. 158 f. This point is well argued by P. H. Nowell-Smith, "Miracles—The Philosophical Approach," *Hibbert Journal* 48 (July 1950): 354–60; reprinted in *New Essays in Philosophical Theology,* ed. A. Flew and A. MacIntyre (London, 1955), pp. 243–53.

34. Modern science and technology have ruled out explanations in terms of free will by an intelligent agent to account for natural phenomena, not because such explanations can be logically refuted—they cannot—but because they have been found to be unfruitful. That an explanation in terms of free will can never be logically eliminated can be shown very simply. Let us suppose a religion in every way identical

with Roman Catholicism but having one additional dogma, namely, that on the eve of the New Year the Pope must celebrate a High Mass in St. Peter's with the proper intention *ex opere operantis* (as distinguished from *ex opere operato*— by the work itself) on which the welfare of society in the coming year, and specifically rainfall or drought, depend. Now the most diehard logical positivist could not possibly deny that this is a meaningful dogma (we know perfectly well how it could be tested and falsified in principle—the celebration of the Mass with the proper intention and drought). But in fact it cannot be falsified, because whatever happens in a particular year is consistent with the dogma: if there is rainfall it was caused by the celebration of the Mass, and if there is drought it was caused by the lack of proper intention. The shift away from explanation in terms of the free will of an agent is related to the transition from a mythological view of natural events to a more scientific attitude, which no longer seeks to know *who* caused certain things, but *what* natural processes brought them about.

35. A. E. Taylor, "The Vindication of Religion," in *Essays Catholic and Critical,* ed. E. G. Selwyn, 3rd ed. (New York, 1950), p. 50. Cf. E. Gilson, *God and Philosophy* (New Haven, 1959), p. 140. The eminent contemporary Thomist scholar, Professor R. Garrigou-Lagrange, O.P., after a careful examination of St. Thomas' "Five ways," similarly concludes: "All these arguments can be summed up in a more general one, based on the principle of causality, which may be stated as follows: That which does not exist by itself can exist only by another, which is self-existent. Now there are beings which do not exist of and by themselves. Therefore, etc." (R. Garrigou-Lagrange, *God: His Essence and His Existence,* appendix to the first volume of the English trans., 1934, p. 381).

36. Eric L. Mascall, *He Who Is* (New York, 1948), p. 44.

37. It has been pointed out to me that Aquinas' strictly theological arguments may not be intended to offer either a scientific or a metaphysical explanation of the world. They do not intend to prove anything; they are rather arguments from convenience (see above, p. 2) to support the mind in accepting a revelation which transcends its powers according to the familiar principle derived from St. Anselm, "fides quaerens intellectum" (*Proslogion,* proem). That may indeed be the case, but if we accept this interpretation, the arguments properly belong to the field of devotional literature. When faith is appealed to, rational argument is out of place.

38. The objection may be raised that in the claim that God is a "Necessary Being," the necessity may not arbitrarily be identified with logical necessity. St. Thomas, it is said, is using the older Aristotelian conception of factual necessity, meaning as applied to beings, that they are not generable or corruptible, or, more technically, that they cannot come into existence via conglomeration, construction, or (re)formation, or pass out of existence via deterioration, destruction, or deformation (see *De Caelo,* bk. I, chaps. 10–12; *Met.,* bk. V, chap. 5, bk. VI, chaps. 1–4, bk. XII, chaps. 1–10). On this view a necessary being is a simple spiritual essence of pure form with no matter, hence incapable of substantial change, i.e., of being other than

it is. It applies to angels and pure spirits, which are all creatures—freely created by and dependent on God—as well as to God. A possible or contingent being, in contrast, is one that can be or not be, i.e., be or not be other than it is; in other words, a being composed of matter and form in its essence which is capable of substantial change, of becoming another essential being than it is now. The proponents of this interpretation of "necessary being" back it by two important considerations. (1) For Aquinas God is not the only necessary being. In a number of passages he concedes the existence of a plurality of created necessary beings, and the notion of an *efficient cause* for what is *logically* necessary seems to make no clear sense. (2) Secondly, in *S.T.*, 1a, Q. 2, art. 3, in the Third Way for Demonstrating the Existence of God, viz., from possible and necessary being, Aquinas argues, fallaciously, that if each thing at some time or other does not exist, then at some time or other, everything does not exist. (Modern logicians label this as the "Quantifier-Shift Fallacy." To see what is essentially wrong with the argument, compare the parallel argument that since all roads lead somewhere, therefore there must be a single place [say, Rome] to which all roads lead. Possible things might have staggered terms of being in such a manner that at no time there was nothing in existence.) But, continues Aquinas, if this were true, nothing would exist now, because what does not exist does not begin to exist except through something that does exist. He concludes, therefore, that not everything has the possibility of being or not being, but "there has to be something necessary in things" (*oportet aliquid esse necessarium in rebus*). But he does not go on to say "and this everyone calls 'God'"; instead he divides such necessary being(s) into two kinds: those (a) who receive their necessity from another (necessary *ab aliter,* i.e., created angels, human souls, and the Aristotelian heavenly bodies), which finally leads us back to (b) a necessary being Who is His own existence. And it is this being alone, he says, which everyone calls "God." But the notion of a *logically* necessary being that has its necessity "caused by another" sounds absurd. Hence, it is argued that for Thomas, the notion of necessary being cannot be an all-or-nothing logical concept, but is a factual notion, capable of degrees and qualifications. The unique quality of God is not necessary being, which He shares with all spiritual beings, but that He possesses His being from Himself and is, as it were, underivatively necessary and unconditioned. This characteristic of God is termed aseity, or being *a se,* i.e., ontologically independent existence (in contradistinction to the created universe and everything, in it which exists *ab alio*). On this interpretation a necessary being is one without a built-in tendency to corruption, while the Necessary Being *per se* (God) is the uncreated incorruptible Being. To summarize in a nutshell: necessary = incorruptible; contingent = corruptible. For this interpretation of necessary being see: Thomas B. Wright, "Necessary and Contingent Being in St. Thomas," *New Scholasticism* 15 (1951): 429–66; Patterson Brown, "St. Thomas' Doctrine of Necessary Being," *Philosophical Review* 73 (1964): 76–90; John Hick, "Necessary Being," *Scottish Journal of Theology* 14 (1961): 353–69; Cornelio Fabro, "Intorno alla

Nozione 'Tomista' di Contigenza," *Rivista di Filosofia Neoscolastica* 30 (1938): 132–49.

We may readily grant that this interpretation has considerable exegetical advantages, but it is far from certain whether it can successfully resolve all our difficulties. In some places, at least, St. Thomas seems to use "necessary being" to mean logically necessary being. In the first Article of the second Question of the First Part of the *Summa Theologiae,* Aquinas inquires whether the existence of God is self-evident. In his reply he points out that some propositions are self-evident in themselves (*propositio per se nota*), though not self-evident to us (*quoad nos*). A proposition is self-evident in itself, Aquinas says, when the predicate follows analytically from the subject because it is included in the essence of the subject (*quia predicatum includitur in ratione subjecti*). This characterization shows that Aquinas takes these propositions to be necessarily true (cf. Kant's analytic judgments). Since he further maintains that the proposition "God exists" is self-evident in itself (but not to us), it is equally clear that he takes the proposition to be logically necessary; hence it appears likely that in the *tertia via,* when he sets out to demonstrate the existence of a necessary being "that all men speak of as God," he may be trying to prove a logically necessary being, a being whose existence is logically involved in the very conception and definition of His nature. Furthermore, as Brown intimates at the conclusion of his article, there are some severe difficulties in the Aristotelian notion of factual necessity in the context of Aquinas' theology. A causally necessary being would presumably be one whose existence is made absolutely necessary by causal laws, or the laws of nature. What this glossing of necessary might mean in the case of God is far from clear, however, since according to Aquinas God freely sets up and maintains the present system of natural laws and causal relations. God instituted these laws in the plenitude of His grace when He freely created the world; but God did not, in instituting these laws, bring Himself or His necessity into existence. Thus even if the textual critics are correct, it is difficult not to identify Aquinas' necessary being with a logically necessary being. Again, according to Aquinas (*S.T.* la, q. 104, a. 4 c) prime matter is a necessary existent and is incorruptible, but is rather the substantial substrate of bodies in which generation and corruption occur. To be sure, Aquinas elsewhere explains that matter is "concreated," i.e., as material beings are created, composed of matter and form. But why this modification and complication of Aristotle, for whom matter as well as the universe is eternal? "Why," asks Cleanthes, in Hume's *Dialogues Concerning Natural Religion,* part IX, "why may not the material universe be the necessarily existent being? . . . We dare not affirm that we know all the qualities of matter; and for aught we can determine, it may contain some qualities which, were they known, would make its non-existence appear as great a contradiction as that twice two is five" (ed. N. K. Smith, p. 190). Just so! If it is proper for the Thomist to maintain, as he must, that since God's essence is His existence, the ontological proof *must* be valid even though it cannot be comprehended by us here on earth as it will be by the blessed *in patria*, then it is equally proper for the materialist to argue that scientists confidently expect to have proof, probably within the next generation, of the necessary existence of matter.

We must consider one other interpretation of necessary being. Fr. Copleston argues that "metaphysical analysis" can show that the proposition "If there is a contingent being, then there must be a necessary being" is a necessary proposition. Aquinas, according to this interpretation, was not seeking to express a relation of logical implication, but of existential dependence on an absolutely necessary being. Aquinas was not confusing causal relations in general with logical entailments: he was asserting a unique relation between finite things and the transfinite transcendent cause on which they depend" (*Aquinas* [London, 1955], p. 115). This is the notion of "creation," the bestowal of existence on contingent beings by God, who did not have to bring them into existence but who did so freely. This, perhaps, is the least objectionable explanation of necessary being and related ideas, but I cannot say that it is a great improvement on the words of Genesis, "In the beginning God created the heavens and the earth." How the nonexistent is made to exist we are not told. The ultimate mystery of the origination of the world cannot be fathomed by us. Man never creates from nothing. He builds a house from bricks, that is all. There is a superficial analogy here, insofar as the house exists where there was none before. But to build a house in this way is not to bring it into existence; the stone, the bricks, and the other building materials already exist. If a man were to create a house, in the sense of "create" which distinguishes it from building, he would have to bring the materials themselves into existence. The production of something out of something else is almost as far from creation as is being from nonbeing. But that is all we have to go on; since creation expresses a *unique* relation, it cannot be given a generic, but only an analogical, description. The *modus operandi* of divine creativity is wholly unimaginable and inconceivable. Man only produces, he does not create, and absolute creation is beyond his ken, outside of his experience. "We reach a point in our analysis of creation where we are forced to admit that a full understanding of God's creative activity exceeds the competence of the human reason. And if we are left with mystery, this is nothing to be surprised at in such a connexion. After all, experience only supplies us with analogies of creative activity in the proper sense. It is not the business of the Christian thinker to eliminate all mystery but rather to point out where the mystery lies" (*ibid.*, pp. 140 f.).

So this is the end of wisdom: *omnia exeunt in mysterium* ("all things pass into mystery"). Now it may very well be that no philosophy can resolve the ultimate mystery of existence. But surely the intellectual appeal of Thomism must be based on the claim that it does, and rival philosophies do not, give an intellectually satisfactory explanation of this mystery. And, as Dr. Broad once remarked in reviewing Professor Tennant's *Philosophical Theology*, if an explanation involves the admittedly unintelligible notion of creation, it is an unintelligible hypothesis supported by a limping analogy which dissolves away when exposed to critical reflection. And what

is more, the introduction of a Creator simply substitutes two mysteries for one, viz.,
the mystery of the Creator's own origin and of the way He creates matter by an
avowedly incomprehensible and supernatural act, for the mystery of the origin of
matter.

39. Martin Heidegger, *An Introduction to Metaphysics,* trans. Manheim (New
Haven, 1959), pp. 6–7.

40. Ernest Nagel, *Sovereign Reason* (Glencoe, Ill., 1954), p. 30. Cf. George Santayana, *Scepticism and Animal Faith* (New York, 1928), p. 284: "Fact can never be
explained, since only another fact could explain it: therefore the existence of a universe rather than no universe, or of one sort of universe rather than another, must be
accepted without demur." See also Terence Penelhum, *Religion and Rationality*
(New York, 1971), p. 44.

41. Nor can I agree that Thomas gave philosophy its formal charter of independence from theology. Let us assume that St. Thomas is right in saying that
Aristotle's argument for the eternity of the world is inconclusive and fallacious. Let
us next suppose that another philosopher or scientist comes along and maintains
that he has discovered a more cogent proof for the eternity of the world. Now since
truth is one and God is truth, the Thomist would have to maintain on *theological
grounds* that the argument of this philosopher is fallacious, or if formally correct,
that it must contain a verifiably false proposition, even before he examines it. But if
so, the validity of a purely philosophical argument is judged by a nonphilosophical
element, and philosophy is consequently in perpetual subordination to theology.

Nowadays the common Thomistic teaching, which seems entirely faithful to the
thought of Aquinas himself, is that revelation regulates philosophy not directly, as a
positive norm, but indirectly, as a negative norm. Thus if something has been
definitely proved by human reason, it is impossible for that thing to be false. But
since God is the creator of all truth (including what can be known by natural human
reason) and cannot contradict Himself, it is impossible that anything could have
been truly proved by reason which contradicts a truth divinely revealed. M. Gilson,
following Aquinas, says that "to any sincere believer who is at the same time a true
philosopher, the slightest opposition between his faith and his reason is a sure sign
that something is wrong with his philosophy. For indeed faith is not a principle of
philosophical knowledge, but it is a safe guide to rational truth and an infallible
warning against philosophical error" (*Reason and Revelation in the Middle Ages*
[New York, 1938], p. 83). Speaking of a thinker in the Thomist tradition, Professor
Gilson remarks elsewhere: "the faith is always there and any conflict between his
faith and his philosophy is a sure sign of philosophic error" (*The Spirit of Medieval
Philosophy* [New York, 1936], p. 6). But this right of veto accorded theology, whereby any conclusion resulting from philosophical speculation which is not in harmony
with faith might be condemned, constitutes a permanent shackle upon the reason.
"From the nature of the case," a critic has well said, "it must be impossible for a
thinker who knows beforehand the prescribed conclusions at which he must arrive,

or with which the results of his own deliberations must at least be capable of being harmonized, not to be continually influenced throughout the development of his thought by the desire to conform to the dictates of an external authority, in spite of the fact that his duty as a philosopher is 'to follow the argument wherever it may lead'" (R. L. Patterson, *The Conception of God in the Philosophy of Aquinas* [London, 1933], p. 371).

42. R. Garrigou-Lagrange, O.P., *God: His Existence and Nature,* Eng. trans. (St. Louis, 1936), vol. 2, p. 101; *idem, The One God,* Eng. trans. (St. Louis, 1943), p. 517. Cf. also J. Maritain, *The Degrees of Knowledge,* trans. Gerald B. Phelan (New York, 1959), p. 234; Joseph Owens, *An Elementary Christian Metaphysics* (Milwaukee, 1963), p. 99.

43. Arthur O. Lovejoy, *The Great Chain of Being* (Harvard University Press, 1936), p. 157. Professor Lovejoy has at great length very ably defended his thesis that Aquinas did not reconcile Aristotle's theism with the theism of Christianity but merely incorporated both into his system, which suffers from incoherences and contradictions. See his discussions with two established Thomists, Professor Henry B. Veatch and President Anton C. Pegis of the Pontifical Institute of Mediaeval Studies, in a series of nine articles in *Philosophy and Phenomenological Research,* vols. 7 (1947) and 9 (1949). A. N. Whitehead has observed that "it may doubted whether any general metaphysics can ever, without the illicit introduction of other considerations, get much further than Aristotle," who did not get "very far towards the production of a God available for religious purposes" (*Science and the Modern World* [Mentor ed., 1948], pp. 173 f.). See also A. E. Taylor, *Aristotle* (New York: Dover, 1955), p. 60. For Maimonides see Jacob Becker, *Maimonides' Philosophical Doctrine* (Hebrew) (Tel-Aviv, 1955), p. 49. Becker contends that Maimonides was an out-and-out Aristotelian and that his professed opposition to Aristotle is merely tongue-in-cheek (*ibid.,* pp. 19 f.). Becker finds support for his views in Kaspi, Efodi, Narboni, and Palquera among the classical commentators on the *Guide.* For the difference between the God of Abraham and the god of Aristotle, see Judah Halevi, *Kuzari* IV, 16 ff. Pascal wrote in the "memorial" of his conversion, which he kept like a talisman in the lining of his coat until his death: "God of Abraham, God of Isaac, God of Jacob, not of the philosophers and scholars" (quoted by Morris Bishop, *Pascal: The Life of Genius* [New York, 1936], p. 172). Contrast the glib assertion of Guttmann above, p. 24.

44. Modern scholars have traced back the image of dwarfs sitting on the shoulder of giants to John of Salisbury, who attributes it to Bernard of Chartres (died ca. 1126) in his *Metal.* bk. III, chap. 4 (in Migne, *P.L.*, vol. 199, p. 900; ed. C. C. J. Webb, p. 136; the passage has been translated into English by Daniel D. McGarry, *The Metalogicon of John of Salisbury* [Berkeley, 1955], p. 167). See F. E. Guyer, "The Dwarf on the Giant's Shoulders," *Modern Language Notes* 45 (June 1930): 398–402; R. Klibansky, "Standing on the Shoulders of Giants," *Isis* 26, no. 71 (December 1936): 147–49; Gilson, *History of Christian Philosophy,* p. 619, n. 71.

The various formulations of the aphorism are entertainingly traced in R. K. Merton's *On the Shoulders of Giants* (New York, 1965).

This parable was popular among Jewish writers, and particularly among rabbinic decisors, who availed themselves of it to justify their disagreement with older authorities. Examples of the aphorism in Hebrew literature are collected by Dov Zlotnik in *PAAJR* 40 (1972): 163–67; this list is supplemented in *Hadoar* 53 (1974): 425 and 299, but still further instances of the image could be cited, cf., e.g., R. Jacob of Lissa, *Sefer Hawwot Da'at*, Introduction.

45. Exodus 22:27 (as interpreted by the LXX, taking the Hebrew *Elohim* in the profane plural sense): Philo, *Vita Mos.* ii. 205, *De spec. leg.* i. 53; Josephus, *Ap.* ii, 237, *Ant.* iv, 207. Cf. Azariah de'Rossi, *Me'or 'Enayim,* "Imre Binah" chap. 5 (ed. D. Cassel, p. 96). K. Kohler has credibly shown that this teaching is not merely apologetically motivated but reflects the true viewpoint of the old Halakah, "The Halakic Portions in Josephus' *Antiquities,*" in *Studies, Addresses, and Personal Papers* (New York, 1931), pp. 79 f.; *contra* G. Allon, *Tarbiz* 6 (1934–35): 30, n. 1. In this connection it may be pointed out that the oldest reference to Jesus outside of the New Testament is found in the description of Josephus, who speaks rather sympathetically about him. I am not referring to the so-called Testimony of Josephus in the *Antiquities* (xviii, 63–64), which is quoted by Eusebius (*Eccl. Hist.*, i, 11), who may have had a hand in forging the passage. That text is generally rejected as an interpolation because it is "too Christian"—there is a hint that Jesus was divine: he is said to have taught the truth, to have wrought miracles, and to have risen from the dead; and the messianic prophecies are expressly referred to him. To imagine Josephus, the Jew and Pharisee turned pagan, writing such things is preposterous. Recently, however, Shlomo Pines, professor of philosophy at the Hebrew University in Jerusalem and translator of Maimonides' *Guide* into English, has called attention to a long-overlooked Arabic version of the same text, which he feels is far closer to what Josephus may have written than the spurious text handed down through the centuries. It is found in a church history first published in 1912 (*Patr. Orient.,* vol. 7, p. 471) and written by Agapius, an obscure bishop of the Eastern Church who flourished in the tenth century. In a monograph published in 1971 by the Israeli Academy of Sciences and Humanities (*An Arabic Version of the Testimonium Flavianum* he gives a translation of the Arabic text (p. 16):

At this time there was a wise man who was called Jesus. And his conduct was good and (he) was known to be virtuous. And many people from among the Jews and from the other nations became his disciples. Pilate condemned him to be crucified and to die.

And those who had become his disciples did not abandon his discipleship. They reported that he had appeared to them three days after his crucifixion and that he was alive. Accordingly he was perhaps the Messiah of whom the prophets have recounted wonders.

Professor Pines notes that a version of Josephus preserved only in an Arabic text is more likely to have escaped Church censorship than the traditional vernacular (Greek) text, and he believes that this more restrained fragment may well be authentic. Saadiah, the first major Jewish philosopher, while rejecting the Christian doctrines of the Trinity and the Incarnation in no uncertain terms (*Amānāt,* ed. Landauer, pp. 86 ff.), yet conducts his controversy on a high plane and in an urbane manner (cf. H. A. Wolfson, "Saadia on the Trinity and Incarnation," in the *A. A. Neuman Festschrift* [Philadelphia, 1962], pp. 547–68), while the famous moralist Baḥya ibn Pakudah, in his *Duties of the Hearts* (*Hidāyah,* ed. A. S. Yahuda, p. 330, 11 ff.), quotes with approval from the Sermon on the Mount (Matt. 5:33, 34, 37) and refers to Jesus as "one of the upright ones" (*ba'ḍu al-afāḍil;* ibn Tibbon, *eḥad min ha-Ḥasidim*). See Emanuel Baumgarten in his introduction (p. xii) to S. G. Stern's edition (Vienna, 1854) of ibn Tibbon's translation of the *Ḥoboth ha-Lebaboth,* and Yahuda, Introduction, pp. 78 f. Speaking of the relation of Judaism to the two great world religions which emanated from it, Judah Halevi suggested the very helpful figure of the seed. The two daughter religions are the tree which grows from the seed of Judaism and overshadows the earth; but the fruit of the tree must contain the seed again, which, though unnoticed is its most valuable part, guaranteeing the perpetuation of the plant. In some such sense, Christianity and Islam exist to spread the knowledge of the biblical God throughout the nations, thereby preparing them for Judaism in the Messianic era (*Kuzari* IV:23). (See the use made of this parable by Franz Rosenzweig in *The Star of Redemption* [*Der Stern Der Erloesung,* first published in 1921], III, pt. ii *ad fin.;* see, also, *Judaism Despite Christianity,* ed. E. Rosenstock-Huessy [University of Alabama Press, 1969], pp. 56 and 112. For reasons readily apparent, the Church Fathers viewed the facts somewhat differently and suggested different metaphors. Augustine developed the theory of the Jews as a witness-people who serve as the "slave-librarian" of the Church. "The Jewish nation," he wrote [*Epist.* cxxxvii, iv, 16; *P.L.* 33:523], "itself rejected because of unbelief, being now rooted out from its own land, is dispersed to every region of the world, in order that it may carry elsewhere the Holy Scriptures, and that in this way our adversaries themselves may bring before mankind the testimony furnished by the prophecies concerning Christ and his Church, thus precluding the possibility of the supposition that these predictions were forged by us to suit the time; in which prophecies also the unbelief of those very Jews is foretold.") The attitude of Maimonides toward Christianity and Islam was more narrow-minded and bigoted; while admitting that "they help bring all mankind to perfection" (*Yad, Melakim* 11:4), he nevertheless considers the Christians to be idolaters (*Yad, 'Akum* 9:4) and refers to Mohammed as "the Madman" (*Epistle to Yemen,* ed. Halkin, p. 14, l. 5 and *passim;* see the editor's discussion in his (Hebrew) introduction, pp. xiii–xxi (especially p. xiv). Nowhere does Maimonides, however, use such scurrilous invective about Mohammed as the founder of Christianity saw fit to use in his denunciation of the Scribes and Pharisees in the twenty-third chapter of the Gospel according to St. Matthew and elsewhere. Moreover, "madman" and similar epithets were customary in Judeo-Arabic literature for the Arabian Prophet, and Maimonides was perhaps merely using terms understandable to his prospective readers, and not expressing his own feelings (see Steinschneider, *Polemische Literatur* [Leipzig, 1877], pp. 202–3). But Maimonides is one of the few rabbinic casuists, decisors, and codifiers who maintain that the Deuteronomic law (23:21) regarding the taking of interest from non-Jews is not merely permissive or directory, but mandatory, and he includes it among the 613 commandments (*Yad, Malwe we-Lowe,* 5:1; *Sefēr ha-Miṣwoth,* affirmative precept #198, see the commentaries *ad loc.*).

46. *'Iḳḳarim,* ed. and trans. Husik, vol. 3, pp. 232 f. I have supplemented Albo's polemic with the trenchant criticism of Philip H. Wicksteed, who makes essentially the same point as Albo but shows a far greater familiarity with Thomist texts. Cf. *The Reactions Between Dogma and Philosophy,* Hibbert Lectures, Second Series (London, 1920), pp. 276–78 and 358–60. In all fairness, it should be pointed out that for all his shortcomings, Albo had a much clearer understanding of Catholic dogma than many modern philosophers who should have known better. One example will suffice. Bertrand Russell says that "the Roman Catholic Church holds that a priest can turn a piece of bread into the Body and Blood of Christ by talking Latin to it" (*Education and the Modern World* [New York, 1932], pp. 67 f.).

47. *De Rationibus Fidei,* i. quoted in *St. Thomas Aquinas Theological Texts,* ed. Thomas Gilby, (New York, 1955), p. 371, no. 620. Cf. *S.T.* 3a, q. 75, a. 4, corp. and ad. 3 (see the commentary of Cardinal Cajetan *in loc. cit.*). Aquinas attempts to get over the other difficulty raised in the quotation from Albo, viz., how one body can be at two different places at the same moment, by saying that the Messiah's body is present within the small consecrated wafer called the Host, not as in place but in the manner of substance (*per modum substantiae*); it is numerically the same body which, without division or distance, is simultaneously in heaven and in the sacrament of the Eucharist, because it is present in the Eucharist illocally (*nullo modo corpus Christi est in hoc sacramento localiter*), in a certain special way which is peculiar to this sacrament. The body of the Messiah is in the sacrament "spiritually" and "invisibly" in an order superior to the order of space. *Ibid.,* q. 76, a. 1, 2, 3, 5; *Sent.* IV. xliv. 2 (2, 5 ad 1); *Quaest. Quodlib.* I, xxii. ad 1. A body may, according to this view, exist in a manner inconceivable to us, and may dispense with the modes under which our senses apprehend and observe it.

Transubstantiation may serve as a paradigm case of the medieval method of argument. The framework of thought has been fixed by the Bible and the Church Fathers. Whatever may appear to be false, either by appearance (as in the wafer) or by rational argument (as in creation), is rendered true by an outside body of information—Church doctrine in transubstantiation, and the Bible in the case of creation. In "Tantum Ergo," a Eucharistic hymn attributed to St. Thomas, the matter is put thus: "Praestat fides supplementum sensuum defectui!" ("Let faith supplement the deficiency of the senses"). Thomas Hobbes was more caustic: "The Egyptian conjurers, that are said to have turned their rods to serpents, and the water into blood, are thought but to have deluded the senses of the spectators by a false show of things; yet they are esteemed enchanters. But what would we have thought of them, if there had appeared in their rods nothing like a serpent, and in the water enchanted nothing like blood, nor like anything else but water; but that they had faced down the king that they were serpents that looked like rods, and that it was blood that seemed water. That was both enchantment, and lying. And yet in this daily act of the priest, they do the very same, by turning the holy words into the manner of a charm, which produces nothing new to the sense; but they face us down, that it has turned the bread into a man; nay more, into a God; and require men to worship it, as if it were our Savior himself present God and man, and thereby commit most gross idolatry. For if it be enough to excuse it of idolatry, to say it is no more bread, but God; why should not the same excuse serve the Egyptians, in case they had the faces to say, the leeks and onions, they worshipped, were not very leeks and onions, but a divinity under their species, or likeness" (*Leviathan,* pt. IV, chap. 44).

48. *Qu. disp. De Anima,* art. 9, ad 17m (Eng. trans. J. P. Rowan [St. Louis, 1949], p. 123); cf. *S.T.* 1a, q. 90, art. 2.

49. "Esse accidentis est inesse et dependere, et compositionem facere cum subjecto per consequens"—*In lib. I Sent.,* d. 8, q. 4, a. 3 sol. Again, Aquinas says expressly; "the dimensive quantity is an accident"—*S.T.* 3a, q. 77, art. 2, obj. 1 (although the passage actually quoted occurs in an objection, Aquinas' reply implicitly accepts its truth).

50. *C.G.* iv, chap. 65; cf. *S.T.* 3a, q. 77, a. 1, 2, 3.

51. "But for myself," says Cardinal Newman of the doctrine of transubstantiation, "I cannot indeed prove it, I cannot tell *how* it is; but I say, 'Why should it not be? What's to hinder it? What do I know of substance or matter? Just as much as the greatest philosophers, and that is nothing at all' . . . The Catholic doctrine leaves phenomena alone. It does not say that the phenomena go; on the contrary, it says that they remain: nor does it say that the same phenomena are in several places at once. It deals with what no one on earth knows anything about, the material substances themselves" (*Apologia* [Modern Library ed., 1950], p. 238). Newman had learned well the lesson which Hobbes taught. "It is with the mysteries of our religion," says Hobbes in *Leviathan,* chap. 32, "as with wholesome pills for the sick, which swallowed whole have the virtue to cure, but chewed are for the most part cast up again without effect." The point is precisely that Aquinas has relied too much on Aristotelian principles and categories to abandon them at this late stage in the argument. By appealing to the omnipotence of God, transubstantiation can be squared with *any* philosophical theory. This is evident from Descartes' reply to Arnauld in the fourth set of *Objections,* where the difficulty is raised that if, as Descartes held, extension is identical to corporeal substance, and if qualities are subjective, it follows that there are no real accidents which can remain after the conversion of the substance. To this Descartes replies: "There is nothing incomprehensible or difficult in

the idea of God, the creator of all things, being able to change one substance into another, and the second substance remaining comprised within the same superficies as that which bounded the former" (*Works,* trans. Haldane and Ross, vol. 2, p. 121). Apparently the Holy Office was not convinced by this reasoning, and Descartes' works remained on the Index of Forbidden Books until after the Second Vatican Council, when the Index was quietly abolished. See also Leibniz's correspondence with the Jesuit theologian Fr. des Bosses, where he demonstrates that his theory of monads could be reconciled with the doctrine of transubstantiation, *Letters to des Bosses,* in L. E. Loemker's *G.W. Leibniz: Philosophical Papers and Letters,* 2nd ed. (Dordrecht, 1969), pp. 596–617.

52. Maimonides' solution of the problem of creation versus eternity of the world is similarly at odds with the Aristotelian principles which he professes to accept. Since according to Aristotle matter is pure potentiality and in itself has no existence, the "prime matter" in Maimonides' system is left in the awkward position of a sort of created nothing, the actuality of pure potency, which is an impossible concept, however one considers it.

5. DEVICES TO BYPASS THE CONFLICT OF SCIENCE AND RELIGION

1. *Guide,* Introduction, p. 10b, Pines trans.

2. Leo Strauss, *Persecution and the Art of Writing* (Glencoe, 1952), chap. 3, pp. 38–94 (reprinted from *Essays on Maimonides,* ed. Salo W. Baron [New York, 1941], pp. 37–91). On the methodology of Maimonides' calculated obscurity by means of (1) contradiction, (2) the misplaced word, and (3) scattering, see also Alvin J. Reines, "Maimonides' Concept of Mosaic Prophecy," *HUCA* 40–41 (1969–70): 325 f. Above all, Maimonides' own directions for the study of his treatise, found at the conclusion of his introduction to the *Guide,* should be carefully studied.

3. Strauss, *Persecution,* p. 74.

4. Cf. Salo W. Baron, *Social and Religious History of the Jews,* vol. 8, p. 314, n. 28.

5. Abraham Nuriel, "The Question of a Created or Primordial World in Maimonides," *Tarbiz* 33 (1963–64): 372–87. Nuriel intends to utilize his method to investigate the exoteric-esoteric views of Maimonides on a variety of philosophical topics.

6. A distinguished contemporary existentialist philosopher characterizes the scholastic method employed by Aquinas as follows: "The method degenerates into a making of countless distinctions leading to endless discussions. Simple facts are befogged, one carefully reasoned claim is set over against another, and both are annulled in favor of whatever vindication or charges happen to be required. The

method further involves distraction by pretended philological thoroughness that drowns you in quotations" (Karl Jaspers, *Der philosophische Glaube angesichts der Offenbarung* [Munich, 1962], p. 85).

7. These propositions, it may be noted, are not accepted in a tentative spirit as principles of a speculative philosophical system, but are treated by Maimonides and his defenders as firmly established and beyond questioning. When the philosopher Ḥasdai Crescas raised some difficulties about one of these propositions, he was curtly rebuffed with the insulting reprimand that "no doubt and objection can be raised except by a perverse fool incapable of understanding" (Shem-Ṭob, Commentary on *Guide* II, Introduction, Prop. 1, end). Professor H. A. Wolfson observes that the implication of the remark is quite clear: "Crescas is a 'perverse fool' and is lacking in good sense and understanding" (*Crescas' Critique of Aristotle* [Cambridge, Mass., 1929], p. 33, where a misprint occurs in the Hebrew text of the quotation).

8. But in Aristotle (*Metaphysics* XII, 8) the argument leads to fifty-five unmoved movers of co-equal divinity and exactly alike in all respects! The notion of a plurality of unmoved movers was not unknown in the Middle Ages and should at least have put Maimonides on his guard against identifying an impassive Prime Mover with the God of Genesis. See the cryptic remark of Ibn Ezra on Eccles. 5:7 and Husik in *Philosophical Essays*, pp. 148 f.; cf. also Aquinas, *S.T.* Ia, q. 32, art. 1, c. and *Sent.* I xxi. 2, 1. W. Jaeger (*Aristotle*, chap. 14) has suggested that starting out as a monotheist, Aristotle came to see that a single source of movement was not sufficient to explain the running of the universe, and frankly adopted, in writings now lost, a polytheistic hypothesis in the interests of natural science.

9. Because of considerations similar to those so cavalierly disposed of by Maimonides, William of Ockham was to deny the demonstrability of God's existence. Cf. *Quodlibet,* VII, 17–23.

10. *Moreh ha-Moreh* (ed. Pressburg, 1837), p. 43; cf. Munk, *Guide,* vol. 1, p. 29, n. 1 and p. 350, n. 1. One does not wish to cavil, but in passing it may be pointed out that Palquera himself commits a logical blunder here. If the premises of a valid argument are false, it does not follow that the conclusion will *necessarily* be false; it may be true. See also the delightful little essay of Husik, "A Question of Logic in Maimonides," in *Philosophical Essays,* ed. Milton C. Nahm and Leo Strauss (Oxford, 1952), pp. 136–40. On the other hand, I. Joel's treatment of Maimonides' logical method (*Religions-philosophie des Moses ben Maimon* [Breslau, 1876], pp. 15 f.) lacks philosophical subtlety and penetration. Munk (p. 350) points out a further difficulty, namely, that according to Maimonides those who believe in the dogma of creation *ex nihilo* can never demonstrate the unity and incorporeality of God. Maimonides offers three further proofs for the existence, unity, and incorporeality of God, all based on principles taken from the *Physics* (VIII, 6) and the *Metaphysics* (XII, 6–8) of Aristotle and his Arabian commentators. These proofs likewise proceed from the assumption of the eternity of the world. The first proof we have discussed in the text. In the third proof the assumption of eternity is necessary for the

argument, which proceeds from the assumption that as far as individuals are concerned, what is possible may or may not be realized, but what is possible with regard to a species whose duration is *eternal* must necessarily come to pass, otherwise the word "possibility" is vain. This idea ultimately goes back to Aristotle, who taught that in things eternal there is no distinction between possibility and actuality. *Physics* III, 4, 203b 30: "In the case of eternal things, what may be must be." (Cf. Maimonides' own explanation in his letter to his translator Samuel ibn Tibbon in *Tarbiz* 10 [1939]: 326 f.) Proof number four is only a variation of the first proof, substituting the more general transition from potency to act for the more restricted transition from rest to movement, as Shem-Ṭob observes in his commentary *ad loc.* The second proof does not, indeed, absolutely require this premise, but the argument is more forceful if it is assumed. From the fact that there are things which are moved but do not move, and things which both move and are moved, it may be inferred that in an *infinite* time span there must be something which moves but is not moved.

11. This truth was not unknown to the medieval thinkers, and the principle is clearly enunciated in a commentary on Aristotle's *Prior Analytics* ascribed to Duns Scotus. See J. Łukasiewicz, "Zur Geschichte des Aussagenkalkuls," *Erkentniss* 5 (1935): 124 (pp. 111–31); reprinted in English under the title "On the History of the Logic of Propositions," in Jan Łukasiewicz, *Selected Works,* ed. L. Borkowski (Amsterdam, 1970), pp. 213 ff. (197–217).

The story is told that the great Cambridge mathematician G. H. Hardy once remarked at a meeting of a professional society that if 2 plus 2 equals 5, then any other statement can be proved. To the challenge of an objector, "Prove that I am the Pope," Hardy replied, "By subtraction of 3 we get 1 equals 2, and therefore you and the Pope, two, are identically you, one."

12. *Guide* I:71, pp. 96b–97a, ed. Munk; Pines trans. In the *Contra Gentiles,* which, of all his works, most nearly resembles a purely philosophical treatise, Aquinas in his proofs of the existence of God swallows Maimonides' grotesque methodology hook, line, and sinker. In bk. I, chap. 13, he raises the objection that his proofs "presuppose the eternity of motion, which Catholics consider to be false." To this he replies: "The most efficacious way to prove that God exists is on the supposition that the world is eternal. Granted this supposition, that God exists is less manifest. For, if the world and motion have a first beginning, some cause must clearly be posited to account for this origin of the world and of motion. That which comes to be anew must take its origin from some innovating cause; since nothing brings itself from potency to act, or from non-being to being" (*On the Truth of the Catholic Faith,* trans. A. Pegis [New York, 1955], pp. 94 f.). Long ago it was said, "if one blind man leads another, they will both fall into a ditch." It seems applicable here.

The claim has been made by some Thomists that all of Aquinas' proofs in the *Summa Theologiae,* which reflects his later, and perhaps more mature, views, abstract from the question of temporal creation. This is not so; the assumption of the eternity of the world is necessary for at least the first three of the *quinque viae.* I am glad to be able to claim for this view the support of such an outstanding Thomist as Professor Gilson, who states my case very forcefully. "St. Thomas' third proof for the existence of God is related to the first in that it assumes, in an even more obvious way, the thesis of the eternity of the world. . . . No doubt, and we have already noted this insofar as St. Thomas is concerned, they [the Jewish philosopher and the Christian philosopher] do not really accept the eternity of the world. But as Maimonides says, they wish 'to confirm the existence of God, in which we believe, by a method of demonstration that is incontestable so as not to found this true and important doctrine upon a basis that anyone can shake and which many can even consider as null and void.' Maimonides and St. Thomas are in complete agreement on this point" (E. Gilson, *The Christian Philosophy of St. Thomas Aquinas* [New York, 1956], p. 70).

13. That is to say, Maimonides is not arguing in the form "p and − p, therefore God exists," which is fallacious, but in the form "p implies God exists, and −p implies God exists, therefore God exists," which is a valid form of inference.

14. Cf. Leo Strauss, in his introductory essay to S. Pines's translation of the *Guide of the Perplexed* (Chicago, 1963), pp. lii ff.

15. *Mekilta,* Tractate Baḥodesh, #5, ed. Lauterbach, vol. 2, p. 231 (abridged), and see Rashi on Exod. 20:2.

16. The expression that I have translated "which confuse opinions" is rendered by Wolfson "which sets minds awondering" (H. A. Wolfson, *The Philosophy of the Kalam* [Cambridge, Mass., 1976], pp. 108 f. and n. 79). The phrase at any rate shows clearly that the Rabad is far from advocating such views himself, and Wolfson has conclusively shown (pp. 109–11) that none of the authoritative spokesmen of Judaism championed a belief in the corporeality of God.

17. *'Or ha-Ḥayyim,* end of chap. 5, quoted by I. Barzilay, *Between Reason and Faith* (The Hague, 1967), p. 139. Compare also the poignant story involving the Cabbalist R. Isaac Luria related by Louis Jacobs. In the days of Luria there was a simple-minded man who read in the Bible that in Temple times the Israelites brought twelve loaves of bread corresponding to the twelve tribes and placed them on a table before the Lord as showbread. In his innocence the unlearned man believed that God somehow ate the bread, and wanting to do a good deed, he instructed his wife to bake twelve loaves every Friday which he then carefully placed before the Holy Ark. Each week the synagogue sexton would take the loaves home, thus confirming the naive old man in his superstition that God had accepted his offering. When this came to the attention of the town rabbi, he reprimanded the man for his credulity and for his primitive conception of God. Deprived of his way of serving God, the man's world collapsed around him. Master Isaac Luria, when he found out about this, cursed the town rabbi for depriving the man of his simple faith. See Louis Jacobs, *Faith,* p. 190, who retells the story from Aaron Arele Roth, *Shomer Emunim* (Jerusalem, 1942/3), pp. 95b–97a.

18. Philip H. Wicksteed, *Reactions Between Dogma and Philosophy,* Hibbert Lectures, Second Series (London, 1920), pp. 274–76 (emphasis supplied). In unguarded moments the Saint is apt to forget these fine distinctions expressed in precise philosophical terminology and almost lapses into tritheistic formulas. *In Joan.,* cap. X, lect. 4, n. 2: "Sed cum in Christo sint tres substantiae, scilicet substantia Verbi, animae, et corporis . . ." (*Opera Omnia,* ed. Frette, Paris, Vivès, vol. 20, p. 136, col. 2). A placard held by a group of devout Catholics at a parade in Milan, Italy, some years ago, read: "God bless the Holy Trinity."

19. The passage "For a God of knowledge is the Lord" (I Sam. 2:3) is interpreted by the rabbis by the remark, "Great is knowledge, since it leads from God to God" (Berakoth 33a, and parallels). In the *Shema',* the Jewish confession of faith, the individual is bidden to love God with all his heart (i.e., intellectual faculties), his soul (i.e., the emotions), and might (i.e., physical capabilities and material resources), the mind being accorded pride of place (Deut. 6:5).

20. Maimonides makes use of the Aristotelian distinction between privation and negation (see, *inter alia, Metaph.* iv, chap. 2, 1004a, 14–16, and Alexander of Aphrodisias, *Metaphysica,* ed. Mich. Hayduck, p. 327, 11. 18–20, commenting on *Metaph.* iv, chap. 6, 1011b, 15 ff.). Privation refers to the absence of a quality or property where it has been or might be expected to be present (e.g., John is blind), negation is used to remove something from a universe of discourse (e.g., the wall is not seeing). Thus, for example, God is "powerful" means God is "not weak." The negation implies that the term in question ("weak") is inapplicable to God; it also means that the affirmative term ("powerful") is equally inapplicable, and that it can be used only in an equivocal sense. It follows that the only true attributes of God are the negative ones because if one says, God is not this, not that, not the other things, He is only denying of Him what He is not, and in negation no plurality is involved no matter how many the negations are.

21. Furthermore, if the human intellect is essentially deficient, then how can we trust our mind when it draws the grand conclusion that the world was made by an omnibenevolent Creator? As the Latin Averroist John of Jandun noted, creation *ex nihilo* is an occurrence which has not been observed. Therefore it cannot be justified by arguments drawn from sensible experience. The universe may have been uncaused and its origination spontaneous. After all, "creation very seldom happens; there has been only one, and that was a very long time ago" (translation primarily adopted from Gilson, *History of Christian Philosophy* [New York, 1955], p. 524). In Catholic teaching, of course, this debilitation of the natural capabilities of the human mind is one of the consequences of Original Sin. Nevertheless in most modern philosophies human intelligence is much more limited in metaphysical capacity than it is in Thomism. Many modern thinkers would question Thomism's naive confidence in reason, especially in its assumption of self-evident principles (e.g., an action cannot contain a greater perfection or a higher order of reality than is possessed by the being

which is the cause of the action). Again, all the proofs for the existence of God make use of the principle of causality, which is extended from the phenomenal sphere to the universe as a whole.

22. In the original Arabic version of the *Guide,* Maimonides employed two terms to designate the divine "will," (1) *irāda* and (2) *mashī'ya.* The translators and commentators on the *Guide,* both medieval and modern, have not differentiated between these terms. Recently however a young Israeli scholar, in an extremely suggestive treatment of this subject, has shown that this usage is intentional and that Maimonides attached a different meaning to each of the above expressions. Maimonides employed *mashī'ya* when he referred to Divine Wisdom, while *irāda* is used in reference to the necessity of Nature. See Abraham Nuriel, "The Divine Will in *More Nevukhim,*" *Tarbiz* 39 (1969–70): 39–61.

23. Cf. *S.T.* 1a, q. 13, art. 5 c; *C.G.* I, 33; *Qu. disp. De Pot.* q. 7, art. 7 c.

24. See Zevi Diesendruck, "Samuel and Moses ibn Tibbon on Maimonides' Theory of Providence," *HUCA* 11 (1936): 341–66.

25. *Ibid.,* p. 345. With all their shortcomings, the medieval commentators on the *Guide* had a far better conception of the task of an expositor and a greater mastery of the "secret" doctrine contained in that enchanted book sealed with seven seals, than their modern counterparts. The superficial and shallow nature of Guttmann's analysis is evident in his cavalier treatment of this topic. He says: "Our explanation of Maimonides' doctrine of providence follows that given by most modern scholars, who rely on chapter 17 of the third section, where the problem of providence is systematically set forth. But Samuel ibn Tibbon, translator of the *Guide,* had already noted in his letter to Maimonides that in chapter III, 23 and in chapter III, 51 there are locutions which yield an exactly contrary theory to that indicated in chapter 17. . . . It is clear that these contradictions were not unintended. Maimonides did not propose a full-scale exposition of his final thoughts on this matter, and therefore—in agreement with the position he adopted at the end of the introduction to the *Guide*— he allowed opinions which were contradictory to each other to stand in various places in the book, thereby arousing the informed reader to discover his true doctrine. The medieval commentators, however, when it came to a discussion of this problem of his esoteric doctrine, were of various opinions concerning its seriousness and application, and so long as there is no convincing and probative hypothesis otherwise, we have no course but to uphold the statements of chapter 17" (Guttmann, *Philosophies of Judaism,* p. 433, n. 99). Incidentally, Guttmann to the contrary notwithstanding, there is a large element of agreement among the early commentators on the *Guide* (Palquera, Kaspi, Narboni, Efodi, and Shem-Ṭob) as to the true nature of its teachings; the differences are largely those of formulation and emphasis.

26. Vajda, *Introduction,* p. 135. See also S. Pines, s.v. "Jewish Philosophy," in *Encyclopedia of Philosophy,* ed. Paul Edwards (New York, 1967), vol. 4, p. 268; *idem,* s.v. "Maimonides," *ibid.,* vol. 5, pp. 129–34 (especially p. 130). For a modern criticism of Maimonides' doctrine of attributes, see Charles Hartshorne and William

L. Reese, *Philosophers Speak of God* (University of Chicago Press, 1953), pp. 116–19; cf. Professor Marvin Fox's remarks on pp. xxviii–xxxiii of his prolegomenon to Abraham Cohen's *The Teachings of Maimonides* (New York, 1968). The same difficulties vitiate Aquinas' attempt to combine the negative theology (*via negationis* or *remotionis*) with the *via eminentiae,* the principle that every "perfection," i.e., every valuable quality which we find in created beings, exists "in a more eminent manner" in God. But this is formally inconsistent with the "way of remotion," since according to this principle, many analogical terms have some positive elements of meaning predicable alike of creatures and of the Creator.

27. A. Altmann in *Tarbiz* 27 (1958): 301–9.

28. It should be noted that Friedlander, in his English rendition of the *Guide,* translates freely "prudence," following in this al-Ḥarizi, who in his Hebrew version toned down the original; the newer translation by S. Pines is more accurate: "divine ruse" or "wily graciousness." The translation "God's deceit" is taken from Simon Rawidowicz, who discusses the concept in the framework of Maimonides' philosophy. See his "Knowledge of God: A Study in Maimonides' Philosophy of Religion," in *Jewish Studies in Honor of the Chief Rabbi, J. L. Landau* (Tel-Aviv, 1936), pp. 93–96 (pp. 78–121), reprinted in *Studies in Jewish Thought* (Philadelphia, 1974), pp. 269–304 (see especially sec. 5); *idem,* "Man and God: Discussions of Maimonides' Theology" (Hebrew), *Moznaim* 3 (1935): 504–6 (493–526). See also J. Becker, *Maimonides' Philosophical Doctrine* (Hebrew) (Tel-Aviv, 1955), pp. 34–47, especially pp. 39 ff. It is probable that this chapter led to a strong opposition to the *Guide.* We have been credibly informed by a contemporary, R. Joseph ben Todros Halevi, a participant in the Maimunist controversy, that Maimonides himself felt that he had overshot his mark and wanted to withdraw the third part of the *Guide.* "Many years ago we were told that our Master, its author, wished to supress the third part of it [the *Guide*], which teaches the motives for the precepts and laws, but was unable to do so since it had already spread to the distant isles—because he thought that he had gone too far in basing himself on tenuous conjectures [lit. 'hanging mountains on a hair' (cf. Hag. 1:8)]"—Kobak, *Ginze Nistarot,* vol. 3 (1872), p. 164. See further Abravanel, *Naḥalat Abot* (New York, 1953), commentary on Abot 3:22, p. 209.

29. Cf. Prov. 25:2, "It is the glory of God to conceal a thing," or as Moffatt renders the passage, "Mystery is God's glory."

30. In his *Varieties of Religious Experience* (p. 37), William James quotes Ernest Renan (*Feuilles détachées,* p. 397) as having ascribed the following statement to St. Augustine: "Lord, if we are deceived, it is by Thee" ("Domine si error est a te decepti sumus"). I have been unable to authenticate this in any of the usual concordances, nor were any readers of the "Queries and Answers" column of the *New York Times Book Review* (September 19, 1965, p. 63) able to help me track down this passage. Fr. Robert P. Russell, O.S.A., of the Augustinian Collegiate Seminary in Villanova, Pennsylvania, who has a very complete card index to Augustinian texts, has since informed me (personal communication dated March 24, 1966) that he believes the

"quote" from Augustine is spurious. See the writer's brief notice in *Notes and Queries,* October 1977, p. 459.

As far as the idea òf ascribing deceit to God is concerned, it may be remarked that although it seems offensive to modern sensibilities, it is by no means foreign to the religious genius. In certain passages in the Bible we find the idea expressed that God is the source of delusion as well as of truth, and that He has recourse to deceit for the purpose of carrying out His plans. Thus God commissioned an evil and "lying spirit" to lure Ahab to his defeat in Ramoth-gilead by deceiving his prophets (I Kings 22:20 ff.); and the priest-prophet Ezekiel expressly proclaims God as threatening to use deception as a means of taking revenge upon idolaters. "If the prophet be deceived and speak a word, I, the Lord, have deceived that prophet, and I will stretch out my hand against him, and I will destroy him from the midst of my people Israel" (Ezek. 14:9). Again, Jeremiah cried out in his anguish: "O Lord, thou hast deceived me, and I was deceived" (Jer. 20:7). For some similar passages see Exod. 7:3; Deut. 2:30; Judg. 9:23; I Sam. 18:10, 19:9, 26:19; I Kings 18:37; Amos 3:6; Isa. 6:10, 19:14, 37:7, 45:7, 63:17; Mic. 1:12; Jer. 4:10, 15:18, 18:11; Job 23:13. For the idea in St. Paul see II Thess. 2:7–12. Paul writes of certain persons who "received not the love of the truth" that "for this cause God shall send them strong delusion, that they should believe a lie." Such difficult texts induced Abraham ibn Dā'ūd to compose his treatise *The Sublime Faith* (*Emūnāh Rāmāh*), as he himself states in the preface to that work. In Chronicles, a late book in the Jewish Bible, certain evil actions which in the earlier Book of Kings are ascribed to God are laid at the hands of Satan. Compare, for example, II Samuel 24:1 with I Chronicles 21:1 regarding the source of the inspiration for King David to commit the sin of taking the census. With this may be compared the vacillation of Descartes, who in the first three essays of his *Meditations on the First Philosophy* shifts back and forth uneasily from a "deceiving God" to a "malignant demon."

According to some versions of the "Ransom Theory" of the Atonement, which was held by Origen, Augustine, Gregory the Great, and most of the Western Fathers, God deceived the devil, by offering him the Redeemer's soul in exchange for the souls of men, although he knew full well that the devil could not possibly keep hold of the Redeemer's sinless soul, which could only cause him torture. On this theory of the Atonement, in which Satan the deceiver is himself deceived, one authority in the place of many may be adduced. St. Gregory of Nyssa boldly says (*Oratio Catechetica,* chap. 26, in Migne, *P.G.,* vol. 45, col. 68): "He who is at once the Just and Good and Wise One used, for the salvation of that which was destroyed, the device of deceit [*tē epinoiā tēs apatēs echrēsato*]."

31. Cf. the trenchant critical comment (*hassagah*) of Rabad of Posquieres on *Yad, Teshubah* 3:7, where Maimonides declares that whosoever conceives God to be a corporeal being is an apostate: "Why does he call such persons apostates? Men better and worthier than he have held this view, for which they believe they have found authority in the Scriptures and in a confusing view of the Haggadah."

32. *Several Letters Written by a Noble Lord* (*Shaftesbury*) *to a Young Man at the University* (London, 1716), p. 30. Cf. A. N. Whitehead, *Religion in the Making* (New York, 1926), p. 15: "Religion is force of belief cleansing the inward parts. For this reason the primary religious virtue is sincerity, a penetrating sincerity." The ideal relation between reverence and truth has been beautifully expressed by George Santayana: "The feeling of reverence should itself be treated with reverence, although not at a sacrifice of truth, with which alone, in the end, reverence is compatible" (*Reason in Religion*[New York, 1905], p. 13).

33. *Guide* III:32 (paraphrased and abridged).

34. Louis Ginzberg, *Students, Scholars and Saints* (Philadelphia, 1928), pp. 205 f.; cf. Judah Halevi, *Kuzari* I:98 and III:23. An incisive criticism of Maimonides' philosophy from an ethical viewpoint was made by Samuel D. Luzzatto in *Kerem Hemed*, III (1838), 67–70 (reprinted in S. D. Luzzatto, *Mehkere ha-Yahaduth* [Studies in Judaism], pt. II [Warsaw, 1913], pp. 167 ff.), who follows in the footsteps of Crescas, *Or ha-Shem* III:24. Luzzatto points out that man's ultimate perfection, according to Maimonides, does not consist of moral qualities or ethical living but in becoming rational *in actu,* that is, in an intellectual knowledge of reality. The non-intellectual, be he ever so virtuous, is excluded from the future existence, which is limited to the thinkers whose acquired intellect (in the philosophical jargon of the Aristotelians) becomes part of the divine active intellect and thus attains perfection and permanence (*Guide* III:27, 51). To be sure, Maimonides insists that until man has attained moral perfection he cannot reach the degree of intellectual perfection needed for the union with the active intellect of which alone immortality consists. But the fact remains that morality as such for Maimonides is only a transitional stage. Salvation or immortality is not an ethical but a purely intellectual state; possession of knowledge makes a man independent of all morality. Furthermore, Maimonides expressly places intellectual perception above moral feelings (*ibid.* I:2). Therefore, it is by no means a travesty of Maimonides' teaching, as Ahad ha-'Am thought ("The Supremacy of Reason," in *Essays, Letters and Memoirs,* trans. Leon Simon [Oxford: East and West Library, 1946], pp. 174 f. [pp. 138–82]), but a necessary corollary of that teaching, to say that the philosopher, *once he has acquired metaphysical knowledge,* may unblushingly commit theft, murder, adultery, and other heinous crimes with perfect impunity and yet win eternal life, since in Maimonides' aristocratic heaven salvation does not depend on merit. To be sure, Julius Guttmann has argued that in his exposition of Jer. 9:22–23 in the concluding chapter of the *Guide,* Maimonides taught that to know God is to imitate Him and to serve Him in the practice of "loving-kindness, justice and righteousness" (J. Guttmann, *Religion and Knowledge* [Jerusalem, 1955], pp. 86 f.). But Guttmann's successor in the chair of Jewish philosophy at the Hebrew University in Jerusalem has rejected this quasi-Kantian interpretation of Maimonides, which would make moral virtues and moral actions of greater importance and value than the intellectual virtues and the theoretical way of life, as completely false (Translator's Introduction to

Guide, p. cxxii). By analyzing the text and collating it with other passages in the *Guide,* a young Israeli scholar has shown that the attributes of action which man is urged to imitate are in no way to be construed as moral attributes. Rather, the prophet in his role as statesman should imitate God both in the bestowal of benefits and in the infliction of suffering for the preservation of the body politic. (See Eliezer Goldman, "The Worship Peculiar to Those Who Have Apprehended True Reality" [Hebrew], *Annual of Bar-Ilan Studies in Judaica and the Humanities* 6 [1968]: 287–313, especially pp. 303 ff.) Maimonides here sets himself in conscious opposition to the entire talmudic-rabbinic literature, which contains not a single instance of the sterner biblical attributes of God being set up as a model for man to copy. Cf. Israel Abrahams, *Studies in Pharisaism and the Gospels,* 2nd Series (Cambridge, 1924), p. 152. Similarly, Maimonides' naturalistic interpretation of Providence had a negative effect on morality, for God's loving care of man is determined by, and in proportion to, his intellectual rather than ethical attainments (*ibid.* III:17–18). This view was especially harsh on the fairer sex, which was considered inferior by Maimonides and incapable of intellectual and spiritual achievements. Mme. C. Sirat, in her recent work on medieval Jewish thought, observes that according to Maimonides, women as a class are included among the reprobate since they are earth-bound and "material," and therefore outside the pale of Providence and beatitude. See Colette Sirat, *Jewish Philosophical Thought in the Middle Ages* (Hebrew) (Jerusalem, 1975), p. 226 n. Julius Guttmann's view (*Philosophies of Judaism,* pp. 178 f.) that Maimonides formulated his Thirteen Principles of Faith out of solicitude for the masses, that they too may attain immortality in the form of union with the "active intellect" by acquiring a minimum of metaphysical truths, is rightfully dismissed by S. M. Urbach (*The Philosophical Teachings of Rabbi Hasdai Crescas* [Hebrew] [Jerusalem, 1961], p. 26, n. 29) with a thoroughgoing reprimand as "philosophical homiletics." David Hartman adds that Guttmann's understanding of Maimonides' reason for formulating the Thirteen Principles of Faith "would make immortality of the soul the function of a mechanical act" (*Maimonides, Torah and Philosophic Quest* [Philadelphia, 1976], p. 229, n. 31).

   It may be noted that a somewhat similar dilemma confronts Pauline Christianity. Since the one essential to salvation is faith in the risen Savior, the true believer is at liberty to indulge in all license with impunity. An impartial reading of I and II Corinthians and the Letter to the Philippians will indeed show that Paul's teachings on practical morality were superior to his theory, but at the expense of his logic. My revered and beloved master, the late and lamented Rabbi Dr. Samuel Belkin, demonstrated that even after his conversion Paul's approach to the rules of conduct reflected Pharisaic principles and that with good reason he still declared himself a Pharisee (Acts 23:6). See "The Problem of Paul's Background," *Journal of Biblical Literature* 54 (1935): 41–60.

   35. In the preceding paragraph I have drawn upon *Some Dogmas of Religion* by J. McT. Ellis McTaggart, sec. 164. See also J. S. Mill, *Three Essays on Religion* (New

York, 1874), pp. 36 f., 176–95. For an appreciative understanding and a more favorable estimate of Maimonides' position than that taken here, see Erich Fromm, *You Shall Be as Gods* (New York, 1966), pp. 116 f., cf. pp. 32 ff. In fairness to Maimonides, it must be admitted that Jewish thinkers in the modern era were no more successful in working out a Jewish philosophy of religion. An anecdote, related concerning the world-renowned leader of the Neo-Kantian school of philosophy, Hermann Cohen, illustrates the futility and ineffectiveness of these lofty speculative structures better than many a critical tractate. The story goes like this: The great philosopher was once delivering a public lecture on the topic, "The Aspiration for Moral Values and the 'Idea' of God in the Religion of Reason Drawn from the Sources of Judaism." A young Polish *yeshivah baḥur* (student in a rabbinical academy) listened to the brilliant lecture attentively and reverently. When Cohen finished, he put the simple question, "Herr Professor, where is there room left in your system for the *Ribono shel 'Olam* (Master of the World—a pious Jew's appellation for God)? At these words, at least so it is told, Hermann Cohen burst into tears like a child and made no attempt to reply. (Samuel H. Dresner, *Prayer, Humility and Compassion* [Philadelphia: 1957], pp. 14 f.). A somewhat different version of the story is found in Strauss, *Philosophie und Gesetz* (Berlin, 1936) p. 39; cf. Franz Rosenzweig, *Jehuda Halevi* (Berlin, 1927), p. 280 (Eng. trans. in N. Glatzer, *Franz Rosenzweig: His Life and Thought* [New York, 1953], p. 282). See also S. W. Baron, *A Social and Religious History of the Jews,* 1st ed. (1937), vol. 2, p. 393.

36. J. S. Mill, *An Examination of Sir William Hamilton's Philosophy,* 4th ed. (London, 1865), chap. 7, pp. 127 ff. See also the excellent treatment of this topic by J. M. E. McTaggart in *Some Dogmas of Religion* (Cambridge, 1906), pp. 213 ff. (he says that Mill's criticism is "one of the great turning points in the religious development of the world"), and by Baron D'Holbach, *Bon Sens* [Good Sense] (1772), sec. 89. The question is treated from a liberal Christian perspective by W. E. Channing, *Works* (Boston, 1886), p. 461.

37. T. L. Penido, *Le role de l'analogie en theologie dogmatique* (Paris, 1931), pp. 96 f.

38. John of St. Thomas, *Cursus Philosophicus Thomisticus,* vol. 1, ed. Beatus Reiser (Turin, 1930), p. 481.

39. H. Lyttkens, *The Analogy Between God and the World* (Uppsala, 1953); George P. Klubertanz, S.J., *St. Thomas Aquinas on Analogy* (Chicago, 1960); Ralph M. McInerny, *The Logic of Analogy* (The Hague, 1962); Battista Mondin, *Principle of Analogy in Protestant and Catholic Theology* (The Hague, 1963).

40. Thomists make great play with the assertions that God is His own essence, that His being and essence are one, and that He is being itself (see, for example, Jacques Maritain's *The Degrees of Knowledge,* trans. Gerald B. Phelan [New York, 1959], chap. 5, pp. 202–44). This involves them in all sorts of inconsistencies. "The distinction between essence and existence, on which the Five Ways depends, involves the recognition of a distinction between the being of things and their qualities; this

distinction . . . is one on which the argument finally founders, since the notion of necessary being is inconsistent with it; yet we now find a further inconsistency. If God *is* being, and his essence is one in which all qualities are identical, then the being that God is is not to be contrasted with all predicates, but *includes* them all. This is one of the greatest philosophical inconsistencies, since the proof of God requires that the distinction on which it depends is maintained until it is finished" (Terence Penelhum, *Religion and Rationality* [New York, 1971], p. 74).

41. Cf. Fr. P. Descoqs, S.J., *Institutiones Metaphysicae Generalis* (Paris, 1925), p. 270.

42. See, for example, J. F. Anderson, *The Bond of Being* (St. Louis, 1949), p. 270.

43. E. Gilson, *The Christian Philosophy of St. Thomas Aquinas* (New York, 1956), p. 105.

44. For the principle "omne agens agit simile sibi" in the context of the Thomist metaphysics, see Battista Mondin, S.X., *The Principle of Analogy in Protestant and Catholic Theology* (The Hague, 1963), pp. 86 ff. In the writer's opinion, the first part of this book gives one of the clearest expositions of Thomistic analogy.

45. See H. W. B. Joseph, *An Introduction to Logic,* 2nd ed. (Oxford, 1916), p. 13.

46. Jacques Maritain, *The Degrees of Knowledge,* trans. G. Phelan (New York, 1959), pp. 230 f. and Appendix III, "What God Is," pp. 422–29, especially p. 426. See the criticism of these elucidations in Gilson, *The Christian Philosophy of St. Thomas Aquinas,* p. 463, n. 37. When two giants disagree, it is not seemly for an outsider to venture into theological thickets and take sides.

47. Neo-Thomists have rightly pointed out that Aquinas means by *motus,* "movement" or "motion," something more general than what we do today; he includes under it any observable change by which an entity tends toward its specific end. Nonetheless, Aquinas was mainly concerned with change in position (i.e., local motion), as is shown in the parallel passage in the *Summa Contra Gentiles,* where he offers the rather unfortunate example of the sun as something which everybody would admit to be in motion.

48. I. Newton, *Mathematical Principles of Natural Philosophy,* trans. A. Motte and revised by F. Cajori (Berkeley, 1946), p. 13.

49. See Anthony Kenny, *The Five Ways* (New York, 1969), p. 28; cf. Edmund T. Whittaker, *Space and Spirit* (London: 1946), appendix.

50. For the background of this principle, see Solomon Pines, "Omne quod movetur necesse est ab aliquo moveri: A Refutation of Galen by Alexander of Aphrodisias and the Theory of Motion," *Isis* 52 (1961): 21–54, and J. A. Weisheipl, "The Principle *Omne quod movetur ab alio movetur* in Medieval Physics," *ibid.* 56 (1965): 26–45.

51. Alasdair MacIntyre, "Is Understanding Religion Compatible with Believing?" in *Faith and the Philosophers,* ed. John Hick (New York, 1964), p. 129. Similarly in the nineteenth century the argument from design was undermined by the theory of organic evolution. Eyes and other adaptive structures have slowly evolved by the accumulation of minute differences which helped to preserve the life of the in-

dividuals possessing them. Nature herself produces adaptations, and no external intelligent agent is needed. As Darwin wrote in his *Autobiography:* "The old argument of design in nature, as given by Paley, which formerly seemed to me so conclusive, fails, now that the law of natural selection has been discovered. We can no longer argue that, for instance, the beautiful hinge of a bivalve shell must have been made by an intelligent being, like the hinge of a door by man" (Darwin, *Autobiography,* ed. N. Barlow [New York, 1959], p. 87).

52. E. A. Burtt, *The Metaphysical Foundations of Modern Physical Science,* rev. ed. (New York, Doubleday Anchor Books, 1955), p. 26; cf. Carl L. Becker, *The Heavenly City of Eighteenth-Century Philosophers* (New Haven, 1932), p. 47. On the difference between the ancient and modern ways of conceptualizing the objects of the sciences, see Jacob Klein, *Greek Mathematical Thought and the Origin of Algebra* (Cambridge, Mass., 1968), pp. 117 ff.

53. *Commentaria in S.T.,* I, q. 2a, 2, ed. L. Urbano (Madrid, 1934), p. 109 (quoted by E. Gilson, *Elements of Christian Philosophy* [New York, 1960], p. 294— needless to say, Gilson does not subscribe to this opinion). For similar expressions of extravagant praise of the Angelic Doctor, see Appendices II and III of *St. Thomas Aquinas,* by J. Maritain (New York, 1958).

On the Jewish side, Crescas' critique of Maimonides' rejection of the possibility of a regress to infinity collapses the Aristotelian and Maimonidean proofs for the existence of an unmoved mover. See *Or Ha-Shem,* bk. I, secs. 1–2, and H. A. Wolfson's magisterial study, *Crescas' Critique of Aristotle* (Cambridge, Mass,. 1929

54. Anthony Kenny, *op. cit.,* pp. 10 ff. and 29, where the references to the learned journals will be found.

Perhaps my references to a few unsatisfactory or questionable attempts by Neo-Thomists to deal with modern science are unfair. Undoubtedly some valuable work has been done in this regard by the River Forest Thomists (such as W. A. Wallace and the late Vincent E. Smith) and by the late Charles De Koninck of Laval University. In extenuation I can only plead that in their estimate of other schools of scientific thought, Thomists are not always conspicuously overcome by Christian charity. In his introduction to a thick two-volume selection of basic Thomist texts, Professor A. C. Pegis speaks ironically of the Platonic school of Chartres, with its "physics without matter" which barred the way to science (*The Basic Writings of St. Thomas Aquinas,* ed. A. C. Pegis [New York, 1944], vol. 1, p. xlvi). But to what science, if any, we may ask, does Thomism open the way? Consider, for example, the Thomist-Aristotelian metaphysical analysis of local motion as *actus imperfecti.* Movement, we are told, is the actualization of a potentiality not fully completed; it is actuality inasmuch as it implies potency in part realized, and it is potentiality inasmuch as the subject, partly actualized, is susceptible of further actuality. The experimental physicist, since he lacks this knowledge, cannot possibly understand motion. In *Philosophical Physics* (New York, 1950), Fr. Vincent E. Smith says: "Motion eludes the empiriological physicist. . . . he cannot claim to be a rival of the philosophical physicist in the study of the mobile world" (p. 34). The reason for this is that "time and motion in empirio-logical physics are not mobile." A critic does well to call nonsense by its rightful name, and I can do no better than quote some of Professor Sidney Hook's devastating comments on these pronouncements which presuppose what Theophrastus called the likeness-theory of cognition, according to which the subject and object of knowledge must resemble each other. "If this means," he says, "that the conceptions of time and motion are not mobile, of course they are not. Our concepts do not have to move to understand motion any more than they have to eat to understand eating. If the reference is to the properties and behavior of moving things, this is precisely what physics tries to discover." As for the metaphysical analysis of motion as a mixture of act and potency, this is aptly characterized as "a mixture of tautology and phantasy." See Sidney Hook, "Scientific Knowledge and Philosophical 'Knowledge,'" in *The Quest for Being* (New York, 1961), pp. 220 f. (pp. 209–28).

55. In choosing examples of the conflict, apparent or real, of Thomism with modern science, it must not be thought that I am visiting the sins of the children on the father. The same reasoning-procedures and thought-patterns found among the Neo-Thomists were at work in the formulation of such concepts as "intellectual vision," "ontological necessity," and "timeless existence," to name just a few.

56. Space does not permit us to consider the other difficulty posed by the theory of evolution, viz., how there can be absolute and unchanging knowledge about anything if reality is evolving. The conceptualistic formal logic of scholasticism deals with an essentially static universe.

57. Maritain, "Co-operation and Justice," *Modern Schoolman* 22 (1944): 6, reprinted with minor changes in J. Maritain, *The Range of Reason* (New York, 1952), chap. 4. See also Maritain's oversubtle dialectical distinction between man as *individual,* and as such subordinate to the claims of the state, and man as a *person,* and as such transcending the claims of the state, in *Freedom in the Modern World* (New York, 1936), pp. 49–53.

58. E. Gilson, *The Christian Philosophy of St. Thomas Aquinas* (New York, 1956), pp. 128 f. In *Qu. disp. De Pot.,* Q. 3, a. 16, ad 17, Aquinas says: "The universe as created by God is the best possible in respect of the things that actually exist; but not in respect of things that God is able to create." Cf. *S.T.* la, Q. 25, a. 6c. and ad 3.

59. Cf. R. L. Patterson, *The Conception of God in the Philosophy of Aquinas* (London, 1933), p. 344. Aquinas' reasoning involves him in inconsistencies. At different times and in different contexts he affirms: (1) that God's goodness made him create the world and the particular things that do in fact exist (*S.T.* la, Q. 19, a. 2; *C.G.* I, 76); and (2) that all of God's actions are free, i.e., exempt from all necessity. To get out of this difficulty Gilson says: "The internal law ruling the essence of the good and bringing it to communicate itself must not be thought of as a natural necessity constraining God" (*Christian Philosophy of Aquinas,* p. 112). But this is true only of an *external* necessity constraining God, not the *logical* necessity entailed by His

being. God's creation of the world is logically necessitated by His own nature and attributes (as Aquinas conceives them).

60. *Guide* III:13; cf. I:69.

61. *S.T.* la, q. 32, a. 1 contra, quoting Ambrose, *De Fide* 1, 10 (*P.L.* vol. 16, col. 543). The special mystery of generation consists of the fact that, whereas all things are made by God, Jesus alone is begotten of God. The uniqueness of God's relation to the second person of the Trinity, as compared to the relation that God bears to the rest of His handiwork, makes of that relation a special mystery. The anti-Christian iconoclast Robert G. Ingersoll has sneeringly caricatured this view: "'The Father is uncreated, the Son uncreated, the Holy Ghost uncreated. The Father incomprehensible, the Son incomprehensible, the Holy Ghost incomprehensible'—And that is the reason we know so much about the thing" (*Works* [Dresden ed.], vol. 1, p. 494).

62. The historian Gibbon has shrewdly remarked: "The subtle, the profound, the irrefragable, the angelic and the seraphic Doctor acquired these pompous titles by filling ponderous volumes with a small number of technical terms, and a much smaller number of ideas." E. Gibbon, *Outline of the History of the World* (ed. 1796), III, p. 184. (The philosophers identified by their honorific titles are, in the order mentioned: Duns Scotus, Richard of Middleton, Alexander of Hales, Thomas Aquinas, and Bonaventure.)

63. A. Geiger, *Lesestücke aus der Mischnah* (Breslau, 1845), pp. 65 f. The text commented upon is found in the Mishnah, Berakoth 1:5.

64. See *Guide,* pt. II, chaps. 32–48. Insofar as Church dogma permitted, Aquinas followed Maimonides very closely. See *S.T.*, 2a, 2ae, q. 171 ff.; cf. the conscientious study of A. Merx in *Die Prophetie des Joel und ihre Ausleger,* pt. II (Halle, 1879), pp. 341–67.

65. Whether, according to Maimonides, Moses was influenced by the imaginative faculty is a moot point hotly debated by the medieval and modern students of the *Guide;* see the commentaries of Efodi (affirmative) and Abravanel (negative) on *Guide* II:36.

66. Graham Wallas, *The Art of Thought* (New York: Harcourt, Brace & Co., 1926), chap. 4, pp. 79–107.

67. *Leviathan,* pt. III, chap. 32 (emphasis supplied). See also Locke, *Essay Concerning Human Understanding,* bk. IV, chap. 16, sec. 4, and chap. 18, sec. 2; and for a modern treatment, Sidney Hook, *The Quest for Being* (New York: St. Martin's Press, 1961), pp. 130 ff.

68. Commentary on Gen. 18:2. Cf. Munk, *Guide,* vol. 2, p. 321, n. 1; see also Aquinas, *S.T.* la, Q. 51, a. 2 c.

69. Abravanel, Commentary on the *Guide,* pt. II, chap. 42; a similar explanation is already found in Gersonides, *Perush al ha-Torah* (ed. Venice, republished by Rabbi Jacob Schurin [Brooklyn, 1958]), Vayishlah = Gen. 32, p. 41b. See Alvin J. Reines, *Maimonides and Abravanel on Prophecy* (Cincinnati, 1970), p. 167.

70. Leonard S. Kravitz, "The Revealed and the Concealed: Providence,

Prophecy, Miracles and Creation in the *Guide,"* *CCAR* 16, no. 4 (October 1969): 15, n. 43 (emphasis in the original).

71. RITBA (= R. Yom-Tob ben Abraham Ishbili), *Sefer ha-Zikkaron,* ed. Kalman Kahane (Jerusalem, 1955/6), pp. 43 f.; cf. Abravanel, Commentary on the *Guide,* vol. 2, chap. 42.

72. A. Flew, "Theology and Falsification," in *New Essays in Philosophical Theology,* ed. A. Flew and A. MacIntyre (London, 1955), p. 97.

73. See *Minḥath Kena'oth* of Abba Mari of Lunel (Pressburg, 1836), letter 81; cf. Responsa of Ibn Adret (ed. Venice), p. 662; B. Halper, *Post-Biblical Hebrew Literature* (Philadelphia, 1921), I, p. 136; Eng. trans. II, pp. 177 f.

74. J. B. S. Haldane, "If . . .," *Rationalist Annual* (London, 1934), pp. 9–14; reprinted in J. B. S. Haldane, *Science and Life* (London: Pemberton Publishing Co., 1968), pp. 12–18. A more academic, if prosaic, criticism of a farfetched hypothesis may be found in David Friedrich Strauss' discussion, in the first volume of his *Das Leben Jesu,* of the attempted reconciliation of the two discrepant pedigrees of Jesus found in the genealogical tables in Matthew and Luke. Strauss examines in detail, and rejects as forced and implausible, the opinion of Sextus Julius Africanus and some of the Latin Fathers that two levirate marriages had taken place among the ancestors of Joseph, in one of the instances of which the husbands were only brothers of the half-blood. The discrepancies in the genealogies are explained by the hypothesis that the names of the generations of Israel were enumerated in a twofold manner, by nature or according to law. When the enumeration is given by nature, the succession is that of physical offspring; it is given according to law wherever another raised up children to the name of a deceased childless brother. Thus neither of the accounts in the two Gospels is in error, since the one is reckoned by nature and the other by law. Strauss does not consider the further difficulty that Jesus, having been born of a virgin, could not have been a scion of the House of David, since Jewish genealogies follow the paternal line, although in the matter of religion the children follow that of the mother. (See D. F. Strauss, *The Life of Jesus Critically Examined,* trans. George Eliot, 2nd ed. [1892], pp. 111–18.)

75. We need not devote much space to this modern-sounding sociological-anthropological explanation of the sacrificial cult, as it is not original with Maimonides but is found in some of the Church Fathers, e.g., Jerome (*In Epist. ad Galates,* IV, 8; *P.L.,* vol. 64, cols. 375–76) and Gregory Nazianzenus (*Orationes Theol.* v. 25, 26; *P.G.* vol. 36, col. 160-a). The attempt of Abravanel (Introduction to his Commentary on Leviticus) to find support for this view of Maimonides in a parable recorded in Midrash Lev. Rabbah xxii:8 is based on a misunderstanding of the text as pointed out in the commentary *Yefeh To'ar in loc.;* cf. David Hoffmann, *Das Buch Leviticus,* I, (Berlin: 1905), pp. 81 ff. In the context of the writings of the Church Fathers this theory at least made some sense; it was part of the familiar antithesis going back to Paul (Rom. 8:15), and beloved still today in the fundamentalist press, between the two Testaments: between the tribal God of the Old Testament and the

loving Father of the New Testament; between the law and grace; and between the fear of slaves and the love of servants. But in an age when even Christian martyrs like Dietrich Bonhoeffer repeatedly warn against a too hasty escape from the so-called Old to the New Testament, this view is definitely outmoded (see *Letters and Papers from Prison,* 3rd ed. [New York, 1967], pp. 10 ff., 155, 185, 205 f.). It would take the learning of a Professor Wolfson to trace the migrations of this doctrine from the Church Fathers to Maimonides. I shall content myself to seeking the help of Col. "Bob" Ingersoll to exorcise the dybbuk from the twelfth-century rabbi: "Suppose you go to the Cannibal Islands to prevent the gentlemen there from eating missionaries, and you found they ate them raw. Of course you do not tell them, in the first place, it is wrong. That would not do. The first move is to induce them to cook them. That would be the first step toward civilization. You would not say it is wrong to eat missionaries, but it is wrong to eat missionaries raw. After you get them to eat cooked missionaries, you will then, without their knowing it, occasionally slip in a little mutton. We will go gradually decreasing missionaries and increasing mutton, until finally, in about what the Bible calls 'the fullness of time,' they will be so cultivated that they will prefer the sheep to the priest" (Robert G. Ingersoll, *Ingersoll's Famous Speeches* [New York, n.d.], p. 305).

76. One of the Ṣūfīs (I have mislaid my reference) trenchantly observed that to call God "righteous" is just as silly, and implies just as much anthropomorphism, as to say that He has a beard, and Ernst Haeckel contemptuously described the God of popular religion as a "gaseous vertebrate" (*Riddle of the Universe,* trans. Joseph McCabe [New York, 1901], p. 288). These remarks are not flippant, but raise a serious challenge to the concept of God and His attributes as expounded by Maimonides. The nature of the challenge is as follows. The Bible portrays God as a being with affections similar to those of a human being. God walks in the garden in the cool of the day (Gen. 3:8); He eats with Abraham (Gen. 18:8); He writes with His own finger upon the tables of stone (Exod. 31:18), and the like. The Bible is replete with expressions of an anthropomorphic and anthropopathic nature, such as the hand of God, His arm, foot, mouth, or ear, or His speaking, walking, or laughing, and so on. Now Maimonides, in his laudable and praiseworthy aim of spiritualizing and "demythologizing" the notion of God, rejects all positive attributes or derives them from the Deity's effects. "All attributes ascribed to God are attributes of His actions" (*Guide* I:54). But the crucial question is whether in so doing he has not completely undermined the basis of ethical monotheism—whether, so to speak, he has not thrown out the baby with the bath-water. Many contemporary philosophers have recently argued that attributes like "righteous," "wise," "powerful," and so forth, cannot be applied to God if God is a purely spiritual Being. These adjectives have significance when they are applied to human beings, who have bodies and whose behavior is publicly observable, but they have no meaning when they are applied to a pure spirit. Paul Edwards, who raises these objections, writes: "It seems to me that all these words [just, good, etc.] lose their meaning if we are told that God

does not possess a body. Anyone who thinks otherwise without realizing this, I think, is supplying a body in the background of his images. For what would it be like to be, say, just without a body? To be just, a person has to *act* justly—he has to behave in certain ways. This is not reductive materialism. It is a simple empirical truth about what we mean by 'just.' But how is it possible to perform these acts, to behave in the required ways, without a body? Similar remarks apply to the other divine attributes" (Paul Edwards, "Some Notes on Anthropomorphic Theology," in *Religious Experience and Truth,* ed. Sidney Hook, [New York, 1961], p. 243). I do not say that it can be seen to be absolutely impossible that a purely spiritual being, a disembodied mind, should have moral and other attributes, but I at least have not the faintest notion how this could be. When I read Maimonides on the divine attributes, I am reminded of the story of the Cheshire Cat in *Alice in Wonderland*—the grinning cat went away and left its grin behind. However that may be, Maimonides deserves credit for having anticipated the view of linguistic philosophers that God's existence cannot meaningfully be asserted before it has been settled whether or not meaningful assertions can be made about His nature and activity. Herein surely lies the answer to the difficulty expressly raised by Isaac Abravanel concerning the paradoxical plan and the apparently illogical order of the *Guide,* which deals with the nature and attributes of God in part one while the very existence of God is proved only in part two! (see "Be'ur Sod ha-Moreh," in *She'eloth Saul* [ed. Venice, 1574], p. 27a; photographically reproduced under the title *Teshuboth* [Jerusalem, 1966/7]). The English translator of the *Guide* remarks: "According to Maimonides it is not by sacrifices or prayers that we truly approach God" (M. Friedlander, *Guide of the Perplexed,* III, p. 294, n. 1). "Rational philosophical thought," says Friedrich Heiler, "destroys the essential presuppositions of a simple prayer. These are: faith in the anthropomorphic character of God, in His real presence, in His changeability, in the reality of personal communion with Him" (*Prayer,* [London, 1932], p. 98). Maimonides' opposition to vocal prayer is expressed in the following manner: "The idea is best expressed in the book of Psalms, 'Silence is praise to Thee' (65:2), which interpreted signifies: silence with regard to You is praise. It is a very expressive remark on this subject; for whatever we utter with the intention of extolling and praising Him contains something that cannot be applied to God and includes derogatory expressions; it is therefore more becoming to be silent, and to be content with intellectual reflection, as the perfect ones have enjoined when they said: 'Commune with your own hearts on your beds, and be silent. Selah' (Ps. 4:5)." (*Guide* I:59) One is reminded of Hegel, who answered his housekeeper when she wondered why he did not go to church, "Meine liebe Frau, das Denken ist auch Gottesdienst." Cf. A. Schopenhauer, *Parerga et Paralipomena,* 2nd ed. (1862), vol. 2, p. 405; see also Becker, *op. cit.,* pp. 74–79.

77. Dr. Nemoy sends me the following note: "I suppose that Maimonides would have replied to you that the Gentiles had eaten such unwholesome victuals since time

immemorial, and would reject any advice to eschew them—in fact, they had been offered the Torah, with its dietary restrictions, before it was offered to the Israelites, and willfully rejected it. By the same token, he would have argued, you should forbid the manufacture and sale of spirits and tobacco products if you yourself eschew them for reasons of health." Dr. Kravitz points out that Nahmanides' views regarding forbidden foods were similar to those of Maimonides. He tries to get over the difficulty in another manner. He calls attention to the Midrash that tells of the physician instructing one patient that he may eat whatever he wishes while telling another that he may eat only certain foods. When asked the reason, the physician replies: "The first patient will die whatever I do, so I let him eat what he wishes. The second will live if he follows my diet" (see Lev. Rabbah XIII. 2 and the parallels listed by Margulies in the critical apparatus in his edition; see also Rashi on Lev. 11:2). A half-hearted rationalism of the type discussed is also typical of Aquinas, especially when he tries to reconcile and harmonize conflicting authorities. To give but one instance, he tried to reconcile the two conflicting accounts of the Evangelists regarding the setting of the Sermon on the Mount. According to Matthew, the wonderful sermon was delivered to the disciples from a mountain; Luke, on the other hand, says that it was delivered to the general public on a plain. There is no contradiction here, says St. Thomas—*distinguo,* I beg to make a distinction: there was a mountain with a level summit, on which, however, a little elevation rose. Jesus gave the discourse to the disciples at the summit of the small elevation, and repeated it to the multitude on the exalted plain.

78. W. R. Smith, *The Religion of the Semites,* 2nd ed. (New York: Meridian Library, 1956), p. 221 n. 343. See also J. Guttmann, "John Spencers Erklaerung der biblischen Gesetze in ihrer Beziehung zu Maimonides," in *Festschrift fuer Simonsen,* pp. 259 ff.

79. J. G. Frazer, *Folklore in the Old Testament,* vol. 3 (London, 1918), p. 117.

80. See S. W. Baron, *A Social and Religious History of the Jews,* 2nd ed., vol. 1 (New York, 1952), p. 328, n. 22 and the literature there cited, and Finkelstein, *The Pharisees,* vol. 2, p. 659, n. 42. Cf. also Abraham ibn Ezra, Standard *Commentary on Exodus,* 23:19.

6. AUTONOMY OF RELIGION AND PHILOSOPHY PREFERABLE TO THEIR SYNTHESIS

1. J. S. Mill, *A System of Logic,* bk. I, chap. 3, #1.

2. See Ibn Dā'ūd, *Emūnāh Rāmāh,* I, 1 (p. 8, ed. S. Weil).

3. See Appendix C, "Kant and Judaism." The distinction between hypothetical

and categorical imperatives is found in the little book entitled *Fundamental Principles [Grundlegung] of the Metaphysics of Morals*. An even more extreme view of the autonomy of ethics is defended by H. R. Prichard. Whereas Kant held that "it is impossible to conceive of anything in the world, or even outside of it, which can be called good without qualification except a good will" (*Fundamental Principles*, first sect., opening words), Prichard maintained that the rightness or obligatoriness of an action is "absolutely underivative or immediate," and that there are no "non-moral reasons" that can be given for it, and, in particular, that it in no way depends on the motives of the agent (the Kantian view). Prichard sets out his views in his essay "Does Moral Philosophy Rest on a Mistake?", in *Moral Obligation* (New York, 1949), pp. 1–17 (originally appeared in *Mind* 21 [1912]: 21–37).

4. Cf. Erwin I. J. Rosenthal, *Griechisches Erbe in der Juedischen Religionsphilosophie des Mittelalters* (Stuttgart, 1959), pp. 18 ff.

5. See Jacob Guttmann, "Die Familie Schemtob in ihren Beziehungen zur Philosophie," *MGWJ* 57 (1913): 177 ff., where several contemporary witnesses are cited; to which may be added, among others, Solomon Al'ami, *Iggereth Musar* (ed. Haberman), pp. 41, 43; Joshua (ben Joseph ibn Vives) Lorki, *Iggereth* (ed. Landau), p. 1. Cf. Benzion Netanyahu, *The Marranos of Spain* (New York, 1966), p. 97: "Faith in Judaism had been *shattered* before it was abandoned; and what had shattered that faith, at least in the initial stages, was not Christianity, but the thoroughgoing, long lasting and corruptive influence of secular philosophy." See also E. Barzilay, *Between Reason and Faith* (The Hague, 1967), especially the introductory and concluding chapters.

6. Deut. 11:16: "Take care lest you become so openminded (or tolerant) that you turn aside and serve other gods and worship them." For this enlightening translation I am indebted to Theophile J. Meek, *Journal of Biblical Literature* 67 (1948): 235 f. Professor Meek points out that the root *pth*, usually translated "deceived," means "to be wide, to be open" and calls attention to Gen. 9:27 and Prov. 20:19, where it is used in this sense. The Septuagint corroborates this interpretation. See also the commentary of S. R. Hirsch *in loc. cit.*

7. Joseph Ya'beṣ, *Or ha-Ḥayyim* (ed. Amsterdam, 1781), chap. 12, p. 23b, quoted by Jacob Guttmann, *Die Religions-philosophischen Lehren des Isaak Abravanel* (Breslau, 1916).

8. *Rosh Amanah* (ed. Koenigsberg, 1861), pp. 29a, 30b, where the author attempts to justify his view by referring to Sanhedrin 99a. Abravanel's position received strong support from R. David ibn Abi Zimra (ca. 1476–1589), Responsa RaDBaZ, no. 344. (This responsum has been translated into English in Louis Jacobs's *Principles of the Jewish Faith* [New York, 1964], pp. 24 f.) The present writer regrets to find himself entirely out of harmony with David Neumark's opinion (*History of Dogmas in Judaism* [Hebrew] [Odessa, 1919], vol. 2, p. 79) that Abravanel was paying mere lip service to orthodoxy. Samuel David Luzzatto, a truly religious spirit, perceived that Abravanel expressed his innermost belief and that

these cardinal statements fully agree with the rest of his concepts (Luzzatto, "Über die angeblichen Plagiate Abrabanel's und Moscato's," in Jost's *Israelitische Annalen*, 1840, p. 24b). Cf. the conscientious study by E. Mihaly, "Isaac Abravanel on the Principles of Faith," *HUCA* 26 (1955): 481–522 (especially p. 487, n. 15), who reaches similar conclusions. The best recent study of Abravanel is found in Barzilay, *Between Reason and Faith* (1967), pp. 61–132. We cannot agree with B. Netanyahu (*Abravanel, Statesman and Philosopher*, 2nd ed. [1968], p. 97) that this position marks a backward step in Jewish philosophical speculation. We rather share the view of Louis Ginzberg (*Jewish Encyclopedia*, s.v. "Abravanel") that Abravanel's entire conception of Judaism "was rooted in a firm conviction of God's revelation in history, and particularly in the history of this selected people." Fashions in theology come and go, but right now this view, which considers the biblical faith as redemptive or "sacred history" (*Heilsgeschichte*), is definitely "in." It is quite true that Abravanel was a child of his age and accepted a mechanical view ("dictation theory") of the verbal inspiration of the Bible, but this is not the distinguishing feature of his position, but rather an aspect which he shared with almost all medieval thinkers, not excluding Maimonides and Aquinas. According to Aquinas, "a falsehood can never underlie the literal sense of Holy Scripture." Consequently, even the smallest assertions of fact, although not directly bearing on questions of faith and morals, are inerrant; for instance, to deny that Elkanah was Samuel's father (I Sam. 1:19–20) would be contrary to the principles of Catholic faith, "for it follows that Divine Scripture would be false" ("Si quis diceret Samuelem non fuisse filium Elcanae; ex hoc enim sequitur Scripturam divinam esse falsam"). *S. T.*, Ia, q. 1, a. 10, ad. 3; *ibid.*, q. 32, a. 4 c.

9. Franz Rosenzweig, *Zweistromland* (Berlin, 1926), p. 54: "[Das] Blutzeugentum [ist] kein Rechenexempel." Rosenzweig is speaking of "the pseudological theory of the unity of God" ("der pseudologischen Theorie der Gotteseinheit"). See also H. M. Kallen, *Judaism at Bay* (New York, 1932), pp. 70 ff. A Christian writer with theological sensitivity observes: "Compare the life of an ordinary American Protestant Christian, for whom religious customs tend toward the vanishing point, with the life of an orthodox Jew, colored by such customs from morning to night. Which is apt to be reminded of God oftener?" (Fleming James, *Personalities of the Old Testament* [New York, 1939], p. 478.) It is significant that in the wake of the moralist (Musar) movement inaugurated by R. Israel Lipkin (Salanter) in the nineteenth century, when there was a revival of the systematic study of Jewish ethico-religious classics in the East European Yeshivoth, the first treatise of Baḥya's *Duties of the Hearts*, which treats of the existence and unity of God, was purposely omitted from study, and the spiritual advisers forbade their charges to study it. In the beginning of his polemical work, *Magen wa-Romaḥ* ([Shield and spear], edited by David Kaufmann in *Beth Talmud* 2 [1881]: 117–25; cf. also, Graetz, *Geschichte*, 4th ed., vol. 4, appendix, n. 4, iii, pp. 424 f.; Yitzhak Baer, *A History of the Jews in Christian Spain* [Philadelphia, 1966], vol. 2, p. 254), R. Ḥayyim ibn Musa, who flourished in

fifteenth-century Spain, accuses the philosophizing preachers and advanced thinkers of being "fifth columnists" who are undermining Judaism from within, and relates the following pathetic story:

> In the days of my youth I once heard a certain preacher expounding God's unity in the critical manner of the philosophers. He would say repeatedly: "If He is not one, then such and such must follow." Finally a certain householder rose, of them that tremble at word of the Lord [Isa. 66:5], and said: "In the massacre in Seville [in 1391], they robbed me of everything I had and beat me and wounded me and left me for dead. All this I bore for my faith in *Hear, O Israel, the Lord our God, the Lord is One.* Now you attack the tradition of our fathers by way of philosophical quibbling, saying, 'If He is not one, such and such will be the case.'" And the householder said: "I believe more in the tradition of our fathers. I do not wish to listen to this sermon." Whereupon he left the synagogue, and most of the congregation with him (trans. after M. Himmelfarb).

10. See Abravanel, 2nd preface to Ezekiel and commentary to chap 1; *idem,* Commentary on the *Guide* (ed. Landau), II, pp. 48 f.; *idem, 'Aṭereth Zeḳenim,* chap. 24; cf. Crescas, *Or ha-Shem, ma'mar* IV, *derush* 10 (p. 90, ed. Vienna); M. L. Malbim in the preface to his commentary on Ezekiel.

11. In the heyday of the Maimunist controversy, Joseph ibn Kaspi flung down the gauntlet at the unsophisticated believers in the Torah and tradition in the good old style by relating the following incident at their expense in his ethical testament (ed. I. Abrahams, *Hebrew Ethical Wills,* pt. 1, pp. 151 f. [chap. 14, pp. 127–61]). It happened once that when he was giving a grandiose party, and all the preparations had been made and completed, luck would have it that a hapless maid put a milk spoon in a meat pot. Not remembering the ritual laws of "mixtures," Ibn Kaspi was forced to leave his guests to go and seek instructions from a rabbi. At first, he relates, tongue in cheek, he felt humiliated at having to consult somebody much younger than he, but upon a nicer consideration of the situation he consoled himself with the thought that there is a need for specialization and division of responsibility. He ends his ironical causerie with the following rhetorical flourish: "Is not the faculty of expounding the existence and unity of God as important as familiarity with the rule concerning a small milk spoon?" This question deserves a straightforward answer. If the medieval philosopher-theologians had succeeded in establishing their position by rational arguments, this claim might be allowable. But as things are, medieval philosophy is a long road leading literally from nothing (*creatio ex nihilo*) to nowhere (*utopia*), so the question is a moot one. For normative Judaism, however, the answer is clear: the *Shulḥan 'Aruk* and its commentaries devote a hundred times as much space—it would not be an exaggeration to say a thousand times as much space—to the "small milk spoon" as they do to expounding the existence and unity of God,

and the responsa literature devoted to the "small milk spoon" is more extensive than the whole literary output of all Jewish philosophers. The "small milk spoon" accomplished its end in the survival of Judaism, and therein history has vindicated it. Even in the post-emancipation period it did more to preserve the Jewish people than all the inane pulpit-rhetoric about ethical monotheism and all the drivel and cant about *die allgemeine Menschenliebe* and universal ethical values.

12. Arthur Eddington, *Philosophy of the Physical Sciences,* (New York, 1939), chap. 2, "Selective Subjectivism." More precisely Eddington's ichthyologist arrives at two generalizations: (1) no fish is less than two inches long; and (2) all fish have gills. Which of these statements, if any, is justified? Eddington says that (1) is qualifiedly justified because the true import of a scientific statement is: With the tools I used, these are the possible observations. With the fish-net used by the scientist, he could not hope to catch fishes shorter than two inches. Although he does not say so explicitly, the scientist makes statements only about phenomena which can be observed. As soon as he ventures beyond that he has given up his role as a scientist and has become a metaphysician. As for (2), with the very same net, the scientist may catch fish without gills; his sample did not contain any, but the possibility of observation of such fish is not ruled out. Hence (2) is not justified, except perhaps in a probability sense. Thus Eddington sees science as limited and argues that there may be realms of existence which are outside the scope of science. In this manner he reconciles, to his satisfaction, science and the existence of a spiritual world and finds room for values in a world of facts. The use of this parable from Eddington is not to be taken as an acceptance of his views of the philosophy of science or religion. See also the illuminating parable of the blind psychologist and the seer of the sun, and how the former tries to convince the latter, employing J. S. Mill's "Method of Difference" (cf. *Logic,* III, viii. 2), and challenging him to see light with his eyes shut, or to fail to see it with them open, that "the sun" is just a projection of his subjective feelings of warmth and perceptions of light, in J. B. Pratt, *The Religious Consciousness* (New York, 1920), pp. 457 f.

It may not be amiss to quote the views of another philosopher of science, whose religious views differ markedly from Eddington's, on the limitations of science and the scientific method. Sir Karl Popper, who is an agnostic, writes in *The Logic of Scientific Discovery* (New York, 1961), p. 111: "The empirical basis of objective science has thus nothing 'absolute' about it. Science does not rest upon rock-bottom. The bold structure of its theories rises, as it were, above a swamp. It is like a building erected upon piles. The piles are driven down from above into the swamp, but not down to any natural or 'given' base; and when we cease our attempts to drive our piles into a deeper layer, it is not because we have reached firm ground. We simply stop when we are satisfied that they are firm enough to carry the structure, at least for the time being." Again, on p. 180, he concludes: "The old scientific ideal of *episteme*—of absolutely certain, demonstrable knowledge—has proved to be an idol. The demand for scientific objectivity makes it inevitable that every scientific statement must remain *tentative for ever.* It may indeed be corroborated, but every corroboration is relative to other statements which, again, are tentative. Only in our subjective experiences of conviction, in our subjective faith, can we be 'absolutely certain.'" Cf. A. N. Whitehead, *Science and the Modern World* (New York: Mentor, 1948), pp. 4, 17, 19 f. These pronouncements (which could be multiplied indefinitely) are not voices crying in the wilderness, but represent the consensus of authorities on the philosophy of science. See Thomas Kuhn, *The Structure of Scientific Revolutions* (New York, 1962), and Paul Feyerabend, *Against Method* (New York, 1975).

Similar limitations of the scientific method hold true in the case of the social sciences and the humanities. A group of scholars in various disciplines have come to the conclusion that the Jewish people represent a unique phenomenon and defy all attempts at explanation by the ordinary categories of interpretation. Professor Flemming James, *Personalities of the Old Testament* (New York, 1939), p. 2, writing a decade before the establishment of the State of Israel, says:

> If we can believe in the possibility of any miracle, two facts in the field of history and in the complex world of today may well bear that name. One is the Jewish people. Since 70 A.D. they have had no nation of their own, but have been scattered throughout the earth, mingling with all peoples yet remaining distinct, existing everywhere as sojourners, generally discriminated against and often persecuted; yet everywhere teeming, aggressive, vigorous, brilliant, a force to be reckoned with; today kept under here and there only by violence, and probably not to be kept under long; a phenomenon seemingly unique in history. The second fact is Judaism, the religion by virtue of which this people are what they are.

Whereas at the turn of the century scholars like Delitzsch, in *Babel und Bibel,* emphasized the alleged lack of originality of the Jews, recent scholarship, especially under the impetus of the late William Foxwell Albright, the greatest orientalist of this century, emphasizes the accuracy of the biblical traditions and how Judaism has stood out from the ancient religions that surround it. We need mention only two authors and the titles of their works: Norman H. Snaith, *The Distinctive Ideas of the Old Testament* (London, 1942), and G. Ernest Wright, *The Old Testament Against Its Environment* (Chicago, 1950). The latter author comes to the conclusion that the prophetic protest against social injustice which was protected by religious sanctions must be conceded to be "without close parallel in the ancient world" (p. 60). The judgment of the sociologist Carl Mayer, "Religious and Political Aspects of Anti-Judaism," in *Jews in a Gentile World,* ed. Graeber and Britt (New York, 1942), p. 315 (pp. 311–28), is similar: "By every known sociological law the Jews should have perished long ago. They should have disappeared or merged with other peoples or changed to such a degree as to become entirely unrecognizable. Yet the Jews still persist." To this may be added the testimony of a noted philosopher, Nicholas Berdyaev, who states that the continued existence of Jewry down the centuries is rationally inconceivable and inexplicable. "I remember," he writes in *The Meaning of History* (New York, 1936), pp. 86 f., "how the materialist interpretation of history, when I attempted in my youth to verify it by applying it to the destinies of peoples, broke down in the case of the Jews, where destiny seemed absolutely inexplicable from the materialistic standpoint. And, indeed, according to the materialistic and positivist criterion, this people ought long ago to have perished. Its survival is a mysterious and wonderful phenomenon demonstrating that the life of this people is governed by a special predetermination, transcending the process of adaptation expounded by the materialistic interpretation of history."

To be sure, the social scientist *qua* social scientist cannot appeal to the supernatural as an explanation any more than the natural scientist can, but it is surely to beg the question to assume that he can interpret the history and destiny of the Jews in purely natural categories. The mere fact that the scientist in the laboratory must assume that every disease has a cause which can in principle be discovered surely does not permit us to conclude that the cure for every disease must be found, much less that any particular scientist can find it. Even Wellhausen, the foremost protagonist of natural explanation for biblical matters, is reluctantly forced to admit in his article "Moab," *Encyclopaedia Biblica,* col. 3177: "Israel and Moab had a common origin and their early history was similar. . . . Still, with all this similarity, how different were the ultimate fates of the two! The history of the one loses itself obscurely and fruitlessly in the sand; that of the other issues in eternity." "Why," Wellhausen asks elsewhere, "did not Chemosh, the god of the Moabites, become the God of righteousness and the Creator of heaven and earth?" And Wellhausen confesses that this is "a question to which one can give no satisfactory answer" ("Die Christliche Religion," in *Kultur der Gegenwart,* ed. J. Wellhausen *et al.,* 2nd ed. [Berlin, 1909], p. 15).

13. A brief summary of Hartmann's thought in English may be found in his *New Ways of Ontology,* trans. R. C. Kuhn (Chicago, 1953). Hartmann's views have a certain affinity to the various theories of emergent evolution developed in the past fifty years, but they are worked out with a richness of detail, and with less of an aura of mystery and of an *ad hoc* character than the other level-theories. Furthermore, Hartmann cannot be suspect of having any apologetic purposes; his thought is marked by a complete absence of religious feeling, and he specifically rejects God and immortality, and any anthropocentric or anthropomorphic interpretation of reality.

14. Cf. A. J. Ayer, *The Central Questions of Philosophy* (New York, 1973), p. 7.

15. *S.T.* 1a, q. 1, a. 8, ad 2; cf. *ibid.* q. 2, a. 2, ad 1. *In Boet. de. Trin.* q. 2, a. 3 resp.: "Sacred doctrine is founded upon the light of faith, philosophy depends upon the light of natural reason; wherefore it is impossible that philosophical truths are contrary to those that are of faith; but they are deficient as compared to them. Nevertheless they incorporate some similitudes of those higher truths, and some things that are preparatory for them, just as nature is the preamble to grace" (trans. R. Brennan).

7. CONCLUSION AND EVALUATION

1. See R. Carnap, *Philosophy and Logical Syntax* (London, 1935), pp. 17 f. Saadiah (*Amānāt,* ed. Landauer, p. 26) uses the following comparison to illustrate the relation between reason and revelation. Someone weighs his money and finds that he possesses a thousand pieces. He distributes different sums to a large number of people, and then, wishing to show his friends quickly how much is left, he says that he has five hundred pieces and offers to prove it by weighing the money that is left in his hands. When he weighs the money in their presence, which takes but little time, and finds that it amounts to five hundred pieces, his friends are obliged to believe what he has told them. But there may be among them a particularly cautious man, who wants to find the amount left over by the method of calculation, i.e., by adding together the various amounts given away and subtracting their sum from the original amounts. Revelation, in this simile, is the weighing process, which gives us an easy "shortcut" to truth by a method which is direct and cannot be questioned. Reason is the process of calculation: a cautious man with plenty of time may use it to verify a truth which has already been proved to him by the easy and quick method of weighing. Obviously, however, calculation cannot change the result which weighing has already produced; and if there is any difference in the results, the weighed money will be neither increased nor diminished, and the mistake must be in the calculation.

2. Quoted by Gotthold Weil, *Juedische Rundschau* 12, no. 6 (February 8, 1907): 54. See also Gershom Scholem, "The Science of Judaism—Then and Now," in *The Messianic Idea in Judaism* (New York, 1971), p. 307. In this connection it may be of interest to mention a story—no doubt apocryphal—which illustrates the essentially museumlike approach of Steinschneider to the Jewish cultural heritage. On his way to Marienbad in search of health, the Russian-Hebrew poet Judah Leib Gordon stayed over in Berlin for three days, and took the occasion to pay his respects to Steinschneider. When he introduced himself as a Hebrew poet, the venerable savant absent-mindedly asked him: "Young man, in what century did you live?" The great bibliographer knit his brow as if trying to recall where he had heard the name before and said: "Wait a minute, and I'll tell you the year you died." In his autobiography Dr. Joseph Klausner, the late professor of modern Hebrew language and literature at the Hebrew University in Jerusalem, relates that Steinschneider only reluctantly permitted his manual on Jewish literature to be translated into Hebrew, and then only on receiving a token royalty which he did not insist on in the case of translations into other European languages, because, he said, for his work to be translated into Hebrew was not a privilege and honor for him but a detriment which he must be compensated for (Joseph Klausner, *My Way Towards Rebirth and Redemption* [Hebrew] [Tel-Aviv, 1946], pp. 51 f.). The self-hatred manifested by the pioneers of the *Wissenschaft des Judentums* and the negative tendencies of much of its scholarship in its early phases is a complicated subject and deserves a critical investigation. In 1818 Zunz, the founder and godfather of the movement, was firmly

convinced that a century later a Hebrew book would be well-nigh impossible to obtain. See Luitpold Wallach, *Liberty and Letters: The Thought of Leopold Zunz* (London, 1959), p. 18. The same writer notes that Zunz regarded the Science of Judaism as a "swan song rather than as the dawn of a new era in Jewish life" (*ibid.,* p. 19).

3. David Hume, *An Enquiry Concerning Human Understanding,* sec. XII, pt. 3, ed. A. Selby-Bigge (Oxford, 2nd ed., 1902), p. 165; ed. C. W. Hendel (New York: Liberal Arts Press, 1955), p. 173.

4. Gilson, *The Unity of Philosophical Experience* (New York, 1937), p. 306.

5. The eminent Cambridge scholar Professor J. L. Teicher has plausibly argued that the fountainhead of medieval Islamic and Jewish philosophy is puzzlement and bewilderment with what Kant was later to describe as the "Antinomies of Reason." He calls attention to the literal identity of the arguments used by Kant with those used by the Muslim philosophical schools, and suggests that there is no better introduction to medieval specualtion than Kant's *Critique of Pure Reason.* "The whole development of Arabic and Jewish philosophy can, indeed, be regarded as one continuous and successful effort to solve the problem of the 'Antinomies of Reason.'" J. L. Teicher, "Avicenna's Place in Arabic Philosophy," in *Avicenna, Scientist and Philosopher: A Millenary Symposium,* ed. G. M. Wickens (London, 1952), p. 33 (pp. 29–48).

6. Fredrick W. Robertson, *Sermons on Religion and Life* (Everyman's ed.), vol. 1, p. 132. The picture of a man whose faith is battling with his doubt as his inner being revolts against a materialistic view of human nature and destiny may be autobiographical and is reminiscent of the preacher's own turmoil during the period of intense questioning and skepticism through which he passed before going to Brighton. The passage shows the literary influence of Tennyson's *In Memoriam,* canto 124, iii, iv. A perceptive writer has discerned the same struggle in Tennyson himself: "Whereas in such matters as love and politics, Tennyson had no doubt as to the truth and value of his compromise and delivered his message in a jaunty and complacent manner which strikes us as both foolish and irritating, yet on religious matters the compromise which he had hoped to evolve broke down before the depth and honesty of his own bitter perplexities, and the result is that we have, not the objective enunciation of a doctrine, but the subjective confession of a tortured human soul" (Harold Nicolson, *Tennyson* [New York: Anchor, 1962], pp. 271 f.).

7. G. Leibniz, *Principles of Nature and Grace, #7.* Martin Heidegger considers this the crucial question for philosophy. See chapter 1 of his *Einführung in die Metaphysik* (Tübingen, 1953), translated by Ralph Manheim as *An Introduction to Metaphysics* (New Haven, 1959).

Linguistic philosophers have sometimes maintained that Bertrand Russell's theory of "description" disposes of the ontological mystery of existence. In modern logic the negative existential proposition has been very fully analyzed. According to Russell, to say that something exists is to say that such-and-such a description has a referent, and conversely to say that something does not exist consists in the fact that such a description has no referent. Now since the denial of an existential proposition is not self-contradictory, it is logically possible that there might be nothing at all. A semantically proper way of translating the super-ultimate question "Why is there anything at all?" is as follows: "Why should not all negative existential statements be true?" If, in fact, all negative existential statements were true, it would then be the case that there be nothing at all. This way of analyzing and construing negative existential statements shows that the original question is insoluble because improperly formulated; there is no conceivable answer to it that would not itself generate the same type of question. Invoking God as the reason that there is something rather than nothing does not solve the fundamental problem, because the question would then immediately arise, "But *why* must there be a God rather than nothing at all? What *reason* is there for this?" If Russell is right, therefore, the original question is meaningless and has given rise to metaphysical theories which have been responses to a false problem. That Russell's analysis has not convinced all contemporary philosophers, not even all those belonging to the linguistic camp, is made abundantly clear by the quotation in the text from Professor Smart. See also Milton K. Munitz, *The Mystery of Existence* (New York, 1965). For Russell's account of the theory, see "On Denoting," *Mind* 14 (1905): 479–93; *Principia Mathematica* (Cambridge, 1910), vol. 1, Introduction, chap. 3 and pp. 173–87; *Introduction to Mathematical Philosophy* (New York, 1919), chap. 16; *Mysticism and Logic* (New York, 1918), chap. 10. The theory is best summarized by Russell himself in his popular *History of Western Philosophy* (New York, 1945), p. 831. For the application of the theory to issues in the philosophy of religion I have availed myself of the illuminating discussions of John Hick (*Scottish Journal of Theology* 12 [1959]: 291–292; *Arguments for the Existence of God* [New York, 1971], pp. 82 f.) and Kai Nielsen (in *Philosophical Interrogations,* ed. Sidney and Beatrice Rome [New York, 1964], pp. 402–3).

    8. J. J. C. Smart, "The Existence of God," in *New Essays in Philosophical Theology,* ed. A. Flew and A. MacIntyre (London, 1955), p. 46. See also Abraham J. Heschel, *Man Is Not Alone* (New York, 1951), p. 12; *idem, God in Search of Man* (New York, 1955), pp. 45 f. In the face of a conflict between logic and experience, to which his theories seemed to have led him, William James announced his determination "*to give up the logic,* fairly, squarely, and irrevocably" (*A Pluralistic Universe* [New York, 1909], p. 212, emphasis in the original). James held that personal religious experience carries authority only for him who has it and not for anyone else, and that while one ought to be cautious of knowledge claims based on such experience, one ought yet to be appreciative of the tendency of such experience to break down the exclusive authority of rationalistic systems which may overlook man's emotional dimensions. "(1) Mystical states, when well developed, usually are, and have a right to be, absolutely authoritative over the individuals to whom they come. (2) No authority emanates from them which should make it a duty for those who stand outside of them to accept their revelations uncritically" (*The Varieties of*

Religious Experience, p. 422). We are here reminded of what Thoreau said: "If a man does not keep pace with his companions, perhaps it is because he hears a different drummer" (*Walden,* XVIII, conclusion).

9. "It is not contrary to reason to prefer the destruction of the whole world to the scratching of my finger" (Hume, *Treatise,* bk. II, pt. iii, sec. 3). Wittgenstein's criticism of metaphysics is more sophisticated. His comparison of metaphysics to a ladder has become classic. "My propositions are elucidatory in this way: he who understands me finally recognizes them as senseless, when he has climbed out through them, on them, over them. (He must, so to speak, throw away the ladder, after he has climbed on it.) . . . Wovon man nicht sprechen kann, darüber muss man schweigen— Whereof one cannot speak, thereof one must be silent." *Tractatus Logico-Philosophicus* (6.54) *ad fin.* Cf. Maimonides' exposition of Ps. 65:2 (Targum), "Silence is praise to Thee, O God," in *Guide* I, chap. 59: a happy agreement.

10. At the very least, Christianity believes in all the dogmas of Judaism and adds to them others of a Christological and ecclesiastical nature.

11. Of course the greenness of grass can be defined in terms of light waves of a certain length, but the light waves themselves are not what we mean by green; the blind physicist knows all about wavelengths, but he cannot tell the color of grass from the color of an orange, while the child playing on the lawn knows nothing about light vibrations but can distinguish green from orange.

12. F. H. Bradley, *Appearance and Reality,* 10th imp. (Oxford University Press, 1966), p. x. If we omit the derogatory epithet "bad," this obiter dictum is as good a definition of philosophy as I have seen. In the considered opinion of G. E. Moore, "unless new reasons never urged hitherto can be found, all the most important philosophic doctrines have as little claim to assent as the most superstitious beliefs of the lowest savages" (*Philosophical Studies* [London, 1922], p. 5). "We do not believe in immortality because we have proved it," declared the British philosopher James Martineau, "but we forever try to prove it because we cannot help believing in it." Very interesting also is the observation of William James: "A Philosophy is the expression of a man's intimate character, and all the definitions of the universe are but the deliberately adopted reactions of human characters upon it" (*A Pluralistic Universe* [New York, 1909], p. 20). Cf. G. B. Shaw, *Saint Joan* (1924), scene V: "*Joan:* My voices come first. I find the reasons after." One recalls the remark attributed to Chief Justice John Marshall: "Judgment for the plaintiff: Mr. Justice Storey will furnish the authorities."

13. William James, *The Will to Believe* (New York, 1897), p. 131.

14. *The Chief Works of Benedict de Spinoza,* trans. with an introduction by R. H. M. Elwes, 2nd ed. (London, 1889), vol. 1, pp. 194 f. (The quotation is from the *Theological-Political Treatise,* chap. 15.) I have singled out Spinoza because he consciously sought to make a break with the past and to create for man "a brave new world" fashioned in the beauty of reason. As a matter of sober fact, the influence of Jewish thought on the system of Spinoza was much greater than he would care to ad-

mit. The full extent of Spinoza's indebtedness to his Jewish predecessors has been carefully documented in Professor H. A. Wolfson's magisterial two-volume study, *The Philosophy of Spinoza* (Cambridge, Mass., 1934). George Eliot (Marian Evans), who could have known only a small part of the evidence relating to the influence of Jewish thought on the pantheistic system of Spinoza, was able to recognize it, through the generosity of her spirit and her amazing intuition. In *Daniel Deronda* she makes Mordecai say: "Baruch Spinoza had not a faithful Jewish heart, though he had sucked the life of his intellect at the breast of Jewish tradition. He laid bare his father's nakedness and said: 'They who scorn him have the higher wisdom.'" Essentially, Spinoza took the deanthropomorphized Deity of Maimonides, combined it with the eternity of matter of Gersonides, the determinism of Crescas, and the immanence of God in all things taught by the Cabbalists, and cast the whole potpourri into the mold of the geometric method. "His reputed God-intoxication," says Professor Wolfson, "was really nothing but a hangover of an earlier religious jag" (*op. cit.*, vol. 2, p. 348).

More recently John Dewey and his followers have turned the "scientific method" into the very apotheosis of philosophy. Dewey himself speaks of the scientific method in terms of religious adoration. Whereas Job in the robust expression of his faith had asserted, "Though He slay me, yet will I trust in Him" (Job 13:15 A.V.), Dewey assures us that "there are a steadily increasing number of persons who find security in *methods* of inquiry, of observation, experiment, of forming hypotheses. Such persons are not unsettled by the upsetting of any special belief, because they retain security of procedure. They can say, borrowing language from another context, though this method slay my most cherished belief, yet will I trust it" ("Fundamentals," *New Republic* 37 [1924]: 275, reprinted in *Characters and Events,* ed. Joseph Ratner [New York, 1929], vol. 2, p. 457). Needless to say, scientists themselves are much less sanguine about the value of the scientific method (cf. above p. 231, n. 12). Friedrich A. Lange showed himself to be the clearer thinker when, in his famous *History of Materialism,* he stated that the scientist *qua* scientist must affirm the scientific method as a methodological principle in natural science. But he also warned of the danger of making a metaphysics out of a method and transforming a technical procedure into a general philosophy.

15. *Flatland,* E. A. Abbot's science fiction classic of life in a two-dimensional world, has suggested to me an analogy regarding this matter, which I have found very helpful. Supposing a scientist from Flatland were to study a fly as it walks across the top of a table. He can accurately predict when the fly will reach the opposite side if it walks at a steady pace. But if the fly flies off the surface of the table and then reappears sometime later at another spot on the table, its behavior will be inexplicable to that scientist; no discoverable law in Flatland can describe its behavior. Nevertheless, this type of phenomenon would not entitle the inhabitants of Flatland to doubt and question the accuracy of the laws of motion on flat surfaces discovered

by their scientists. Similarly, just because science and philosophy are unable to deal satisfactorily with all issues, this does not permit us to question the solid results which these disciplines have achieved.

The limitations of a rational interpretation of reality have been recognized by thinkers who have no theological ax to grind. In one of his books, the British philosopher C. E. M. Joad speaks of Truth, Goodness, and Beauty as the Three Dowagers of Philosophy. In the past, philosophers considered the idea of truth (or reality) the most fundamental concept in philosophy. However, James Mark Baldwin (the editor of the *Dictionary of Philosophy and Psychology*), in *A Genetic Theory of Reality* (1915), develops a philosophical system in which beauty is the key to every facet of reality. According to this theory, aesthetic appreciation is the highest and absolute vehicle of human apprehension and reveals truths otherwise unobtainable. The ultimate aspect of reality is only realized in achieving and enjoying the beautiful. The upshot of Baldwin's metaphysical system, for which he invents the name Pancalism, is that a thing is true and good *because* it is beautiful. The aesthetic appreciation, rather than reason or will, is thus the ultimate organ of reality. It is only fair to add that in Baldwin's opinion the religious conception fails in that it lends itself to a dualism which it cannot overcome. It is unsuccessful in achieving a unity, because as an ideal, God is a postulate beyond the grasp of intellectual apprehension, while insofar as He is actual, He is not ideal, but remains a finite person along with other persons.

16. Cf. the standard talmudic objection: "Why do I need a biblical text?—The matter is founded on reason!" (Kethuboth 22a, Baba Kamma 46b, Niddah 25a). See also the comments of R. Beşalel Ashkenasi (*Shittah Meḳubeṣet, Zebaḥim* 75b, #1), and the writer's remarks in the rabbinical journal of *Beth Yitzchak* (New York, 1953), pp. 100 f. See further, Joseph B. Soloveitchik, "The Man of Halakah" (Hebrew), *Talpiyot* 1, nos. 3–4 (1944): 700–702 (pp. 651–735). The essay contains a fine characterization and sketch of the talmudic scholar (*talmid ḥakam*) by my distinguished master and beloved teacher, who is preeminent in talmudic learning among contemporary scholars.

17. Every revelation is, of course, *ipso facto* supernatural, but we are here limiting our attention to the *content* of an alleged revelation. Interestingly enough, some modern Jewish thinkers like Rosenzweig and his followers have blessed us with the problem of a vacuous revelation devoid of content.

18. *In Galat.* 3:6 (Weimar ed.), vol. 40, pt. 1, p. 363, 1. 25. "In all who have faith in Christ," Luther says elsewhere, "reason shall be killed; else faith has no place with them; for reason fights against faith" (*Works* [Erlangen ed.], vol. 44 [1850], p. 157).

19. H. M. Rolton, *Studies in Christian Doctrine* (London, 1960), pp. 166 ff. (emphasis in the original). Cf. also Kierkegaard's doctrine of Christian faith as a "leap into the absurd."

20. On this mysterious rite, see the interesting essay of Joseph L. Blau, "The Red Heifer: A Biblical Purification Rite in Rabbinic Literature," *Numen* 14 (1967): 70–78.

21. Although in their context the concluding sentences of Hume's essay *Of Miracles* are grotesque, yet standing alone they are a competent summary of traditional Christian teachings and of impeccable orthodoxy. "Upon the whole we may conclude that the Christian religion not only was at first attended with miracles, but even at this day cannot be believed by a reasonable person without one. Mere reason is insufficient to convince us of its veracity. And whoever is moved by faith to assent to it, is conscious of a continued miracle in his own person, which subverts all the principles of his understanding, and gives him a determination to believe what is most contrary to custom and experience."

Louis Jacobs, *Faith* (London, 1968), Appendix II, "Jewish Parallels to the Tertullian Paradox," pp. 201–9, has attempted to find statements in Jewish sources stressing the incompatibility of faith and reason, but his examples are very late (Rabbi Naḥman of Bratzlav, who died in 1811, and the Ḥabad school of Ḥasidism) and not very cogent.

22. George Foot Moore, *Judaism*, vol. 3 (Harvard University Press, 1930), p. 60. Some of the ideas and the exposition in the preceding paragraphs are taken from an essay entitled "The Orthodox Position" (Cambridge, 1915), written by the late Mr. Herbert Martin James Loewe, sometime Reader in Rabbinics at Cambridge University, and from an unpublished lecture of Dr. Azriel Rosenfeld.

Perhaps, like most generalizations, this one about the basic difference between Judaism and Christianity is in need of some qualification. Catholicism and the more traditional forms of Protestantism do impose restraints on the conduct of an individual which impede the free exercise of his faculties in such spheres as, for example, birth control and Sunday Mass attendance. Nevertheless these restraints are of secondary importance in comparison to proper beliefs and the profession of the correct creed. The Inquisition executed thousands of persons for holding heterodox views on the Trinity but not one for immoral or unethical conduct. Ultimately the generalization goes back to the distinction which Moses Mendelssohn made between the "revealed religion" (*Glaubenslehre*) of Christianity and the "revealed law" (*Gesetzgebung*) of Judaism. Among all the Jewish laws, he points out, there is none that says: "Thou shalt believe" or "Thou shalt not believe"; all say "Thou shalt do" or "Thou shalt not do." "The spirit of Judaism," he says in a letter written in 1782, "is conformity in deeds and freedom of thought in doctrinal matters" (Letter to Abraham Nathan Wolf, in *Gesammelte Schriften*, vol. 5 [Leipzig, 1844], pp. 602–3; Eng. trans. by Alfred Jospe in *Jerusalem and Other Jewish Writings by Moses Mendelssohn* [New York, 1969], p. 137).

The distinction is elaborated by Mendelssohn in chapter 2 of his *Jerusalem* (ed. Alfred Jospe, pp. 61–73). While Mendelssohn's distinction has frequently been criticized and questioned, I think that it is essentially sound. In the first place, as Mendelssohn quite properly points out, the distinction is by no means original with him but has its roots in the medieval religious philosophers and mystics. Secondly, we see this phenomenon in our own day in the Reconstructionist movement. This movement adheres to a great many traditional Jewish laws that it observes in the form of religious "folkways," while subscribing to a naturalist-humanist conception of God, interpreting it as the sum total of those forces which help us live better and richer lives.

23. Medieval theologians universally held that the damned will greatly outnumber the saved even among adult Catholic Christians and that the overwhelming majority of the human race will go to eternal perdition. Father F. X. Godts, a Belgian Redemptorist priest, has collected exhaustively the judgments of medieval theologians as to the small number of mankind who shall be saved. Fr. Godts gave his treatise the characteristic title "What Have the Saints Taught Concerning the Paucity of Those That Shall Be Saved?" (*De paucitate salvandorum quid docuerint Sancti* [Roulers, 1899]). St. Thomas himself, for all his moderation, accepts as a fact too universally known to need proof that the damned would far outnumber the saved. He contrasts "some" who shall be saved with "very many" who shall be damned (*aliquos . . . plurimos: S.T.,* 1a, q. 23, art. 7 ad 3). See the study of the Cambridge medievalist George Gordon Coulton, *St. Thomas Aquinas on the Elect and the Reprobate* (London, 1927). With this contrast the teaching of the rabbis that every Israelite will ultimately be saved: "All Israel have a share in the world to come" (Mishnah, Sanhedrin 11:1—in the numeration of the Jerusalem Talmud, 10:1). In the Middle Ages the opinion came to prevail that every human soul would be redeemed and that the righteous Gentiles would enjoy the felicities of the world to come. Thus Maimonides: "The pious of the nations of the world [Gentiles] have a share in the world to come" (*Yad, Teshubah* 3:5). And again: "Not only the tribe of Levi, but every human being born into this world whose spirit moves him and whose intellect guides him to devote himself to the service of the Lord . . . becomes sanctified with supreme sanctity. God is his portion and his eternal inheritance, and He will provide sufficiently for his needs as He did for the priest and the Levite of yore" (*Yad, Shemitah we-Yobel* 13:13). See L. Zunz, *Zur Geschichte und Literatur* (Berlin, 1845), pp. 371–89; cf. Jacob Katz, "The Vicissitudes of Three Apologetic Passages" (Hebrew), *Zion* 23–24 (1958–59): 174 ff. (pp. 174–93).

W. E. H. Lecky, at the conclusion of volume 1 of his *History of Rationalism,* first published in 1865, observes: "Whenever the doctrine of exclusive salvation is generally believed and realized, habits of thought will be formed around it that are diametrically opposed to the spirit of enquiry and absolutely incompatible with human progress. An indifference to truth, a spirit of blind and at the same time wilful credulity, will be encouraged, which will multiply fictions of every kind, will associate enquiry with the ideas of danger and of guilt, will make men esteem that impartiality of judgment and study which is the very soul of truth an unholy thing, and will so emasculate their faculties as to produce a general torpor on every subject."

24. For a philosphical critique of these doctrines, see Kant, *Religion Within the Limits of Reason Alone,* trans. Greene and Hudson (Chicago, 1934). See also Edward Westermarck, *Christianity and Morals* (London, 1939), pp. 150, 157, 162–64, 398, 402.

25. William Empson, *Milton's God,* rev. ed. (London, 1965), p. 251.

26. Circumcision in particular became the subject of ribald mockery. M. Theodore Reinach was one of the most liberal nineteenth-century scholars. In a very learned tome entitled *Textes d'auteurs grecs et latins relatifs au Judaisme* (1895), he collected every fragment written by Greek and Latin writers on Jews. On the left column of the page, the original text is printed, on the right the translation. But when he came to some of the coarse and loose epigrams of Martial, he thought that they were better left in the decent obscurity of a learned tongue. He says: "La circoncision, facile sujet de plaisanterie, est encore mentionée dans les passages suivants qu'on nos dispensera de traduire" (p. 288, n. 1). What is even more surprising is that the editors of the Loeb Classical Library completely omitted or shamelessly bowdlerized these same passages in the English translation, being content in one place to remark that a knowledge of the vulgar tongue is desirable in understanding Martial.

27. Quoted by Charles Francis Potter, *The Preacher and I* (New York, 1951), p. 316. Incidentally, Darrow was not quite as clever as he possibly imagined himself to be. The rabbis knew as well as Darrow that it does not matter to God what we eat and what we avoid. "For, indeed, what difference does it make to God," they ask, "how we slaughter an animal or of what kind of food we partake, except that He desires by such laws and regulations to benefit His creatures, to purify their hearts, and to ennoble their character" (*Tanḥuma,* "Shemini," ed. Buber, p. 30; Genesis Rabbah 44:1 [see the parallels listed by Theodor-Albeck, pp. 424–25, and Maimonides' use of the passage in *Guide* III:26]; cf. G. F. Moore, *Judaism,* vol. 2, pp. 7, 77, and 161).

28. The contrast drawn between Judaism and Christianity in their respective attitudes toward science perhaps needs some qualification. Certain rabbis declared that in the event of a conflict of views between the rabbis and scientific or medical authorities, the views of the latter are to be disregarded and those of the rabbis adhered to. Typical of this school of thought is R. Isaac ben Sheshet Perfet (acronym, RIBaSh, 1326–1408). In his Responsa #447 (p. 276, ed. 1878), he says: "With regard to the Torah and its commandments, we should not base our judgment on the words of natural scientists and physicians; for if we believed their words, it would be as though the Torah were not—God forbid—of divine origin. . . . Rather, we rely on our sages of blessed memory even if they tell us that right is left . . . and not on the Greek and Arab scholars, who speak only on the basis of their own

reasoning or on the basis of some experiment. . . . as it says [Niddah 30b] 'I bring you proof from the Torah, and you bring proof from some fools!' . . ."

The biblical allusion in this excerpt is to Deuteronomy 17:11: "You shall not turn aside from the verdict which they declare to you, either to the right hand or to the left." On this text Rashi (quoting the Sifre) comments, "Even if they tell you that right is left and left is right." See, however, the emendation of Elijah Wilna reading: "Even if it *appears to you* that they are telling you that right is left and left is right." This emendation is supported by the Jerusalem Talmud, Horayoth 1:1, 45d, where it is stated: "You might infer that if they tell you that right is left and left is right, you are to listen to them, therefore Scripture says 'to the right or to the left'—if they tell you the right is right and the left is left." Isaac Arama, *'Aḳedat Yiṣhak,* sec. Yethro, chap. 43, concludes that the Sifre refers to the Great Sanhedrin, that is, the Supreme Court in Jerusalem, and in a case of emergency legislation, where judgment was rendered not by scriptural prescription. In such instance the individual should submit to the opinion of the majority, as an emergency measure, even though he differs from their opinion. This merely indicates the duty of the individual to obey the majority in communal and state matters. On this passage see also the remarks, which bear careful examination, of Joseph Albo, *'Ikkarim* III:23. In all fairness to R. Isaac ben Sheshet, it must be pointed out that he was himself well versed in contemporary philosophy and rhetoric and was far from being narrow-minded. Professor Baer points out that his fundamental objections to philosophy and science are found only in those of his writings written after the great persecutions and massacres of 1391. See Yitshak (Fritz) Baer, *A History of the Jews in Christian Spain* (Philadelphia, 1966), vol. 2, pp. 75 f. and p. 465, n. 23. On the whole this attitude is perhaps more typical of some forms of Christianity than of normative Judaism. With the sentiment expressed one may compare the words of St. Ignatius Loyola, the founder of the Society of Jesus: "In order to be entirely of one mind with the Catholic Church, we must," he said, "if anything appears to our eyes white, which it declares to be black, also declare it to be really black" (Constitution of the Jesuits, par. vi, cap. 1, sec. 1, cf. C. J. Cadoux, *Catholicism and Christianity* [London, 1928], p. 122 n.).

Some thinkers of this school of thought denounced the Copernican system as heretical, because the Bible said that the earth was fixed and the sun moving. Over two hundred years after Copernicus published definite proof of the heliocentric system, the famous Rabbi Jonathan Eybeschitz stated emphatically that Copernicus and his followers had inherited falsehood, and "the earth standeth still for ever" (Eccles. 1:3—*Ya'aroth Debash,* Sermon for 7th Ab 5504 [= 1744]; ed. Lemberg 1863, p. 36; cf., also, Tobias Katz, *Ma'aseh Tubiah,* "'Olam ha-Galgalim" iii). The attitude of Maimonides (*Guide,* III:15 end) on scientific questions was more sound and reasonable; see, however, *Yad, Hilkoth Sheḥitah* 10:12 f.

In general it is fair to say that in his halakhic works Maimonides not only hewed close to the law, but was, in fact, a rigorist, even when he could have a choice between rigor and leniency; and, always with notable exceptions, he did not allow his scientific training to affect his strict adherence to talmudic rule. It may be that in his philosophical and medical works he gave himself greater freedom of action, relying on the greater liberality of his prospective readership in those two fields; but this was not generally the case in the field of Halakah. See, for example, the Introduction to the *Book of Holiness* in the Yale Judaica Series, English trans. by Rabinowitz-Grossman (New Haven, 1965), p. xxix: "While Maimonides valued man-made science highly, he believed that it should be limited to its proper sphere; worldly wisdom, he thought, cannot outweigh the wisdom of the Torah, but should rather be subservient to it. He therefore held that the rulings of the Sages, being of Scriptural derivation, are inherently true, even if in some cases scientific knowledge, in a particular day and age, may seem to contradict them. Human knowledge is at best imperfect, and what is considered a scientific fact today may in any case be found to be not so tomorrow, whereas divine wisdom is perfect and immutable." But cf. *supra* p. 183, n. 3.

29. Philosophical analysis, however, can show that certain essential Christian claims about the Godhead and the relation between Persons of the Trinity embody conceptual confusion rather than legitimate paradox. See Ronald W. Hepburn, *Christianity and Paradox* (New York, 1958).

30. The same criticism can be made of Buber and the Jewish existentialists. Although Buber tried to promote understanding and possessed a magnetic personality, the net effect of his philosophy is reactionary.

Buber attempted to preclude any rational criticism of his position. This he tried to do by utilizing his distinction between I-It and I-Thou relations. An I-It relationship, in Buber's terminology, refers to an attitude toward a person or thing as a means capable of being employed to further one's interests or goals. It is much more difficult to say exactly what Buber meant by an I-Thou relationship. His authorized translator, Professor Walter Kaufmann, accuses him of deliberate obscurity, saying of *I and Thou* that "a lack of clarity is almost indispensable [to the survival of the book]" (W. Kaufmann, preface to *I and Thou,* by Martin Buber [New York, 1970], p. 20; cf. pp. 18 and 19). His translator further reproaches Buber with oversimplification in reducing man's manifold relation to reality to the twofold division I-It and I-Thou. People crave tidy formulas; what they want "is an oversimplification, a reduction of a multitude of possibilities to only two. But if the recommended path were utterly devoid of mystery, it would cease to fascinate men" (*ibid.,* p. 10). *"Mundus vult decipi,"* he reiterates again and again in his preface, "the world wants to be deceived." Suffice it to say for our purposes that an I-Thou relationship is a relation to a person, or even to an animal, plant, or stone, that is characterized by mutuality, openness, directness, and presentness.

Now leaving aside Buber's deliberate obscurity and oversimplification, however important, it is clear that every objective critique of his thought can be dismissed as belonging to the realm of I-It, which has no bearing on the realm of I-Thou. The Buberite is thus provided with an "insulated theory" and a dialectical device which can short-circuit any attempted objective criticism of his thought. Maurice Friedman, one of Buber's most devoted disciples and an authoritative expositor of his thought, admits as much when he says: "It is the presentness of the I-Thou relation which shows most clearly the logical impossibility of criticizing I-Thou knowing on the basis of any system of I-It" (Maurice S. Friedman, *Martin Buber: The Life of Dialogue* [Chicago, 1956], p. 168).

This dialectical ploy has the effect of what Cardinal Newman called "poisoning the wells." In his *Apologia* Newman recounts the details of his famous controversy with Charles Kingsley. The latter challenged Newman's integrity by suggesting that truth did not possess the highest value for a Roman Catholic priest—unfailing devotion to the Church was regarded above truth. Newman protested that such an assumption made it possible for an opponent to state his case. He just has no ground to stand on. How could Newman prove to Kingsley that he prized truth above anything else if Kingsley argued from the premise that he did not. So long as the proffered definition of the situation is imposed on him, he has no way to turn; Newman would be logically "hamstrung." There is no possible sort of argument by which he could extricate himself from the charge laid upon him. But as Newman pointed out, no accusation can be accepted on its face if it is impossible to see how it stacks up against contrary, or apparently contrary, evidence. And the same surely holds true for a philosophical theory or overall world-view. For a trenchant criticism of Buber, see Ronald W. Hepburn, *Christianity and Paradox* (New York, 1968), chaps. 3 and 4, and Paul Edwards' Lindley Lecture, *Buber and Buberism: A Critical Evaluation* (Lawrence: University of Kansas Press, 1970).

31. *Yad, Kiddush ha-Ḥodesh* 17:24, translation with some minor verbal changes adapted from Solomon Gandz in the Yale Judaica Series. Sense and context require the addition of the words in brackets; cf. E. Baneth, "Maimuni's Neumondsberechnung," *Berichte über die Lehranstalt für die Wissenschaft des Judenthums in Berlin* 21 (1903): 174, n. 12.

32. The term "category mistake" was first coined by Professor Gilbert Ryle. See (1) his *The Concept of Mind* (New York, 1949), index, s.v. "category-mistake"; (2) his paper "Categories," in *Proceedings of the Aristotelian Society,* 1938–39, now reprinted in *Essays on Logic and Language,* 2nd series (Oxford, 1955), pp. 65 ff.; (3) his inaugural lecture, "Philosophical Arguments," given in Oxford in 1945.

33. Franz Rosenzweig, *Briefe* (Berlin, 1935), pp. 581–82. The translation of the first part of the quotation is taken from N. N. Glatzer, *Franz Rosenzweig: His Life and Thought* (New York, 1953), p. 158; the second part is taken from the rendering in Will Herberg, *Judaism and Modern Man* (New York, 1951), p. 249. See also Jakob J. Petuchowski, "The Supposed Dogma of the Mosaic Authorship of the Pentateuch," *Hibbert Journal* 57 (July 1959): 356–60; Milton Steinberg, *Anatomy of a Faith,* ed. Arthur A. Cohen (New York, 1960), pp. 260 and 167, and Emanuel Rackman, *One Man's Judaism* (New York, 1970), pp. 18, 175 f. See Appendix D, "The Keystone in S. R. Hirsch's Philosophy of Judaism."

34. See above, pp. 24 ff.

35. See Isaac Breuer, *Die Welt als Schöpfung und Natur* (Frankfurt A. M., 1926), chap. 8, pp. 52 ff. The year 5686 A.M. (*anno mundi* = "in the year of the world") in the Hebrew calendar corresponds to 1926 in the Gregorian calendar, the year when Breuer's work was published. Breuer's thesis is reminiscent of Philip Gosse's refutation of the theory of evolution in *Omphalos* (1857). According to Gosse, trees were created full-blown with annular rings, and rocks were created complete with fossils just as they would have become if they had been due to volcanic action or to sedimentary deposits. What Charles Kingsley wrote to Philip Gosse regarding his argument applies equally, *mutatis mutandis,* to Breuer's thesis: "Assuming the act of absolute creation—which I have always assumed as fully as you—shall I tell you the truth? It is best. Your book is the first that ever made me doubt it, and I fear that it will make hundreds do so. Your book tends to prove this—that if we accept the fact of absolute creation God becomes *Deus quidam deceptor.* . . . It is not my reason but my conscience which revolts here" (Edmund Gosse, *Life of P.H. Gosse* [London, 1890], pp. 280–81). For a view regarding evolution similar to Breuer's, see the Lubavitcher Rebbe's (Rabbi M. M. Schneerson) "Letter on Evolution" (New York, 1962), substantially reprinted in *A Science and Torah Reader,* ed. Y. Kornreich (New York, 1970), pp. 19–27.

36. The source of this aphorism has not been established. Kaufmann, *Attributenlehre,* n. 190, pp. 326 f., enumerates many parallels from Arabic, Jewish, and Christian sources, but one could add many more, for example, Saadiah, *Amānāt* I, 4 (ed. Landauer, p. 71); *Musare ha-Pilosofim* (ed. Lowenthal, p 13). For a modern version of this aphorism, cf. Samuel H. Dresner, *Three Paths of God and Man* (New York, 1960), p. 13. Joseph ibn Ṣaddiḳ, a twelfth-century Jewish philosopher, offers a peculiar argument for the unknowability of God. To know a thing, he says, we must know its cause. The distinguishing metaphysical attribute of God, however, is *aseitas* (uncaused existence), and He is therefore unknowable (*Microcosm,* ed. Horovitz, p. 48).

37. Maimonides, *Eight Chapters,* end (Gorfinkle trans.); Aquinas, *De Veritate,* II, 1 ad 9; cf. *C.G.,* I, 12; *S.T.,* Ia, q. 2, a. 2, ad 3; *Expositio Super Librum Boethii De Trinitate,* q. 1, a. 2, ad 4; *De Potentia,* q. 7, a. 5, ad 14; St. Augustine, *Sermones* 41 de V.D., cited by John A. O'Brien, *Truths Men Live By* (New York, 1945), p. 104. The Anglican divine Richard Hooker, in his *Ecclesiastical Polity* (bk. I, 2), admirably sums up the consensus of the medieval thinkers: "Dangerous it were for the feeble brain of man to wade far into the doings of the Most High; Whom although to know be life, and joy to make mention of His name; yet our soundest knowledge is to know that we know Him not as indeed He is, neither can we know Him: and our safest eloquence concerning Him is our silence, when we confess without confession that His glory is inexplicable, His greatness above our capacity and reach. He is above, and we upon earth; therefore it behooveth our words to be wary and few."

38. In order that I may not be misunderstood, let me make it clear that I believe that this assurance of the rightness of one's convictions is a common human failing affecting all thinkers of whatever school (in the words of the prophet Jeremiah [9:25] "the circumcised as well as the uncircumcised") and is not the peculiar failing of religious philosophers. Professor Edwin A. Burtt (*In Search of Philosophical Understanding* [New York, 1965], p. 106) has cited chapter and verse illustrating this assurance from the writings of Bradley, Russell, and Wittgenstein. I should like to add an example of my own. Morris R. Cohen edited with his son Felix a textbook of readings in legal philosophy which appeared in 1951, not long after the elder Cohen's death, under the title *Readings in Jurisprudence and Legal Philosophy.* It is a fat volume of almost a thousand pages covering the field from the earliest times to the present day and containing selections from Aristotle to Von Ihering. In this tome, fully one-third of the selections are devoted to the writings of the two Cohens, father and son. And the son had the naivete to remark in the preface that the main factor of selection was the preference of students. I suppose the mediocre students selected Aristotle, Kant, and Hegel, while the brilliant A students opted for the Cohens, senior and junior.

39. The "naturalist" philosopher Professor F. J. E. Woodbridge, late of Columbia University, has expressed himself clearly on this point. "Obviously that which is acknowledged to be superior to Nature cannot be proved to exist in the way existence is proved or disproved in Nature. Could it be, it would cease to be supernatural. Its existence must be supernatural existence" (F. J. E. Woodbridge, *An Essay on Nature* [New York, 1940], p. 306).

40. G. W. F. Hegel, *Lectures on the Philosophy of Religion,* trans. E. B. Speirs and J. B. Sanderson, vol. 2 (New York, 1962), pp. 338 f. Cf. Maimonides, *Yad, Yesode ha-Torah* 8:1 and *Guide* III:24. Even if the existence of God is assumed, miracles cannot be utilized to prove the truth of any one religion, for their evidence rests upon the assumption that God possesses a moral character which excludes the possibility that He may, for one reason or another, work miracles on behalf of a falsehood. The weakness of miracles as a foundation for theological beliefs was clearly demonstrated in the aftermath of the Six Day War in Israel in 1967. The rabbis affiliated with the National Religious Party (Mizrachi) saw in the Israeli military victory not only a miracle, but the very "beginning of the redemption" (*'athalta di-ge'ulah*), the final "happening" before the advent of the Messiah. On the other hand, the extreme rightist group known as the Neturei Karta (Guardians of the City) saw in the victory not the hand of God, but only natural events. Their spokesman, the Satmarer Rebbe, explained that "miracles" are miracles only when they are in accord with the Torah and Halakah; otherwise, like the miracles of the Egyptian magicians, they are the deceptions of Satan. Indeed, military victories are special opportunities for the seductions of Satan. See the *Kunteras al ha-Ge'ulah we'al ha-Temurah,* which applied the Rabbi of Satmar's teaching to the aftermath of the Six Day War

(Jerusalem, 1968; especially p. 69; cf., also, pp. 7 and 34 f.). In this situation the laity was understandably disturbed and perplexed. "Who shall decide when doctors disagree?" The ideology of the Neturei Karta is summarized in English in a hostile and very unsympathetic spirit by Dr. Norman Lamm, in an article in the Fall 1971 issue of *Tradition,* and with candor and reverence by Y. Domb, *The Transformation* (London, 1958).

41. A. S. B. Michelson, *Dober Shalom* (Przemysl, 1910), p. 78, quoted in Louis I. Newman, *The Hasidic Anthology* (New York, 1934), pp. 307 f. This moral is the theme of Bruce Marshall's clever and frequently witty satirical novel, *Father Malachy's Miracle,* whose significance has been noted by no less eminent a theologian than the late Karl Barth in volume 4 of his *Kirchliche Dogmatik.*

42. Cf. I. Heinemann, "Das Ideal der Heiligkeit usw.," *Jeschurun* 8 (1921): 99–120, and Bruno Italiener, "The Musaf Kedushah," *HUCA* 26 (1955): 413—25.

43. Rudolf Otto, *The Idea of the Holy,* trans. J. H. Harvey, 2nd ed. (Oxford, 1950), pp. 60 f. (emphasis in the original).

44. *Ibid.,* pp. 63, 71, 202, App. III; *idem, Religious Essays* (Oxford, 1931), pp. 25–26.

45. In his commentary on Sanhedrin 10:1 (p. 203, ed. J. Kafiḥ), Maimonides puts the matter in the following way: "Know that just as a blind man can form no idea of colors, nor a deaf man comprehend sounds, nor a eunuch feel the passion for sexual intercourse, so bodies cannot comprehend the delights of the soul." (This passage is shamelessly bowdlerized in Leon Roth, *The Guide of the Perplexed, Moses Maimonides* [London, 1948], pp. 114 f.)

It was not without reason that targumist and liturgist were to recreate the scene of Isaiah's Temple experience in terms of an antiphonal chorale at a coronation that recalls Handel's account of the mystic trance which he experienced as he was enraptured out of his corporeal senses and saw Heaven opened up when he penned the "Hallelujah" chorus with its multitudinous reverberations. The Aramaic paraphrase (Targum pseudo-Jonathan) interprets the triune refrain of the angelic choir: "Holy—in the highest heavens, His divine abode; holy—upon earth, the work of His might; holy—forever and unto all eternity is the Lord of hosts." But the words, like the ineffable quality of the numinous, are incapable of interpretation.

46. Friedrich Nietzsche, *Human, All too Human,* I.

47. F. R. Tennant, *Philosophical Theology* (Cambridge, 1930), vol. 1, pp. 290 ff.; chap. 12; vol. 12, pp. 95, 243 ff. See also George Nakhnikian, "On the Cognitive Import of Certain Conscious States," in *Religious Experience and Truth,* ed. Sidney Hook (New York, 1961), pp. 156–64. Alvin Plantinga, in his impressive study, *God and Other Minds* (New York, 1968), champions the thesis that belief in other minds and belief in God are in the same epistemological boat; hence if either is rational so is the other. But obviously our belief in fellow-subjects is rational; so, therefore, is the theist's belief in God. Cf. Tennant, *op. cit,* vol. 1, pp. 88 f. G. K. Chesterton used to

counter doubts about the existence of God by demanding proof of the existence of one's next-door neighbor.

48. The Spanish Carmelite St. Teresa of Avila, perhaps the greatest female mystic, assures us (as do other Christian mystics) that after her ecstatic intellectual Vision, which was vouchsafed to her in the Seventh Habitation of the soul, she learned to understand the deep mystery of the Blessed Trinity and to comprehend how God can be three Persons. Far be it from me to question the truth of her assertion, but surely she would not have recognized the revelation as that of the Trinity if she had not already known something about the Trinity. Would a vision of the Holy Trinity have appeared to her great-grandfather, who was Jewish? (see Homero Seris, "Nueva genealogia de Santa Teresa (artículoreseña)," *Nueva Revista de filología hispánica* 10 [1956]: 365–84). I have read a fair amount of the literature containing the testimony of the mystics, but I have never come across a Jewish mystic who had a vision of the Blessed Virigin or a Christian mystic who meditated on the elevation of Mohammed's coffin.

49. Otto, *Idea of the Holy,* p. 11, n. (emphasis in the original).

50. C. D. Broad, *Religion, Philosophy and Psychical Research* (London, 1953), p. 198. Elsewhere Broad has revived Bergson's view that the brain is essentially an organ of limitation, its primary function being to channelize attention unto those parts of the exterior world which may be biologically useful to man.

51. William James, *The Varieties of Religious Experience* (New York: Longmans, Green & Co., 1903), p. 25.

52. For Ezekiel see Edwin C. Broome, "Ezekiel's Abnormal Personality," *Journal of Biblical Literature* 65 (1946): 277–92.

53. Babylonian Talmud, Ḥagigah 14b.

54. St. John of the Cross, *Ascent of Mount Carmel,* bk. II, chap. xxix, 4.

55. Cf. C. D. Broad, *Religion, Philosophy and Psychical Research* (London, 1953), pp. 190–201. On the unanimity of the mystics' reports on certain key points, see the detailed examination of Walter Stace in chapter 2, "The Problem of the Universal Core," in *Mysticism and Philosophy* (Philadelphia, 1960), pp. 41–133. See also Bergson's discussion of mysticism in chapter 3 ("Dynamic Religion") of his *Two Sources of Morality and Religion* (New York, 1935).

56. K. Kohler, *Jewish Theology* (New York: Macmillan, 1918), p. 70 (emphasis in the original). A much more weighty authority than Kohler, R. Elijah Gaon of Wilna, expressed his considered opinion that the *Kuzari* is an authoritative and authentic exposition of normative Judaism. See the passage from the *Tosefet Maʿaseh Rav* of R. Baer b. Tanḥum quoted on p. 5 of M. T. Genizi's edition of the *Kuzari* with a new commentary, published in Tel-Aviv in 1969. Gershom Scholem speaks felicitously of Halevi as the "most Jewish of Jewish philosophers" (*Major Trends* [New York, 1946], p. 24).

57. J. B. Watson, *Behaviorism* (New York: People's Institute Pub. Co., 1924), pp.

1, 2, cf. p. 289. A more balanced estimate of the claims of both science and religion, endeavoring to maintain the strictly scientific point of view without giving the religious man cause for just complaint, was made by James B. Pratt. Professor Pratt was careful to distinguish psychological observations from metaphysical hypotheses, and laid down the limits of psychology quite properly when he said that "it must content itself with a description of human experience, while recognizing that there may well be spheres of reality to which these experiences refer and with which they are possibly connected, which yet cannot be investigated by science" (J. B. Pratt, *The Religious Consciousness* [New York, 1920], p. 42).

58. In all fairness it must be stated that Freud tried to separate the question of the psychological origin of religion from that of its truth or falsity, saying that "it does not lie within the scope of this inquiry to estimate the value of religious doctrines as truth" (Freud, *The Future of an Illusion* [New York, 1949], p. 57). Unfortunately the epigones were not as circumspect.

59. *Yad, Matnoth 'Aniyim* 10:18 (see Karo in his commentary *Kesef Mishneh, ad loc.,* for the talmudic references); commentary on Abot 4:5. In the nineteenth century, R. Moses Sofer still showed great misgivings about accepting remuneration from the community. See *Hatam Sofer, Hoshen Mishpat,* no. 164. Many outstanding halakic authorities refused to hold any communal offices. As late as the eve of the destruction of East European Jewry in the wake of the Second World War, R. Israel Meir Kahan of Radin, known as the Hafeṣ Hayyim, for example, eked out a meager livelihood by running a small grocery store. He closed his shop as soon as he had earned enough to provide his family with the necessaries for one week, lest the faithful flock to it to the detriment of his competitors. Dr. Nemoy takes exception to this line of apologetics. He writes: "Behaviorists might claim that the rabbis were motivated by their superiority complex over against the *'Am ha-'areṣ* (the ignorant and negligent *vulgus*), who constituted the overwhelming majority, and regarded themselves as the elite. Even if the profit therefrom was not economic, there was still the honor and deference of a superior caste, a powerful inducement surely."

60. W. E. Hocking, *The Meaning of God in Human Experience* (New Haven: Yale University Press, 1912), p. 143. Perhaps this state of facts can be illustrated by puzzle pictures with which the gestalt psychologists have experimented. The same ambiguous pattern of lines, curving and straight, can be interpreted as a duck's head facing left or as a rabbit's head facing right. Again in the same picture two people, or the same person at different times, may quite properly perceive a white flower or a Maltese cross, a vase or a pair of faces. The use of these illustrations should not suggest to the reader that I trifle with the subject. No less influential a philosopher than Ludwig Wittgenstein devotes a great deal of space to such puzzles in his posthumous *Philosophical Investigations* (New York, 1953), pp. 194 ff. See also Joseph Jastrow, *Fact and Fable in Psychology* (New York, 1900), p. 295.

61. A. E. Taylor, *The Faith of a Moralist,* Series II (London: Macmillan, 1937), pp. 381 ff. Professor Taylor acknowledges his own indebtedness to another luminous

thinker, Dr. E. R. Bevan, whose acute essay, "Christianity in the Modern World," appears in *Hellenism and Christianity* (London, 1921), pp. 249 ff. The present writer has utilized this analysis in a discussion of the religious situation in present-day Israel. See "Faith and Doubt" (Hebrew) in *Deoth: A Religious-Academic Periodical,* Fall 1971, pp. 51 ff.

62. From the middle benediction of the Sabbath *'Amidah.* The essence of a religion is always best seen in its liturgy. When the soul makes ready to pour out its most intimate and profound thoughts, no distressing discord of controversy is heard, and the noises of life cannot find entrance.

63. To the best of my knowledge, no thoroughgoing, conclusive, factual studies have ever been made of the religious beliefs of scientists and other intellectuals. James Leuba, a psychologist and an authority on mysticism, did make a survey of the belief in a personal God and immortality among various scientific men listed in Cattell's *American Men of Science.* The result of his survey was published in book form in *The Belief in God and Immortality* (Boston: Sherman, French Co., 1916), and summarized, together with some subsequent studies of his, in an article entitled "Religious Beliefs of American Scientists," *Harper's Magazine* 169 (1934): 291–300. His findings were that disbelief was more widespread among the more eminent men in every branch of science objectively classified (viz., those starred in Cattell's directory because they were considered preeminent by their colleagues). These findings have been questioned by other investigators. In particular, strong exception has been taken to his treatment (in good Orwellian fashion) of some scientists as "more equal" than others. Leuba was greatly impressed with his finding (*O sancta simplicitas!*) that among psychologists, "who may be supposed to have more knowledge bearing upon ultimate questions than other scientific men," one finds the smallest number of believers. However this may be, a study made of the opinions of the Fellows of the Royal Society at about the same time gives a quite different impression. In *The Religion of Scientists,* ed. C. L. Drawbridge (London: Ernest Benn, 1932), the findings show that the vast majority of the fellows believe in a personal God and immortality. Therefore, unless truth varies (as Pascal once humorously suggested) with the degrees of latitude or longitude, not much weight can be put on the results of such surveys. While I do not mean to claim scientific validity for my personal observations, these do bear out the opinion of Professors Bevan and Taylor that at all levels of intelligence and education we find the believer and the unbeliever side by side.

64. See R. M. Hare, "Theology and Falsification," in *New Essays in Philosophical Theology,* ed. A. Flew and A. MacIntyre (New York, 1955), pp. 99–103, and his article "Religion and Morals" in *Faith and Logic,* ed. Basil Mitchell (London, 1957), pp. 176–93.

65. Waismann, "How I See Philosophy," in *Contemporary British Philosophy* (Third Series), ed. H. D. Lewis (New York: Macmillan, 1956), p. 480. Cf. J. N. Findlay, in Flew and MacIntyre, *op. cit.,* p. 71: " . . . there can be nothing really

'clinching' in philosophy: 'proofs' and 'disproofs' hold only for those who adopt certain premises, who are willing to follow certain rules of argument, and who use their terms in certain definite ways."

66. A. MacIntyre, "The Logical Status of Religious Belief," in MacIntyre *et al.,* *Metaphysical Beliefs,* 2nd ed. (New York, 1970; the essay first appeared in 1957), p. 187; see also MacIntyre's discussion in *Difficulties of Christian Belief* (London, 1959), p. 77. I agree with what Professor MacIntyre has written, even if he has given up this view; and I can truly say that Mohammed has kept the faith even though Allah himself has strayed and departed from it.

67. Berakoth 33b.

68. St. Gregory, *In Evang.,* 11 hom. 26 (*P.L.* 76: 1197) quoted in *S.T.* 1a, q. 1, art. 8, obj. 2.

69. E. Gilson, *Reason and Revelation* (New York, 1938), pp. 73 f.

70. D. Mercier, *A Manual of Scholastic Philosophy,* vol. 1 (London, 1916), p. 401; for the Thomist source of this doctrine, see, for example, *S.T.* 2a, 2ae, q. 4, a. 2, ad 1, etc., and the passage from the *De Veritate* quoted in the text.

71. The many facets of this problem are explored in W. D. Hudson, ed., *The Is-Ought Problem* (London, 1969). See Appendix E, "The Fatherhood of God as the Foundation of Morality."

72. John Locke, *An Essay Concerning Human Understanding,* "Epistle to the Reader."

73. John Hick, *Philosophy of Religion* (Englewood Cliffs, 1963), p. 58; *idem, Arguments for the Existence of God* (London, 1970), p. 101; cf. William James, *Varieties of Religious Experience,* p. 74. See also Mordecai M. Kaplan, *The Future of the American Jew* (New York: Macmillan, 1948), p. 171. With a minor change, Saadia's formulation of the time argument for creation can be used to prove the impossibility of the existence of an Eternal Being (i.e., God), and Anselm's ontological argument has been inverted by Professor J. N. Findlay, in one of the phases of his speculation, to disprove God's existence; if it is *possible,* in some logical and not epistemological sense, that there is no God, then God's existence is not merely doubtful but *impossible,* since nothing capable of nonexistence could be God at all. See J. N. Findlay, "Can God's Existence Be Disproved?", chap. 4 in *New Essays in Philosophical Theology,* ed. Flew and MacIntyre (London, 1955), where the views of G. E. Hughes and A. C. A. Ranier may also be found. Cf. also Paul Henle, "Uses of the Ontological Argument," *Philosophical Review* 70 (1961): 102–9; R. Puccetti, "The Concept of God," *Philosophical Quarterly* 14 (1964): 237–45. Logically it is possible to construct an ontological proof for the nonexistence of the devil, the absolutely imperfect being. Cf. W. K. Grant, "Ontological Disproof of the Devil," *Analysis* 17 (1957): 71–72; D. Haight and M. Haight, "An Ontological Argument for the Devil," *Monist* 54 (1970): 218–20.

Hume and Kant, by showing that all proofs for the existence of God ultimately contracted to the ontological proof, in effect showed that all proofs are functions of definitions and in the final analysis mere tautologies.

74. See above pp. 2 ff.

75. The entire paragraph in which this quotation occurs deserves to be quoted in full. "If we think of the existence of our friends; it is 'direct knowledge' which we want; merely inferential knowledge seems a poor affair. To most men it would be as surprising as unwelcome to hear it could not be directly known whether there were such existences as their friends, and that it was only a matter of (probable) empirical argument and inference from facts which are directly known. And even if we convince ourselves on reflection that this is really the case, our actions prove that we have confidence in the existence of our friends which can't be derived from an empirical argument (which can never be certain) for a man will risk his life for his friend. We don't want merely inferred friends. Could we possibly be satisfied with an inferred God?" (J. Cook Wilson, *Statement and Inference* [London, 1926], vol. 2, p. 853). The essay from which this quotation is taken was first written in 1897 and delivered to an Oxford society in that year. See also A. S. Eddington, *Science and the Unseen World* (New York, 1929), p. 70.

76. Kaufmann Kohler, *Jewish Theology* (New York, 1918), p. 30. Maimonides and his school are guilty of bad, that is, unhistorical, exegesis when they attempt to force the speculative meaning upon the biblical "knowledge of God" (*Yad, Yesode ha-Torah* I, 1–6; *Guide* I:39, III:28 and 51). The biblical "knowledge of God" means obedience to the Divine Will, an effort of the will and not an intellectual pursuit. See, e.g., Jer. 9:23, Prov. 3:6, I Chron. 28:9 (according to Judah Halevi, *Kuzari* V:21, the Karaite schismatics placed an intellectual meaning on the knowledge spoken of in this verse). Cf. D. Rosin, *Die Ethik des Maimonides* (Breslau, 1876), p. 101. "To know" is a very imperfect translation of the Hebrew verb *yada'*, which should rather be rendered "to experience," "to be intimate with"; in Gen. 4:1 it is not that Adam *knew* his wife, Eve, the reference is not to an intellectual apprehension, but something rather more meaningful, sensuous, and pleasurable.

77. Cf. Mishnah, Berakot 9:5: "It is incumbent on a man to bless God for misfortune even as he blesses him for good fortune."

78. The messianic prophecies in Deutero-Isaiah were misunderstood as a result of too literal interpretation of poetic language. So the evangelists transformed the Redeemer into a quack doctor who can instantaneously heal organic bodily defects, and his followers into faith healers in order that the messianic prophecies "might be fulfilled" (Mark 16:17 ff.). literally.

79. Undoubtedly the blind man will be greatly consoled by being told (see *Guide* III:10; *S.T.* 1a, q. 49, a. 1) that blindness is a privation, merely the lack of sight, and nothing positive, and that insofar as he is, he is perfect. It has been suggested, however, that this kind of comfort is not available to the sufferer from malaria. He suffers from too much of something, namely protozoans of the genus *Plasmodium*. See Wallace I. Matson, *The Existence of God* (Ithaca, 1965), pp. 142 f.

Maimonides, and to a lesser degree Aquinas, is at a peculiar disadvantage vis-à-vis both simple believers in the Bible and certain other religious philosophers. The former conceive God as a loving Father in whom they trust; their attitude is not merely cognitive or intellectual, but affective, and hence their faith has a "warm" and "heartfelt" character. On the other hand, some other religious philosophers can affirm that it is the essence and character of God to be all-good and all-loving. In this way the sting is taken out of human pain and suffering, even if no intellectual solution to the problem of evil is provided. But the only class of attributes which Maimonides will allow are those which describe God by His actions. Limiting our knowledge of God this way, I do not see how our picture of reality can differ substantially from that drawn by J. S. Mill in his well-known essay on "Nature."

> In sober truth, nearly all the things for which men are hanged or imprisoned for doing to one another, are Nature's everyday performances. Killing, the most criminal act recognized by human laws, Nature does once to every human being that lives; and in a large proportion of cases, after protracted tortures such as only the greatest monsters whom we read of ever purposely inflicted on their living fellow creatures. . . . Next to taking life . . . is taking the means by which we live; and Nature does this on the largest scale and with the most callous indifference. A single hurricane destroys the hopes of a season; a flight of locusts or an inundation desolates a district; a trifling chemical change in an edible root starves a million of people" (J. S. Mill, *Three Essays on Religion* [New York, 1874], pp. 28, 30).

80. Satan's intrigues are not an answer to the problem of evil. The "prologue in heaven," according to Goethe's correct interpretation, is but a literary expedient. In general it may be said that in medieval Jewish thought mysticism was more successful than rationalism in dealing with the problem of evil. In particular, the Lurianic Kabbalah, with its concepts of *Şimşum* (the contraction of the divine essence) and *Shevirath ha-Kelim* (the bursting of the vessels through which the divine essence is channeled), has attempted to show why evil is endemic in the world. Unfortunately the Jewish new learning (*Juedische Wissenschaft*) of the nineteenth century was strongly biased against anything that smacked of mysticism and Kabbalah. The learned bibliographer Moritz Steinschneider declared in the pages of the *Monatsschrift*, "Die eklektischen Lorianer habe ich gar nicht beruecksichtigt" (*MGWJ* 40 [1896]: 132); while the historian Heinrich Graetz described the Jewish mystics as obscurantists whose religion was the "alcohol bottle" practiced in a small conventicle (*Shtibl*), "that is, a dirty little chamber" (*History of the Jews,* Eng. trans., vol. 5, pp. 380 ff.). With the utmost good will, I fail to understand why the good Lord in the plenitude of His grace is more apt to reveal Himself in the pages of the *Monatsschrift fuer die Geschichte und Wissenschaft des Judentums,* or for that matter in a brush fire, than through the medium of an alcohol bottle. "Is anything too hard or wonderful for the Lord?!" (Gen. 18:14; Jer. 32:27). As Bishop Butler said in his *Sermon on the Character of Balaam:* "Things and actions are what they are, and the consequences of them will be what they will be; why then should we desire to be deceived?" (Joseph

Butler, *Fifteen Sermons,* no. vii, #16, in *Works,* ed. W. E. Gladstone [1897], vol. 2, p. 114). In his discussion of mysticism in lectures XVI and XVII of his *Varieties of Religious Experience,* William James states that in his considered opinion, "the drunken consciousness is one bit of the mystic consciousness, and our total opinion of it must find its place in our opinion of that larger whole" (p. 387). Cf. the more recent claim made by Aldous Huxley (in *The Doors of Perception* [New York, 1954]) that mescalin is a short cut to the beatific vision. See further the penetrating study of Huston Smith, "Do Drugs Have Religious Import?" *Journal of Philosophy* 61 (1964): 517–30. Professor Smith endeavors to demolish Professor R. C. Zaehner's refutation of Huxley in his work *Mysticism Sacred and Profane* (New York, 1956). According to Smith, phenomenological experiences induced by drugs can be, and often are, indistinguishable from religious experiences that occur naturally. It is extremely difficult for one like myself, who has experienced no direct religious illumination in a mystical experience, whether of the natural kind or the chemical kind induced by hallucinogenic drugs, to decide between these conflicting claims. Nevertheless in my opinion Professor Zaehner is right in maintaining that a true mystical experience is always "given" and cannot be induced or prolonged by an effort of the will, though anyone can deliberately cultivate a way of life which will leave himself open to these experiences and enlarge the range and content of their revelation. The openness of an individual to become conscious of an immediate knowledge of God can be increased by the process of self-discipline and prayer, but self-discipline and prayer cannot of themselves compel it (cf. Maimonides' theory of prophecy). An unimpeachably Orthodox rabbi and a Lubavitcher Hasid, Zalman M. Schachter, has found the mystic quest in LSD (which the British scholar Robert Graves has identified with the biblical manna); see 'The Conscious Ascent of the Soul," in *The Ecstatic Adventure,* ed. Ralph Metzner (New York, 1968), pp. 96–123. See also Walter Houston Clark, *Chemical Ecstasy, Psychedelic Drugs, and Religion* (New York, 1969). It is significant that the "Death-of-God Rabbi," Richard L. Rubenstein, acknowledges the conscious influence of the Lurianic Kabbalah on his thinking. See *After Auschwitz: Radical Theology and Contemporary Judaism* (New York, 1966), pp. 184, 219 f., 248, and *passim.*

81. *G.K.C. as M. C.: Thirty-Seven Introductions,* by G. K. Chesterton (London, 1929), pp. 44 ff. (pp. 34–62); reprinted under the title, "Man Is Most Comforted by Paradoxes," in Nahum N. Glatzer, ed., *The Dimensions of Job* (New York, 1969), pp. 233 f. (pp. 228–37). See also Martin Buber, *At the Turning* (New York: Farrar, Strauss, & Young, 1952), "The Dialogue Between Heaven and Earth," pp. 61 f.

82. E. Gilson, *The Spirit of Medieval Philosophy* (New York, 1936), p. 51.

83. E. Gilson, "Maimonide et la philosophie de l'*Exode,*" *Medieval Studies* 13 (1951): 223–25. In *S.T.* 1a, Q. 13, a. 11, ad 1, Aquinas carefully, and quite properly, distinguishes the name HE WHO IS from all other Divine names which are "derivative" (i.e., derived from actions). The sacred Tetragrammaton, YKWK (for the spelling which substitutes the letter *K* for *H,* see J. Z. Lauterbach, "Substitutes

for the Tetragrammaton," *PAAJR* [1930–31]: 39), indicates God's essence and hence is a *nomen proprium* (proper name). HE WHO IS indicates the same idea by a descriptive periphrasis and not in the form of a *nomen proprium*.

84. David Kaufmann, *Geschichte der Attributenlehre* (Gotha, 1877), p. 471. See his exposition of Maimonides' views in detail, pp. 364–470.

85. The Vulgate rendering of *Ehyeh* in Exod. 3:14.

86. E. Gilson, *The Spirit of Medieval Philosophy* (New York, 1936), p. 51.

87. *Ibid.*, p. 433, n. 9.

88. Anthony Kenny, *The Five Ways* (New York, 1969), pp. 94, 95.

89. In acknowledgment to the feminist movement in theology, I must apologize for always referring to God simply in the masculine gender. Long before "women's liberation," the mastermind among the prophets conceived of God in feminine terms. "Like one whom his mother comforts," the unknown writer called Deutero-Isaiah makes God declare (Isa. 66:13), "so will I Myself comfort you." Cf. also 49:15.

90. See Berakoth 9b; cf. also the rabbinic commentaries on Exod. 3:14, and Judah Halevi, *Kuzari* IV:3; Naḥmanides on Exod. 3:14 expressly rejects Maimonides' interpretation.

91. See *The Writings of Martin Buber,* ed. Will Herberg (New York, 1956), p. 261; the quotation is from *Israel and the World* (New York, 1948), p. 23. The key text Exod. 3:14 plays a large part in Buber's thought as can be judged by his numerous references to that passage. Cf. Donald J. Moore, *Martin Buber: Prophet of Religious Secularism* (Philadelphia, 1974), pp. 15 f. and p. 243 n. 33 and the references there given.

92. Alfred Lord Tennyson, *In Memoriam,* Prologue, 1. 16; cf. Mishnah, Aboth 2:4.

93. H. H. Price, *Belief* (New York, 1969), Series 2, Lecture 9, pp. 426–54. The lecture first appeared under the title "Belief In and Belief That," in *Religious Studies* 1 (1966): 5–27. In the first chapter of his analytical study, *Faith* (London, 1969), Louis Jacobs has examined the two kinds of belief from the Jewish point of view.

94. Query as to whether the distinction between "belief-that" and "belief-in" does not in some way correspond to the biblical Hebrew *he'emin le* and *he'emin be*. The construction with the prefix *be* is usual when the object of faith is God (e.g., Gen. 15:6, Exod. 14:31, Num. 14:11, 20:12, etc.); the construction *le* is found only twice in reference to God; Deut. 9:23, Isa. 43:10.

95. F. H. Bradley, *Appearance and Reality,* 9th imp. corrected (Oxford, 1966) p. 130.

96. C. E. M. Joad, *A Critique of Logical Positivism* (London, 1950), p. 152.

97. Charles A. Bennett, *The Dilemma of Religious Knowledge* (New York, 1931), p. 49.

98. Naturalistic humanism has never been able to resolve the relation between the realm of value and the realm of fact; it is overwhelmed by the problem of finding

a place for "values in a universe of chance" (to use Charles S. Peirce's apt phrase). J. W. Krutch, in his brilliant study, *The Modern Temper* (New York, 1929, especially chaps. 3–5), has shown that the tension between the concern for values and the search for truth is inherent in the humanist philosophy. That such is indeed the case can be corroborated by an interesting controversy between the two leading naturalist philosophers in the first half of this century, John Dewey and George Santayana. Santayana, in reviewing Dewey's Carus Lectures for 1922, *Experience and Nature,* pronounced Dewey's naturalism to be "half-hearted," for the reason that he seeks to bring the ends, aims, and values which men cherish directly into nature. This results, in Santayana's view, in giving Dewey's philosophy an anthropocentric character quite inconsistent with naturalism, for nature seems to take no account of human values. When human values are incorporated into the realm of nature, man is immediately given a pontifical role with respect to the rest of nature. He becomes the measure of all things, and we have a new kind of anthropocentric "lay religion" (see "Dewey's Naturalistic Metaphysics," *Journal of Philosophy* 22 [1925]; 673–88). Dewey, on his part, in making rejoinder to this criticism called Santayana's naturalism "broken-backed." He finds that Santayana does not make man truly a part of nature because he makes no place in nature for man's values and ideals. In Santayana's philosophy, as Dewey points out, human values and ideals are somehow an "alien" efflorescence of existence which can never have any effect upon the course of reality (John Dewey, in *ibid.* 24 [1927]: 57–64). This controversy did not arise from a misunderstanding of a rival exposition of the same philosophy, which could easily be clarified, but has its origin in a deep-seated dilemma which is endemic to the naturalistic way of thinking. That this is so is evident from the fact that Santayana reprinted his critique with a few minor changes more than a dozen years later in Paul Arthur Schilpp, ed., *The Philosophy of John Dewey* (Evanston and Chicago, 1939), pp. 245–61 (cf. *ibid.,* pp. 530–34, where Dewey's original reply is essentially repeated).

The dilemma at the heart of naturalism has led many thinkers to the viewpoint that all human ideals and institutions are subject to criticism and judgment from a transcendent and spiritual Absolute, and that human experience can best be explained and integrated by theism, rather than by humanism. Man is, observes Reinhold Niebuhr, "in the position of being unable to comprehend himself in the full stature of freedom without a principle of comprehension that is beyond his comprehension" (*The Nature and Destiny of Man* [New York, 1941], vol. 1, p. 125).

99. L. Wittgenstein, *Philosophical Investigations,* 3rd ed. (Oxford, 1967), I:124.

8. EPILOGUE

1. Keith Ward, "Recent Thinking on Christian Beliefs," *Expository Times* 88 (1976): 68.

2. Herbert Loewe, in Appendices I and II to C. G. Montefiore's *Rabbinic Literature and the Gospel Teachings* (London, 1930), pp. 383 f., 377; cf. *ibid.*, p. 246 (Loewe's note) and *idem.*, "Pharisaism," in *Judaism and Christianity*, vol. 1, *The Age of Transition*, ed. W. O. E. Oesterley, pp. 160 ff.

3. Since that time a spate of volumes have appeared dealing with various and "authentic" postures of Jewish faith after the Holocaust. Those which I have read have not redounded to the greater glory of God or to the philosophical acumen of their authors, and with the psalmist we may pray, "Silence is praise to Thee, O God" (Ps. 65:2). Brief but sharp criticisms of Buber's notions of the "eclipse of God" and Fackenheim's "commanding Voice at Auschwitz" may be found in Paul Edward's *Buber and Buberism: A Critical Evaluation* (Kansas, 1970), pp. 44–49. The remarks of a beloved teacher, the late Reinhold Niebuhr, formerly Professor of Christian Ethics at the Union Theological Seminary, in his foreword to the American edition of Leon Poliakov's *Harvest of Hate* (New York, 1954), have a truer ring to them.

> My personal conviction is that the tragedy [of the Holocaust] is too enormous to permit us to treat it as a fund for whatever moral lessons we desire to preach. I think one must read it with a contrite sense, transcending all moral lessons, that it was our humanity which was capable under certain historical conditions, of sinking to this inhumanity. We will no doubt be diligent to avoid repeating the historical conditions which made these noxious fruits possible. We will be assiduous in our lessons on the brotherhood of mankind, but these lessons must not allow us to exhaust the meaning of this terrible record of human depravity.

4. H. Loewe, *s.v.* "Demons and Spirits (Jewish)," Hastings's *Encyclopaedia of Religion and Ethics*, vol. 4, p. 614a. See also W. O. E. Oesterley, *Judaism and Christianity*, vol. 1, p. 205.

5. Bacon, *Novum Organum* I. 46; the story is found in Cicero, *De Natura Deorum* III. 27.

6. "The Ideas of Pharisaism," in *Judaism and Christianity*, vol. 2: *The Contact of Pharisaism with Other Cultures*, pp. 17 f. See also John E. McFayden, "Telescoped History," *Expository Times* 36 (1925): 103–9, and Johannes Hempel, *Gott und Mensch im A.T.*, (Stuttgart, 1936), p. 161; "The greatest offering that Israel made to God was the sacrifice of its pride in its own past in order to justify Him and His righteousness."

7. Loewe, *s.v.* "Disease and Medicine (Jewish)," *Encyclopaedia of Religion and Ethics*, vol. 4, p. 756a.

8. F. Rosenzweig, *Briefe* (Berlin, 1935), pp. 73–75 (letter to his converted cousin Rudolf Ehrenberg, November 1, 1913). See Nahum N. Glatzer, *Franz Rosenzweig: His Life and Thought* (Philadelphia, 1953), pp. 341 ff., xix, xxv, and Jacob Taubes,

"The Issue Between Judaism and Christianity," in *Arguments and Doctrines,* ed. Arthur A. Cohen (New York, 1970), pp. 402–18.

9. Rosenzweig, *The Star of Redemption,* trans. Willaim W. Hallo (New York, 1970), p. 416.

10. H. Loewe, *A Rabbinic Anthology* (London, 1938), p. lxxx f.

11. In a recent perceptive study, Michael G. Berenbaum has shown that Rosenzweig's views are hopelessly and dangerously outdated and that his appeal rests on his affirmation of the principle of the Halakah and his return to Judaism (see "Franz Rosenzweig and Martin Buber Reconsidered," *Response* 10, no. 4 [1976–77]: 25–40). What is rather surprising is that Dr. Louis Finkelstein, the Chancellor emeritus of the Jewish Theological Seminary of America and an eminent rabbinic scholar, expressed a view very similar to Rosenzweig's. He speaks of "the twin religions [*sic*] of rabbinic Judaism and Christianity" (*Akiba: Scholar, Saint and Martyr* [New York, 1936], p. 6). Elsewhere he says: "The Judeo-Christian tradition is one system, of which Judaism is the core and Christianity the periphery" (*Tradition in the Making* [New York: Jewish Theological Seminary, 1937] p. 12).

12. C. G. Montefiore, *Rabbinic Literature and the Gospel Teachings* (London, 1930), p. 206 (this passage as well as many others in the book is from the pen of Loewe, cf. Preface, p. viii).

13. *Ibid.,* Appendix I, "On Faith," p. 379.

14. *Mekilta,* tractate *Shirata,* chap. 3, on Exod. 15:2. See the insightful comment of R. Isaac Adarbi (*Dibrē Shalom* [Venice, 1586], p. 135b, sermon on section "Beshallaḥ"), who explains that the Midrash deals with religious experience and does not concern itself with the intellectual comprehension of the divine.

15. F. R. Tennant, *Philosophical Theology,* vol. 2 (Cambridge, 1928), p. 205.

16. H. Loewe, "The Jewish Background to the Christian Liturgy," *Expository Times* 29 (1927–28): 69 f. (pp. 65–71; the article is a discussion of W. O. E. Oesterley's book bearing the same title). See also Loewe's remarks in *Encyclopaedia Britannica* (1943 ed.), vol. 13, p. 167b; *Encyclopaedia of Religion and Ethics,* vol. 7, p. 596a.

While Loewe's work on the New Testament has been largely neglected, it can by no means be dismissed as mere apologetics. It is significant that the Anglican clergyman and scholar James Parkes invited him to write the foreword to his book *Jesus, Paul and the Jews* (London, 1936), which was published by the Student Christian Movement.

17. It used to be said of a certain scholar that in the pulpit he was Canon X and in the lecture hall he was Professor X. The same decidedly is not true of Loewe. His book-length article on Judaism in Hastings's *Encyclopaedia of Religion and Ethics* may usefully be supplemented by his essay "The Orthodox Position," written about the same time (1915).

18. *Encyclopaedia of Religion and Ethics,* vol. 7, pp. 585, 607.

19. Loewe in Montefiore's *Rabbinic Literature and the Gospel Teachings,* p. 246; *idem,* "The Ideas of Pharisaism," in *Judaism and Christianity,* ed. Loewe, vol. 2, p. 29; *Encyclopaedia of Religion and Ethics,* vol. 5, pp. 605 f., "Expiation and Atonement (Jewish)." As George Foot Moore put it in his magisterial study, *Judaism,* vol. 2 (Cambridge University, 1927), p. 388: "The Rabbis are very liberal with homiletical damnation."

20. Mordecai M. Kaplan, "What Judaism Is Not," *Menorah Journal* 1, no. 4, (October 1915): 209 (pp. 208–16).

21. Mordecai M. Kaplan, *The Greater Judaism in the Making* (New York, 1960), chap. 10, pp. 268 ff. The founder of Reconstructionism has sometimes seen fit to reconstruct quotations to make cheap shots. On p. 269 he quotes Loewe as saying: "All that revelation means is the silent imperceptible manifestation of God in history." What Loewe had said is "Revelation is," etc. (*A Rabbinic Anthology,* p. lxxiii).

22. "The Orthodox Position" (Cambridge, 1915), pp. 15 f. (emphasis in the original); cf. *A Rabbinic Anthology,* pp. lviii and lxxix.

23. "The Orthodox Position," pp. 17 f. A more extended citation is quoted with strong approval by Chief Rabbi Joseph H. Hertz in *Affirmations of Judaism* (London, 1927), p. 61. Loewe practiced what he preached. He used to spend the High Holidays in London in the historic Sephardi Synagogue at Bevis Marks, where he acted as lay preacher on the solemn Day of Atonement.

24. H. Loewe, *Israel Abrahams* (Cambridge, 1944), p. 65. See the preface of this biography, where the wife of Herbert Loewe states that the interpretation by her late husband of the life and writings of his predecessor at the same time throws much light on the writing and ideals of his pupil and successor. Cf. also *A Rabbinic Anthology,* p. lxxiv.

25. Salomon Reinach, *Orpheus: A History of Religions* (New York, 1930), p. 3. Another good example of a persuasive definition is the concept of the conscience of "Catholic Israel," which is utilized by the leaders of Conservative Judaism to justify the religious practices currently in vogue in their congregations and actually observed by their members. But who is included in the category of Catholic Israel? If the concept includes all Jews, then we should eliminate all 613 commandments of the Torah since they are violated by most Jews today. Indeed, the worshippers of the Golden Calf could justify their behavior by the doctrine of Catholic Israel! On the other hand, if the category includes only those religious Jews who observe the Halakah (Jewish law), then we would have to exclude the vast majority of Conservative Jews. In practice it includes the members of the Rabbinical Assembly (the Conservative rabbinical body) and the leaders of the Conservative movement, but not the members of the ultra-Orthodox (Aggudist) *Mo'eṣet Gedolē ha-Torah* (Council of Outstanding Torah Sages). But a definition of Catholic Israel which excludes the Ḥafeṣ Ḥayyim, the Ḥazon 'Ish, and the Rogachover, but includes the members of the Rabbinical Assembly, must be termed bizarre.

26. *A Rabbinic Anthology,* p. lv. This is by no means the first time that the "orthodoxy" of a traditionalist has been attacked by a critic who is much laxer in his observances than the party criticized. David Neumark, a professor at the Hebrew Union College in Cincinnati and a radical reformer who did not consider the Abrahamic Covenant (circumcision) an essential rite in Judaism, attacked the orthodoxy of the biblical scholarship of David Hoffmann, the rector of the Orthodox Rabbinical Seminary in Berlin (see *The Philosophy of the Bible* [Cincinnati, 1918], pp. xxiv f.).

27. *A Rabbinic Anthology,* p. lxi.

28. M. M. Kaplan, *The Greater Judaism in the Making* (New York, 1960), p. 373.

29. M. M. Kaplan, *The Future of the American Jew* (New York, 1948), p. 202 and *passim; idem, The Meaning of God in Modern Jewish Religion* (New York, 1937), especially chap. 2, "God as the Power That Makes for Salvation."

30. Compare Milton Steinberg's pointed criticism of Kaplan's idea of God: "Does God really exist or is he only man's notion? Is there anything objective which corresponds to the subjective conception? And who adds up 'the sum' in 'the sum total of forces that make for salvation'? Is the sum added up 'out there' or in the human imagination?" (*Anatomy of Faith* [New York, 1960], p. 183).

31. Tanḥuma (Buber), section "Yitro" on Exod. 20:2; cf. the parallel Midrash cited above p. 49.

31a. The version of the interpretation given in the text is the one related by the great Hebrew novelist and storyteller S. J. Agnon, *Atem Re'item* (Jerusalem, 1962), p. 164; a somewhat different version can be found in Louis I. Newman, *The Hasidic Anthology* (New York, 1934), p. 441, no. 2.

32. What elements in the Pentateuch are Mosaic is discussed by Loewe with great learning in his Presidential Address to the Society of Old Testament Study, "Mosaic Revelation," delivered in January 1939. Jewish tradition is concerned not so much with the channel of revelation as with the fact that the product came from God. The Divine, rather than the Mosaic, authorship of the Pentateuch is a fundamental Jewish belief. A *Baraitha* (Sanhedrin 99a) states: "'Because he has despised the word of the Lord' [Num. 15:31]—this refers to him who maintains that the Torah is not from Heaven. And even if he asserts that the whole Torah is from Heaven, excepting a particular verse, which [he maintains] was not uttered by God but by Moses himself, he is included in 'because he has despised the word of the Lord.'" Cf. Jakob J. Petuchowski, "The Supposed Dogma of the Mosaic Authorship of the Pentateuch," *Hibbert Journal* 57, no. 227 (July 1959): 356–60.

33. *A Rabbinic Anthology,* p. lxiv.

34. Spinoza, *Theologico-Political Treatise,* chap. vii. "Of the Interpretation of Scripture," severely criticized Maimonides' principles of exegesis, which, he says, "twist and explain away the words of Scriptures," and he scornfully dismisses Maimonides' method of "interpretation" as "harmful, useless, and absurd." On this topic see Leo Strauss, *Spinoza's Critique of Religion* (New York, 1965). Isaac Husik

has shown that at times Spinoza himself is guilty of the same method of interpretation which he execrates in Maimonides. See "Maimonides and Spinoza on the Interpretation of the Bible," in *Philosophical Essays,* ed. Milton C. Nahm and Leo Strauss (Oxford, 1952), pp. 157–59 (pp. 141–59).

35. *A Rabbinic Anthology,* p. lxxxii.

36. *Rabbinic Literature and the Gospel Teachings,* p. 383.

37. Saul Lieberman, *Shkiin* (Hebrew), 2nd ed. (Jerusalem 1970), pp. 81–83.

38. Abraham J. Heschel, *God in Search of Man* (New York, 1956), p. 247. It must be admitted that at times Samson R. Hirsch, the founder of Neo-Orthodoxy, avails himself of a similar "either/or" argument. See, *inter alia, Judaism Eternal: Selected Essays from the Writings of S. R. Hirsch,* trans. Dr. I. Grunfeld, vol. 2 (London, 1956), p. 216.

39. C. S. Lewis, *Mere Christianity* (New York: Macmillan Paperbacks, 1960), p. 56.

40. *Judaism* 11, no. 2 (Summer 1962): 206 f.

41. "The Orthodox Position" (Cambridge, 1915), p. 14. There is a slip of the pen in the quotation from John Keble, it should read: "The trivial round, the common task, / Would furnish all we ought to ask" (*The Christian Year,* "Morning," st. 10).

Mention might be made in this connection of Loewe's edition of the *Zemiroth* (Sabbath table songs), *Medieval Hebrew Minstrelsy* (London, 1926). At the time of his death, Loewe was preparing a revised and enlarged edition of this work.

42. Louis Ginzberg, "The Significance of the Halakah for Jewish History," in L. Ginzberg, *On Jewish Law and Lore* (Philadelphia, 1955), pp. 86–88 (pp. 77–124), cf. p. 21. This lecture was originally delivered in Hebrew before the faculty and student body of the Hebrew University in 1928 and published in 1931. Loewe makes no reference to this lecture; at this stage it cannot be determined whether this was due to his lack of acquaintance with it or to his reluctance to engage in polemics. At any rate, it was republished with Ginzberg's approval and without any changes—in the preface there is a reference to some opinions which Ginzberg no longer maintained—more than a decade after Loewe's *"Render Unto Caesar"* appeared.

43. For a scathing exposure of the pseudo-scholarship permeating Ginzberg's essay and his unwarranted assumptions, see Jacob Neusner, *The Rabbinic Traditions* (Leiden, 1971), pt. 3, pp. 338–41.

44. This point was kindly called to my attention by Professor David Halivni (Weiss). The *Talmudic Encyclopedia* (Hebrew), vol. 7 (Jerusalem, 1956), *s.v. Dina de-Malkuta,* col. 308 top, and the literature there cited, likewise confirms Loewe's contention that the principle that the law of the land was to be obeyed applied also to the Gentile rulers who governed the Holy Land.

45. Herbert Loewe, "Scholars, Builders and Peace," in *Occident and Orient: Gaster Anniversary Volume* (London, 1936), pp. 380–86. See also Loewe's note at the top of p. 536 of *A Rabbinic Anthology,* edited by him and C. G. Montefiore.

46. Robert Gordis, "'Increasing Peace in the World," *Jewish Quarterly Review*

67, no. 1 (July 1976): 44–46. The writer pointed this out to the editor, who in a private communication, dated February 4, 1977, acknowledged the fact, saying, "Surely Dr. Gordis did not do this intentionally and it is most unfortunate that it has happened," but that the journal did "not wish to engage in polemics" and therefore could not print any correction or rectifications. It seems to me to be an antisocial policy to acknowledge an error in private, but to refuse to make any sort of *amende honorable* in print. How different was the attitude of the rabbis, who said, "Whoever reports a thing in the name of him who said it brings deliverance into the world" (Aboth 6:6).

47. An all-to-brief excerpt from this opuscule will be found in Louis Jacobs's excellent collection, *Jewish Thought Today* (New York, 1970), pp. 66–70.

APPENDIX B

1. Aage Peterson, "The Philosphy of Niels Bohr," *Bulletin of the Atomic Scientists* 19, no. 7 (September 1963): 8.

APPENDIX D

1. Cf. Julius Guttmann, "The Principles of Judaism" (Hebrew), in *Religion and Knowledge* (Jerusalem, 1955), pp. 259 ff.; English trans. by D. W. Silverman in *Conservative Judaism* 14, no. 1 (1959): 3 f.

The problem of justifying the verbal inspiration of a revealed scripture is a very formidable one. "And the Lord spake unto Moses, saying." What clear and simple words. But are they so? What do they mean according to Maimonides?

In answering these questions I shall closely follow the interpretation of the Orthodox scholar Professor Michael Wyschogrod, *Tradition* 9, nos. 1–2 (1967): 149 ff., to whom I am considerably indebted.

In chapter 65 of the first part of the *Guide,* we are told of the "inadmissability of the attribute of speech in reference to God." Now ordinarily when we use the word "speak" with reference to a human being, we mean that a certain person had the kinesthetic sensations of opening his mouth and vibrating his vocal cords in such a way as to create undulating air waves which travel to our ear and cause certain sound-sensations which convey the speaker's meaning. But when applied to God the word "speak" cannot mean this, simply because God is not a physical being with a mouth and vocal cords. To say that God "spoke" means, according to Maimonides, that He manifested His will by means of a "created voice" (*ḳol nibra'*) which reached the ears of Moses or the Israelites in a supernatural manner. The very simple phrase, "And the Lord spake unto Moses, saying," is not so clear and simple as it seems.

Nevertheless, if this were the extent of Maimonides' problem, he would be comparatively well off. He could then argue that while God does not speak in exactly the same sense in which human beings do, because there is no physical action involved, He speaks in the sense that He conveys His ideas and His desires to His listeners. And since the purpose of speaking is generally not to exercise one's vocal cords but to convey ideas, the sense in which God speaks is close enough to the usual, human sense in which that word is used to make its use with reference to God understandable and legitimate.

But now Maimonides must substantiate two basic assumptions: (1) that human language is of such a nature that it is possible to formulate precise and completely adequate statements concerning the moral, spiritual, and metaphysical verities of our universe, not only for our contemporaries but for future generations as well; and (2) that if God is going to make a significant revelation of Himself and His plan for salvation, He must do so by an infallible, verbally inspired document. Until both these assumptions are justified, Maimonides' philosophy lacks even the shadow of a foundation.

Maimonides cannot prove the first assumption by showing that *all* human language is capable of such precision in meaning as to serve as the vehicle of an infallible divine revelation because he himself has devoted a large portion of the first part of the *Guide* to analyzing homonymous expressions. But neither, it seems, could he prove that the language of the Bible meets this test because it differs markedly from the rest of human language and linguistic usage. To do so he would have to use biblical texts to authenticate the Bible before he had proved its authority. (This popular but logically fallacious method is epitomized in the remark attributed to a certain professor at an English university, who is said always to have commenced his initial lecture on biblical Hebrew with the words, "Gentlemen, this is the language which God spoke.") But even if such a proof were forthcoming, Maimonides would be confronted with a new problem. He has destroyed the human side of the bridge between God and man. How can man understand precisely and exactly this language that is so idiosyncratic and peculiar, and differs so radically from the language of everyday? How indeed except by studying the *Guide of the Perplexed!* But surely the *Guide* is not written in language as precise and exact as that of the alleged original revelation. Otherwise how account for the various, and often mutually exclusive and contradictory, interpretations of its meaning found among its classic commentators? We have thus already come a very long way from the assertion that the phrase "And the Lord spake unto Moses, saying" is as clear and simple as it seems.

Now let us deal with the second assumption. Granted that God *could* make such a revelation, it does not follow that He *did* make such a revelation. Would Maimonides be prepared to say that God cannot choose any mode but propositional revelation for communicating His purposes to mankind? And if God could choose some other mode for the revelational process, how can Maimonides be so sure that He did not? And why is it so great a virtue to believe that God is (to use Coleridge's phrase, *salva reverentia*) a "supernatural Ventriloquist"? Furthermore, to paraphrase Rousseau, why should God have found Moses the son of Amram in order to speak to Moses the son of Maimun?

We must sadly conclude, therefore, that Maimonides has failed to substantiate these disputable assumptions even formally.

Franz Rosenzweig had the great merit of perceiving these issues clearly, even if he could offer no new solutions. In a letter dated June 5, 1925, addressed to Martin Buber, he wrote: "The primary content of revelation is revelation itself. 'He came down' [on Sinai, Exod. 19:25]—this already concludes the revelation; 'He spoke' [*ibid.* 20:1] is the beginning of interpretation, and certainly 'I am' [v. 2]" (F. Rosenzweig, *On Jewish Learning,* ed. N. N. Glatzer [New York, 1955], p. 118).

2. *Yad, Teshuvah* 3:8; the source of Maimonides is Sanhedrin 99b. Suppose that a pre-Masoretic manuscript of the Torah were found whose authenticity was established beyond doubt by radio-carbon dating and paleography. Suppose now that it differed from our standard Bibles. Which would be more upsetting, if the verse "Timna was a concubine" or the verse *"Shema Yisrael!* Hear, O Israel!" were missing? Is there a single Jew in the whole world who cannot perceive the vast difference between these verses? Did any martyr go to his death proclaiming his faith in a sentence such as "Timna was a concubine" as thousands did with the *Shema'* on their lips? Yet the Halakah has never clearly formulated the existential and emotional difference between these passages.

3. See the *Introduction to Perek Helek* in his *Commentary on the Mishnah,* Sanhedrin, chap. 10, the eighth Principle, ed. J. Kafiḥ, pp. 214 f. For similar remarks by Aquinas, see p. 229, n. 8, end. The classical Jewish religious texts generally fail to distinguish between ethical and ritual commandments. "The commandments, 'Thou shalt love thy neighbor as thyself,' and 'A garment of diverse kinds, of linen and wool, shall not come upon thee,' stand side by side in the same paragraph" (Michael Friedlander, *The Jewish Religion,* American ed., revised and enlarged [New York, 1946], p. 239).

4. S. R. Hirsch, *The Nineteen Letters,* trans. B. Drachman (New York, 1969), p. 143 (adapted). See I. Grunfeld, *Judaism Eternal: Selected Essays from the Writings of S. R. Hirsch* (London, 1956), vol. 1, pp. xxxiv ff.; see also Samuel A. Hirsch, "Ein Wort ueber S. R. Hirschs wissenschaftliche Methode," in the *S. R. Hirsch Jubilaeums Nummer des "Israelit,"* 1908, pp. 33 f.; R. Katzenellenbogen, "Studies in the *Nineteen Letters* and *Horeb*" (Hebrew), in *Rabbi S. R. Hirsch: His Teaching and Method,* ed. Jonah Immanuel (Jerusalem, 1962), pp. 94 f. This view has been tacitly adopted as stock-in-trade by many Jewish thinkers who do not accept Hirsch's system as a whole. The great rabbinic scholar, the late Professor Louis Ginzberg, in his lecture on "The Religion of the Pharisee," delivered before the Harvard Divinity School, paraphrases this analogical argument at length without mentioning Hirsch by name, as if this view were typical of the Pharisees at the time of Jesus! (see L. Ginzberg, *Students, Scholars, and Saints* [Philadelphia, 1928], pp. 404f.).

5. *Horeb,* trans. I. Grunfeld (London, 1962), vol. 1, p. 331, ellipsis in the original.

6. See the very important study by H. Koester, "Nomos and Phusis," in *Studies in the History of Religions,* vol. 14 (1968), ed. Jacob Neusner, pp. 522–45 (especially pp. 531 ff.). See also the rabbinic exposition of Jer. 33:25 in Lev. Rabbah 35:4 and parallels; but the doctrine of natural law is apparently not found in the Hebrew Scriptures. However this may be, the same confusion seems to underlie the Thomist natural law theory. It has been credibly shown that the whole natural law argument begs the question, since in effect we are being told that we ought to act in certain ways because it is natural to do so and also that this concept of the natural is the one we ought to use. See Frederick A. Olafson, "Essence and Concept in Natural Law Theory," in *Law and Philosophy,* ed. Sidney Hook (New York, 1964), pp. 234–40.

7. Moritz Schlick, *The Problems of Ethics* (New York, 1939), p. 247. Cf. Norman Campbell, *What Is Science?* (New York: Dover, 1952; originally published 1921), chap. 7; Hans Reichenbach, *The Rise of Scientific Philosophy* (1951), chap. 10.

8. See S. Schechter, "Higher Criticism—Higher Anti-Semitism," in *Seminary Addresses and Other Papers* (Cincinnati, 1915), pp. 35–39.

9. Geiger, in *Wissenschaftliche Zeitschrift für Jüdische Theologie* 3 (1837): 75–78, 88 (74–91). Geiger points out that Hirsch is simply arguing in a circle in attempting to prove the factuality of the Sinaitic revelation as recorded in Exodus, that he is using the authority of the very document whose authority he was seeking to substantiate before he had proved its authority.

At bottom Hirsch's argument is a variation of the historical proof which was very popular among the medieval Jewish thinkers. This circular argument states that the Bible itself authoritatively asserts that Moses spoke the word of God; the trustworthiness of Moses was tested and established "for ever" because all Israel heard God proclaim the Ten Commandments on Mount Sinai (*Ma'amad Har Sinai*). The public character of the Sinaitic revelation and the uninterrupted continuity of Jewish tradition preclude the possibility of error or deception. That all Israel—an assembly of 600,000 men, exclusive of women and children—heard God proclaiming the Ten Commandments we learn from the Book of Exodus, which reports an authentic tradition going back to the event (Saadiah, *Amānāt* [ed. Landauer], pp. 25, 125–28; Ibn Dā'ūd, *Emūnāh Rāmāh* [ed. Weil], pp. 80 f.; Maimonides, *Yad, Yesode ha-Torah* 8:1 f.; *idem, Moreh Nebukim* II:35; Judah Halevi, *Kuzari* I:87; cf. I:25, 97, IV:11; Aaron Halevi of Barcelona, *Sefer ha-Ḥinnuk,* Introduction [beginning]; Albo, *'Iḳḳarim* I:18, Jacob Anatoli [d. 1256] *Malmad ha-Talmidim,* p. 192; Naḥmanides and Ibn Ezra on Exodus 19:9). This argument became so stock-in-trade that it is found in almost all medieval Jewish thinkers.

Circular or not, the argument served the medieval Jewish theologians as a powerful and coercive weapon in their controversies with Christian or Moslem opponents. In the scholastic rivalry between the theologians of the three great monotheistic faiths, Judaism, Christianity, and Islam, the Jews had a peculiar advantage. While the Christians, on the one hand, repudiated the divine character of the sacred writings of the Moslems, and the Jews, on the other, denied the divine source of both the New Testament and the Koran, no one questioned the divine inspiration of the Hebrew Bible. In it, it was universally agreed in the Middle Ages, God had truly spoken to man. But the Christians and the Moslems claimed that the Torah had become inoperative and was superseded by a new revelation, or at any rate had been absorbed and perfected by it. To answer this, the Jewish theologians laid great stress on the publicity attaching to the revelation on Mount Sinai and to the miracles related in the Torah, and on the uninterruptedness of the Jewish tradition. They justly pointed out that if such supersession had taken place, it must have been by a revelation at least as convincing as that on Mount Sinai. The burden of proof was thus shifted to the Christians and Moslems to demonstrate that such a revelation had indeed taken place. Granting the underlying assumptions which the Jewish thinkers shared with their opponents, this line of reasoning is legitimate.

But in modern times the argument cannot support the weight put upon it. Maimonides prefaces his code with a list of the individual bearers of tradition derived from the Mishnah, Aboth 1, and other rabbinic sources. But there are gaps in the supposedly uninterrupted chain of the forty generations of teachers from Moses to the completion of the Talmuds. Even such a staunch traditionalist as David Hoffmann has to admit that there is a link missing between Antigonos and the two Joses. The Mishnah in Aboth 1:3 f. reads: "Antigonos of Socho received the tradition from Simeon the Righteous . . . Jose ben Jo'ezer of Zeredah and Jose ben Johanan of Jerusalem received it from *them*," etc. "From *him*" would be expected, and C. Taylor, in his edition of the text (p. 135), lists some manuscripts which make this conjectural emendation. (See also *Magen Avot,* the commentary of R. Simeon ben Ẓemaḥ Duran in loc.) But I think the conclusion of scholars who infer that a name or names are missing here cannot be gainsaid. Here, then, there is a missing link in the carriers of the oral tradition. (See David Hoffmann, "Bemerkungen zur Kritik der Mishna," *Magazin für die Wissenschaft des Judentums* 8 [1881]: 125–27; G. F. Moore, "Simeon the Righteous," in the *Israel Abrahams Memorial Volume* [New York, 1927], pp. 348–64 [Moore independently comes to the same conclusion as Hoffmann, whose earlier article he does not seem to have seen]; see also the masterly study of Salo W. Baron, "The Historical Outlook of Maimonides," in *History and Jewish Historians* [Philadelphia, 1964], pp. 152 ff., and the corresponding notes [pp. 109–63, reprinted from *PAAJR* 6 [1935]: 5–113.)

In order to avoid misunderstandings, I must emphatically state here that I absolutely do not want to suggest that the rabbinic tradition is not reliable—it is perhaps the most reliable that has come down to us. I am not at all impressed with the theory of Is. Loeb ("Sur le chapitre Ier des Pirke Abot," *Revue des Etudes Juives* 19 [1889];: 188–201) that the chain of the carriers of the rabbinic tradition is a myth and a late fabrication, nor with the thesis of E. Bickerman ("La chaine de la tradition pharisiene," *Revue Biblique* 59 [1952]: 44 f.) that it is modeled after the paradigm of the Greek philosophical schools, who traced their pedigree by means of supporting

"chains." On the contrary, the same canon of historical criticism which authorizes
the assumption of a gap here and there in the list of the bearers of tradition favors
the authenticity of the list as a whole; if the list had been a late fabrication, fictitious
names would have been supplied to fill the gaps. For the authenticity of the chain of
tradition from Moses to talmudic times, see Louis Finkelstein, *New Light from the
Prophets* (New York, 1969), especially chap. 10, "The Pre-exilic Origin of Mishna
Abot 1:1," and for the trustworthiness of the rabbinic tradition as a whole, see M. H.
Segal, *A Grammar of Mishnaic Hebrew* (Oxford, 1927), pp. 19 f.; Hebrew version
(Tel-Aviv, 1936), pp. 17 f. Professor Segal calls attention to the rule which antedates
the age of Hillel, a contemporary of Jesus, that it is not sufficient for a disciple to
deliver the substance of a practical or theoretical ruling; he must quote the exact
words and use the very diction of the master from whom it had been learned (cf.
Mishnah, Eduyyoth 1:3, with the commentaries *ad loc.*, especially *Meleketh
Shelomoh* of R. Solomon Adeni). I trust, therefore, that I will not be misunderstood
when I say that the rabbinic tradition is most reliable, but not infallible.

In view of this it is rather suprising that the present Lubavitcher Rebbe, Rabbi
Menachem Schneerson, avails himself of the medieval argument to prove "scientifically" that the Torah is divine: "Such an historic event was the Revelation at
Mount Sinai, which has been reported in an identical way by millions of people—
men, women, and children; people from all walks of life and backgrounds, who
witnessed it themselves, and then faithfully reported it to their children, generation
after generation, *without interruption* to this day. At no time, even during the worst
pogroms and massacres of the Jews, were there less than millions of Jews faithfully
maintaining this tradition. In fact, at no time in our history was there a break in the
chain of Jewish tradition from Sinai down to the present day. This makes the giving
of the Torah the most *authenticated of all historical events in human history*" (*A
Thought for the Week* 3, no. 4 [October 31, 1969]: 7–8, emphasis in the original).

Assessment and criticism of the argument. This reasoning, if valid, would equally
prove that the reigning Pope in Rome is the Vicar of the founder of Christianity and
that his pronouncements are infallible when he speaks *ex cathedra* on matters of
faith and morals. Using New Testament texts as a basis and tradition and history for
the interpretation and confirmation, Catholic dogmatic theology sets out to show
that the founder of Christianity instituted a visible Church, that he gave his Church
an hierarchial constitution, that he established Simon Peter as its visible head and
the apostles as its rulers, that he intended Peter and the apostles to have permanent
successors in pope and bishops. The Roman Catholic Church alone, it is thus maintained, has kept the structure of the Church as instituted by its founder and is alone in
unbroken continuity with the first apostolic community (and continuity implies, in
accordance with the philosophy of Aristotle, only differences of degree, but not of
kind). Here the argument ends and the circle is completed. He who is outside the circle of faith is, since he lacks the divine guidance of the Church, not in a position
logically to dispute this argument.

So much for the purported continuity of the tradition; next let us consider the millions of alleged "witnesses" to the original revelation itself on Mount Sinai. The point of departure of the Lubavitcher Rabbi is, of course, the statement that Israel went out of Egypt with a force of 600,000 fighting men, which would imply a total population between two and three million people. In Exod. 12:37 we are told that there were about 600,000 men, besides women and children, and a "mixed multitude" that went up from Egypt. In Num. 1:46 the number of males, aged twenty years and over, is given more precisely as 603,550, plus women and children and Levites. But the same census reports that the number of male first-born was 22,273 (Num. 3:43); and since it is fair to suppose that the number of families in which the first-born child was a female would be about the same, then the total number of families that had any children was 44,456. Now if "first-born" means first-born to the mother (cf. 3:12), then, since the number of first-born and of mothers must be identical, there were 44,546 mothers. But from this number (assuming the number of women over twenty years of age was the same as that of men, i.e., 600,000) it follows that only one women in thirteen or fourteen over twenty was a mother! Nevertheless, the Hebrews in Egypt who went down as seventy in number are said to have increased to some two and one-half millions in four generations. Still further, it would follow that there were from forty to fifty children to a family. The Bible does indeed often speak of the fruitfulness of the Hebrew women (Exod. 1:7), and the rabbis have preserved a tradition that in Egypt Jewish women gave birth to as many as six children at one time (according to some even as many as sixty or seventy—see the Midrashim quoted by M. Kasher in *Torah Shelemah, in loc.*). But such assumptions concerning fecundity border on the miraculous, and while this does not by any means invalidate the biblical tradition (and far be it from me to say that the revelation on Mount Sinai did not take place), it does show that, judged by ordinary canons of historicity, the giving of the Torah is far from being the most authenticated event in *human* history. Finally, it may be remarked that the Lubavitcher Rabbi has failed to locate the mountain in the Sinaitic peninsula around the foot of which millions of "witnesses" could have congregated.

10. It is disingenuous, to say the least, on the part of Hirsch to dismiss all those who do not conform to his views of *Trennungsorthodoxie* as Sadducees, for the retort can well be made, as it was made by Geiger at the time, that Hirsch and his followers are Talmud-Karaites. When Gotthold Salomon, the preacher of the Hamburg Reform Congregation had the audacity to announce that "the age also is a Bible through whose mouth God speaks to Israel" ("auch die Zeit sei eine Bibel, durch deren Mund Gott zu Israel spricht," *Protokolle der ersten Rabbinerversammlung,* 91 [Braunschwieg, 1844]), we can dismiss him with Heinrich Heine as a clown and charlatan who wants to beat up tradition with a razor and a bicycle-chain, and pour the ocean of Judaism into a neat little hand-basin. But I am not so sure that the same criticism could not be leveled at the more moderate view, which holds that Judaism has passed through an evolution and yet maintained an organic unity with the past in

its concept of a growing and developing Torah. The contention can even be made that Hirsch's static conception of the Law as having arisen on Sinai, fixed and immutable for all time, is pagan and un-Jewish. The Laws of the Medes and Persians are indeed unalterable (Dan. 6:9), and Pallas Athene, the patron goddess of Athens, sprang full grown from the head of Zeus, but the Torah is an ever-growing and flourishing "tree of life," and "matters not revealed to Moses were revealed to R. Akiba and his colleagues" (Num. Rabbah 19:6 and parallels). The greater rabbinic casuists and respondents, while always considering Maimonides and the *Shulḥan 'Aruk* as valid guides to Jewish practice, never held them to be final and infallible sources of the Halakah but only evidences of the religious law, the evidence being rebuttable. Cf. L. Ginzberg, *Students, Scholars and Saints* (Philadelphia, 1928), p. 141 and 277, n. 40; S. J. Zevin, *Ishim we-Shitoth* (Tel Aviv, 1952), p. 18. On the development of the Law and the need of interpreting it in the spirit of the times, see (1) The legend recountered in Men. 29b, which has Moses seated behind the eighth row of R. Akiba's pupils and listening but not able to comprehend their discussions. The Torah has unfolded itself and developed to such an extent that Moses could not recognize the traditions which R. Akiba expounded in his name. (The implications of this legend are well brought out by J. Z. Lauterbach, "The Talmud and Reform Judaism," *American Israelite* 58, no. 18 [1911–12]: 1); (2) R. Judah the Patriarch's justification for his innovation involving the relaxation of the law of tithes in Beth-Shean (*sc.* Scythopolis in Lower Galilee) in Hullin 6b–7a; (3) The rabbinic comment on Deuteronomy 17:9, "And you shall come . . . to the judge who is in office in those days," implying that the religious leaders of each generation are empowered to legislate through the Oral Law for their own time in the light of contemporary circumstances, Rosh ha-Shanah, Tosefta 2 (1). 3; Babli 25a–b; also Asheri on Sanhedrin 4:6, and *idem,* Responsa 55:9; cf. also Vidal in his commentary *Maggid Mishneh* on Maimonides' Code, end of *Hilkoth Shekhenim.* On this subject, the debate between the Rev. Joseph Strelitski and Raphael Leon in pt. 2, chap. 15, of Zangwill's *Children of the Ghetto* is more worth reading than most nonfictional discussions.

11. Joseph L. Blau, *Modern Varieties of Judaism* (Columbia University Press, 1966), Preface, p. viii and *passim; idem,* "Tradition and Innovation," in *Essays on Jewish Life and Thought Presented in Honor of Salo W. Baron* (New York, 1959), pp. 95–104. Professor Blau's thesis has been adumbrated to a certain extent by C. Guignebert, who felicitously speaks of "the persistent illusion of all religions which make progress while they imagine themselves to be immovable" (*The Jewish World in the Time of Jesus* [New York, 1939], p. 167), but Blau has shown the deeper and profounder analysis and the finer elaboration.

12. Dr. Noah H. Rosenbloom has offered extensive evidence of the influence of the dialectical modes of Hegelian thought on Hirsch. Cf. "The *Nineteen Letters of Ben Uzziel*—A Hegelian Exposition," *Historia Judaica* 22 (April 1960): 23–60; *idem,*

The Religious Philosophy of Samson Raphael Hirsch (Philadelphia, 1976), index, *s.v.* "Hegel, Hirsch and," especially pp. 181–83. For other foreign influences on Hirsch's thought, see Howard I. Levine, "Enduring and Transitory Elements in the Philosophy of S. R. Hirsch," *Tradition* 5 (1963): 293–95.

APPENDIX E

1. Walter Kaufmann, *Religion in Four Dimensions* (New York, 1976), p. 114.

Bibliographical Note

Maimonides. An excellent and comprehensive survey and evaluation, by the pen of a master, of works on the philosophy of Maimonides which have been published since the early 1930s will be found in Georges Vajda, "La philosophie Juive du Moyen Age," in *Hebrew Union College Annual* 45 (1974): 208–23. The older literature is listed by the same author in *Juedische Philosophie* (no. 19 in the series *Bibliographische Einfuehrungen in das Studium der Philosophie*), ed. I. M. Bocheński (Berne, 1950), pp. 20–24. A selected bibliography of works on Maimonides in English is appended to Isadore Twersky's *A Maimonides Reader* (New York, 1972), pp. 483–90.

Aquinas. The standard and almost exhaustive bibliography for works published up to 1920 is Pierre Mandonnet and Jean Destrez, *Bibliographie Thomiste,* rev. ed. M. D. Chenu (Paris, 1960). A good, up-to-date, annotated bibliography is provided by Ralph McInerny, *St. Thomas Aquinas* (Boston, 1977), pp. 186–89.

Index of Ideas, Names, and Terms

Eve, 253
Evil, 109, 254
Evolution, theory of, 105, 220–21
Existentialism, 23, 92, 93, 137
Exodus, Book of, 266
Eybeschitz, Jonathan, 243
Ezekiel, Book of, 80, 216, 249
Ezra, Abraham Ibn, 80, 152, 161, 162, 210, 227

Fackenheim, Emil F., xix, 160, 258
Fabro, Cornelio, 200
Faith, 25, 90, 93, 99, 105, 106, 113, 235, 251
   and reason, 199, 239, 240
Fakhry, M. 198
Fall, 21, 193
al-Fārābī, 1, 189, 195
Fate, 21
Father Brown, 22
Fatherhood of God, 50, 169, 170–75 passim, 253
Faulhaber, Cardinal, 189
Feldman,Seymour, 195
Feyeraband, Paul, 232
Fichte, Johann Gottlieb, 167
Fideism, xii, 5
Findlay, J. N., 251, 252
Finkelstein, Louis, 185–86, 259, 268
fiqh, 150
First Cause, 34, 36, 43, 46, 47, 54, 63, 64, 210
Fleisher, David, xix
Flew, A., 224
Fosdick, Harry Emerson, 197
Fox, Marvin, 10, 215
Frankel, Zacharias, 159
Frazer, James G., 75
Free will, 198–99
Freud, Sigmund, 103, 105, 250
Friedländler, Michael, 69, 195, 215, 226
Friedman, Maurice A., 185, 245
Fromm, Erich, 219

Gabirol, Solomon Ibn, xvi, 156

Galileo Galilei, 65
Gallagher, Donald A., 192
Gallagher, Thomas Aquinas, xix
Gandz, Solomon, 245
Gardner, John W., xviii
Garrigou-Lagrange, R., 199, 204
Geiger, Abraham, 70, 71, 166, 223, 266, 269,
   *Urschrift und Uebersetzungen der Bibel,*153
Gersonides, 195, 223, 238
al-Ghazzālī, 182
Gibbon, Edward, 223
Gilson, Etienne, 22, 61, 63, 85, 111, 156, 193, 194, 203, 204
   The Christian Philosophy of St. Thomas Aquinas, 59, 66, 110, 146, 212, 220, 221
   History of Christian Philosophy in the Middle Ages, xvi, 22, 24, 213
   The Spirit of Medieval Philosophy, 110, 180, 191
   "Sur la problematique thomiste de la vision beatifique," 192
   Unity of Philosophical Experience, 22, 86
Ginzberg, Louis, 57, 141–42, 180, 185, 229, 262, 265, 270
God
   in Aquinas, 4, 19, 25, 36,61, 192, 193–94
   in Aristotle, 2, 43
   attributes, 9, 62, 225, 253–54
   belief in, 102–5, 114
   in Bible, 2–3, 108, 110, 179–80, 216
   creator, 54, 174. *See also* Creation *ex nihilo*
   essence of , 54, 110, 111, 112
   existence of, xiv, 2–4, 9, 43, 64, 76, 96, 105, 106, 115, 179–80, 194, 236, 252
   gender of pronominal references to, 256
   goodness of, 57, 108, 160, 161